col. r.s. beard

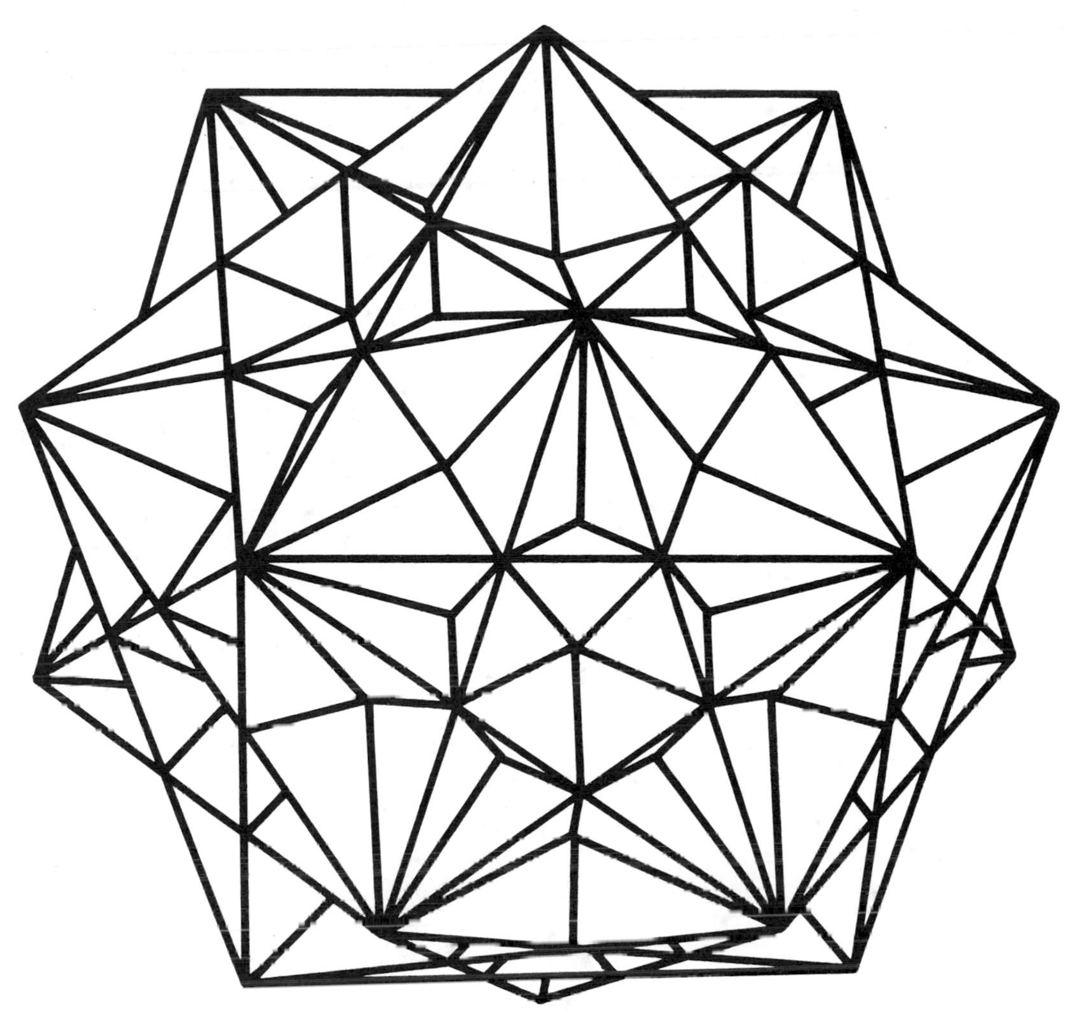

patterns in space

CREATIVE PUBLICATIONS, INC. PALO ALTO, CALIFORNIA

This edition of Patterns in Space is a minor modification of the collection of drawings originally made available through the Fibonacci Association in 1971. By agreement with the Fibonacci Association all rights to Patterns in Space belong exclusively to Creative Publications.

Library of Congress Catalog Number 73-81130

Printed in the United States of America

ISBN: 0–88488–015–X

DEDICATION

This book is dedicated to my good wife, Dr. Helen-Mar Wheeler Beard, with whom I have shared two grand homes and much botanizing all over California, high, low, wet and dry.

R.S.B.

B - R. - 0
BEARD
09412
鬍鬚
D - S. - 2

ABOUT THE AUTHOR

By any standard, Robert Stanley Beard is a remarkable man. Since graduating from M.I.T. in 1905, he has been a successful railroad engineer, city engineer, career Army engineer, and creator of beautiful geometrical designs. At the age of 90, his hand is steady, his eyes keen, and his sense of humor acute. Scarcely a day goes by but that he devotes several hours to plane or solid geometrical problems with model making a specialty. For nearly three decades he has shared his collections of polyhedra with the mathematical community. One set of these models is on permanent display at Teachers College, Columbia University and another at the University of California at Berkeley. He often appears at professional meetings and has authored some thirty papers on various aspects of design.

The present volume is truly unique. At least I have found it so, since it is the only book that I own which captivated my daughter at 7 and my father-in-law at 77! Not only does Colonel Beard show us some unusual designs, but he also tells us how the constructions were made. Such material is especially refreshing since so little in modern school curricula emphasizes the esthetical and constructional aspects of geometric figures.

After scanning this book for the first time, I was reminded of Edna St. Vincent Millay's poem which begins: "Euclid alone has looked on Beauty bare." Perhaps if she had known R. S. Beard, she would have modified that line ever so slightly.

John D. Hancock
California State University
Hayward, California

PREFACE

Much like Uncle Tom's Topsy, this book 'was never born. It just growed.' It grew under the notion that each of us should keep helping things along as best he can to justify our existence. Way back, Plutarch said that the mind is not a vessel to be filled but a fire to be ignited. Shortly after the Second World War left me benched for age, much was being said about geometry being the most disliked of high school studies in spite of its importance in the education of scientists and engineers. Even President Hoover had made some comments about this situation.

Geometry had been a prime factor in my existence ever since the horse and buggy days of the Spanish American War. These disparaging remarks struck a sympathetic chord in my genes and spurred me to explore what might be done to generate some internal radiation in the minds and hearts of students of geometry.

Work along these lines created an opportunity in 1950 to join in organizing a mathematical laboratory for the Institute of Mathematics of Yeshiva University at the invitation of Dr. Jekuthiel Ginsburg, head of the Institute and Editor of *Scripta Mathematica.* The drawings in this book are largely an outgrowth of my five years of conducting that laboratory, the first years jointly with Dr. Hermann von Baravalle.

In 1952 I constructed an elaborate set of polyhedra as my assignment on an ad hoc committee to organize a New York City Mathematical Museum. These models became a permanent exhibit at Teachers College of Columbia University. A second more elaborate set of polyhedra has since been constructed for a permanent exhibit at the Lawrence Hall of Science, University of California, Berkeley.

This, then unfinished, book was first assembled in 1963 with the advice and encouragement of Jens L. Lund, Supervisor of the Teaching of Mathematics, School of Education, University of California, Berkeley, and Brother Alfred Brousseau of St. Mary's College and Managing Editor of the Fibonacci Quarterly. Both of these men are former presidents of the California Mathematics Council.

Dale G. Seymour, President of Creative Publications, has been interested in this project from its California beginnings. He has published much of the material in several of his books and also in the form of colored posters based on individual drawings. Creative Publications is now editing the book, adding a number of my new drawings and indexing the book for publication in permanent form.

Col. Robert S. Beard

TABLE OF CONTENTS

TABLE OF CONTENTS CONTINUED

section 1

POLYGONS

Drawing the Polygons.

The figures numbered 5_R, 5_S and 5_W show how to draw regular pentagons when radius, R, of circumscribing circle, side, S, or width, W, of pentagon is given. $k = \frac{1}{2}\sqrt{5} - \frac{1}{2} = 0.618034$.

Given dimensions are made unity and are marked thus: ←[1]→ .

In prime numbered figures, such as $7'_R$, the construction is a close approximation.

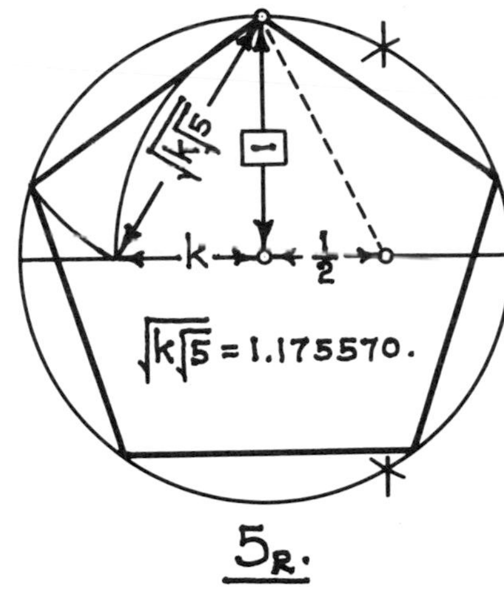

5_R.

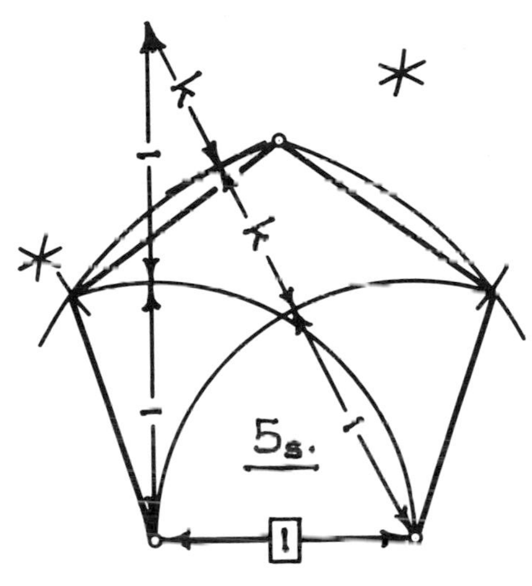

5_S.

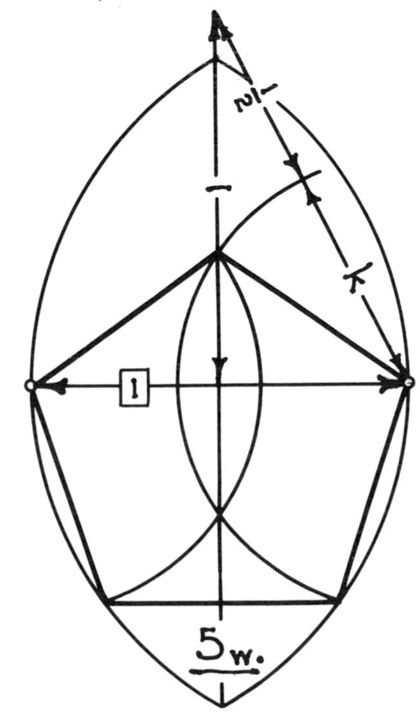

5_W.

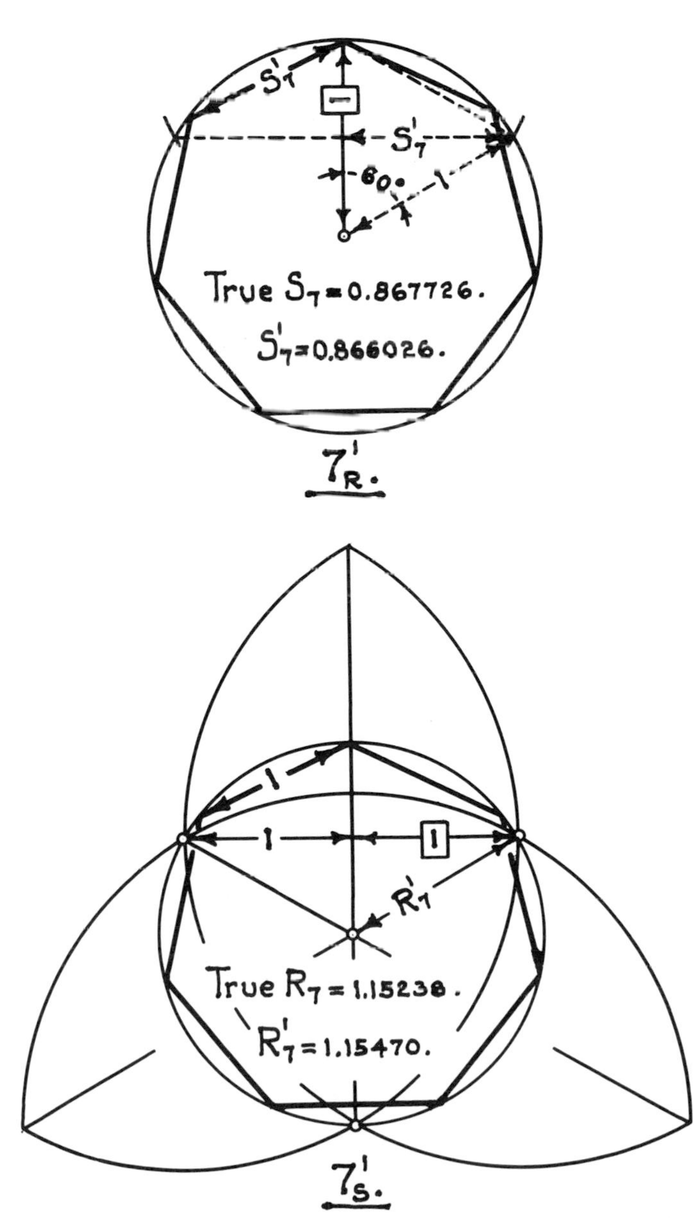

$7'_S$.

Drawing the Polygons.

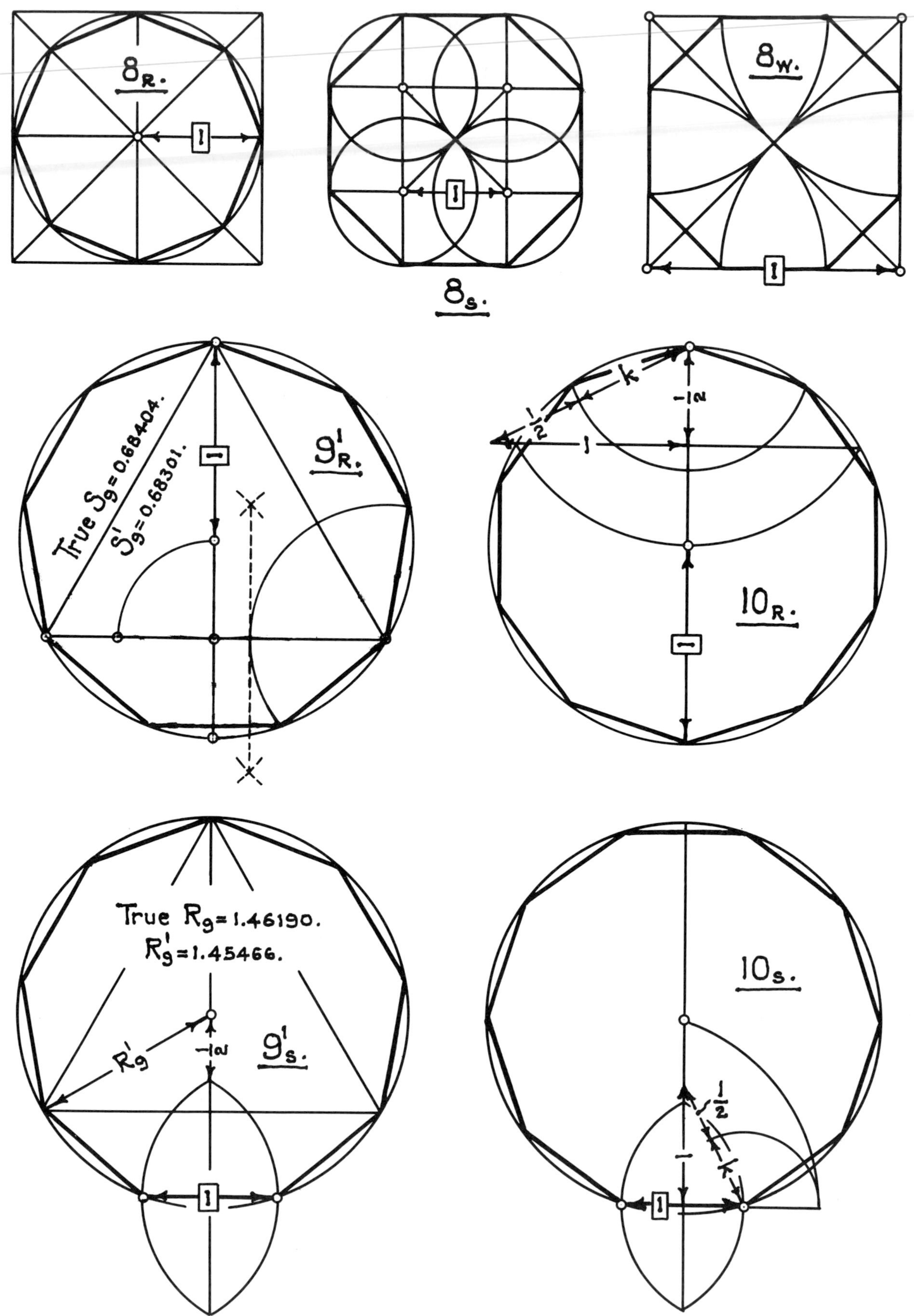

DRAWING THE POLYGONS.

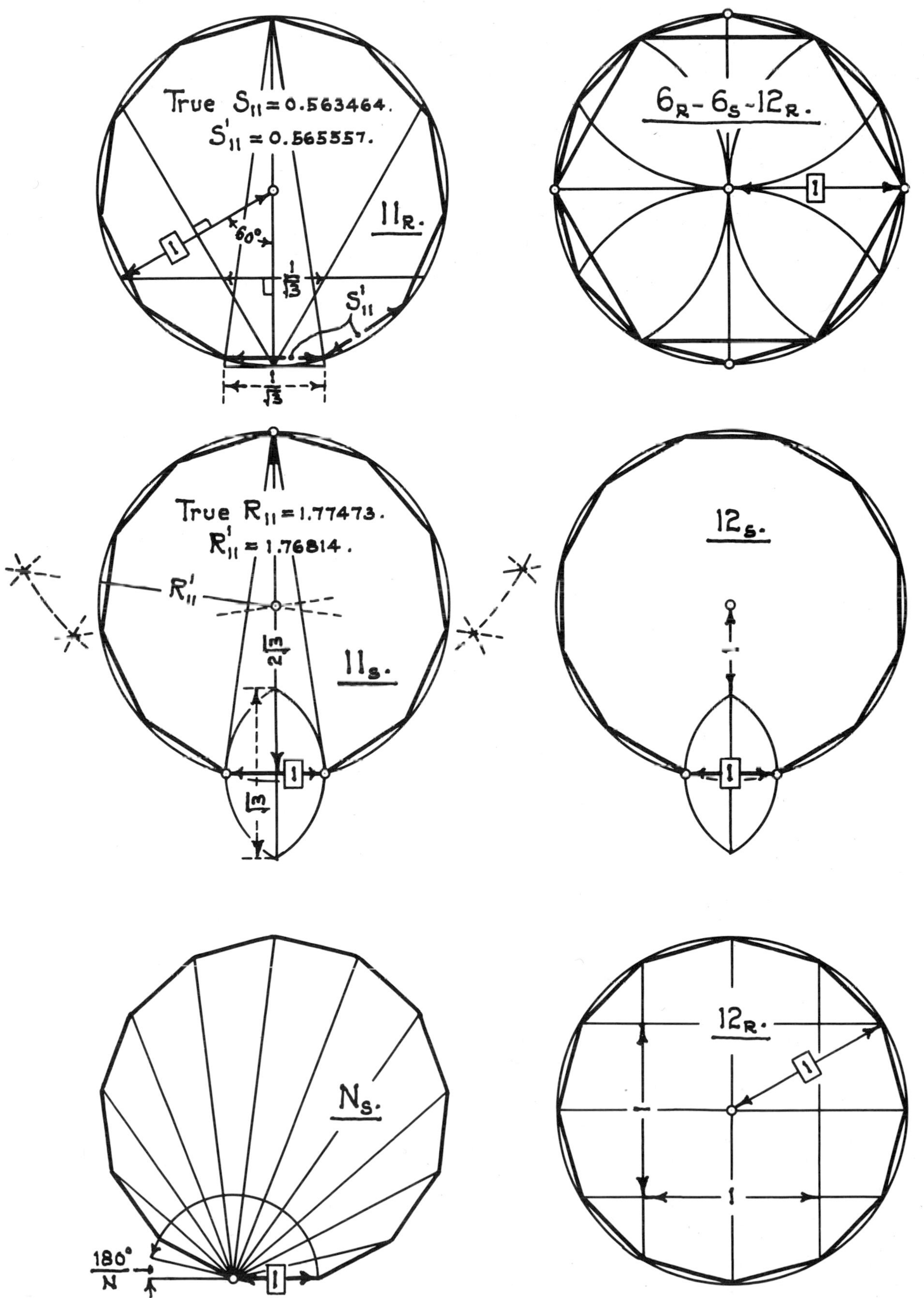

DRAWING THE POLYGONS.

An n sided regular polygon with sides of a given length, s, can be inscribed in a circle of xs radius.

A circle of given radius, r, circumscribes an n sided regular polygon with sides of yr length.

RSB.

n	$\frac{360°}{n}$	x	y	n	$\frac{360°}{n}$	x	y
3	120°	0.5774	1.732	20	18°	3.196	0.3129
4	90°	0.7071	1.414	21	17°09'	3.355	0.2981
5	72°	0.8506	1.176	22	16°22'	3.513	0.2846
6	60°	1.0000	1.0000	23	13°59'	3.672	0.2723
7	51°26'	1.1525	0.8678	24	15°	3.831	0.2611
8	45°	1.3066	0.7654	26	13°51'	4.148	0.2411
9	40°	1.4619	0.6840	28	12°51'	4.468	0.2239
10	36°	1.6180	0.6180	30	12°	4.783	0.2091
11	32°44'	1.7747	0.5635	32	11°15'	5.101	0.1960
12	30°	1.9318	0.5176	34	10°35'	5.419	0.1845
13	27°42'	2.089	0.4786	36	10°	5.737	0.1743
14	25°43'	2.247	0.4450	42	8°34'	6.694	0.1495
15	24°	2.405	0.4158	48	7°30'	7.645	0.1308
16	22°30'	2.563	0.3902	60	6°	9.554	0.1047
17	21°11'	2.721	0.3675	72	5°	11.462	0.0872
18	20°	2.879	0.3473	84	4°17'	13.372	0.0748
19	18°57'	3.038	0.3292	96	3°45	15.282	0.0654

Diagonals of Regular Polygons.

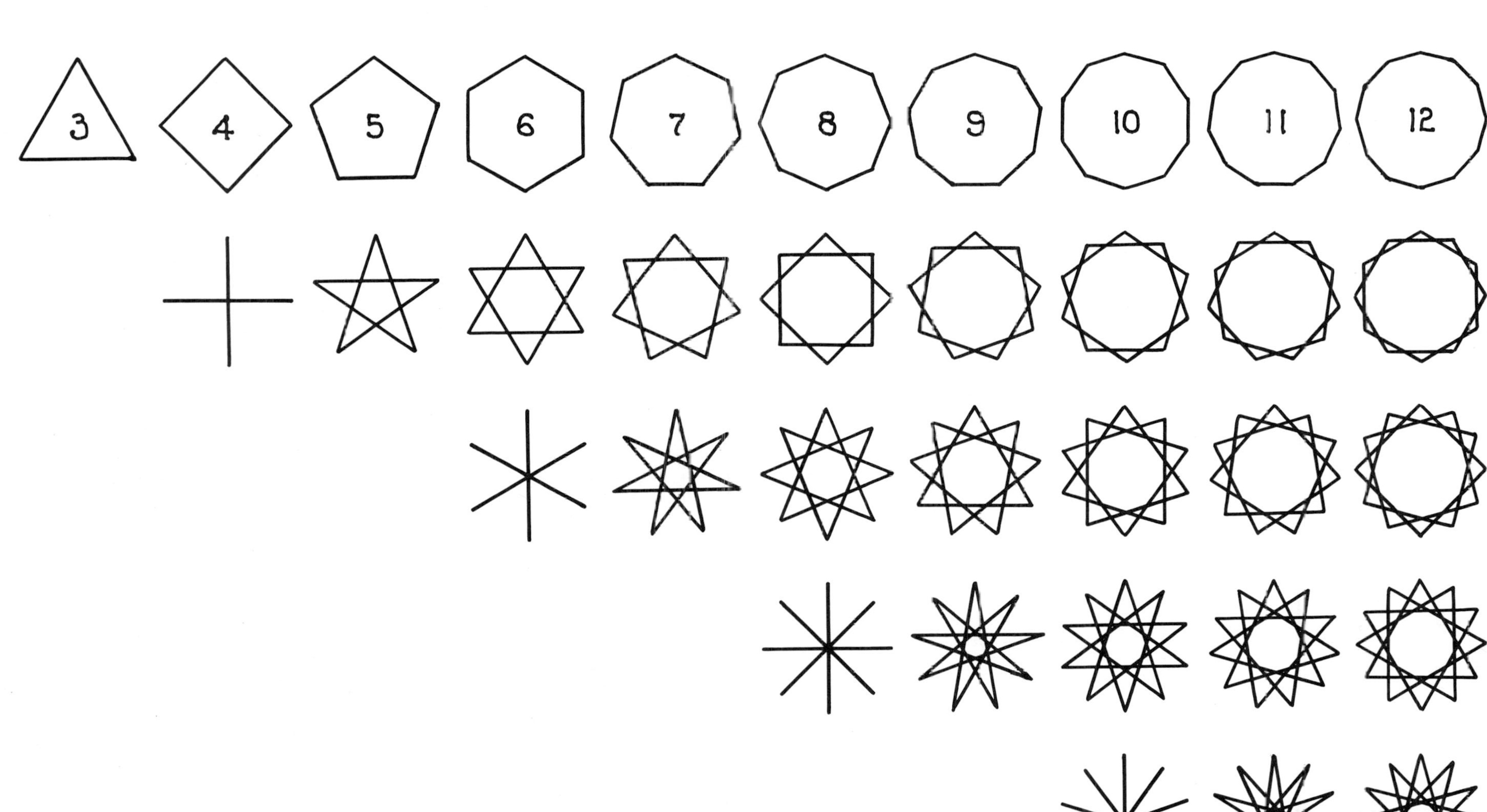

Diagonals of 24 Sided Polygon.

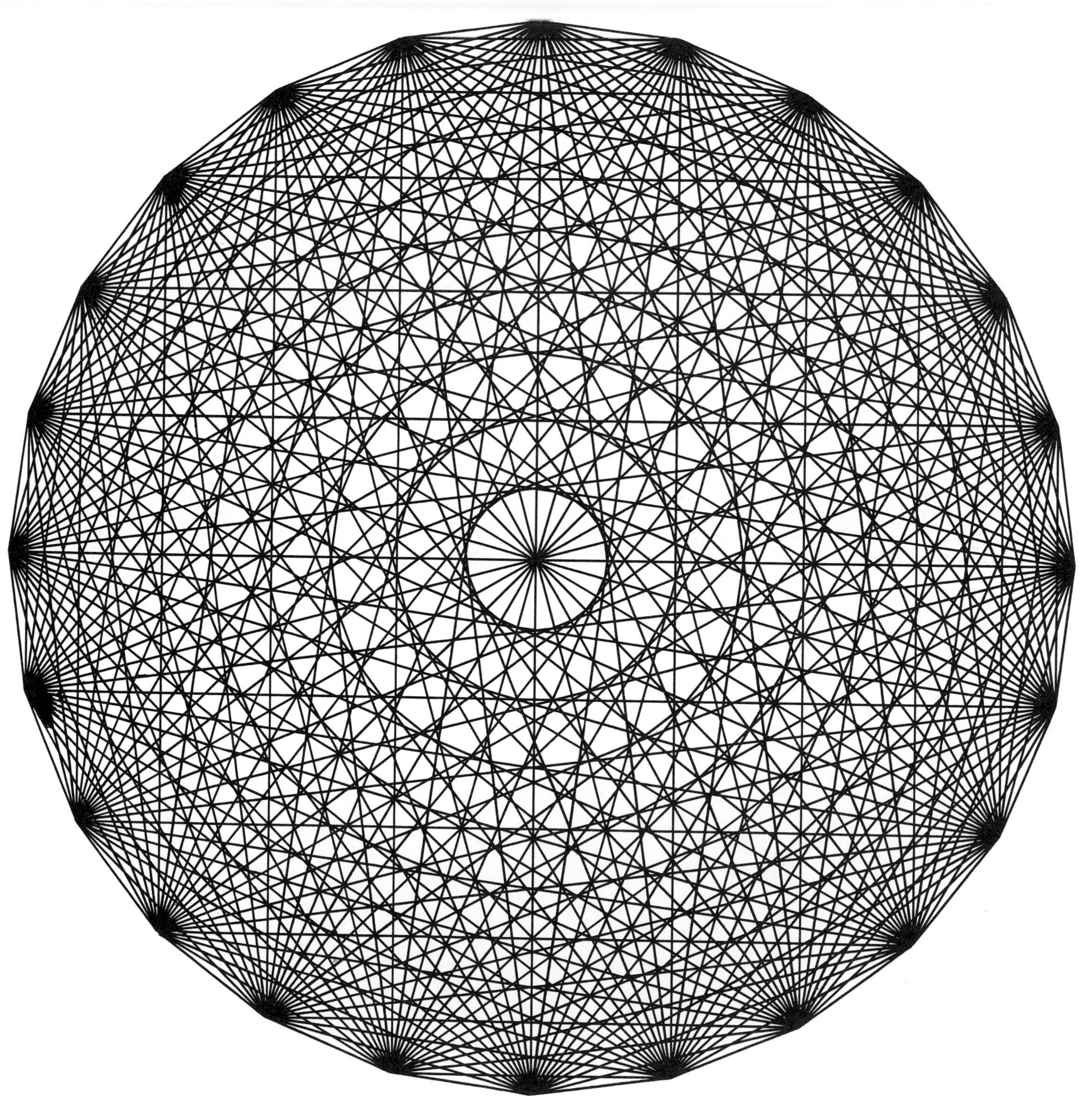

Two Sets of Diagonals in 24 Sided Polygon.

The diagonals that intersect on circle A intercept one side of the bounding polygon. The diagonals that intersect on circle B intercept two sides of the polygon. And so on. Points a,b,c,d,etc are the centers of circles A,B,C,D,etc respectively. The centers of the last nine circles lie on the vertical axis below point h in the reverse order of points h to z.

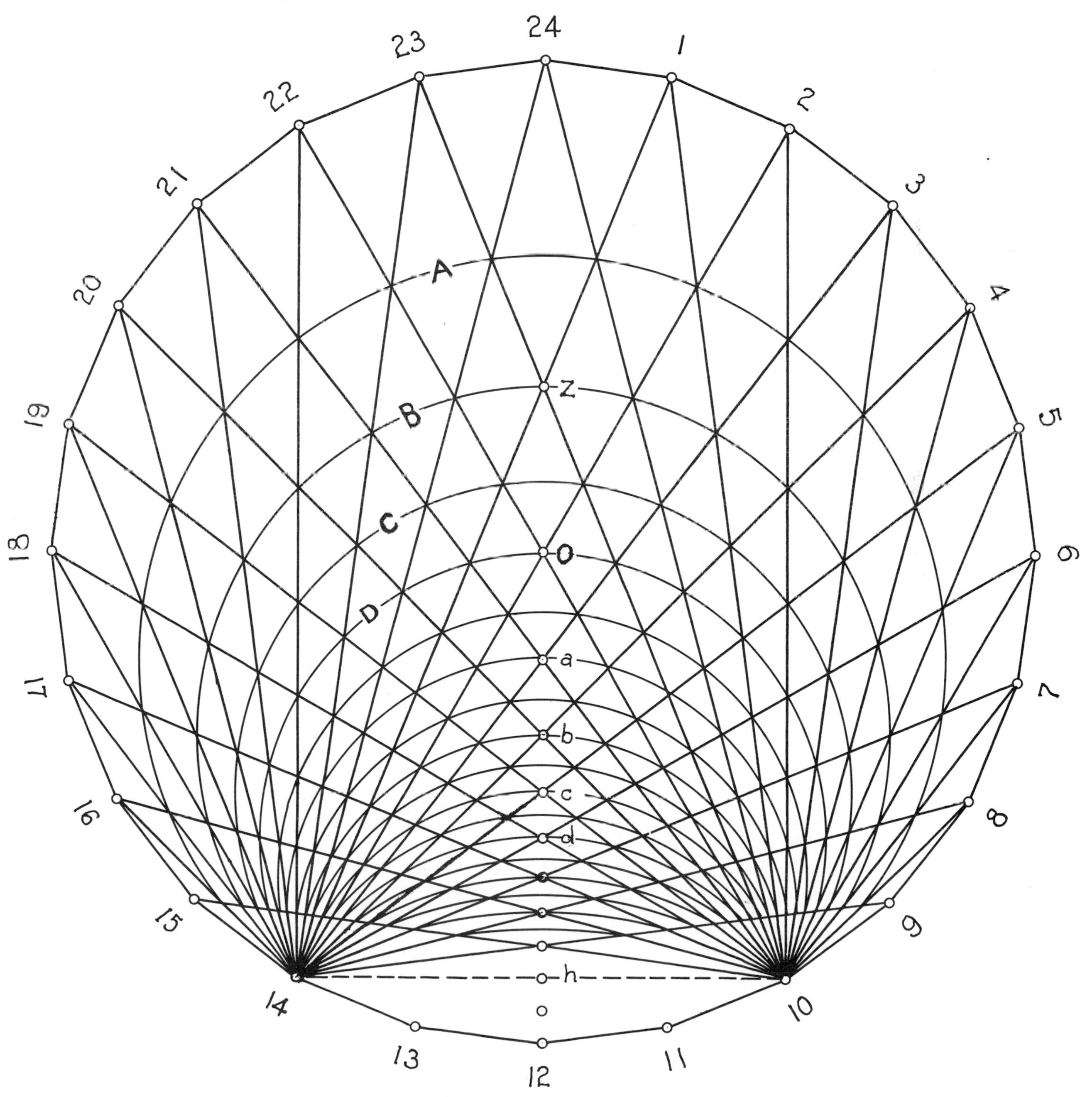

Series.–Diagonals in 24 Sided Polygon.

This tessellation transforms a line drawing into a surface effect. Treating the drawing of the full set of diagonals as a projection of the earth on its equatorial plane sets the poles at its center. The $7\frac{1}{2}°$ circles of latitude lie in its concentric polygons. Its diameters become the circles of longitude at 15° intervals. A multicolored drawing of this polygon with all diagonals can have a separate color for each interior polygon if diagonals of the same length are colored alike.

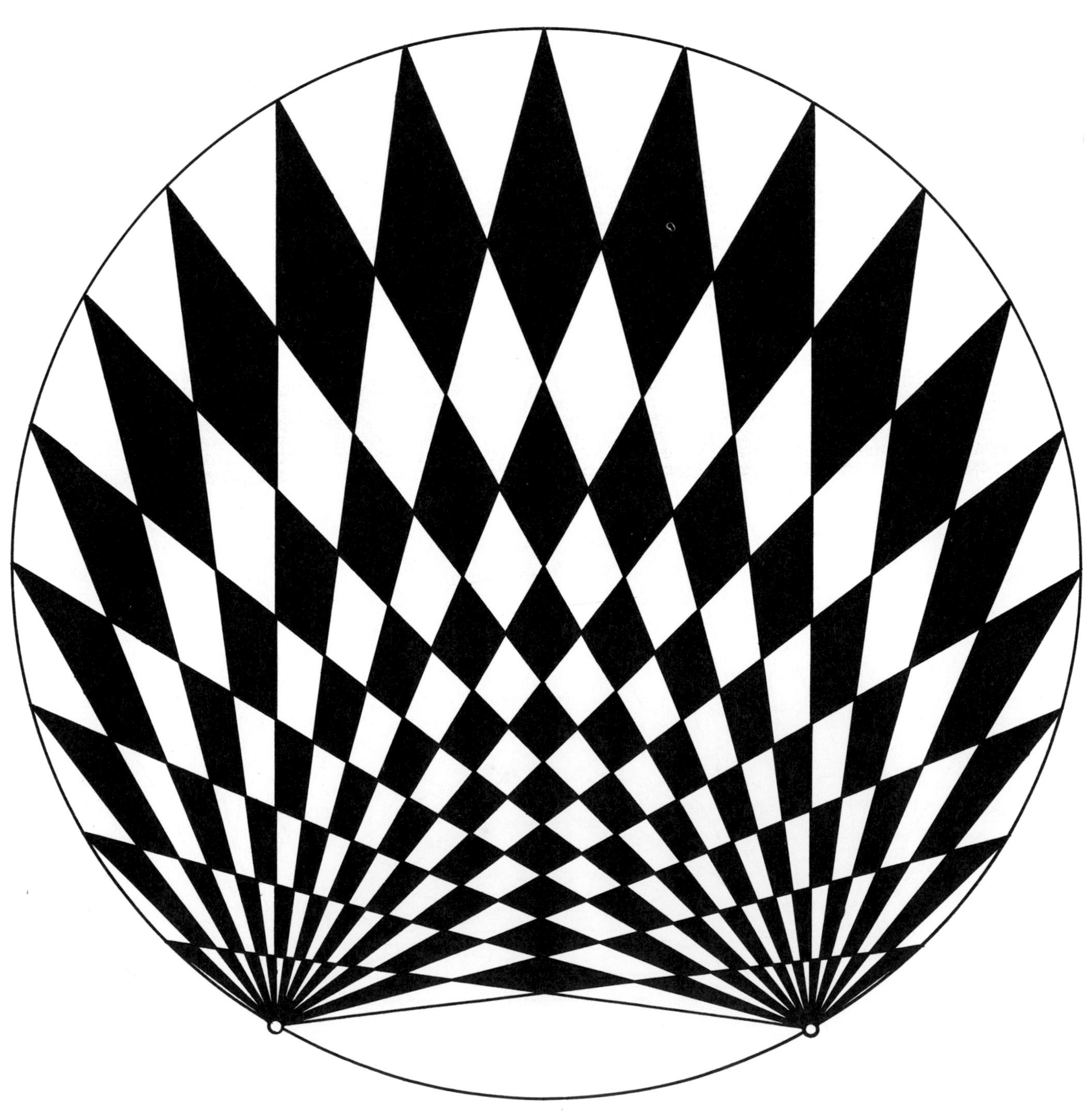

Two Sets of Diagonals in 24 Sided Polygon in Duplicate.

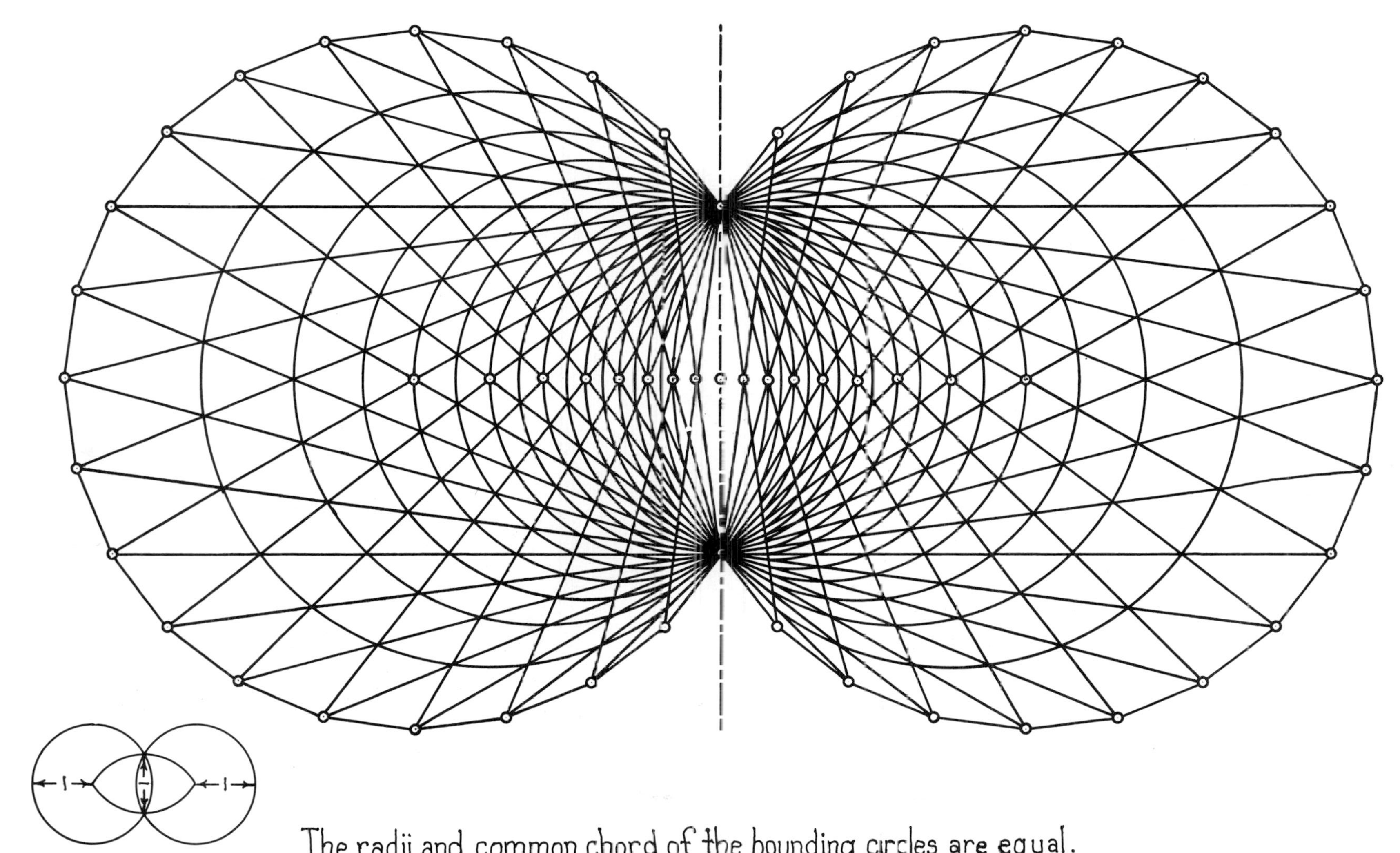

The radii and common chord of the bounding circles are equal.

Each encircled interior point is the center for a circular arc in each half of this twin figure.

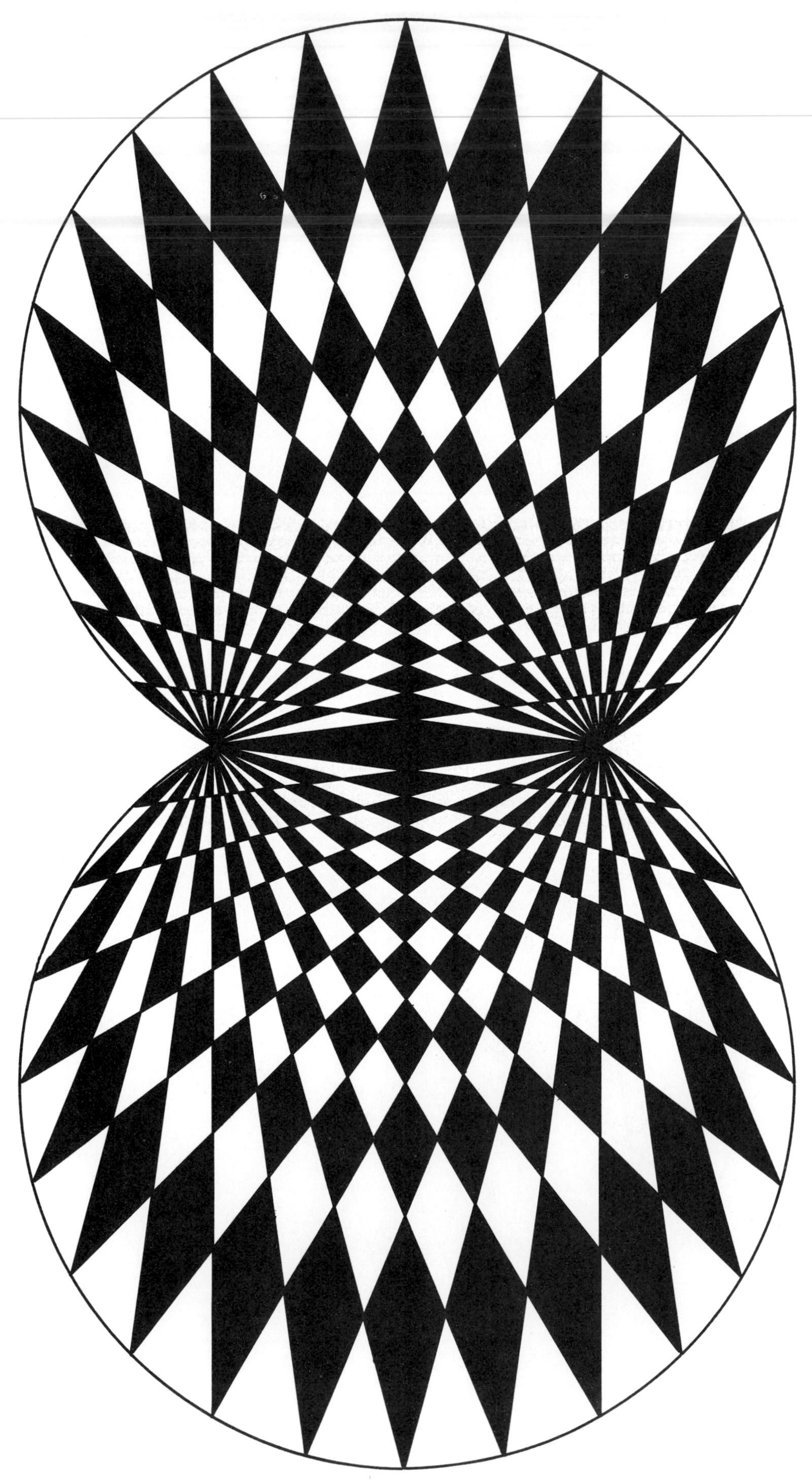

A Right Triangle Cut into n^2 Equal Parts.

Divide each leg of triangle into n equal parts and follow construction shown here for $n=7$.

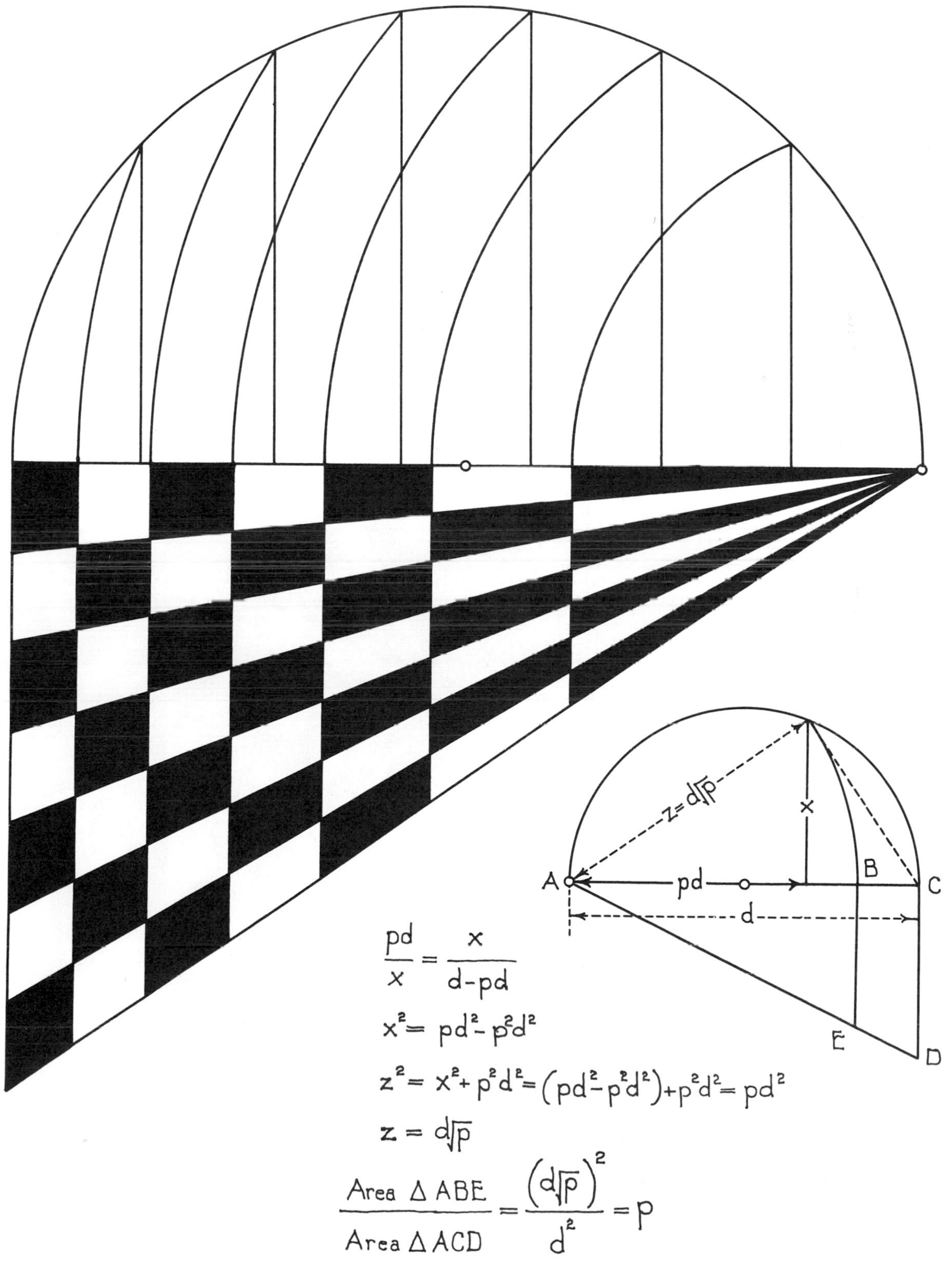

$z=d\sqrt{p}$
x
A
pd
B
C
d
E
D
$\frac{pd}{x}=\frac{x}{d-pd}$
$x^2=pd^2-p^2d^2$
$z^2=x^2+p^2d^2=(pd^2-p^2d^2)+p^2d^2=pd^2$
$z=d\sqrt{p}$
$\frac{\text{Area } \Delta \text{ ABE}}{\text{Area } \Delta \text{ ACD}}=\frac{(d\sqrt{p})^2}{d^2}=p$

Subdividing a Square.

The interior squares divide the figure into four equal areas.
All unit spaces have equal areas.
Use this construction on the altitude of any triangle.

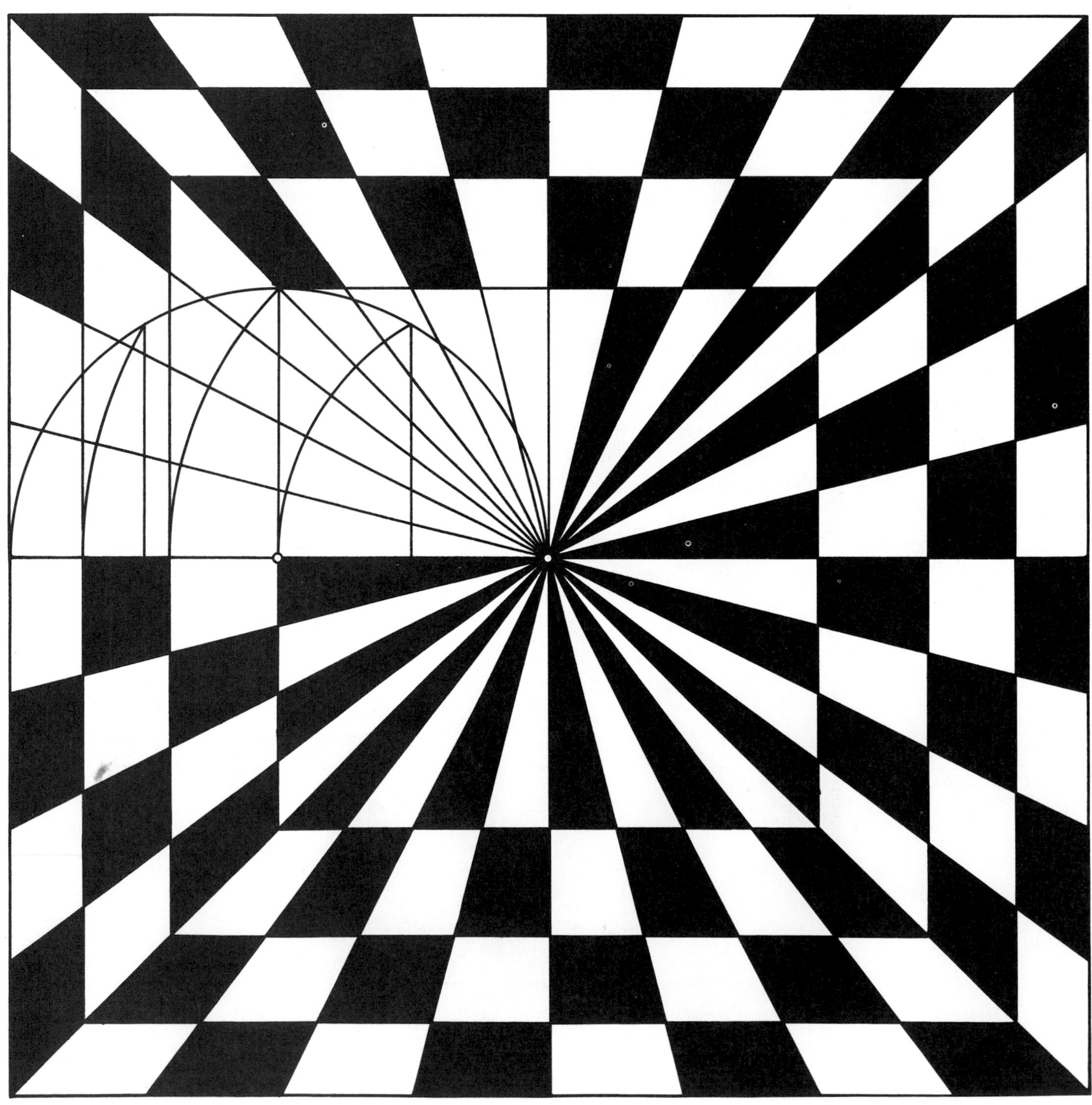

Five Concentric Hexagons.

Ratio of sides of hexagons. $1 - \sqrt{2} - \sqrt{3} - \sqrt{4} - \sqrt{5}$.
Ratio of areas of hexagons. 1 - 2 - 3 - 4 - 5 .
All unit spaces have equal areas.

THE NONAGON.

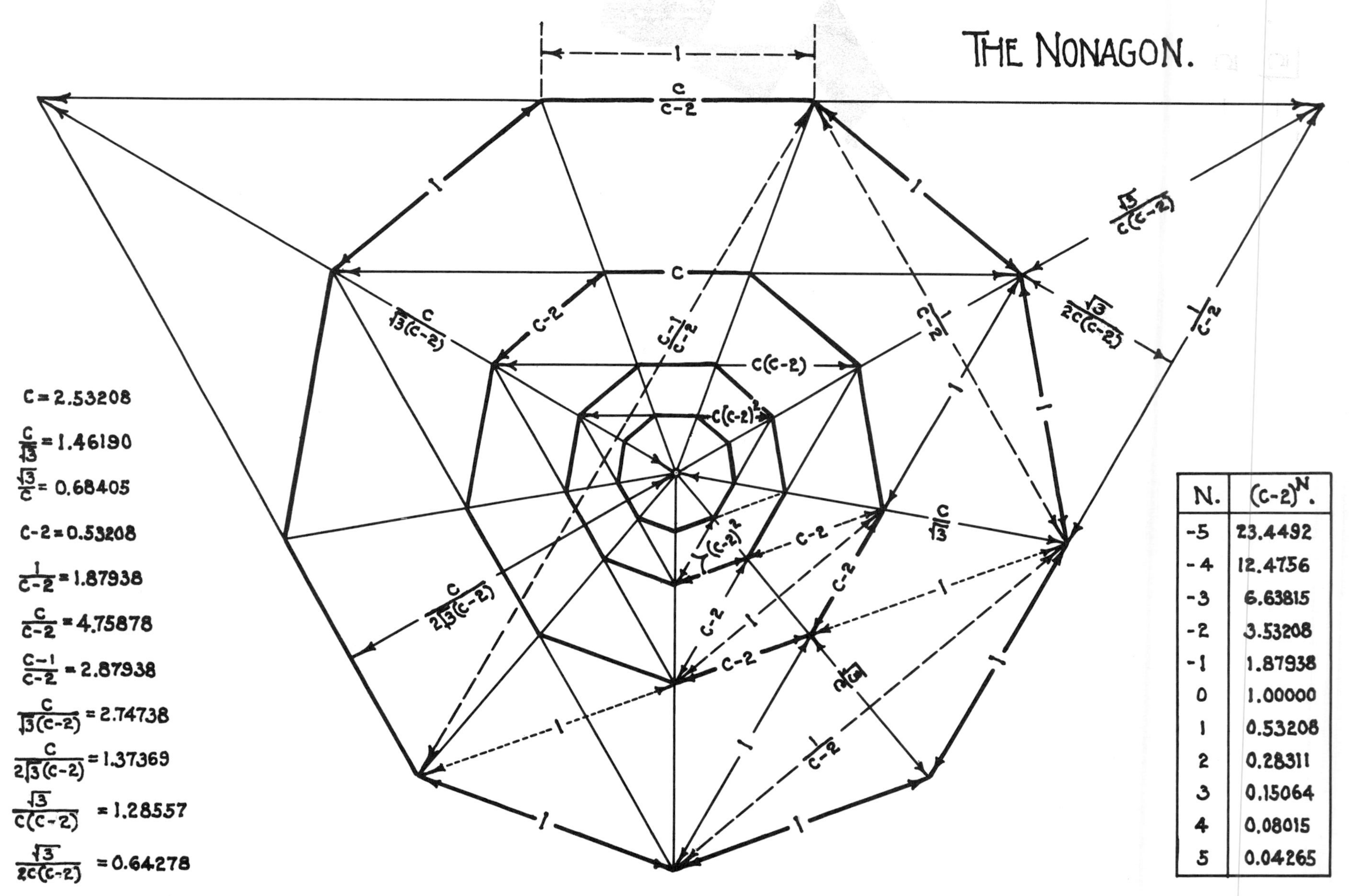

N.	$(c-2)^N$.
-5	23.4492
-4	12.4756
-3	6.63815
-2	3.53208
-1	1.87938
0	1.00000
1	0.53208
2	0.28311
3	0.15064
4	0.08015
5	0.04265

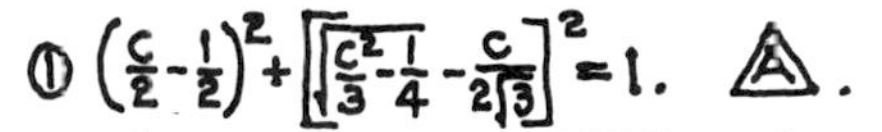

THE NONAGON.

① $\left(\frac{C}{2}-\frac{1}{2}\right)^2+\left[\sqrt{\frac{C^2}{3}-\frac{1}{4}}-\frac{C}{2\sqrt{3}}\right]^2=1.$ △.

② $\frac{C^2}{4}-\frac{C}{2}+\frac{1}{4}+\frac{C^2}{3}-\frac{1}{4}-\frac{C}{\sqrt{3}}\sqrt{\frac{C^2}{3}-\frac{1}{4}}+\frac{C^2}{12}=1.$

③ $\frac{2}{3}C^2-\frac{1}{2}C-1=C\sqrt{\frac{C^2}{9}-\frac{1}{12}}.$

④ $\frac{4}{9}C^4-\frac{2}{3}C^3-\frac{13}{12}C^2+C+1=\frac{C^4}{9}-\frac{C^2}{12}$

⑤ $\frac{1}{3}C^4-\frac{2}{3}C^3-C^2+C+1=0.$

⑥ $\underline{C=2.53208}$

⑦ $\frac{C}{\sqrt{3}}=1.46190$

⑧ $2\sqrt{C^2-\frac{3}{4}}=4.75877$

⑨ $2\sqrt{\frac{C^2}{3}-\frac{1}{4}}-\frac{C}{\sqrt{3}}=1.28557$

⑩ $\sqrt{\frac{C^2}{3}-\frac{1}{4}}-\frac{C}{2\sqrt{3}}=0.642785.$ $1_o=1.00669.$

$\frac{3}{C^2}=3-C.$ $(C+1)(C^3-3C^2+3)=0.$ $(C+1)(C-2)^2=1.$ $\frac{C^3}{3}=C^2-1.$ $\sqrt{C+1}=\frac{1}{C-2}.$

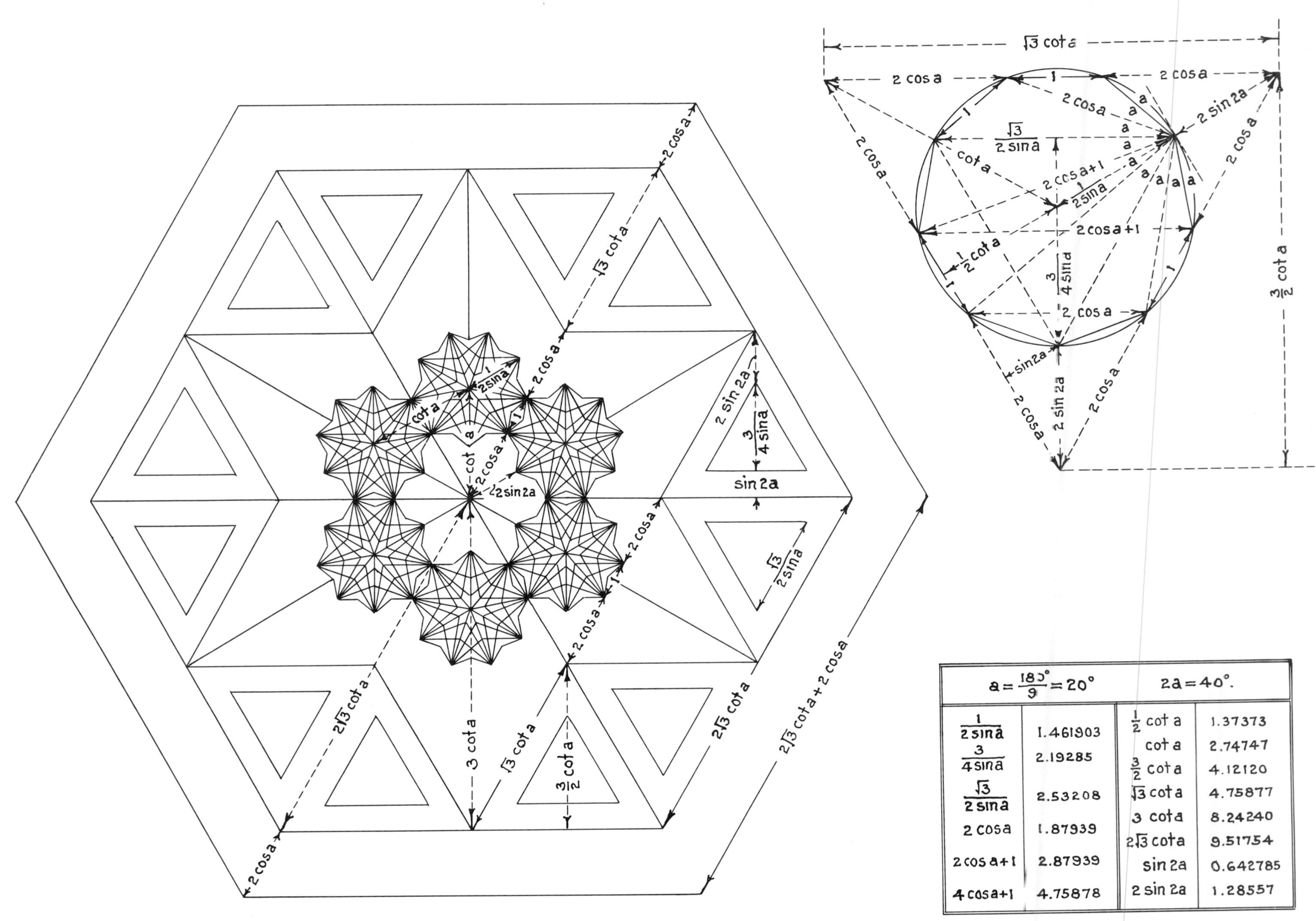

$a = \frac{180°}{9} = 20°$		$2a = 40°$	
$\frac{1}{2 \sin a}$	1.461903	$\frac{1}{2} \cot a$	1.37373
$\frac{3}{4 \sin a}$	2.19285	$\cot a$	2.74747
$\frac{\sqrt{3}}{2 \sin a}$	2.53208	$\frac{3}{2} \cot a$	4.12120
$2 \cos a$	1.87939	$\sqrt{3} \cot a$	4.75877
$2 \cos a + 1$	2.87939	$3 \cot a$	8.24240
$4 \cos a + 1$	4.75878	$2\sqrt{3} \cot a$	9.51754
		$\sin 2a$	0.642785
		$2 \sin 2a$	1.28557

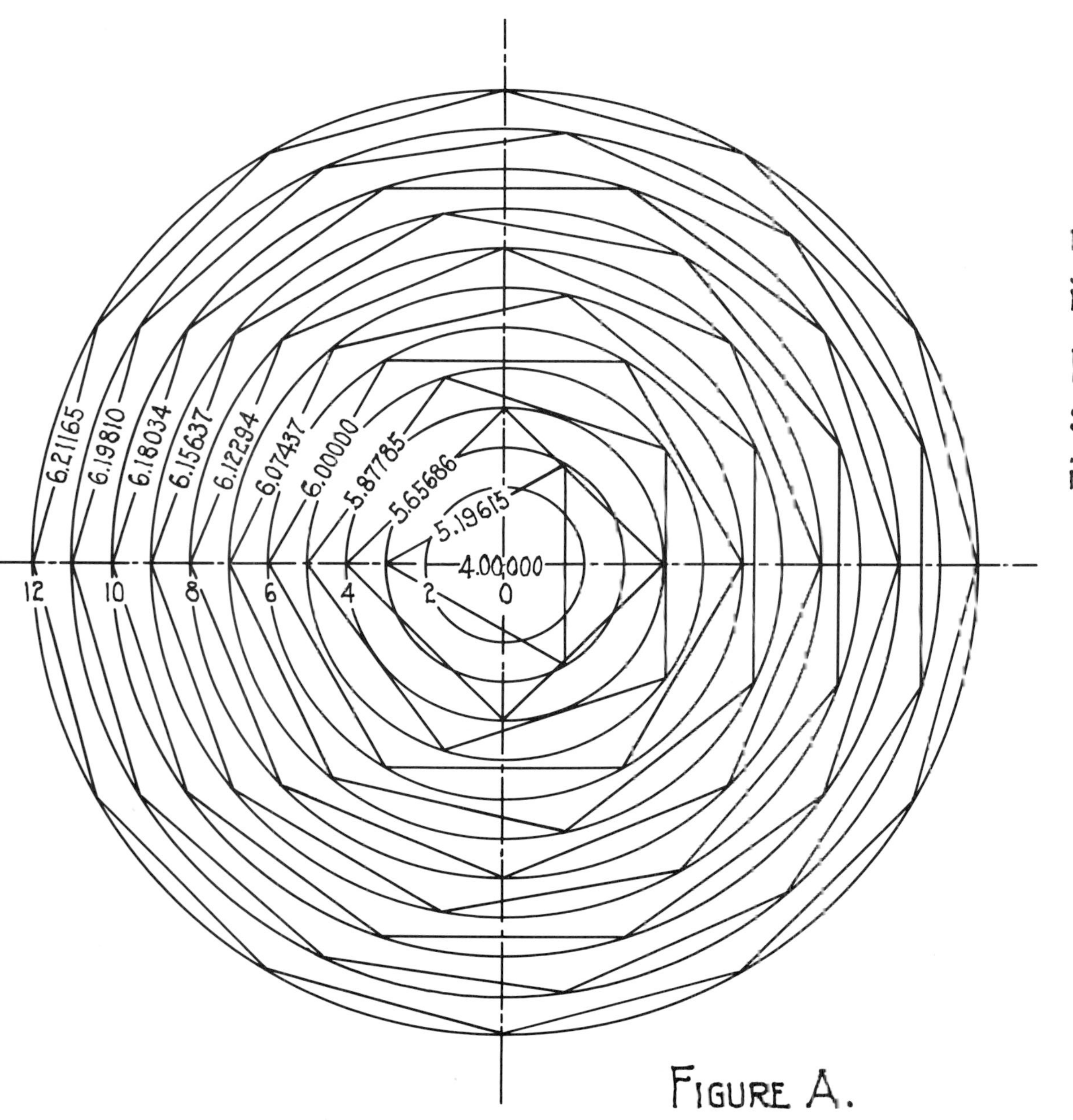

FIGURE A.

THE VALUE OF 2π.

In Figure A, the radius of any circle, n, is n units long and an n sided regular polygon is inscribed in the circle. S_n, the side of the polygon, is measured in terms of the unit subdivisions of the radius. S_n approaches 2π in value as n increases. 2π = 6.28318531.

SIDES OF REGULAR POLYGONS.

$$S_n = 2n \sin\frac{180^\circ}{n}.$$

n.	S_n.	n.	S_n.
2	4.00000	10	6.18034
3	5.19615	11	6.19810
4	5.65686	12	6.21165
5	5.87785	36	6.27520
6	6.00000	360	6.28310
7	6.07437	3600	6.28317
8	6.12294	10800	6.28319
9	6.15637	∞	2π

All S_n arcs are 2π long.

section II

TESSELLATED POLYGONS

Reprinted from Scripta Mathematica, Vol. XVII, Nos. 1–2. March–June, 1951

TESSELLATED POLYGONS

By Colonel Robert S. Beard

Any regular polygon P_n of n sides of length s each can be tessellated into a pattern of diamonds with sides of length $^1/_2 s$.

When n is an even number, P_n yields $n\left(\frac{n}{2} - 1\right)$ such diamonds of which n are grouped around the center of the polygon and the others form alternating belts of n diamonds each. This is illustrated by the tessellation of the eight polygons on plate 1.

When n is an odd number, P_n is tessellated into $n\left(\frac{n-1}{2}\right)$ diamonds. In this case the n central diamonds overlap to form an n pointed star, the width of which $= {}^1/_2 s$. The tessellation of eight such polygons is shown on plate 2.

When n is even, P_n can also be tessellated into diamonds with sides $= s$ instead of $^1/_2 s$. This is illustrated on plate 3. When n is of the form $4k + 2$, the tessellation yields $\frac{n}{4}\left(\frac{n}{2} - 1\right) = 2k^2 + k$ diamonds. If $n = 4k$ the number of diamonds is $^1/_8 n^2 = 2k^2$.

A method for tessellating a regular polygon into $s/2$ diamonds is illustrated by the pentagonal Figures A and B.

Let O be the center and R the radius of the circumscribed circle. With O as a center and $^1/_2 R$ as a radius draw another circle. Draw the radii OD OE, OF, OG, OH intersecting the smaller circle in the points C_1, C_2, C_3, C_4, C_5. From each of these points as a center and $^1/_2 R$ as a radius draw a circle.

We shall prove that the circumference of each of these circles is divided by its points of intersection with the other circles into five equal parts.

Denote by J the intersection of the circles C_1 and C_2 and consider the quadrilateral JC_1OC_2. By construction each of its sides $= {}^1/_2 R$, hence it is a rhombus whose acute angle $C_1OC_2 = {}^1/_5 \cdot 360° = 72°$, and $DC_1J = C_1OC_2 = 72°$. Hence arc $DJ = {}^1/_5$ of the circumference C_1.

Circles C_3 and C_1 intersect at W. The quadrilateral WC_1OC_3 is another diamond and its side WC_1 is parallel to the radius OF. Angle DOF is $= {}^2/_5$ of 360° by construction, and so is its corresponding angle DC_1W. Angle JC_1W = difference between the angles DC_1W and $DC_1J = 72°$. Hence the arc $JC = {}^1/_5$ of the circumference C_1.

By similar reasoning each of the arcs DN and NZ is $^1/_5$ of C_1 and the remaining arc ZW must be of the same length.

Hence $DJWZN$ is a regular pentagon inscribed in C_1. Its side is evidently equal to $^1/_2 s$.

The same is true about the circumferences of the circles C_2, C_3, C_4, and C_5. Each one of them is cut into five equal parts, giving rise to a regular pentagon equal to the one inscribed in C_1.

As a by-product of this construction, we get also the five diamonds $DJVN$, $JEKW$, $KFLX$, $LGMY$, $MHNZ$, and five diamonds $JWYV$, $KWZX$, $LYVX$, $MYWZ$, $NZXV$. The overlapping parts of this second group of diamonds form the stellar pentagon $VWXYZ$. In each of these figures the side $= {}^1/_2$.

In the same way the tessellation of any regular polygon can be demonstrated. When the bounding polygon has an even number of sides, all polygons inscribed in the $R/2$ circles have a common vertex at the center O, and there is no overlapping.

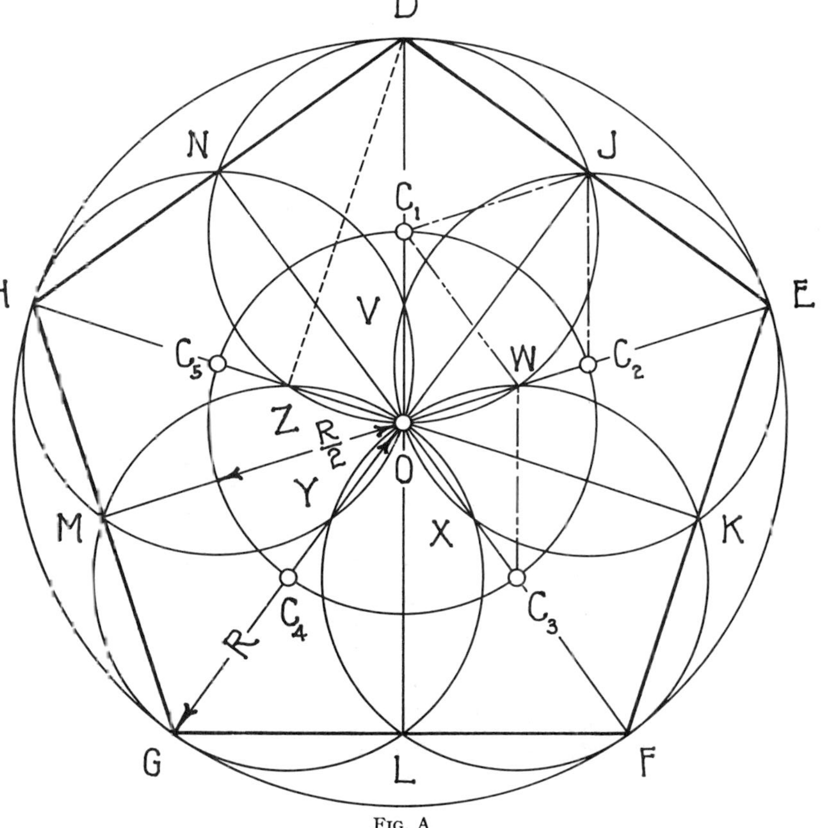

Fig. A

In Fig. A, DNO and DZO are right angles as DO is a diameter of the circle C_1. Denoting $180/n$ by α we have in Fig. B: $DON = \alpha$, $ON = R\cos\alpha$. Similarly $DOH = 2\alpha$, $OZ = R\cos 2\alpha$.

The corresponding points J, K, L, M, and N lie in a circle of radius $R\cos\alpha$ centered at O and the points V, W, X, Y, and Z lie on a concentric circle of radius $R\cos 2\alpha$.

It develops that if radii are drawn to each of the vertices and the midpoints of the sides of a regular polygon, the corners of all of its $s/2$ diamonds are located at the intersections of these $2n$ radii with concentric circles whose

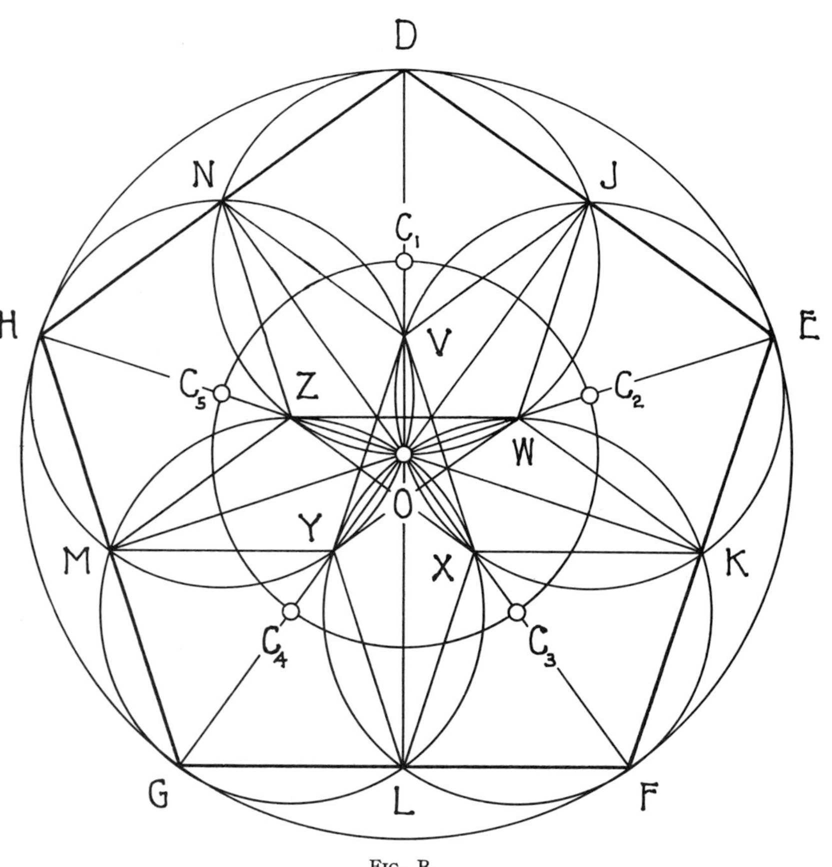

Fig. B

radii are R, $R \cos \alpha$, $R \cos 2\alpha$, $R \cos 3\alpha$, . . . $R \cos \left(\frac{n-1}{2}\right) \alpha$ or $R \cos \left(\frac{n}{2} - 1\right) \alpha$ for odd- and even-sided polygons, respectively.

In each even-sided regular polygon, the $\frac{1}{2}s$ diamonds meeting at the center of the figure are of the same size and number and therefore of the

same total area as the outer belt of diamonds. The same relationship holds between the diamonds that are adjacent to the central diamonds and those adjacent to the outer belt, and so on.

A belt of squares occurs midway between the center and perimeter of the regular polygons having a number of sides divisible by four.

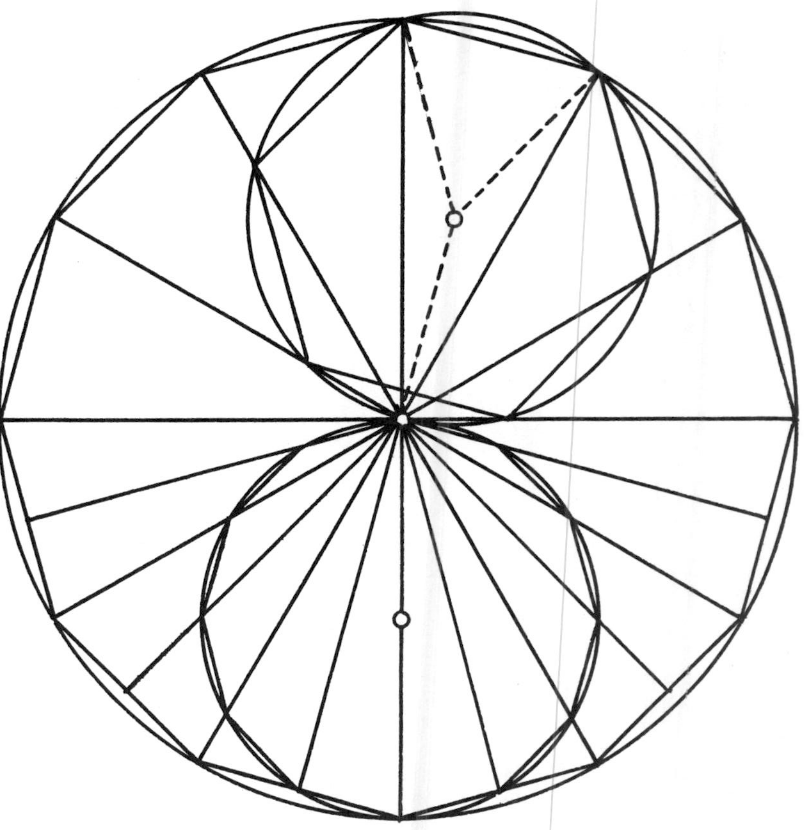

Rhombic Subdivision of Dodecagon.

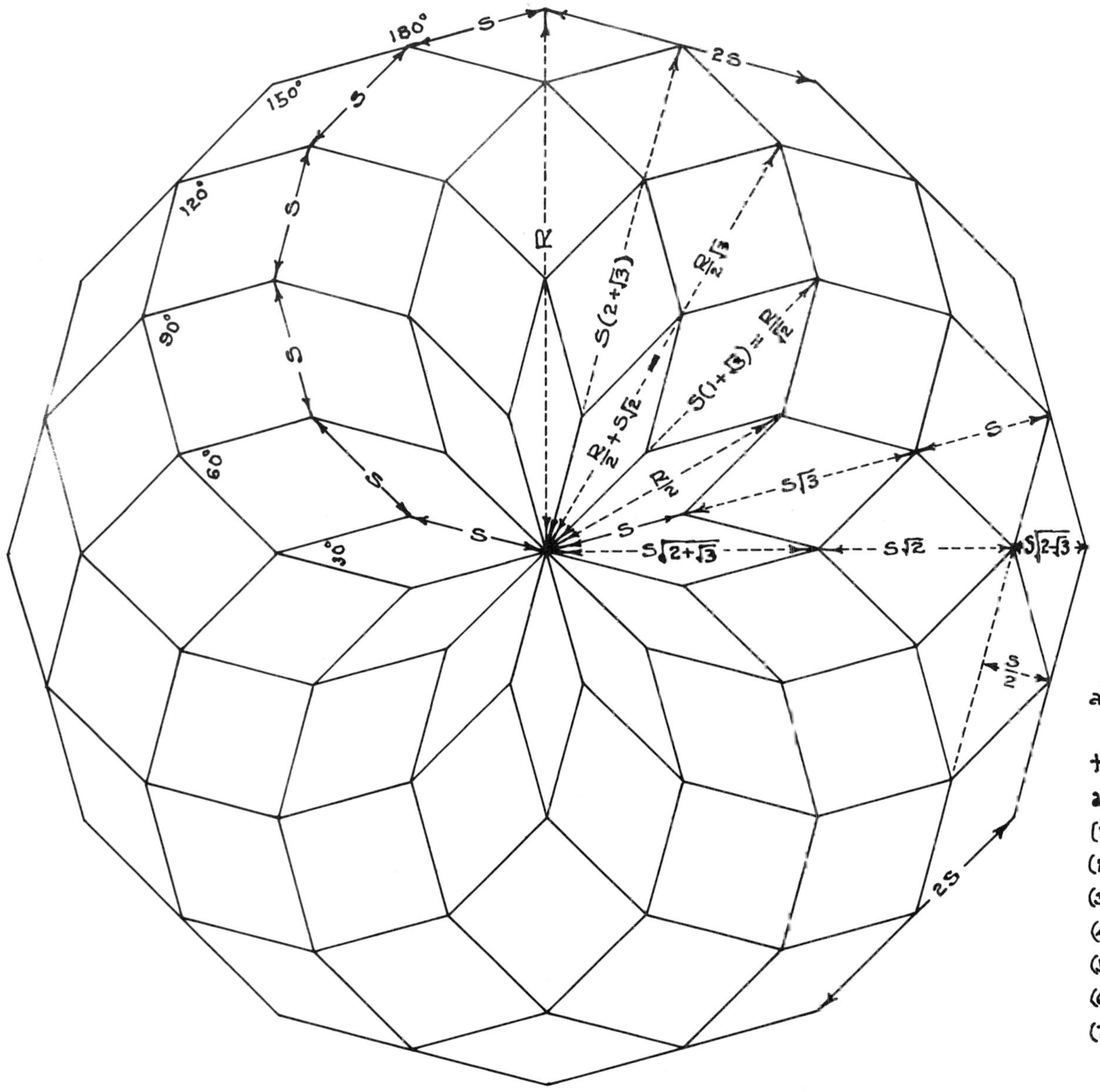

Coordinates for Plotting the Dodecagon.

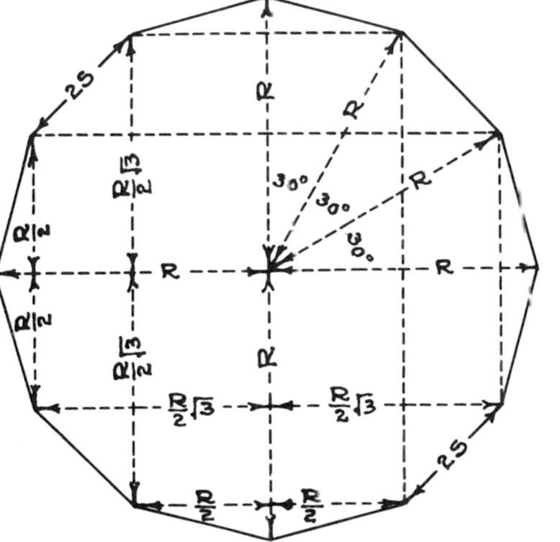

The sixty unit squares and diamonds composing the dodecagon all have sides of the same length, s.

All angle points in this figure are located on the radii drawn to the corners of the dodecagon and to the midpoints of its sides. Each angle point is located at one of the following distances from the center:

(1.) $0 = 0.000000$

(2.) $S = 1.000000\,S = 0.258819\,R.$

(3.) $\frac{R}{2} = 1.931852\,S$

(4.) $S(1+\sqrt{3}) = 2.732051\,S = \frac{R}{\sqrt{2}}$

(5.) $\frac{R}{2} + S\sqrt{2} = 3.346066\,S = \frac{R}{2}\sqrt{3} = S\sqrt{\frac{3}{2}}(\sqrt{3}+1).$

(6.) $S(2+\sqrt{3}) = 3.732051\,S.$

(7.) $R = 3.863703\,S = \frac{S}{\sin 15^\circ} = 2S\sqrt{2+\sqrt{3}} = \frac{2S}{\sqrt{2-\sqrt{3}}} = S\sqrt{2}(\sqrt{3}+1) = \frac{2S\sqrt{2}}{\sqrt{3}-1}$

All interior angle points are the intersection points of twelve circles with radii of $\frac{R}{2}$ centered on the points of the star.

Unit Areas. Squares – S^2. 30° diamonds. – $\frac{S^2}{2}$.

60° diamonds – $\frac{S^2}{2}\sqrt{3}$

Total Area. – $12S^2 + 24\times\frac{S^2}{2} + 24\times\frac{S^2}{2}\sqrt{3} = 12S^2(2+\sqrt{3}).$

Perimeter. — 24S.

$\sin 15^\circ = \frac{1}{2\sqrt{2+\sqrt{3}}} = \frac{1}{2}\sqrt{2-\sqrt{3}}$, $\cos 15^\circ = \frac{1}{2}\sqrt{2+\sqrt{3}}$, $\tan 15^\circ = \frac{1}{2+\sqrt{3}}$, $\cot 15^\circ = 2+\sqrt{3}$.

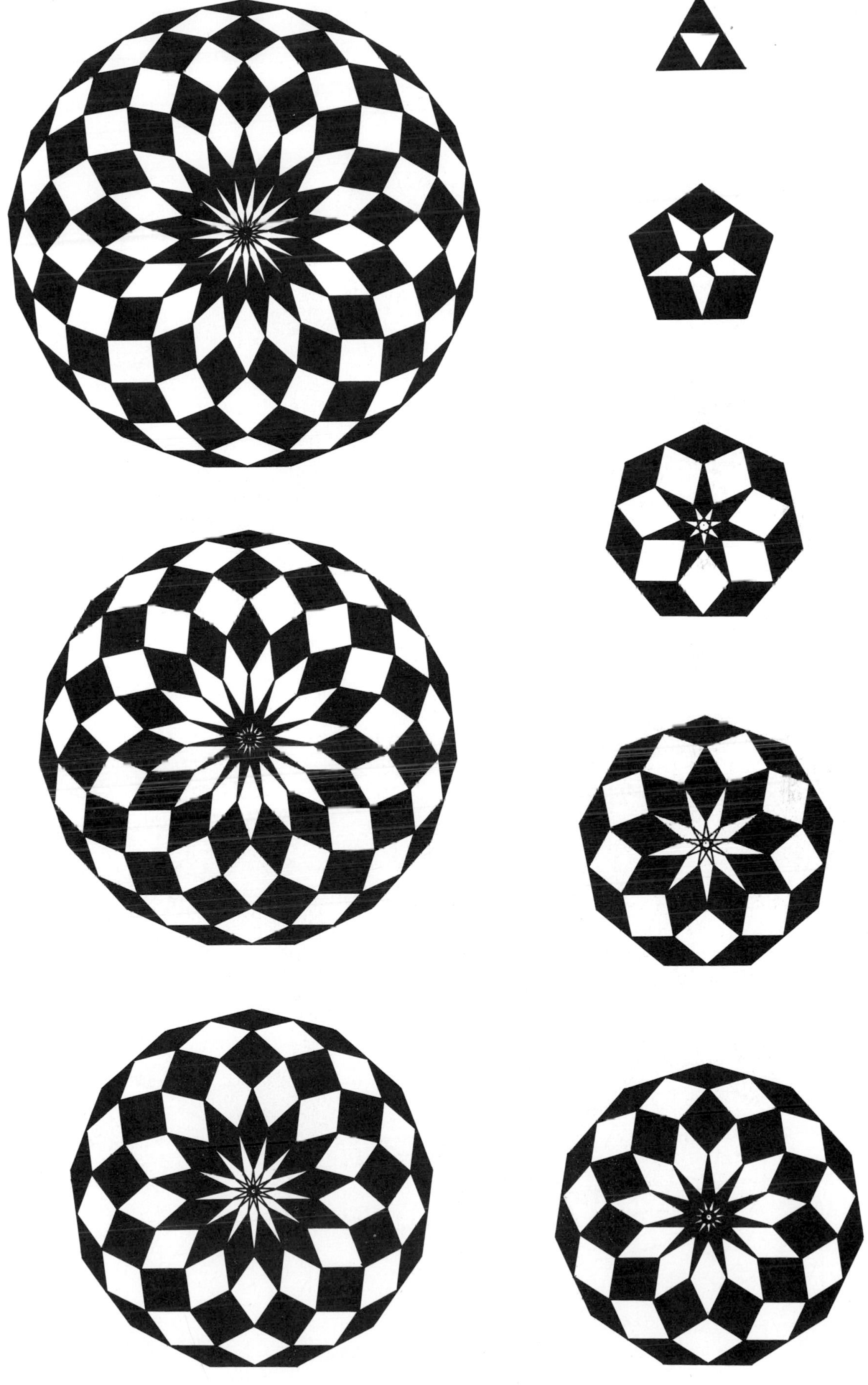

A Rose of Squares in 32 Spirals.

Growth factor – 1.273. $\frac{1}{1.273} = 0.7857.$

Tangent circles centered on vertices of diamonds.

section III

POLYHEDRA PATTERNS

POLYHEDRA MODEL CONSTRUCTION TECHNIQUES

This study of polyhedra logically starts with the definition of a regular solid and my graphic proof that the triangle, cube, octahedron, dodecahedron and icosahedron are the only regular solids that can be constructed. Patterns for constructing these solids are included in this section.

The tetrahedron has four regular triangle faces. The three extra triangles in the pattern are used in all of these patterns for strength and accuracy of construction.

The dimensions for eight sets of the five regular solids are shown on page 59. Set No. 3, equal blister spheres with a 5" cube, is recommended for exhibition purposes. This makes their edges as follows: P4–10", P6–5", P8–7.07", P12–2.70" and P20–4.37". The truncated polyhedra should be cut down from solids of the same size. The compound polyhedra, that is the two tetrahedra, the cube plus octahedron and the dodecahedron plus icosahedron should be constructed with regular solids of the same size. The cases for these figures are a cube, rhombic dodecahedron, and triacontahedron with edges of 7.07", 4.33" and 2.57" respectively.

A desirable size for each of the remaining solids can be determined by reference to tables in the book.

Large exhibition polyhedra models can be cut from 28½ x 45 inch sheets of heavy Manila tag. They can be purchased from paper dealers or printing firms. Variety stores carry smaller sized sheets.

The patterns for each model can be drawn accurately to the desired size on a record sheet. A shortened needle forced into the eraser end of a lead pencil is a good tool with which to punch needle holes through the vertices of the record patterns to transfer the figures to work sheets. A cork board or sheet of celotex prevents needle damage.

Weights can be used to hold the paper sheets in place on the table. The patterns can be cut out of the work sheets with scissors. The interior lines are creased without any scoring. A triangle or straight edge is held along the line to be creased and the paper is turned up against the edge with a strong wide blade knife. It is then turned over the full 180° and creased sharply with the knife. Much of the time the outer edge of the turned over flap can be fitted to an equal adjoining face of the drawing to insure accurate sharp creasing.

The various elements of the patterns are glued together, with Duco, Bond's Universal Cement No. 527, Ambroid or a similar type of cement. These types of cement will prevent paper warping.

Apply cement to both surfaces to be glued. Press them together for a time to insure full adhesion. Apply the cement with a narrow flat wooden spreader. Excess glue can be cleaned from the hands with acetone.

Although considerable time is required to apply colored facings to the polyhedron it is worth the effort because it can be used to emphasize the distinctive features. It also increases the strength and adds much to the attractiveness of the models.

PLATO'S FIVE REGULAR POLYHEDRA

TETRAHEDRON

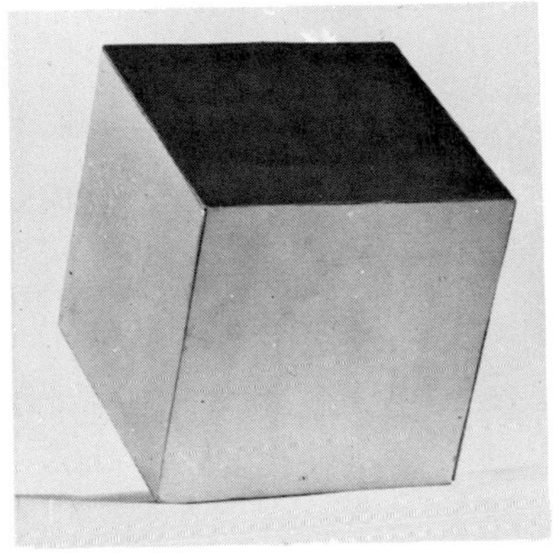

HEXAHEDRON (CUBE)

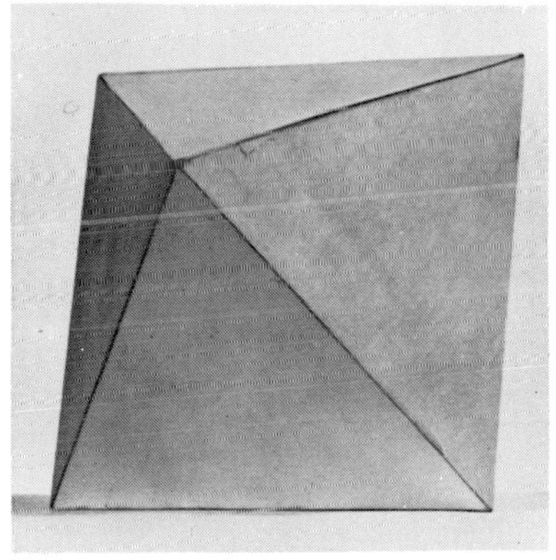

OCTAHEDRON

DODECAHEDRON

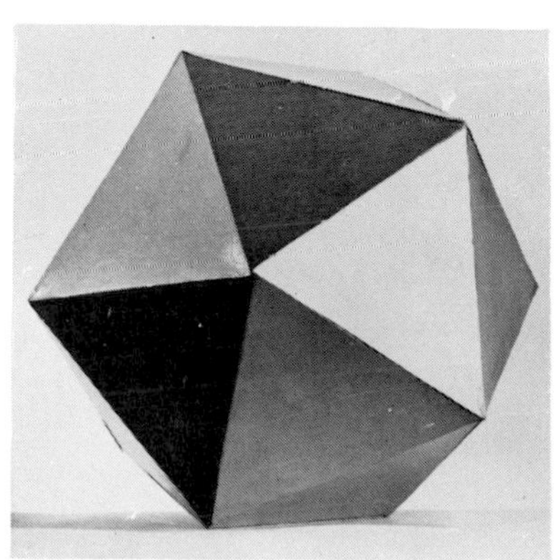

ICOSAHEDRON

Patterns for Plato's Five Regular Solids.

Cut out crosshatched areas ◁|||. Cut dotted straight lines ----. Crease solid lines ——.
Paste unit areas together in alphabetical order, (A to A, A′ to A′, B to B --- C over A to A, etc.).
Make two each of P12 and P20 and trim one of each down to heavy solid lines.
When solids are in 10 cm cover spheres $S_4 = 8.16$ cm, $S_6 = 5.77$ cm, $S_8 = 7.07$ cm, $S_{12} = 3.57$ cm and $S_{20} = 5.26$ cm.

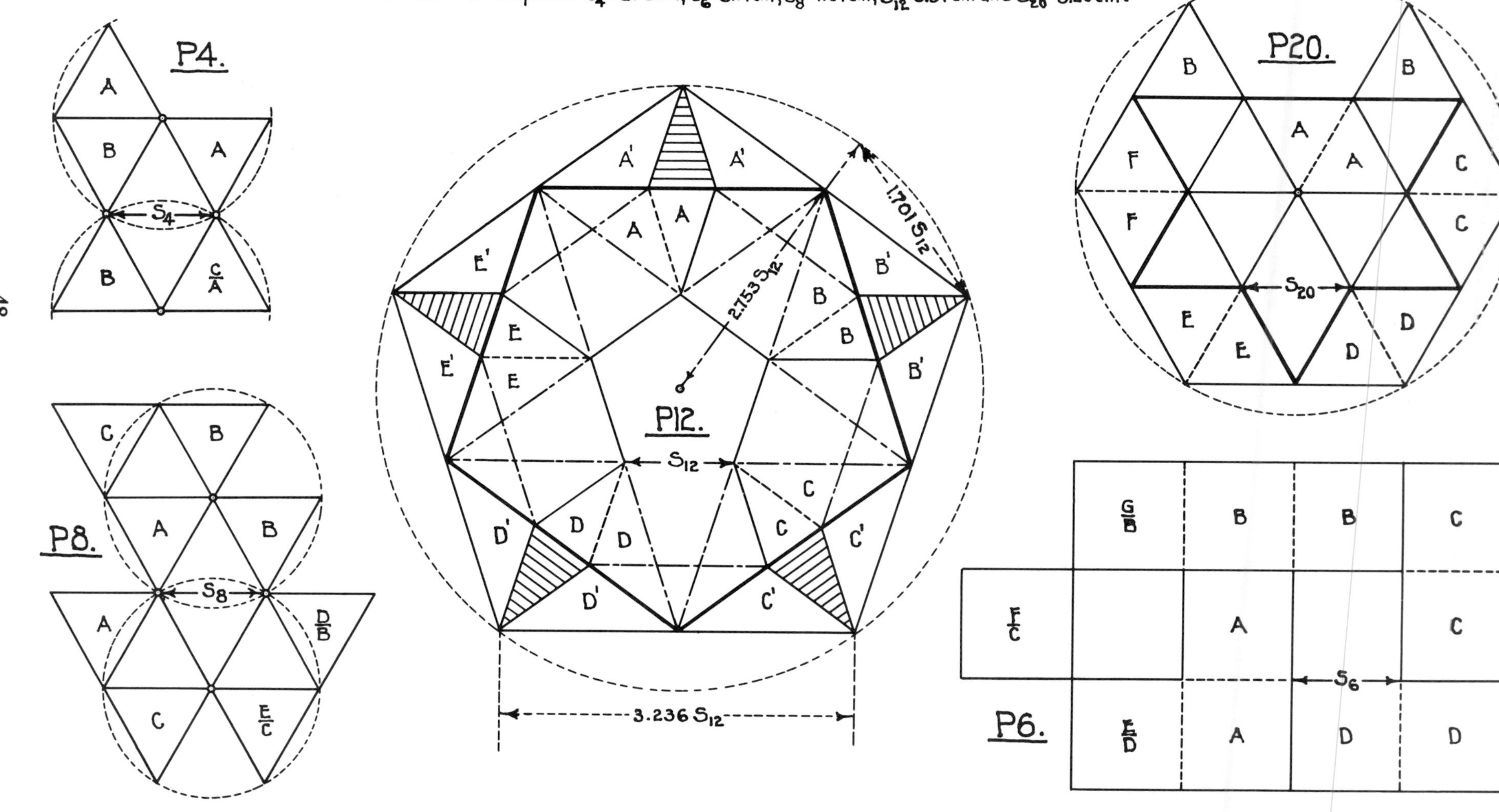

PLATO'S FIVE REGULAR SOLIDS.

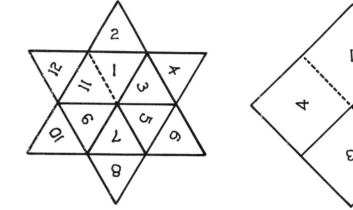

Visual Determination of Total Number.

A regular solid is faced with regular polygons of the same shape and size with all faces meeting at equal convex angles.

The number of different corners that can be formed with three or more like polygons determines the number of regular solids.

Pattern A. Six regular triangles meet at the center with angles totaling 360°. All six triangles lie in one plane and form no corner.

When the pattern is coiled to make triangles 1 and 11 coincide one of the 12 five triangle corners of the icosahedron is formed.

The pattern can be formed into an octahedron with its 6 four triangle corners when it is coiled to make triangles 1 and 9 coincide.

It can form a tetrahedron with its 4 three triangle corners when coiled to make triangles 1 and 7 fit together.

Pattern B. Four squares fill the space around a point in a plane and can form no corner.

Coil pattern and make squares 1 and 4 coincide to form half of the cube which has 8 three square corners.

Pattern C. When pentagons 1 to 5 are revolved on the sides of pentagon 0 to make the shaded gap triangles coincide with the equal triangles within the adjoining pentagons, the pattern will form half of a dodecahedron which has 20 three pentagon corners.

Pattern D. Three hexagons fill the space around a point in a plane. They cannot form a corner without distortion.

Three regular polygons of more than six sides cannot meet at a point without overlapping.

Evidently the tetrahedron, cube, octahedron, dodecahedron and icosahedron are the only regular solids.

Demonstration Patterns.

Cut dotted lines-----. Crease solid lines ——.

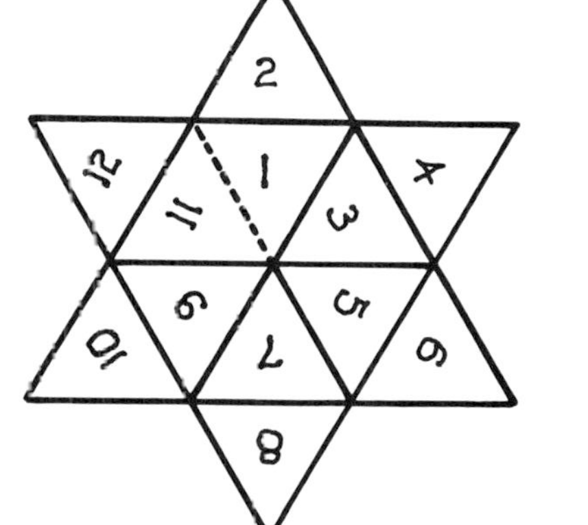

Pattern A.

Pattern B.

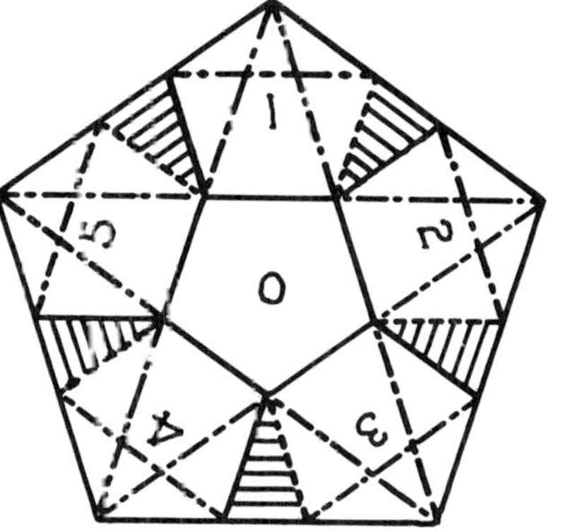

Pattern C.

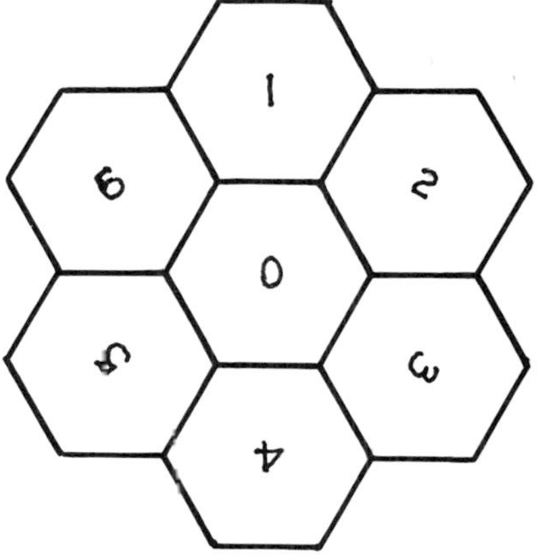

Pattern D.

Dodecahedron.

Sides slope one horizontal to two vertical.

Length of Edges $= r\sqrt{k\sqrt{5}} = 1.176r$.

$k = \frac{1}{2}\sqrt{5} - \frac{1}{2} = 0.618$. $\frac{1}{k} = 1 + k = 1.618$.

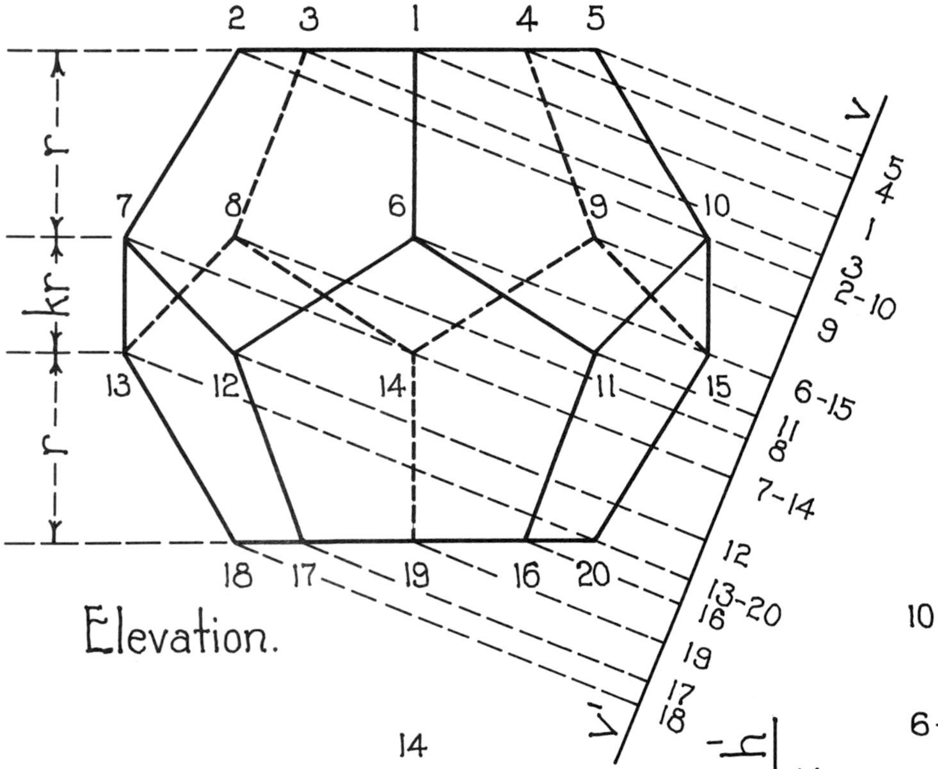

Elevation.

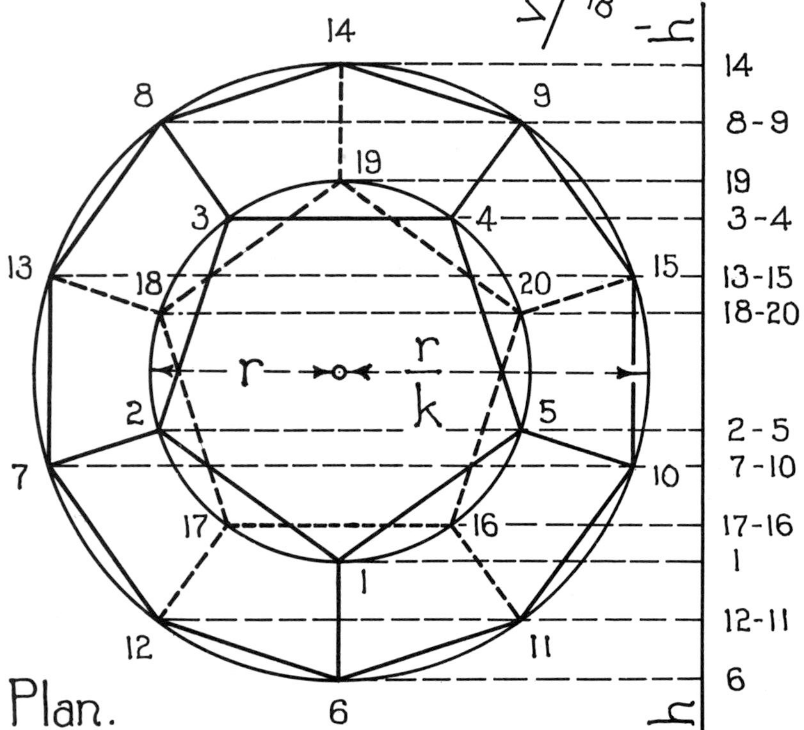

Plan.

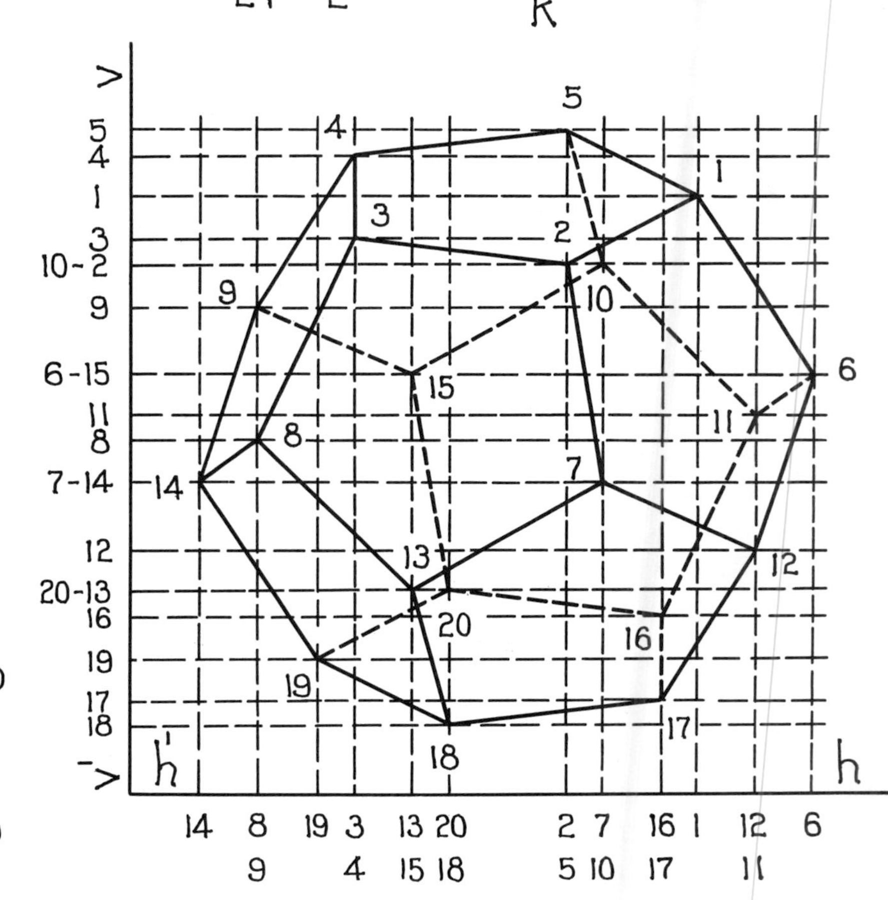

General View.

Icosahedron.

Length of Edges $= r\sqrt{3} = 1.732\,r$.

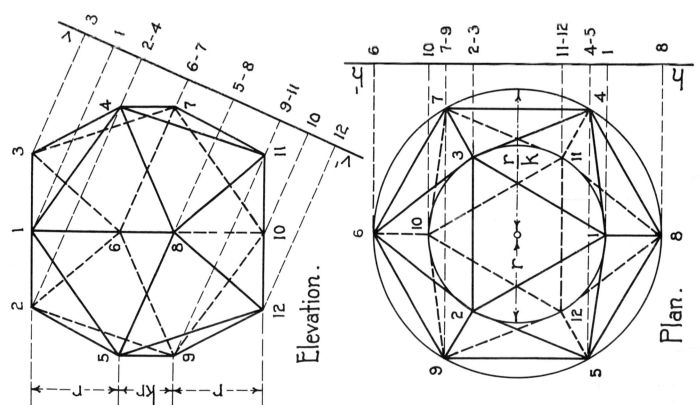

Elevation.

Plan.

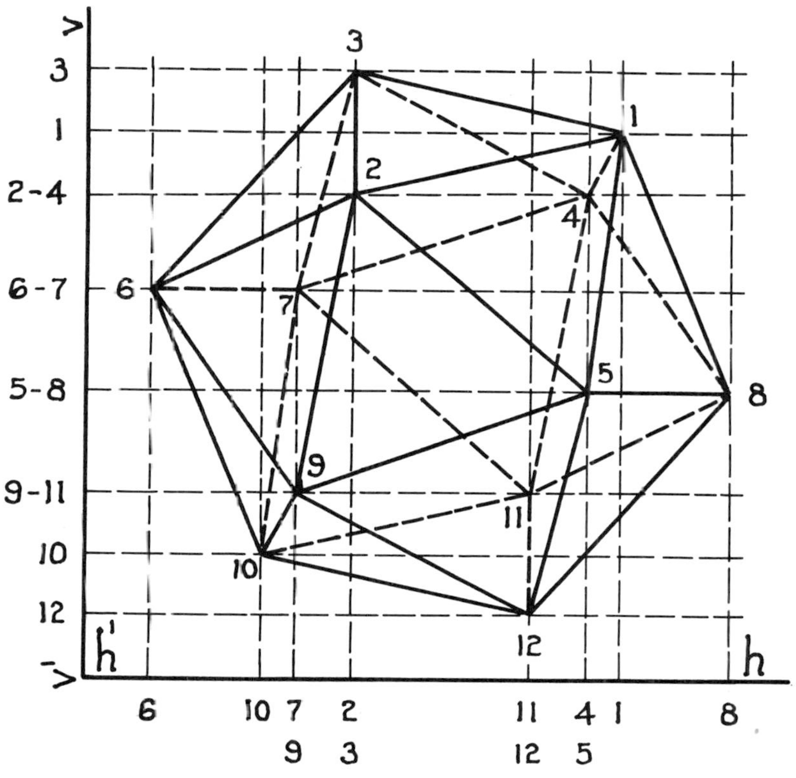

General View.

Tetrahedron - P4.

$\frac{s}{3}$P4 connects c.g.'s of faces.

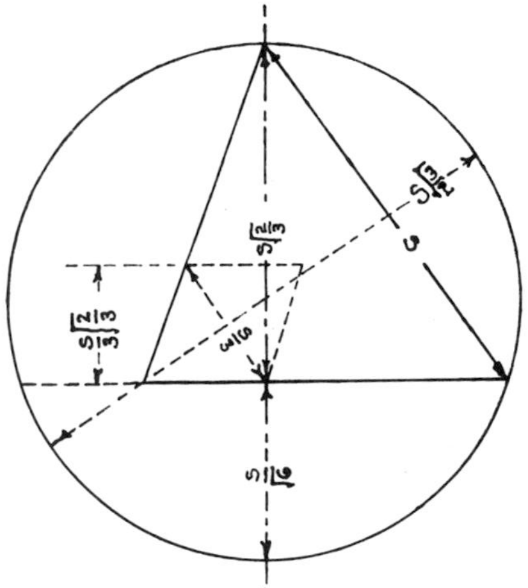

Elevation.

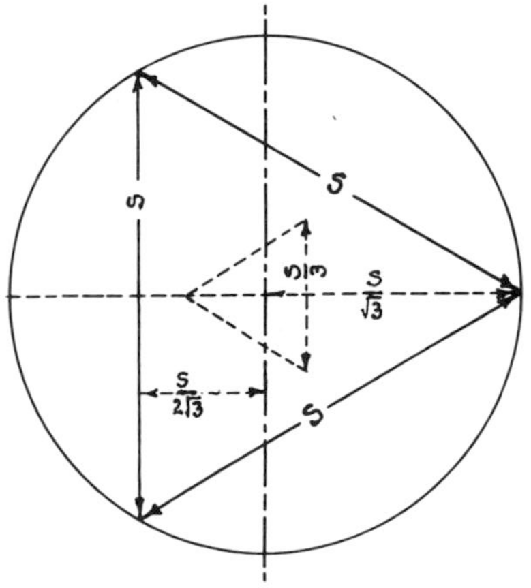

Plan.

Octahedron - P8.

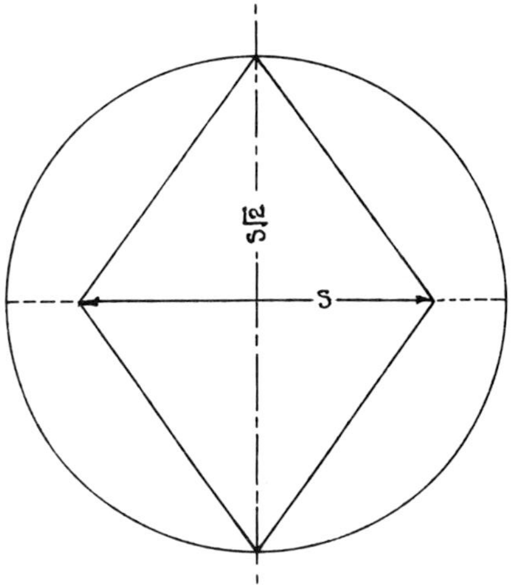

Face Elevation.

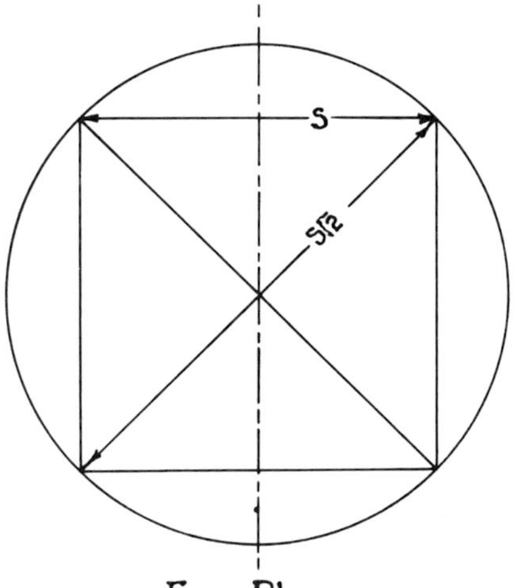

Face Plan.

Octahedron - P8.

Corners are c.g.'s of $s\sqrt{2}$ P6 faces.

$\frac{s\sqrt{2}}{3}$P6 connects centers of P8 faces.

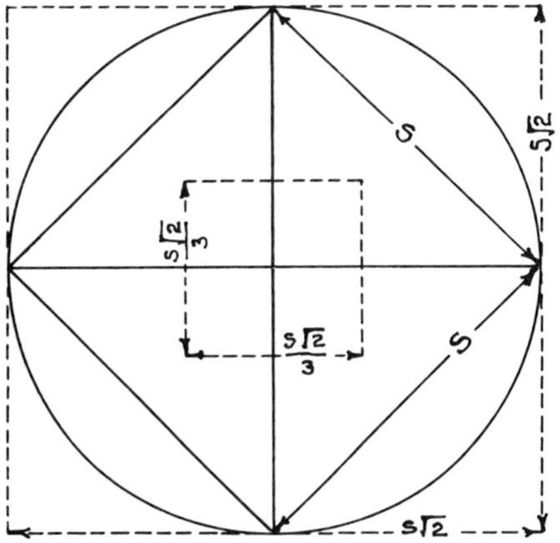

Diagonal Elevation.

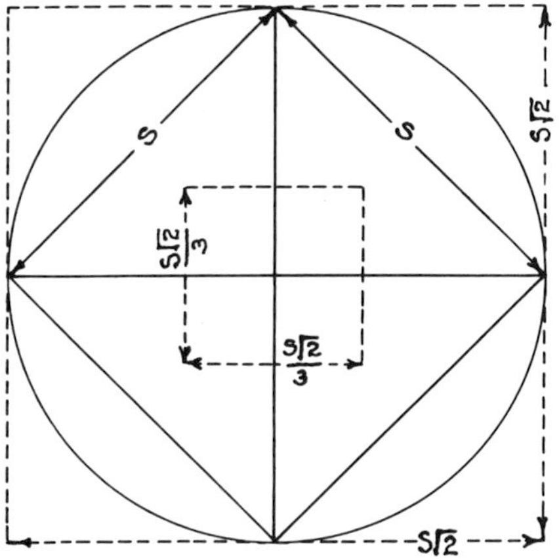

Diagonal Plan.

Dodecahedron - P12.

$\frac{s}{\sqrt{5}k^2}$ P20 connects c.g.'s of P12 faces.

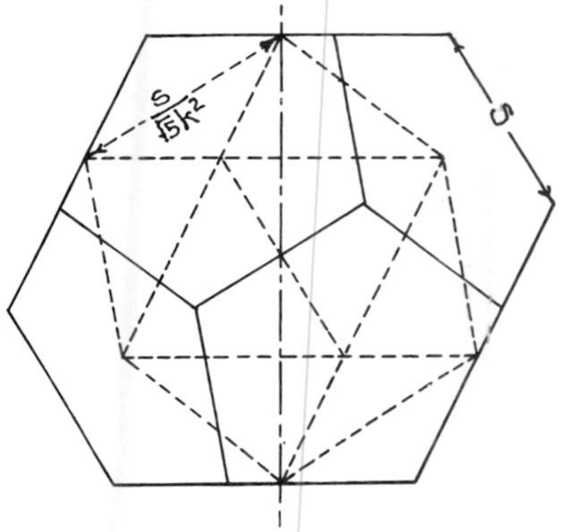

Icosahedron - P20.

$\frac{s}{3k}$ P12 connects c.g.'s of P20 faces.

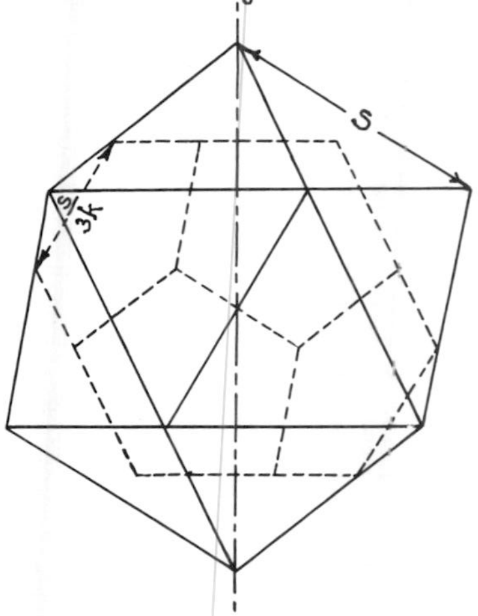

PLATO'S FIVE REGULAR SOLIDS

		TETRAHEDRON P4				CUBE P6				OCTAHEDRON P8				DODECAHEDRON P12				ICOSAHEDRON P20			
NAMES		TETRAHEDRON P4				CUBE P6				OCTAHEDRON P8				DODECAHEDRON P12				ICOSAHEDRON P20			
FACE POLYGONS	FACES	4 Triangles				6 Squares				8 Triangles				12 Pentagons				20 Triangles			
FACE POLYGONS	INTERIOR ANGLES	60°				90°				60°				108°				60°			
FACE POLYGONS	SIDES–S*	S	$D\sqrt{\frac{2}{3}}$	$B\sqrt{2}$	$\theta\sqrt{6}$	S	$\frac{D}{\sqrt{3}}$	$\frac{B}{\sqrt{2}}$	θ	S	$\frac{D}{\sqrt{2}}$	B	$\theta\sqrt{\frac{3}{2}}$	S	$D\frac{k}{\sqrt{3}}$	Bk^2	$\theta\sqrt{\sqrt{5}k^5}$	S	$D\sqrt{\frac{k}{\sqrt{5}}}$	Bk	$\theta k^2\sqrt{3}$
FACE POLYGONS	ALTITUDE	$\frac{S}{2}\sqrt{3}$	$\frac{D}{\sqrt{2}}$	$B\sqrt{\frac{3}{2}}$	$\frac{\theta}{\sqrt{2}}$	S	$\frac{D}{\sqrt{3}}$	$\frac{B}{\sqrt{2}}$	θ	$\frac{S}{2}\sqrt{3}$	$\frac{D}{2}\sqrt{\frac{3}{2}}$	$\frac{B}{2}\sqrt{3}$	$\frac{3\theta}{2\sqrt{2}}$	$\frac{S}{2}\sqrt{\frac{\sqrt{5}}{\sqrt{k^3}}}$	$\frac{D}{2}\sqrt{\frac{\sqrt{5}}{3k}}$	$\frac{B}{2}\sqrt{k\sqrt{5}}$	$\frac{\sqrt{5}}{2}k\theta$	$\frac{S}{2}\sqrt{3}$	$\frac{D}{2}\sqrt{\frac{3k}{\sqrt{5}}}$	$\frac{1}{2}Bk\sqrt{3}$	$\frac{3}{2}k^2\sqrt{\theta}$
FACE POLYGONS	WIDTH	S	$D\sqrt{\frac{2}{3}}$	$B\sqrt{2}$	$\theta\sqrt{6}$	S	$\frac{D}{\sqrt{3}}$	$\frac{B}{\sqrt{2}}$	θ	S	$\frac{D}{\sqrt{2}}$	B	$\theta\sqrt{\frac{3}{2}}$	$\frac{S}{k}$	$\frac{D}{\sqrt{3}}$	Bk	$\theta\sqrt{\sqrt{5}k^3}$	S	$D\sqrt{\frac{k}{\sqrt{5}}}$	Bk	$\theta k^2\sqrt{3}$
FACE POLYGONS	AREA OF EACH FACE	$\frac{S^2}{4}\sqrt{3}$	$\frac{D^2}{2\sqrt{3}}$	$\frac{1}{2}B^2\sqrt{3}$	$\frac{3}{2}\epsilon^2\sqrt{3}$	S^2	$\frac{D^2}{3}$	$\frac{B^2}{2}$	θ^2	$\frac{S^2}{4}\sqrt{3}$	$\frac{D^2}{8}\sqrt{3}$	$\frac{B^2}{4}\sqrt{3}$	$\frac{3}{8}\theta^2\sqrt{3}$	$\frac{5}{4}S^2\sqrt{\frac{1}{\sqrt{5}\ k^3}}$	$\frac{5}{12}D^2\sqrt{\frac{k}{\sqrt{5}}}$	$\frac{5}{4}B^2\sqrt{\frac{k^5}{\sqrt{5}}}$	$\frac{5}{4}\theta^2\sqrt{\sqrt{5}k^7}$	$\frac{S^2}{4}\sqrt{3}$	$\frac{D^2k}{4}\sqrt{\frac{3}{5}}$	$\frac{1}{4}B^2k^2\sqrt{3}$	$\frac{3}{4}\theta^2k^4\sqrt{3}$
FACE POLYGONS	RADIUS OF BOUNDING CIRCLE	$\frac{S}{\sqrt{3}}$	$\frac{D}{3}\sqrt{2}$	$B\sqrt{\frac{2}{3}}$	$\theta\sqrt{2}$	$\frac{S}{\sqrt{2}}$	$\frac{D}{\sqrt{6}}$	$\frac{B}{2}$	$\frac{6}{\sqrt{2}}$	$\frac{S}{\sqrt{3}}$	$\frac{D}{\sqrt{6}}$	$\frac{B}{\sqrt{3}}$	$\frac{\theta}{\sqrt{2}}$	$\frac{S}{\sqrt{k\sqrt{5}}}$	$D\sqrt{\frac{k}{3\sqrt{5}}}$	$B\sqrt{\frac{k^3}{\sqrt{5}}}$	θk^2	$\frac{S}{\sqrt{3}}$	$D\sqrt{\frac{k}{3\sqrt{5}}}$	$\frac{Bk}{\sqrt{3}}$	θk^2
FACE POLYGONS	RADIUS OF LINING CIRCLE	$\frac{S}{2\sqrt{3}}$	$\frac{D}{3\sqrt{2}}$	$\frac{B}{\sqrt{6}}$	$\frac{\theta}{\sqrt{2}}$	$\frac{S}{2}$	$\frac{D}{2\sqrt{3}}$	$\frac{B}{2\sqrt{2}}$	$\frac{\theta}{2}$	$\frac{S}{2\sqrt{3}}$	$\frac{D}{2\sqrt{6}}$	$\frac{B}{2\sqrt{3}}$	$\frac{\theta}{2\sqrt{2}}$	$\frac{S}{2\sqrt{k^3\sqrt{5}}}$	$\frac{D}{2\sqrt{3\sqrt{5}k}}$	$\frac{B}{2}\sqrt{\frac{k}{\sqrt{5}}}$	$\frac{\theta k}{2}$	$\frac{S}{2\sqrt{3}}$	$\frac{D}{2}\sqrt{\frac{k}{3\sqrt{5}}}$	$\frac{Bk}{2\sqrt{3}}$	$\frac{\theta k^2}{2}$
SOLIDS	INTERNAL ANGLES: ADJOINING FACES	70° 31′ 44″				90°				109° 28′ 16″				116° 33′ 54″				138° 11′ 32″			
SOLIDS	INTERNAL ANGLES: MAJOR AXIS AND FACE	19° 28′ 16″				35° 15′ 52″				35° 15′ 52″				52° 37′ 22″				52° 37′ 22″			
SOLIDS	INTERNAL ANGLES: MAJOR AXIS AND EDGE	35° 15′ 52″				54° 44′ 08″				45°				69° 05′ 41″				58° 16′ 57″			
SOLIDS	HEIGHT (above any face)	$S\sqrt{\frac{2}{3}}$	$\frac{2}{3}D$	$\frac{2B}{\sqrt{3}}$	2θ	S	$\frac{D}{\sqrt{3}}$	$\frac{B}{\sqrt{2}}$	θ	$S\sqrt{\frac{2}{3}}$	$\frac{D}{\sqrt{3}}$	$B\sqrt{\frac{2}{3}}$	θ	$\frac{S}{\sqrt{\sqrt{5}\ k^5}}$	$\frac{D}{\sqrt{3\sqrt{5}k^3}}$	$\frac{B}{\sqrt{k\sqrt{5}}}$	θ	$\frac{S}{\sqrt{3}\ k^2}$	$\frac{D}{\sqrt{3\sqrt{5}k^3}}$	$\frac{B}{\sqrt{3}k}$	θ
SOLIDS	SURFACE (total area)	$\sqrt{3}\ S^2$	$\frac{2D^2}{\sqrt{3}}$	$2B^2\sqrt{3}$	$6\theta^2\sqrt{3}$	$6S^2$	$2D^2$	$3B^2$	$6\theta^2$	$2S^2\sqrt{3}$	$\sqrt{3}\ D^2$	$2B^2\sqrt{3}$	$3\theta^2\sqrt{3}$	$\frac{15S^2}{\sqrt{\sqrt{5}\ k^3}}$	$5D^2\sqrt{\frac{k}{\sqrt{5}}}$	$15B^2\sqrt{\frac{k^5}{\sqrt{5}}}$	$15\theta^2\sqrt{\sqrt{5}k^7}$	$5S^2\sqrt{3}$	$D^2k\sqrt{15}$	$5B^2k^2\sqrt{3}$	$15\theta^2k^4\sqrt{3}$
SOLIDS	VOLUME	$\frac{S^3}{6\sqrt{2}}$	$\frac{D^3}{9\sqrt{3}}$	$\frac{B^3}{3}$	$\theta^3\sqrt{3}$	S^3	$\frac{D^3}{3\sqrt{3}}$	$\frac{B^3}{2\sqrt{2}}$	θ^3	$\frac{1}{3}S^3\sqrt{2}$	$\frac{D^3}{6}$	$\frac{1}{3}B^3\sqrt{2}$	$\frac{1}{2}\theta^3\sqrt{3}$	$\frac{\sqrt{5}\ S^3}{2\ k^4}$	$\frac{D^3}{6k}\sqrt{\frac{5}{3}}$	$\frac{1}{2}B^3k^2\sqrt{5}$	$\frac{5}{2}\theta^3\sqrt{\sqrt{5}k^7}$	$\frac{5}{6k^2}S^3$	$\frac{D^3}{6}\sqrt{\frac{\sqrt{5}}{k}}$	$\frac{5}{6}B^3k$	$\frac{5}{2}\theta^3k^4\sqrt{3}$
SOLIDS	DIAMETERS OF CONCENTRIC SPHERES: COVER–D*	$S\sqrt{\frac{3}{2}}$	D	$B\sqrt{3}$	3θ	$S\sqrt{3}$	D	$B\sqrt{\frac{3}{2}}$	$\theta\sqrt{3}$	$S\sqrt{2}$	D	$B\sqrt{2}$	$\theta\sqrt{3}$	$S\frac{\sqrt{3}}{k}$	D	$Bk\sqrt{3}$	$\theta\sqrt{3\sqrt{5}k^3}$	$S\sqrt{\frac{\sqrt{5}}{k}}$	D	$B\sqrt{k\sqrt{5}}$	$\theta\sqrt{3\sqrt{5}k^3}$
SOLIDS	DIAMETERS OF CONCENTRIC SPHERES: BLISTER–B	$\frac{S}{\sqrt{2}}$	$\frac{D}{\sqrt{3}}$	B	$\theta\sqrt{3}$	$S\sqrt{2}$	$D\sqrt{\frac{2}{3}}$	B	$\theta\sqrt{2}$	S	$\frac{D}{\sqrt{2}}$	B	$\theta\sqrt{\frac{3}{2}}$	$\frac{S}{k^2}$	$\frac{D}{k\sqrt{3}}$	B	$\theta\sqrt{k\sqrt{5}}$	$\frac{S}{k}$	$\frac{D}{\sqrt{k\sqrt{5}}}$	B	$\theta k\sqrt{3}$
SOLIDS	DIAMETERS OF CONCENTRIC SPHERES: LINING–Θ	$\frac{S}{\sqrt{6}}$	$\frac{D}{3}$	$\frac{B}{\sqrt{3}}$	θ	S	$\frac{D}{\sqrt{3}}$	$\frac{B}{\sqrt{2}}$	θ	$S\sqrt{\frac{2}{3}}$	$\frac{D}{\sqrt{3}}$	$B\sqrt{\frac{2}{3}}$	θ	$\frac{S}{\sqrt{\sqrt{5}\ k^5}}$	$\frac{D}{\sqrt{3\sqrt{5}\ k^3}}$	$\frac{B}{\sqrt{k\sqrt{5}}}$	θ	$\frac{S}{\sqrt{3}\ k^2}$	$\frac{D}{\sqrt{3\sqrt{5}k^3}}$	$\frac{B}{k\sqrt{3}}$	θ

*S is side of face polygon. D, B and Θ are diameters of the concentric cover, blister and lining spheres. *Cover Sphere.* All corners of a Platonic solid are contained in the surface of its cover sphere. P6, P8, P12 and P20 are D high when balanced on one corner. P4 is then only 2/3D high.

Blister Sphere. All edges of a Platonic solid are tangent to its blister sphere at their midpoints. The lining circle of each face of the solid bounds the blister of this sphere on that face. These solids are all B high when balanced on one edge.

Lining Sphere. All faces of a Platonic solid are tangent to its lining sphere at their midpoints. P6, P8, P12 and P20 are Θ high when resting on one face. P4 is then 2Θ high.

The Golden Section Ratio ($k = 0.618$)

Plato's Regular Solids in Nesting Ratios.

Solids.	Faces.	Sides of faces in S_{20}* units. ($k=\frac{1}{2}\sqrt{5}-\frac{1}{2}=0.618034$).
Tetrahedron.- P4.	4 Triangles.	$\sqrt{2}/k^2 = 3.702459$.
Cube. —— P6.	6 Squares.	$1/\sqrt{3}k^2 = 0.872678$.
Octahedron.- P8.	8 Triangles.	$1/\sqrt{2}k^2 = 1.851230$.
Dodecahedron.- P12.	12 Pentagons.	$1/\sqrt{3}k = 0.539345$.
Icosahedron.- P20.	20 Triangles.	$1 = 1.000000$.

P4 faces contain four P8 and four P20 faces. P8 faces contain eight P20 faces.
P6 corners are centers of P8 faces. P12 corners are centers of P20 faces.
The five diagonals of each P12 face are edges of five P6's formed by such diagonals.
Lining spheres of P4, P8 and P20 and cover spheres of P6 and P12 have diameters of $\frac{1}{\sqrt{3}k^2}$.

*S_{20} is length of side of P20 face. It is the unit of length on this drawing.

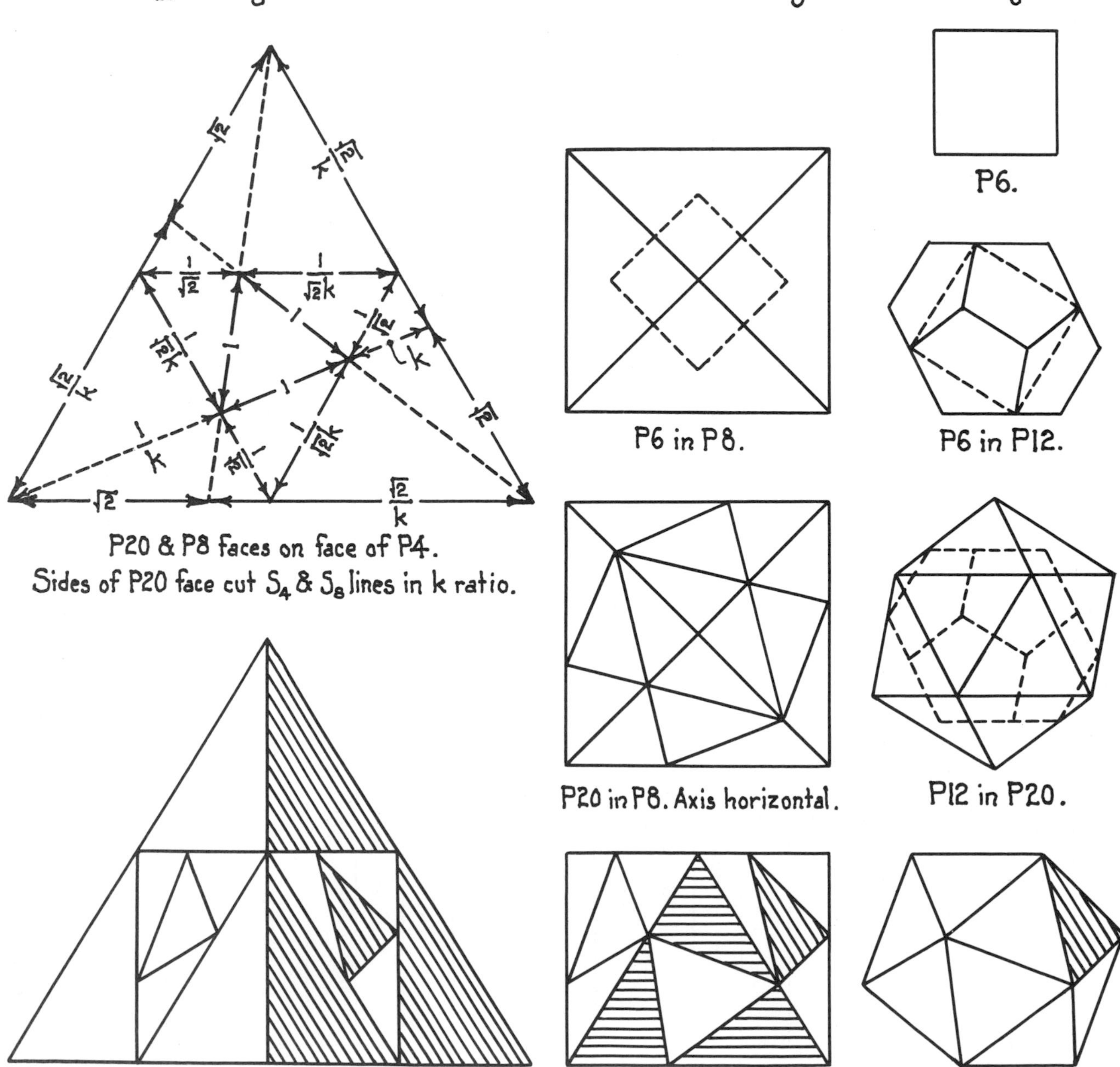

P20 & P8 faces on face of P4.
Sides of P20 face cut S_4 & S_8 lines in k ratio.

P20 & P8 in P4.

P20 in P8 as in P4.

P20 as in P4 & P8.

Dual Cubes and Octahedra.

Centers of faces of each solid are vertices of next smaller solid. Ratio of like solids - 3 to 1. Figure turned 15° clockwise and tilted 15°.

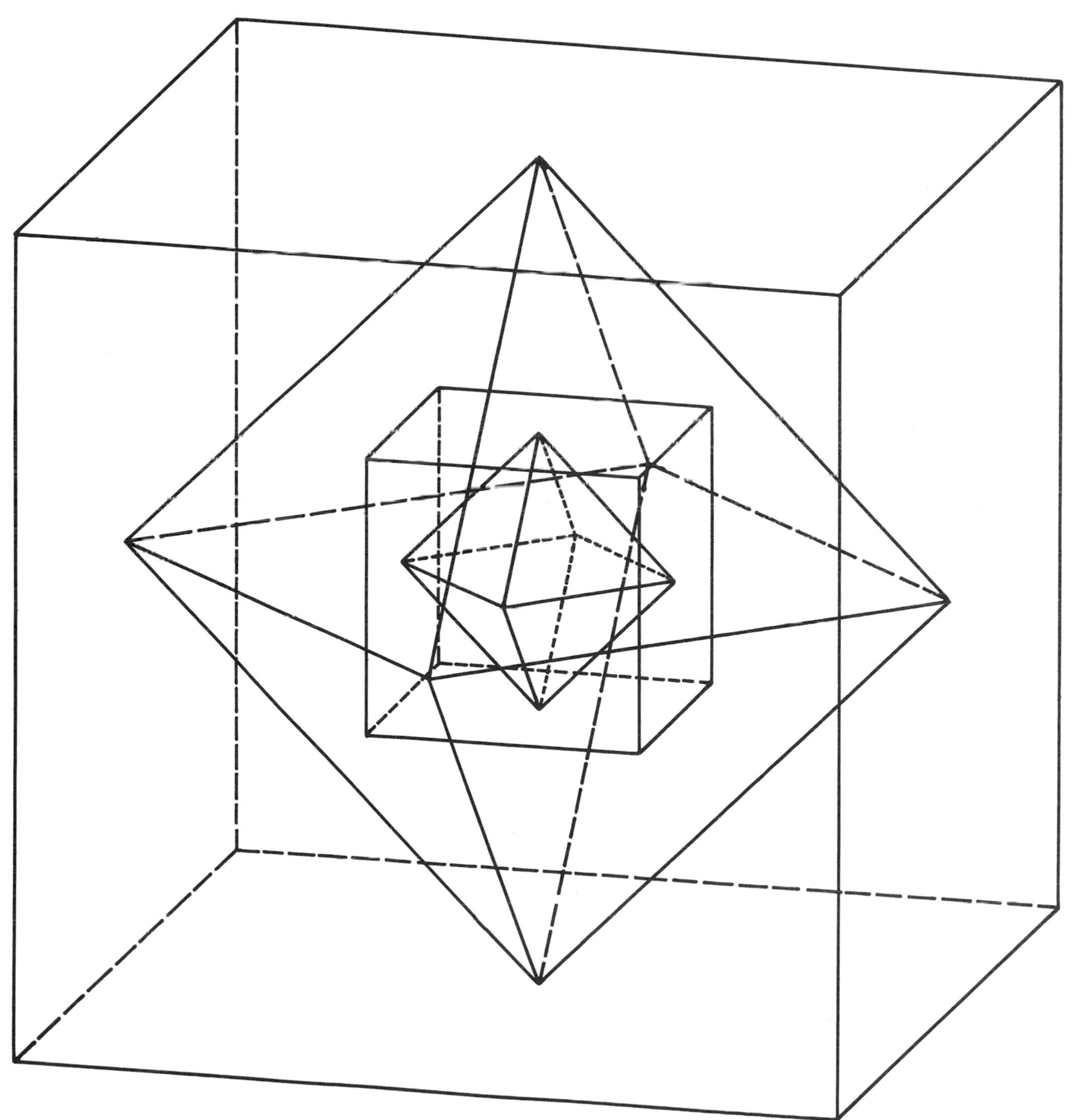

KEPLER'S SOLAR SYSTEM POLYHEDRA.

In 1595 Johannes Kepler was overwhelmed with the belief that he had deeply penetrated the secrets of the Creator with his notion that the orbits of the six planets then known were great circles of inscribing and circumscribing spheres of Plato's five regular solids.

This orbital spacing as conceived by Kepler has been computed in units of the earth's distance from the sun and is tabulated herewith for comparative purposes.

Distances from the sun.			Intervening solids.	
Planet.	Kepler.	Modern.	Name.	Edge.
Saturn	6.539	9.54		
			Cube.	7.550
Jupiter	3.775	5.20		
			Tetrahedron.	6.165
Mars	1.258	1.52		
			Dodecahedron.	0.898
Earth	1.000	1.000		
			Icosahedron.	1.051
Venus	0.795	0.723		
			Octahedron.	1.124
Mercury	0.459	0.387		

VOLUME OF THE REGULAR SOLID BLISTERS.

Diameters of blister and lining spheres are B and θ. Side of face polygon is s. Middle ordinate of spherical segment is m. B, θ, s and m have separate values for each of the regular solids.

Volume of any spherical segment, $V_{ss} = \pi m^2\left(r - \frac{m}{3}\right)$.

In the regular solid blister $r = \frac{B}{2}$ and $m = \frac{B}{2} - \frac{\theta}{2}$.

$$V_B = \pi\left(\frac{B-\theta}{2}\right)^2\left[\frac{B}{2} - \frac{B-\theta}{6}\right] = \frac{\pi}{24}(B-\theta)^2(2B+\theta) = \frac{\pi}{24}\left(2B^3 - 3B^2\theta + \theta^3\right).$$

General Formula. $V_B = \pi\left(\frac{B^3}{12} - \frac{B^2\theta}{8} + \frac{\theta^3}{24}\right)$.

THE TETRAHEDRON. – P4.

$s = B\sqrt{2}$. $\theta = \frac{B}{\sqrt{3}}$. $B = \frac{s}{\sqrt{2}}$.

$$V_{B4} = \pi\left(\frac{B^3}{12} - \frac{B^2}{8}\times\frac{B}{\sqrt{3}} + \frac{1}{24}\times\frac{B^3}{3\sqrt{3}}\right) = \pi B^3\left(\frac{1}{12} - \frac{1}{8\sqrt{3}} + \frac{1}{72\sqrt{3}}\right).$$

$$V_{B4} = \pi B^3\left(\frac{1}{12} - \frac{1}{9\sqrt{3}}\right) = 0.060265\,B^3 = 0.021307\,s^3.$$

THE CUBE. – P6.

$s = \theta = \frac{B}{\sqrt{2}}$. $B = s\sqrt{2}$.

$$V_{B6} = \pi\left(\frac{B^3}{12} - \frac{B^2}{8}\times\frac{B}{\sqrt{2}} + \frac{1}{24}\times\frac{B^3}{2\sqrt{2}}\right) = \pi B^3\left(\frac{1}{12} - \frac{1}{8\sqrt{2}} + \frac{1}{48\sqrt{2}}\right).$$

$$V_{B6} = \pi B^3\left(\frac{1}{12} - \frac{5}{48\sqrt{2}}\right) = 0.030399\,B^3 = 0.085982\,s^3.$$

THE OCTAHEDRON. – P8.

$s = B$. $\theta = B\sqrt{\frac{2}{3}}$.

$$V_{B8} = \pi\left(\frac{B^3}{12} - \frac{B^2}{8}\times B\sqrt{\frac{2}{3}} + \frac{1}{24}\times\frac{2}{3}B^3\sqrt{\frac{2}{3}}\right) = \pi B^3\left(\frac{1}{12} - \frac{1}{8}\sqrt{\frac{2}{3}} + \frac{1}{36}\sqrt{\frac{2}{3}}\right).$$

$$V_{B8} = \pi B^3\left(\frac{1}{12} - \frac{7}{72}\sqrt{\frac{2}{3}}\right) = 0.012414\,B^3 = 0.012414\,s^3.$$

THE DODECAHEDRON. – P12.

$s = Bk^2$. $\theta = \frac{B}{\sqrt{k\sqrt{5}}}$. $B = \frac{s}{k^2}$.

$$V_{B12} = \pi\left(\frac{B^3}{12} - \frac{B^2}{8}\times\frac{B}{\sqrt{k\sqrt{5}}} + \frac{1}{24}\times\frac{B^3}{k\sqrt{5}\sqrt{k\sqrt{5}}}\right) = \pi B^3\left(\frac{1}{12} - \frac{1}{8\sqrt{k\sqrt{5}}} + \frac{1}{24\sqrt{5k^3\sqrt{5}}}\right).$$

$$V_{B12} = \pi B^3\left(\frac{1}{12} - \frac{3k\sqrt{5}-1}{24\sqrt{5k^3\sqrt{5}}}\right) = 0.0083228\,B^3 = 0.149348\,s^3.$$

THE ICOSAHEDRON. – P20.

$s = Bk$. $\theta = \frac{B}{k\sqrt{3}}$. $B = \frac{s}{k}$.

$$V_{B20} = \pi\left(\frac{B^3}{12} - \frac{B^2}{8}\times\frac{B}{k\sqrt{3}} + \frac{1}{24}\times\frac{B^3}{3k^3\sqrt{3}}\right) = \pi B^3\left(\frac{1}{12} - \frac{1}{8k\sqrt{3}} + \frac{1}{72k^3\sqrt{3}}\right).$$

$$V_{B20} = \pi B^3\left(\frac{1}{12} - \frac{9k^2-1}{72k^3\sqrt{3}}\right) = 0.00166448\,B^3 = 0.00705084\,s^3.$$

THE VOLUME OF SPHERICAL SEGMENTS.

THE PRISMOIDAL FORMULA.

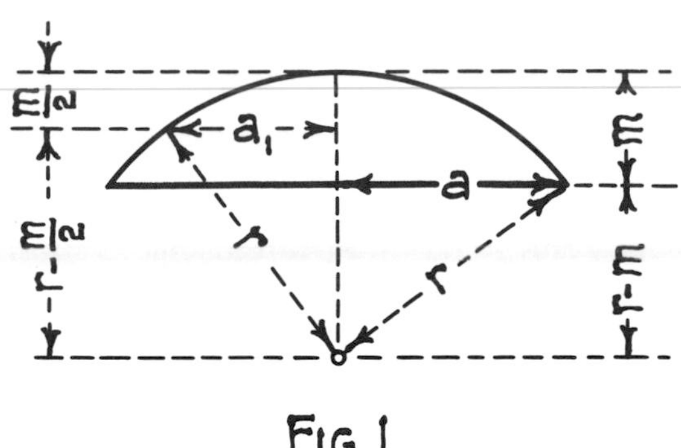

FIG. 1.

$$\text{Volume} = \frac{H}{6}(A_T + 4A_M + A_B).$$

H = height of solid. A_T, A_M and A_B are the areas of top, midsection and base.

SPHERICAL SEGMENTS WITH ONE BASE.

The spherical segments with one base, figures 1 and 2, have a height of m. a and a_1 are the radii of the base circle and midsection.

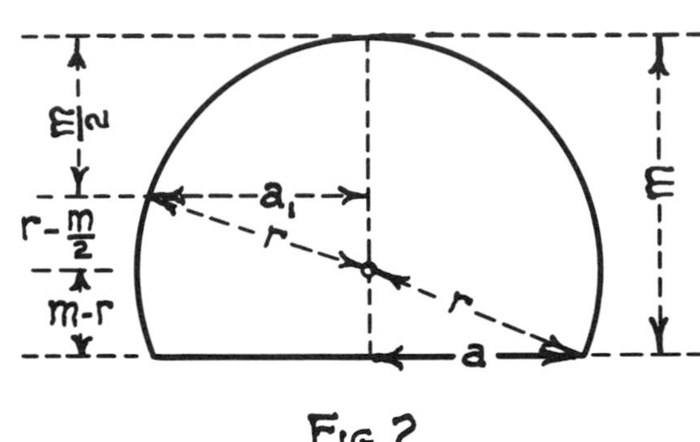

FIG. 2.

$$a = \sqrt{r^2 - (r-m)^2} \text{ (Fig. 1.) or } = \sqrt{r^2 - (m-r)^2} \text{ (Fig. 2.)}$$

$$a = \sqrt{r^2 - r^2 + 2rm - m^2} = \sqrt{2rm - m^2}$$

$$a = \sqrt{m(2r-m)}.$$

$$a_1 = \sqrt{r^2 - (r - \tfrac{m}{2})^2} = \sqrt{r^2 - r^2 + mr - \tfrac{m^2}{4}}$$

$$a_1 = \sqrt{m(r - \tfrac{m}{4})}$$

In figuring the volume of the one base segments, V_{SS1}, by the prismoidal formula, $H = m$, $A_T = 0$,

$$A_M = \pi a_1^2 = \pi m(r - \tfrac{m}{4}),$$

$$A_B = \pi a^2 = \pi m(2r-m).$$

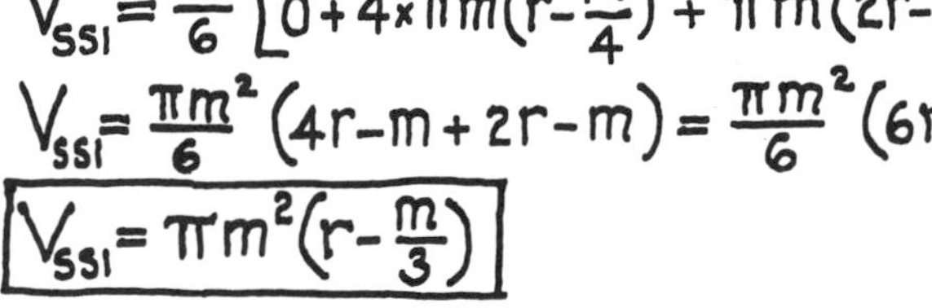

$$V_{SS1} = \frac{m}{6}\left[0 + 4 \times \pi m(r - \tfrac{m}{4}) + \pi m(2r-m)\right]$$

$$V_{SS1} = \frac{\pi m^2}{6}(4r - m + 2r - m) = \frac{\pi m^2}{6}(6r - 2m)$$

$$\boxed{V_{SS1} = \pi m^2(r - \tfrac{m}{3})}$$

SPHERICAL SEGMENTS WITH TWO BASES.

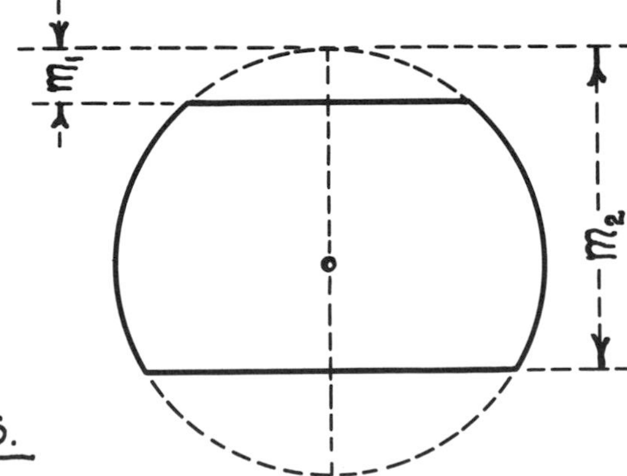

FIG. 3.

$$V_{SS2} = \pi\left[m_2^2(r - \tfrac{m_2}{3}) - m_1^2(r - \tfrac{m_1}{3})\right]. \text{ (Fig 3.)}$$

TOTAL VOLUME OF SPHERE.

$$V = \pi(2r)^2(r - \tfrac{2r}{3}) = \tfrac{4}{3}\pi r^3. \quad (m = 2r \text{ in formula } V_{SS1}.)$$

Eight Sets of Plato's Five Regular Solids.

Set No.	Characteristic of Set.	Length of Edges in Set.*				
		P4**	P6	P8	P12	P20
1	Edges equal.	1.0000	1.0000	1.0000	1.0000	1.0000
2	Circumscribed spheres equal.	1.4142	1.0000	1.2247	0.6180	0.9106
3	Blister spheres equal.	2.0000	1.0000	1.4142	0.5402	0.8740
4	Inscribed spheres equal.	2.4495	1.0000	1.2247	0.4490	0.6616
5	Heights equal.	1.2247	1.0000	1.2247	0.4490	0.6616
6	Surfaces equal.	1.8612	1.0000	1.3161	0.5391	0.8324
7	Volumes equal.	2.0396	1.0000	1.2849	0.5072	0.7710
8	Solids cut consecutively from cube.	1.4142 (1)	1.0 & 1/3 (5)	0.7071 (2)	0.2060 (4)	0.3820 (3)

* Ratio of edges to edges of cube in set.

** P4 - Tetrahedron. P6 - Cube. P8 - Octahedron. P12 - Dodecahedron. P20 - Icosahedron.

The Cube and Its Three Concentric Spheres.

General View of Cube.

Turned 30°. Tilted 30°.

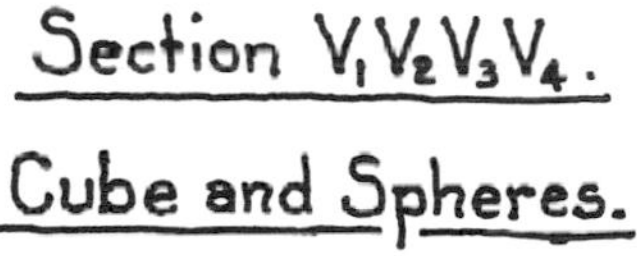
Section $V_1V_2V_3V_4$.

Cube and Spheres.

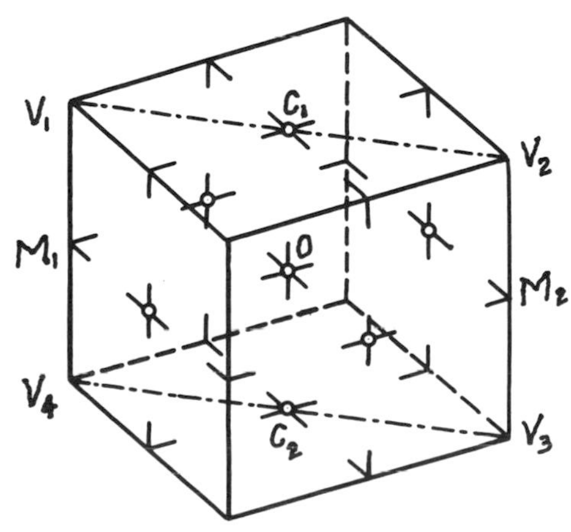

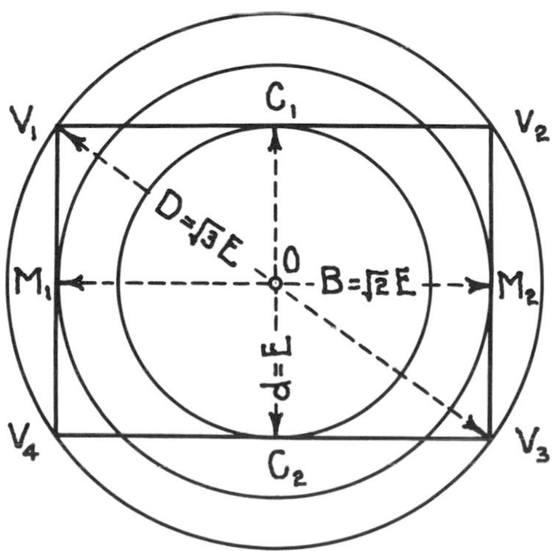

Vertices of cube, V, lie in circumscribed sphere of diameter, D.
Blister sphere of diameter, B, is tangent to edges, E, at midpoints, M.
Inscribed sphere of diameter, d, is tangent to faces at centers, C.

ARCHIMEDEAN POLYHEDRA

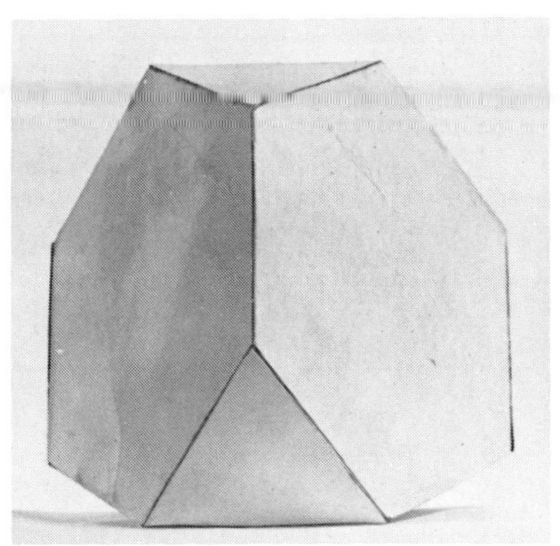

TRUNCATED
TETRAHEDRON

TRUNCATED CUBE

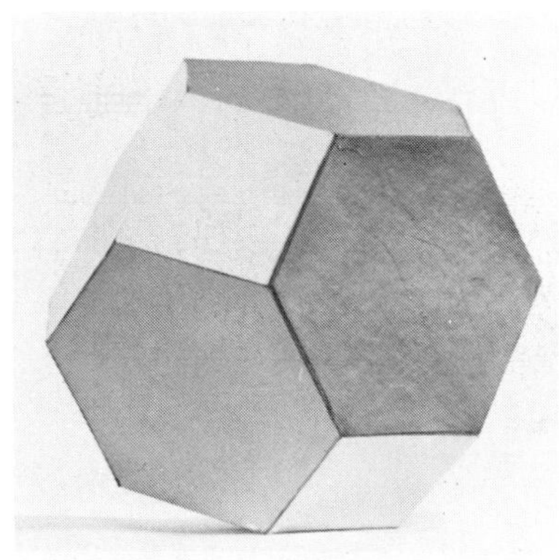

TRUNCATED
OCTAHEDRON

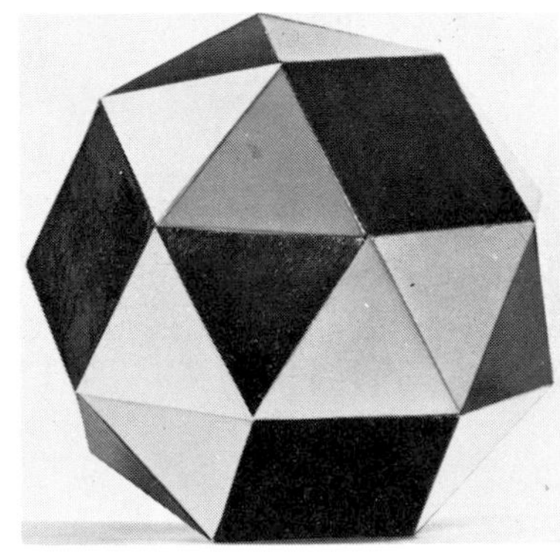

SNUB CUBE

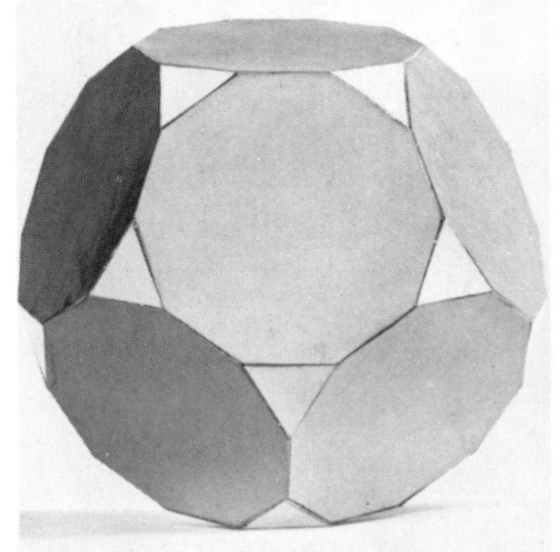

TRUNCATED
DODECAHEDRON

TRUNCATED
ICOSAHEDRON

ARCHIMEDEAN POLYHEDRA

SMALL RHOMBICUBOCTHEDRON

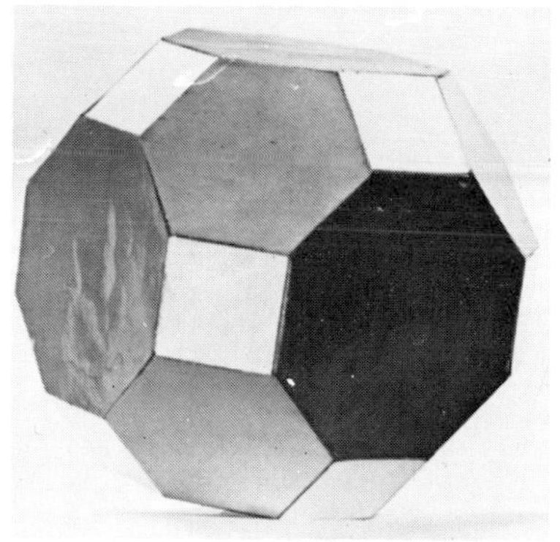

GREAT RHOMBICUBOCTAHEDRON
(TRUNCATED CUBOCTAHEDRON)

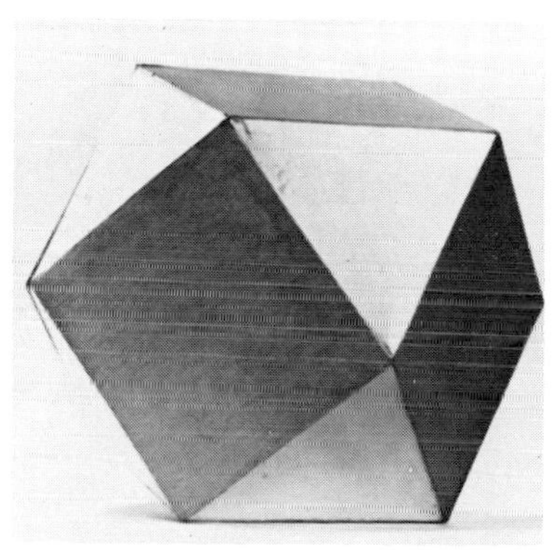

CUBOCTAHEDRON

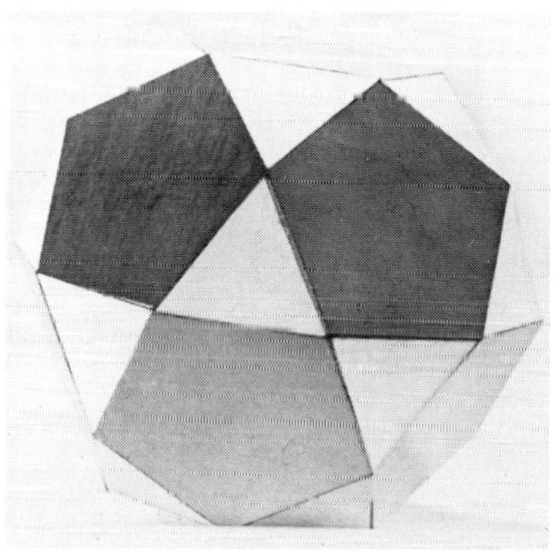

ICOSIDODECAHEDRON

SNUB DODECAHEDRON

SMALL RHOMBICOSIDODECAHEDRON

GREAT RHOMBICOSIDODECAHEDRON
(TRUNCATED ICOSIDODECAHEDRON)

Pattern for Truncated Tetrahedron.

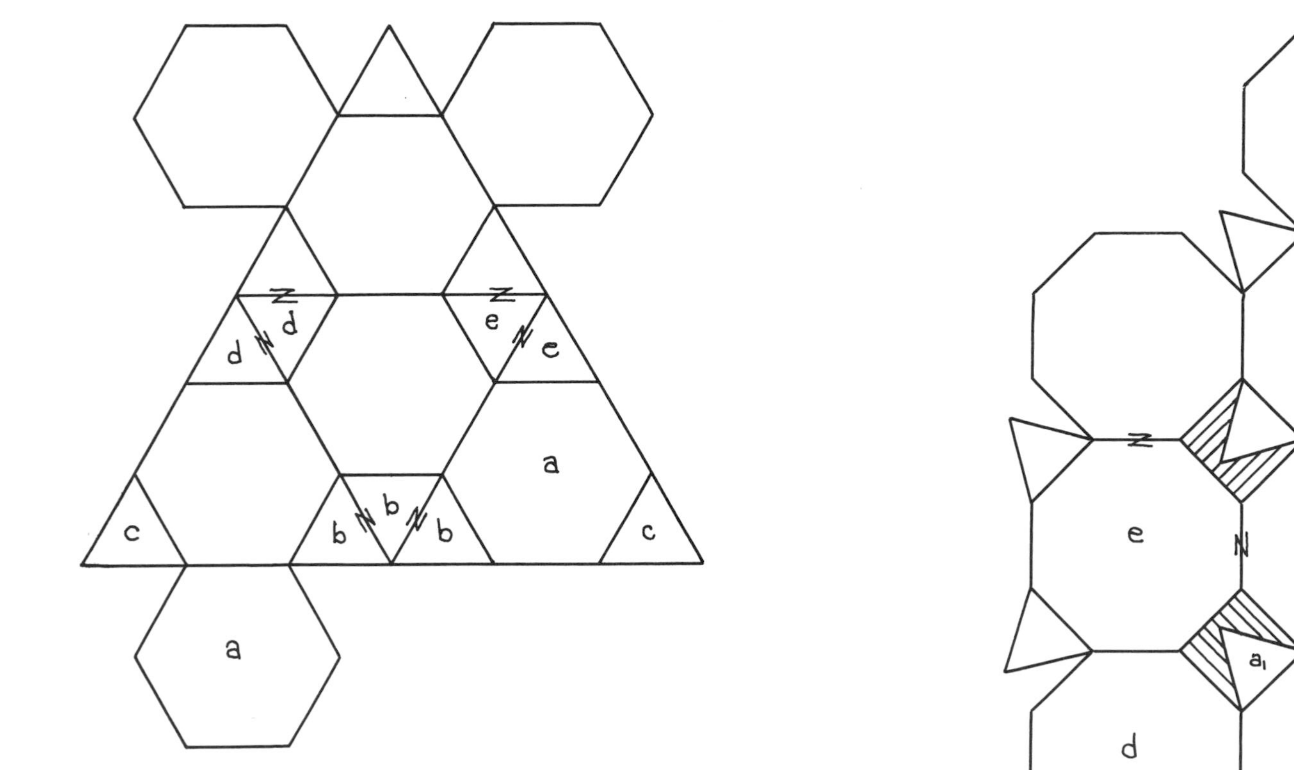

Construction.

These truncated polyhedra are cutback tetrahedra and cubes having 3 and $\sqrt{2}+1$ times longer edges respectively.

In each pattern all of the unit areas are regular polygons.

When the like lettered unit areas are pasted together in alphabetical order, it can readily be seen how to complete each of these truncated polyhedra.

Code: Crease —. Cut ─Z─

$\sqrt{2}+1=2.414$. $\sqrt{3}+\sqrt{2}+1=4.146$.

Cut out crosshatched areas.

a_2 ←1.00→ ←$\sqrt{2}+1$→ a_1 ←$\sqrt{3}+\sqrt{2}+1$→ a_3 a a_4

Cube Pattern A.

Patterns for Truncated Cube.

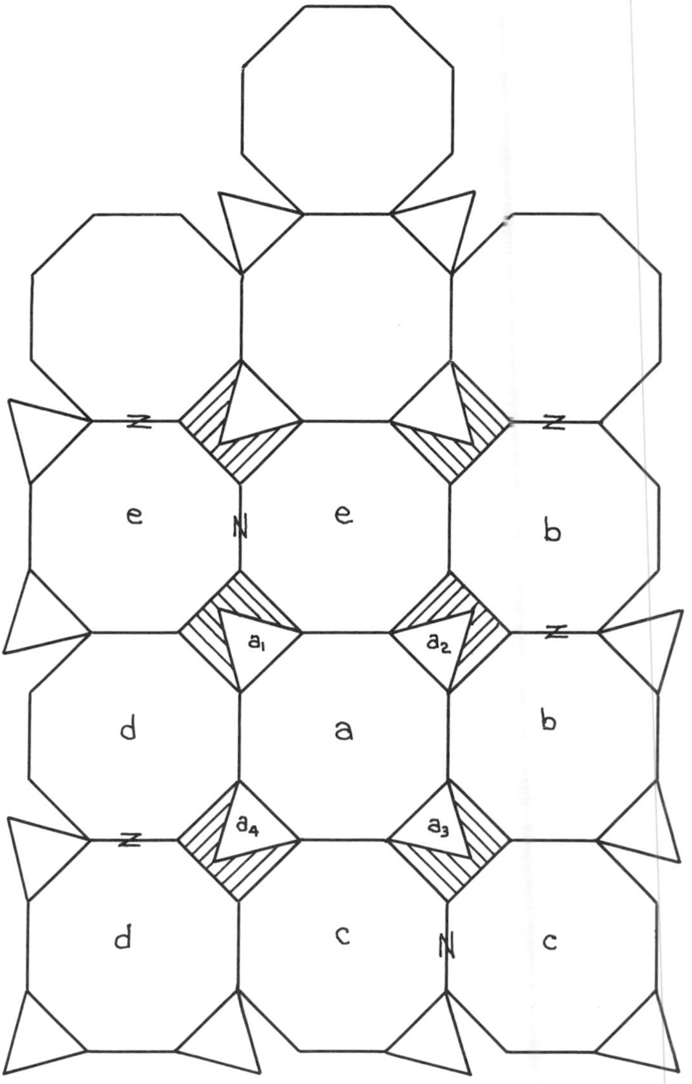

Cube Pattern B.

Pattern for Truncated Octahedron.

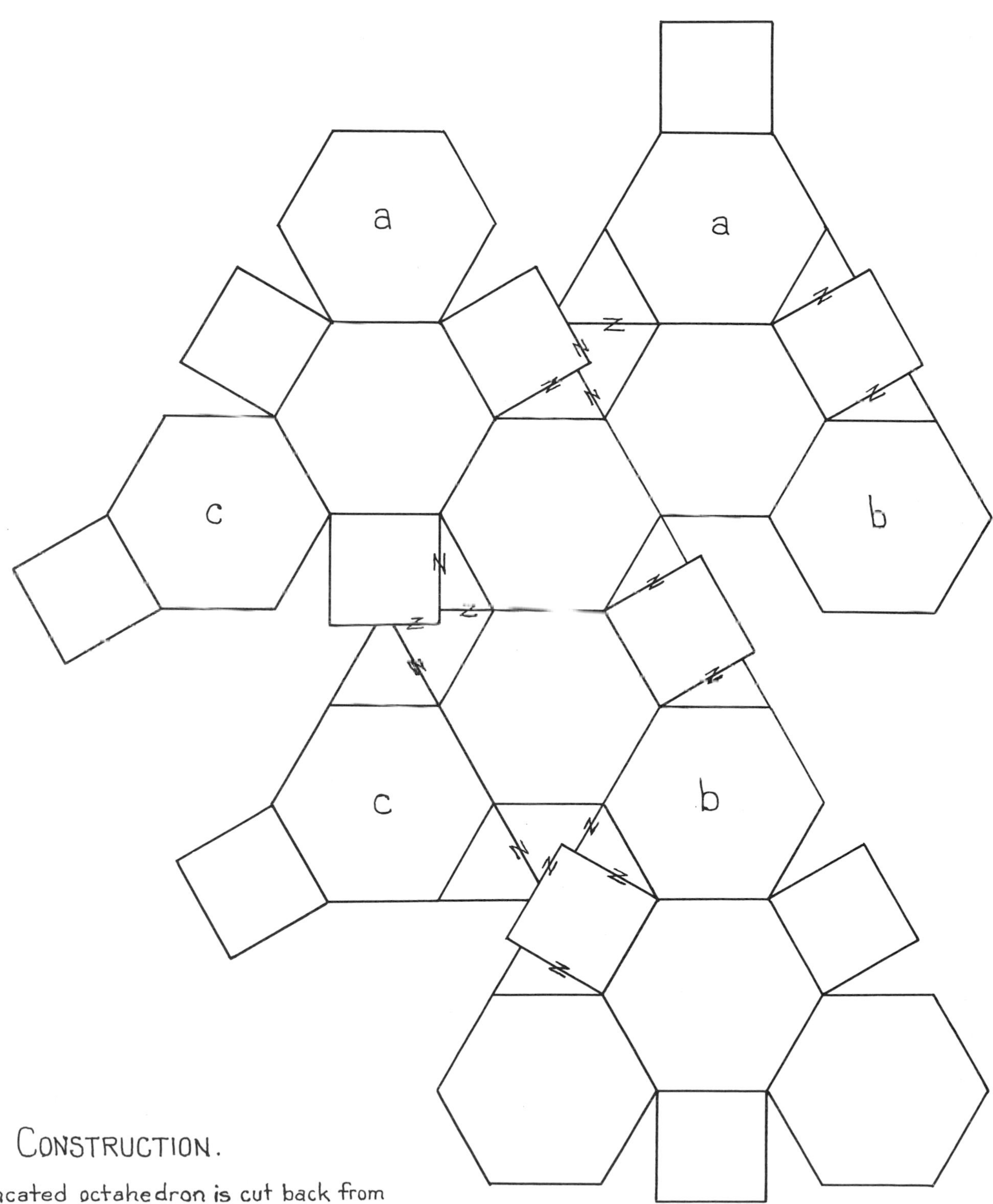

Construction.

The truncated octahedron is cut back from a regular octahedron with three times longer edges.

Paste the like lettered hexagons together in alphabetical order.

Code: Crease ——. Cut -z-.

Patterns for Truncated Dodecahedron.

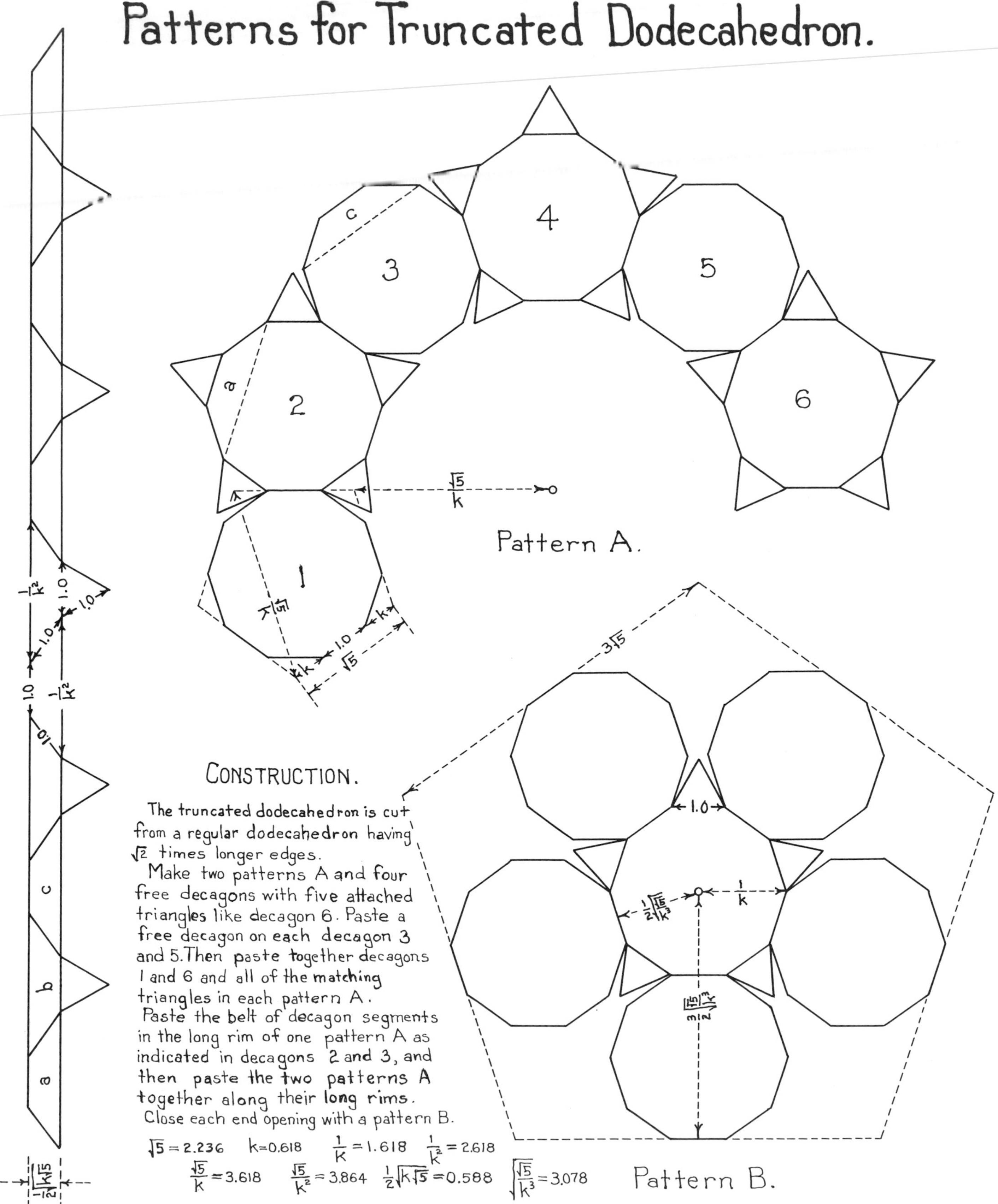

CONSTRUCTION.

The truncated dodecahedron is cut from a regular dodecahedron having $\sqrt{2}$ times longer edges.

Make two patterns A and four free decagons with five attached triangles like decagon 6. Paste a free decagon on each decagon 3 and 5. Then paste together decagons 1 and 6 and all of the matching triangles in each pattern A.

Paste the belt of decagon segments in the long rim of one pattern A as indicated in decagons 2 and 3, and then paste the two patterns A together along their long rims.

Close each end opening with a pattern B.

$\sqrt{5} = 2.236$ $\quad k = 0.618$ $\quad \frac{1}{k} = 1.618$ $\quad \frac{1}{k^2} = 2.618$

$\frac{\sqrt{5}}{k} = 3.618$ $\quad \frac{\sqrt{5}}{k^2} = 3.864$ $\quad \frac{1}{2}\sqrt{k\sqrt{5}} = 0.588$ $\quad \sqrt{\frac{\sqrt{5}}{k^3}} = 3.078$

Patterns for Truncated Icosahedron.

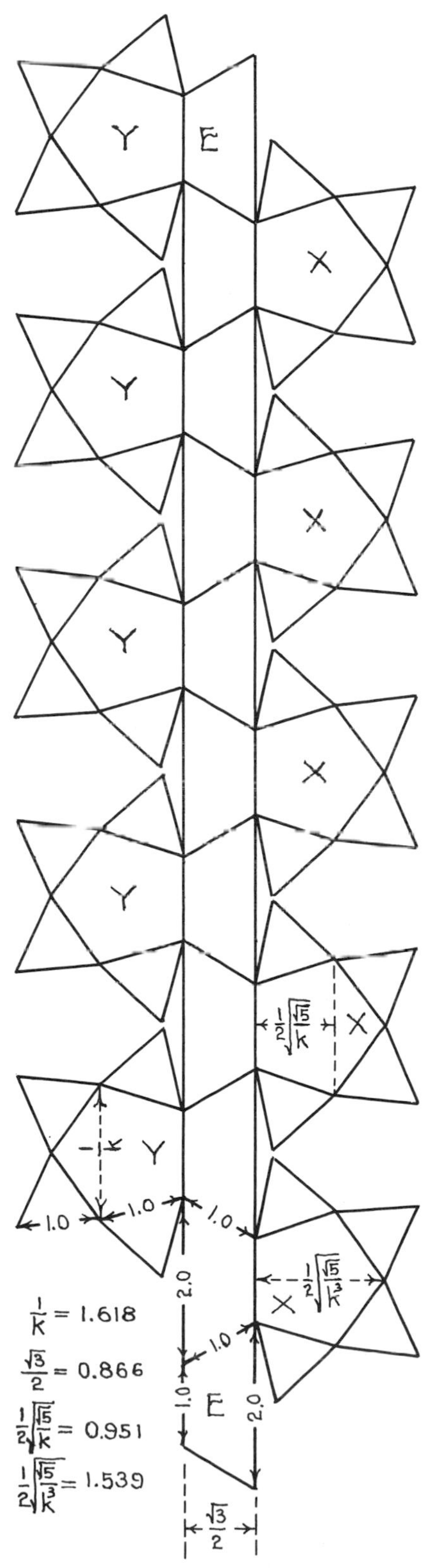

Pattern A.
Make one.

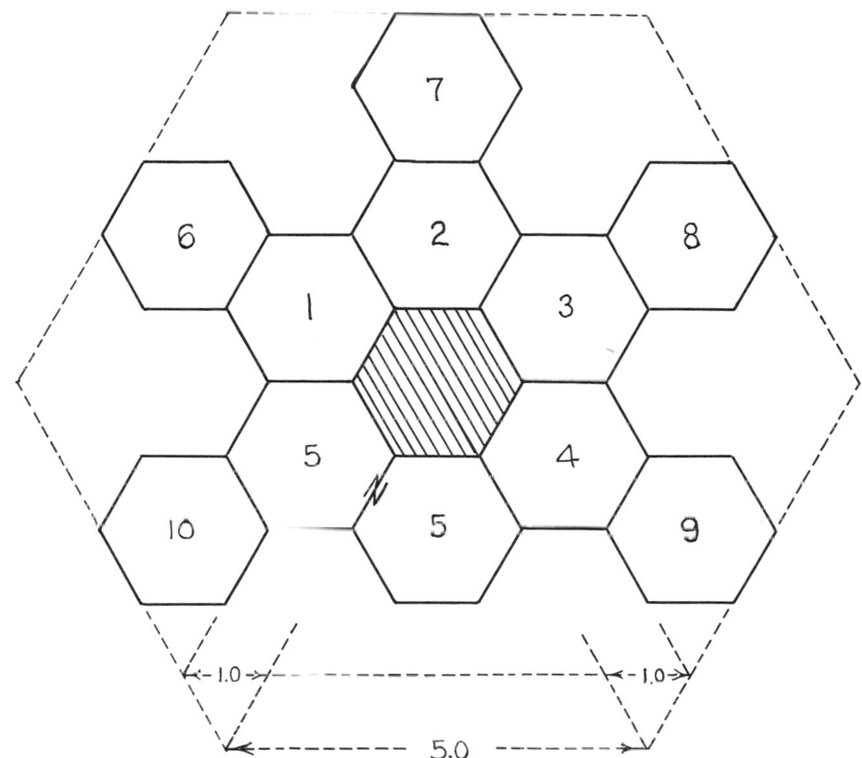

Pattern B.
Make two.

Pattern C.
Make two.

Construction.

The truncated icosahedron is cut back from a regular icosahedron with three times longer edges.
1. Paste together the two hexagons 5 in each pattern B. **2.** Paste together the half hexagons E at ends of belt pattern A. **3.** Paste the outer halves of hexagons 6 to 10 of one pattern B to outside of matching alternate half hexagons in belt pattern A. **4.** Clip a bent down pentagon X to each pair of pasted units as the operation progresses. **5.** Paste the triangles with the five alternate pentagons Y to the first pattern B after freeing the clipped down pentagons X. **6.** Paste the other pattern B to matching half hexagons in pattern A. **7.** Paste the loose triangles of pattern A to pattern B. **8.** Close the ends with patterns C.

Code: Crease —— Cut —≠— Cut out crosshatching.

THE SNUB CUBE.

The snub cube has 6 square faces and 32 triangular faces. It has 24 vertices and 60 edges of length, [S]. Each of its eight 'free' triangular faces shares vertices with three separate square faces.

Figure A is the base of the pyramid formed by the four triangles and half of the square meeting at each vertex. The radius, [r], of its circumscribing circle is a root of the equation, $14r^6 - 20r^4 + 8r^2 - 1 = 0$. $r = 0.928191 4S$.

Four triangles are based on each square face. See figure B. Their outer vertices form a [C] sided square. $C = 1.685018\,S$.

$P = 0.958981\,S$. $M = 0.804859\,S$. $J = 0.521387\,S$. $P^2 = M^2 + J^2$.

A cube of height, [Q], is formed by extending the six square faces. $Q = J + M + P = 2.285227\,S$.

The octahedron formed by extending the eight 'free' triangular faces has a $2P+Q$ major axis. Figure C shows one of its faces. Its height is $2.426712\,S$ when resting on one face.

Interior angles between square and triangular faces measure 142°59'26" and between adjoining triangular faces measure 153°14'08".

Total Surface $= 19.85641\,S^2$. Total Volume $= 7.88948\,S^3$.

Diameter of cover sphere $= 2.687427\,S$.

Diameter of blister sphere $= 2.494446\,S$.

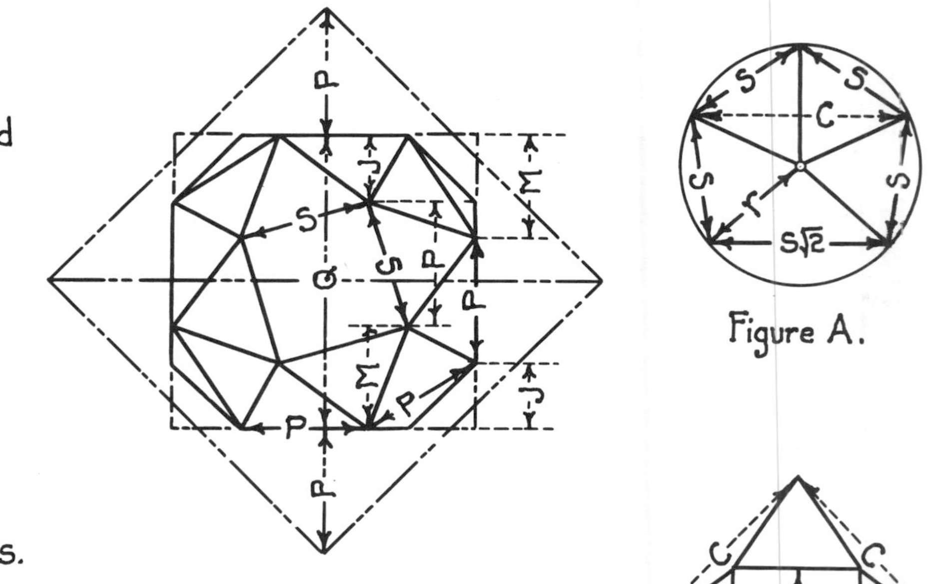

Elevation.

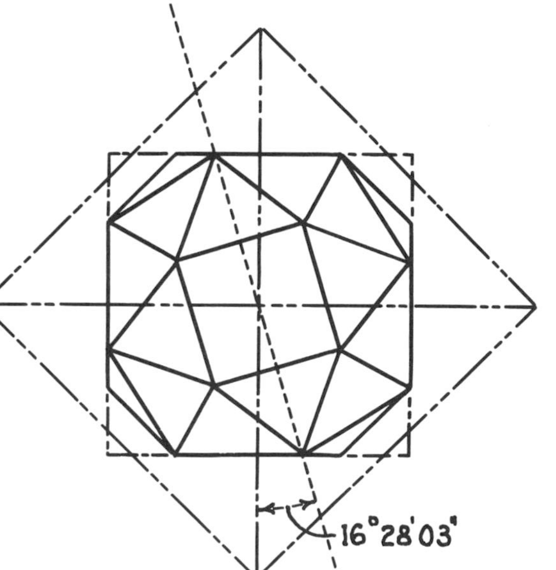

Plan.

Figure A.

Figure B.

Figure C.

PATTERNS FOR THE SNUB CUBE.

Cut the patterns along all dotted lines. Crease them along all solid lines.
Paste unit areas together in consecutive order. (1' to inside of 1, 2' to inside of 2, etc.)
Paste together corresponding unit areas along edges of patterns A and B.

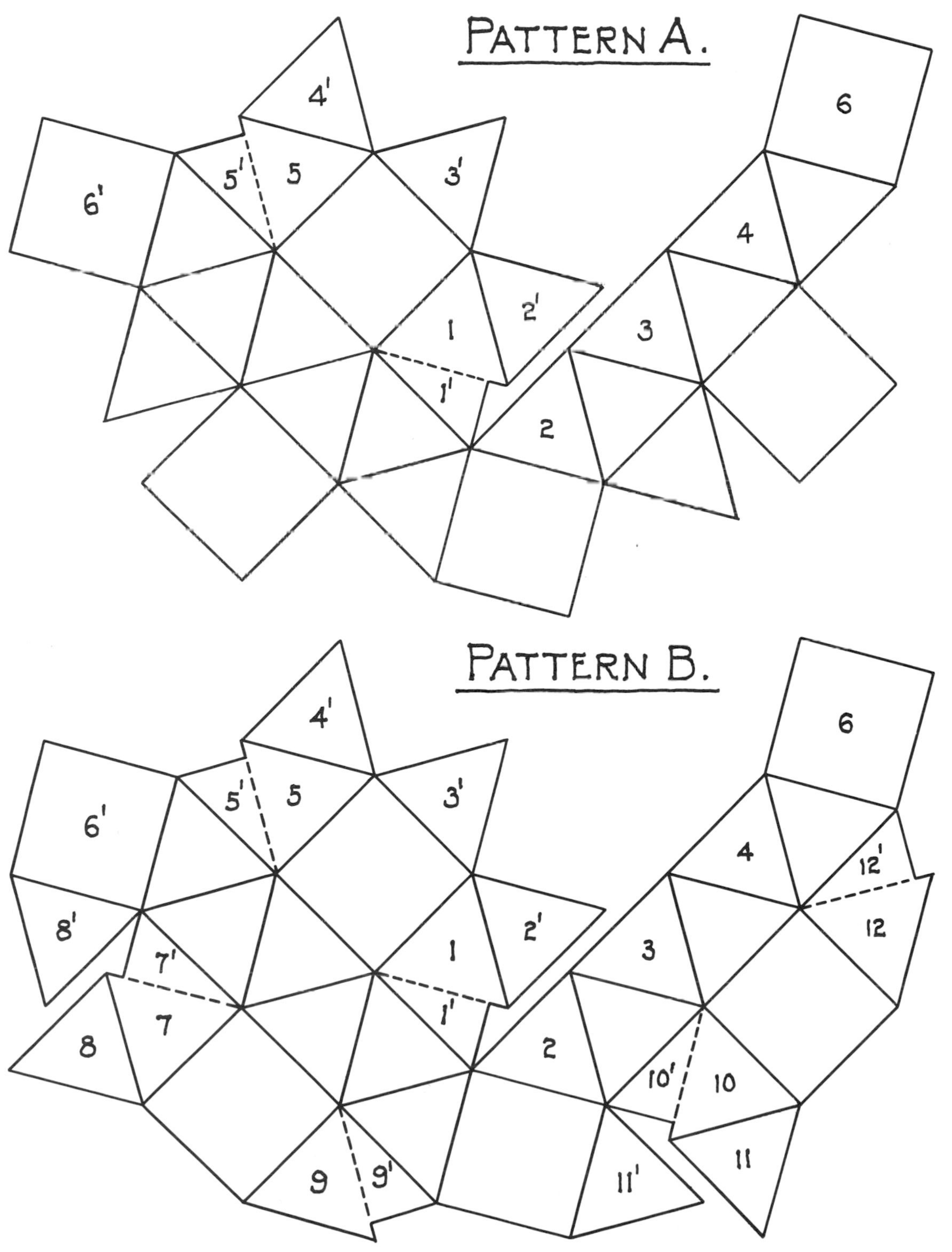

Patterns.

Cuboctahedron.

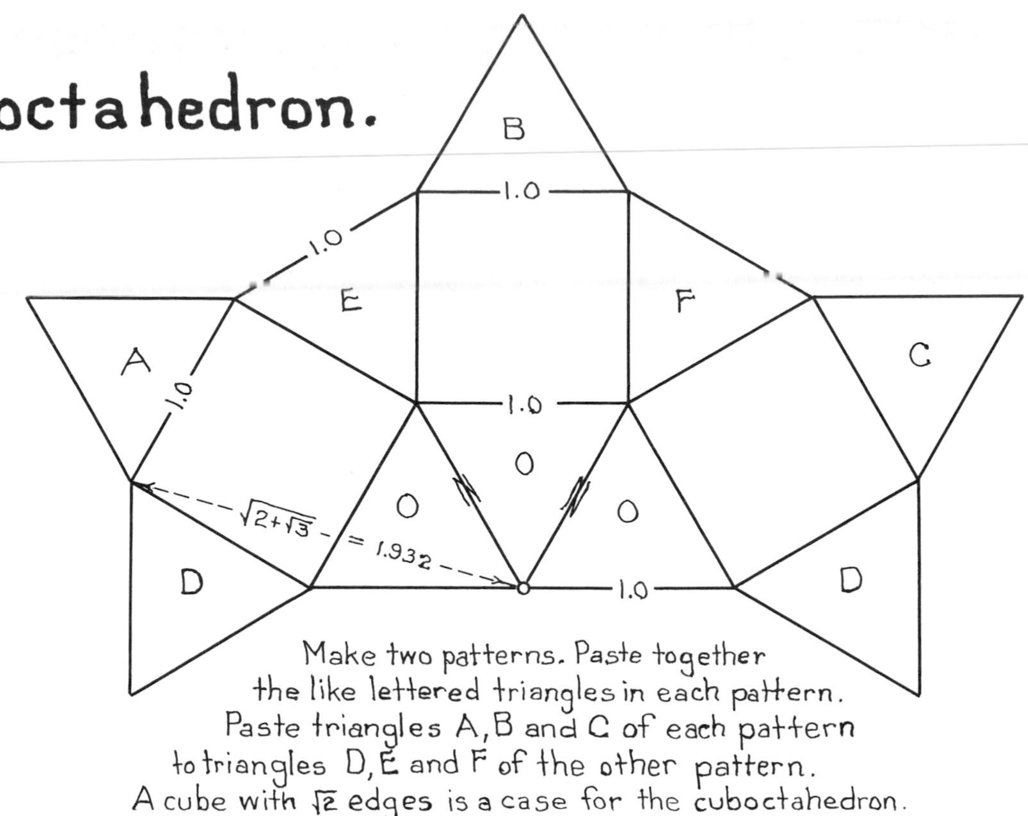

Make two patterns. Paste together the like lettered triangles in each pattern. Paste triangles A, B and C of each pattern to triangles D, E and F of the other pattern. A cube with $\sqrt{2}$ edges is a case for the cuboctahedron.

Icosidodecahedron.

Make two patterns. Paste together the like lettered triangles in each pattern. Paste triangles 1, 2, 3 4 and 5 of each pattern to triangles 6, 7, 8, 9 and A of the other pattern. Close each of the two end openings with a pentagon 1 and its five connected triangles. A dodecahedron with 2k edges is a case for this icosidodecahedron.

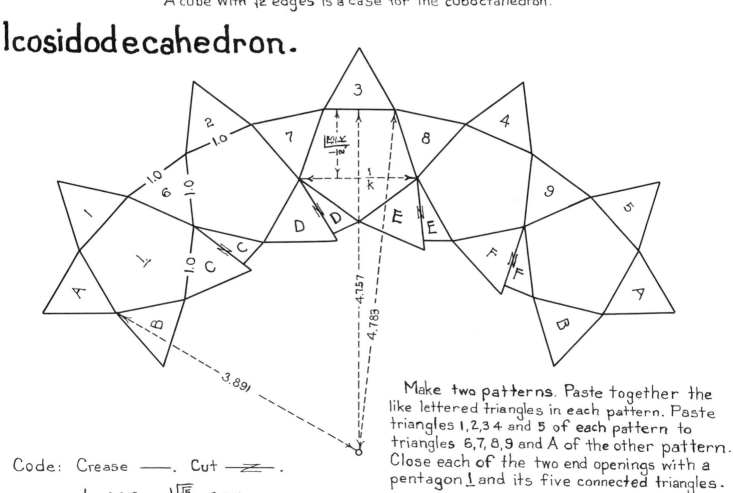

Code: Crease ——. Cut —≠—.

$\frac{1}{k} = 1.618$ $\frac{1}{2}\sqrt{\frac{\sqrt{5}}{k}} = 0.951$

Patterns for Truncated Cuboctahedron.
(Great Rhombicuboctahedron)

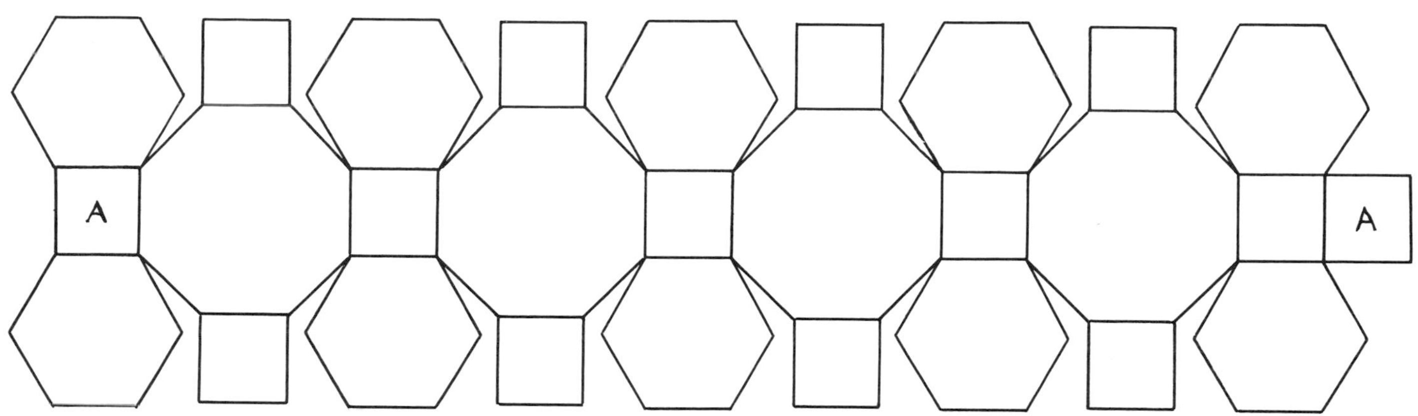

Pattern A.
Make one.

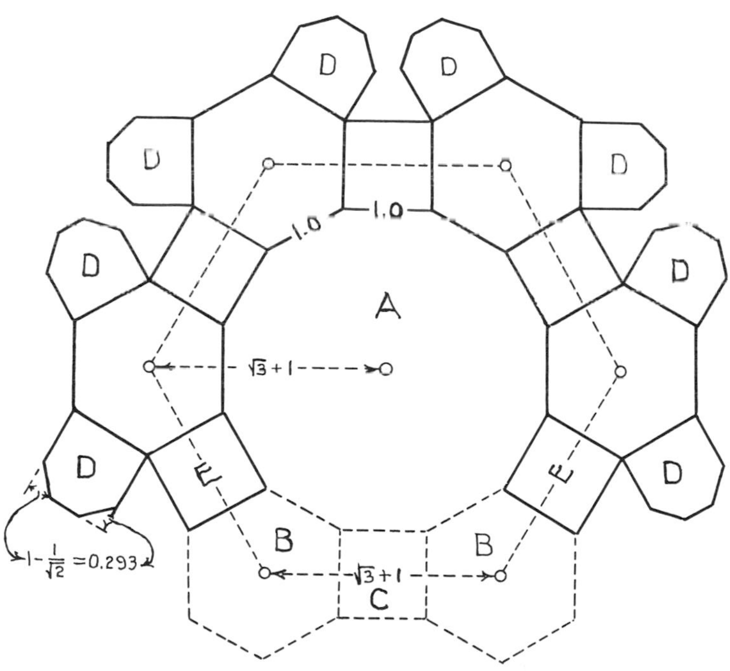

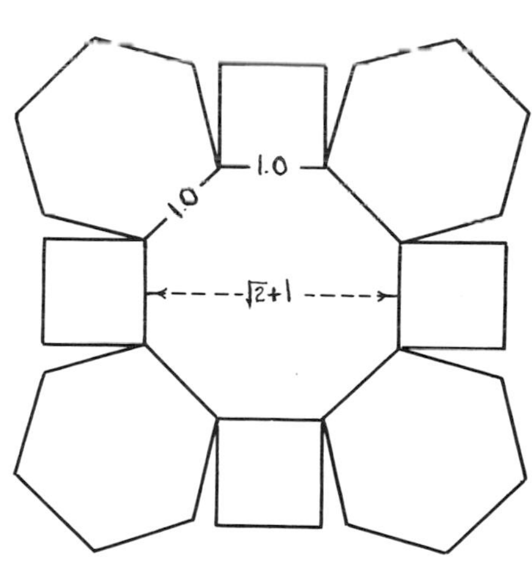

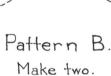

Pattern B.
Make two.

Pattern C.
Make two.

Note. The edges of the cube case for this figure are $2\sqrt{2}+1$ or 3.828 long.

Construction.

In pattern B, cut out the central dodecagon A, two hexagons B, square C and two corners of each square D. In pattern A, paste the end squares A together. Paste together the two squares E of each pattern B. Paste matching rims of patterns A and B together. Close the two open ends with patterns C.

Small Rhombicosidodecahedron Patterns.

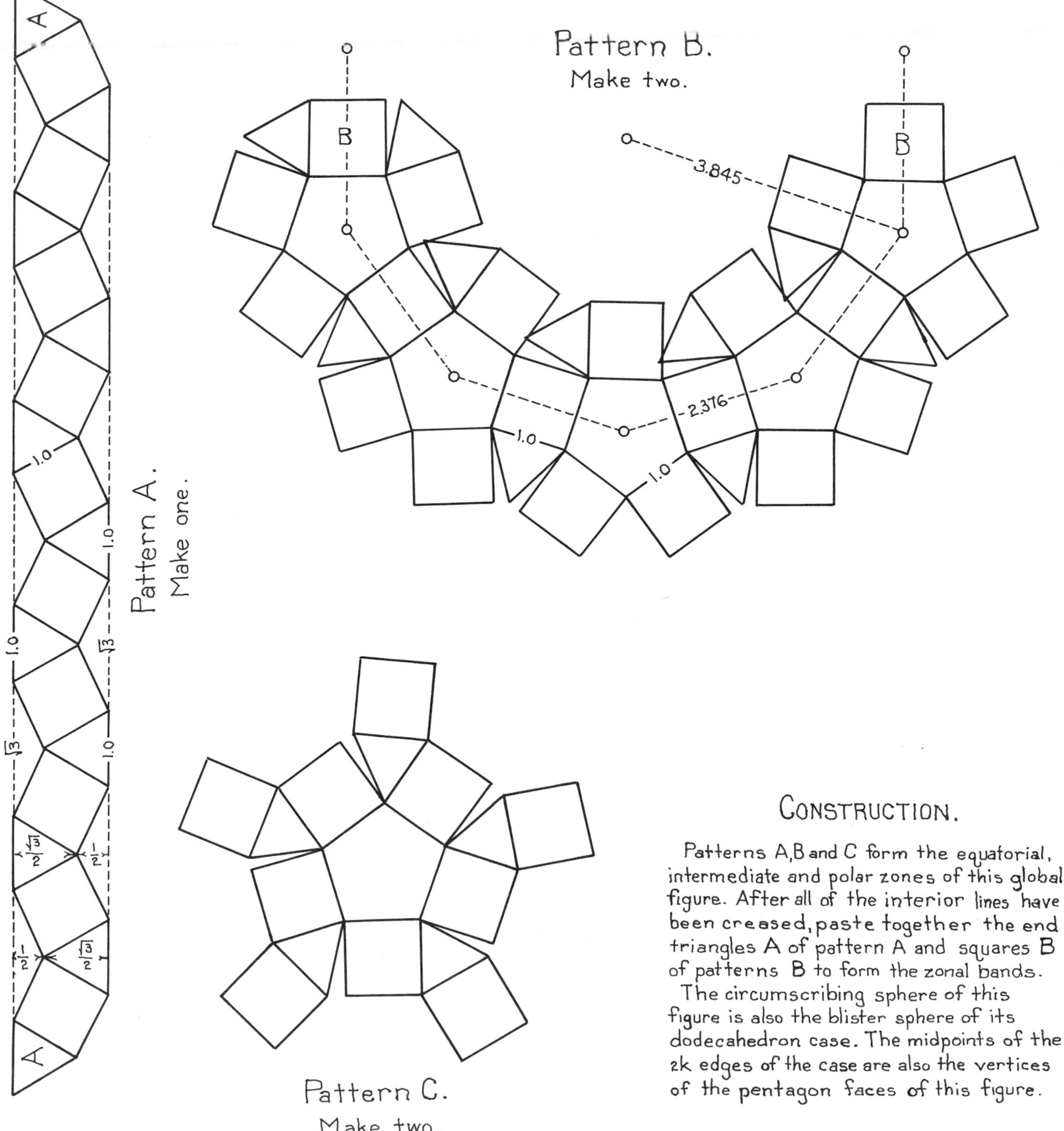

Construction.

Patterns A, B and C form the equatorial, intermediate and polar zones of this global figure. After all of the interior lines have been creased, paste together the end triangles A of pattern A and squares B of patterns B to form the zonal bands.

The circumscribing sphere of this figure is also the blister sphere of its dodecahedron case. The midpoints of the 2k edges of the case are also the vertices of the pentagon faces of this figure.

Truncated Icosidodecahedron Patterns.
(Great Rhombicosidodecahedron)

Pattern B.
Make two.

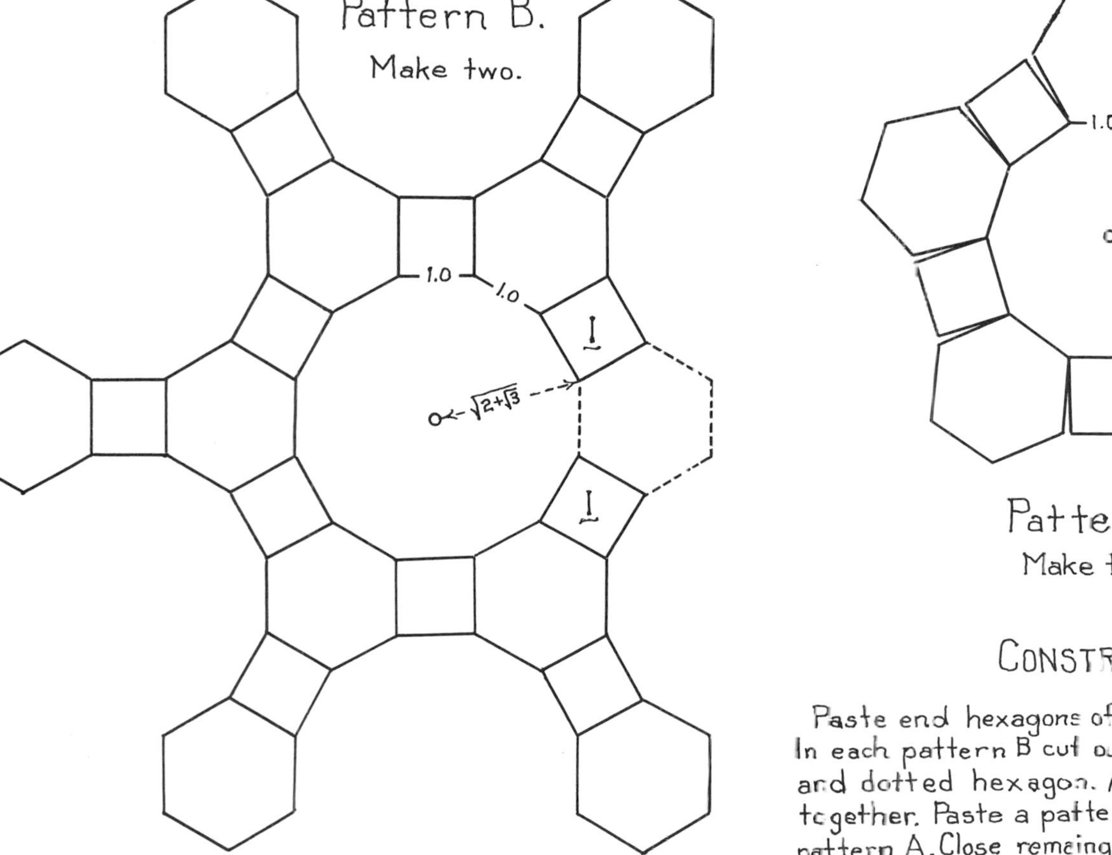

1.0
1.0
$\frac{1}{k}$

Pattern C.
Make twelve.

Construction.

Paste end hexagons of pattern A together. In each pattern B cut out the central dodecagon and dotted hexagon. Also paste squares 1 together. Paste a pattern B to each side of pattern A. Close remaing openings with patterns C. An icosahedron with $\frac{3}{k}$ edges is a case for this figure.

$\frac{1}{k} = 1.618$. $\frac{3}{k} = 4.854$ $\sqrt{2+\sqrt{3}} = 1.932$.

Pattern A.
Make one.

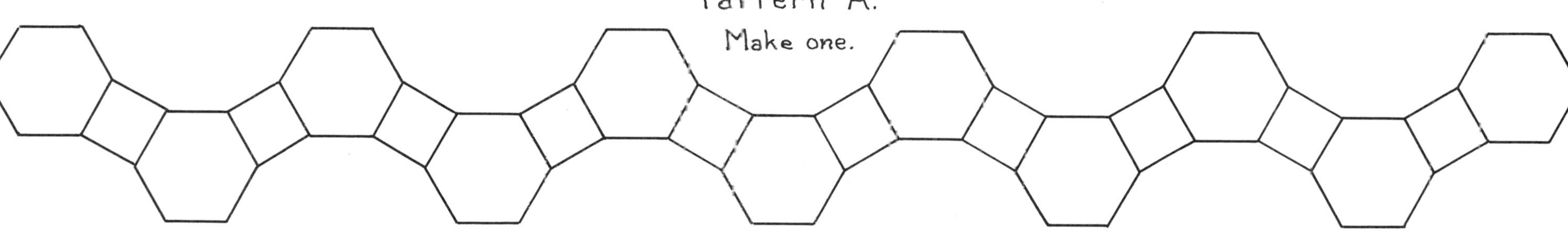

Snub Dodecahedron Patterns.

Pattern B.
Make one.

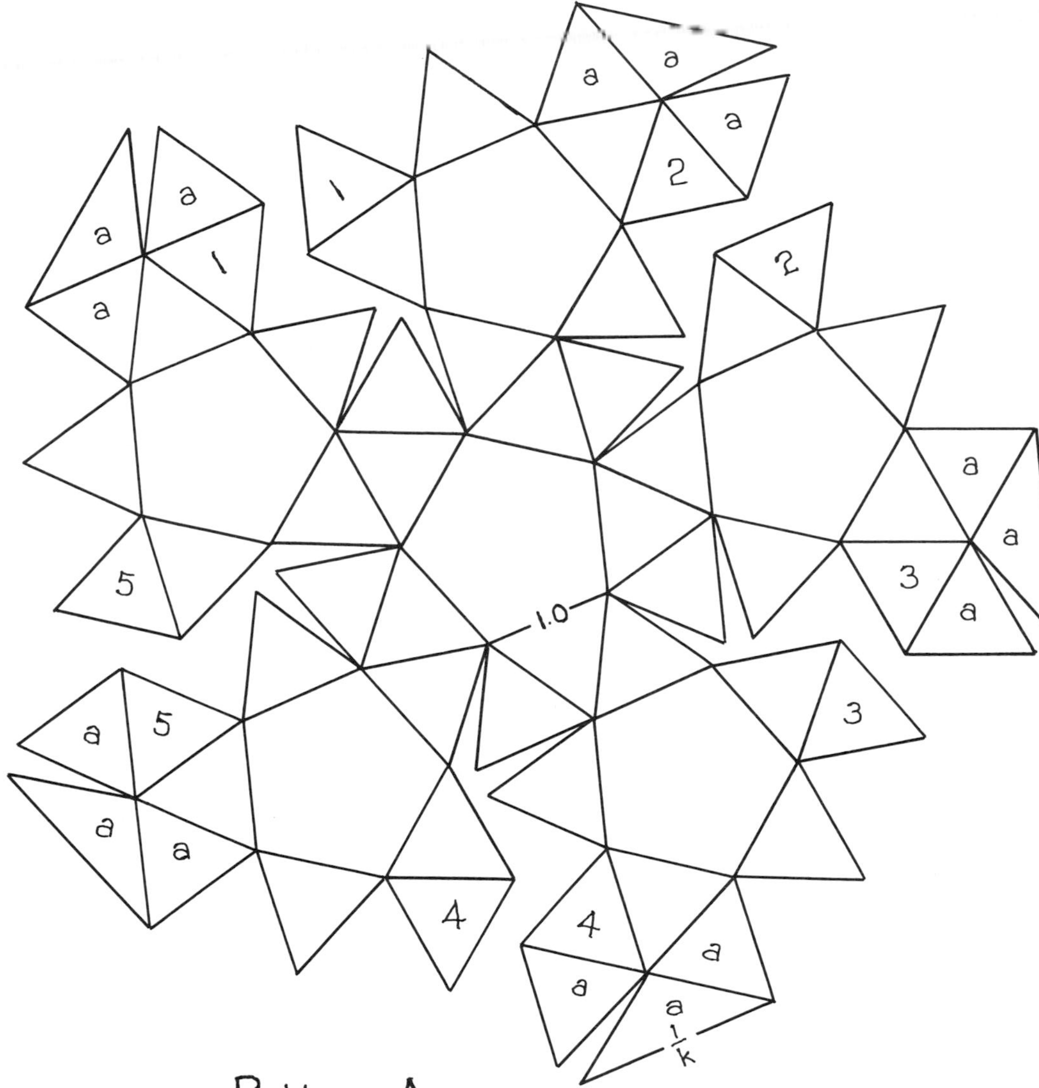

Pattern A.
Make two. Omit triangles a from one.

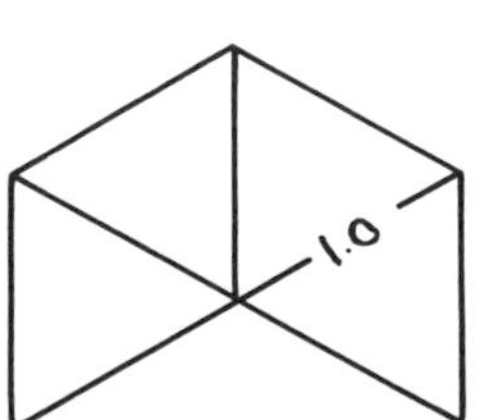

Pattern C.
Make ten.

Construction.

Paste together the like numbered triangles of both patterns A. Paste pattern B on the inside of the rim of the larger pattern A leaving a free edge of alternate 1 and $\frac{1}{k}$ segments. Secure all faces of the two half sections with 10 patterns C pasted inside. Paste the half sections together to complete the figure.

The diamonds connecting the adjoining pentagonal faces in this figure will be tilted equally in the opposite direction if all creasing is reversed. $\frac{1}{k} = 1.618$

Small Rhombicuboctahedron Pattern.

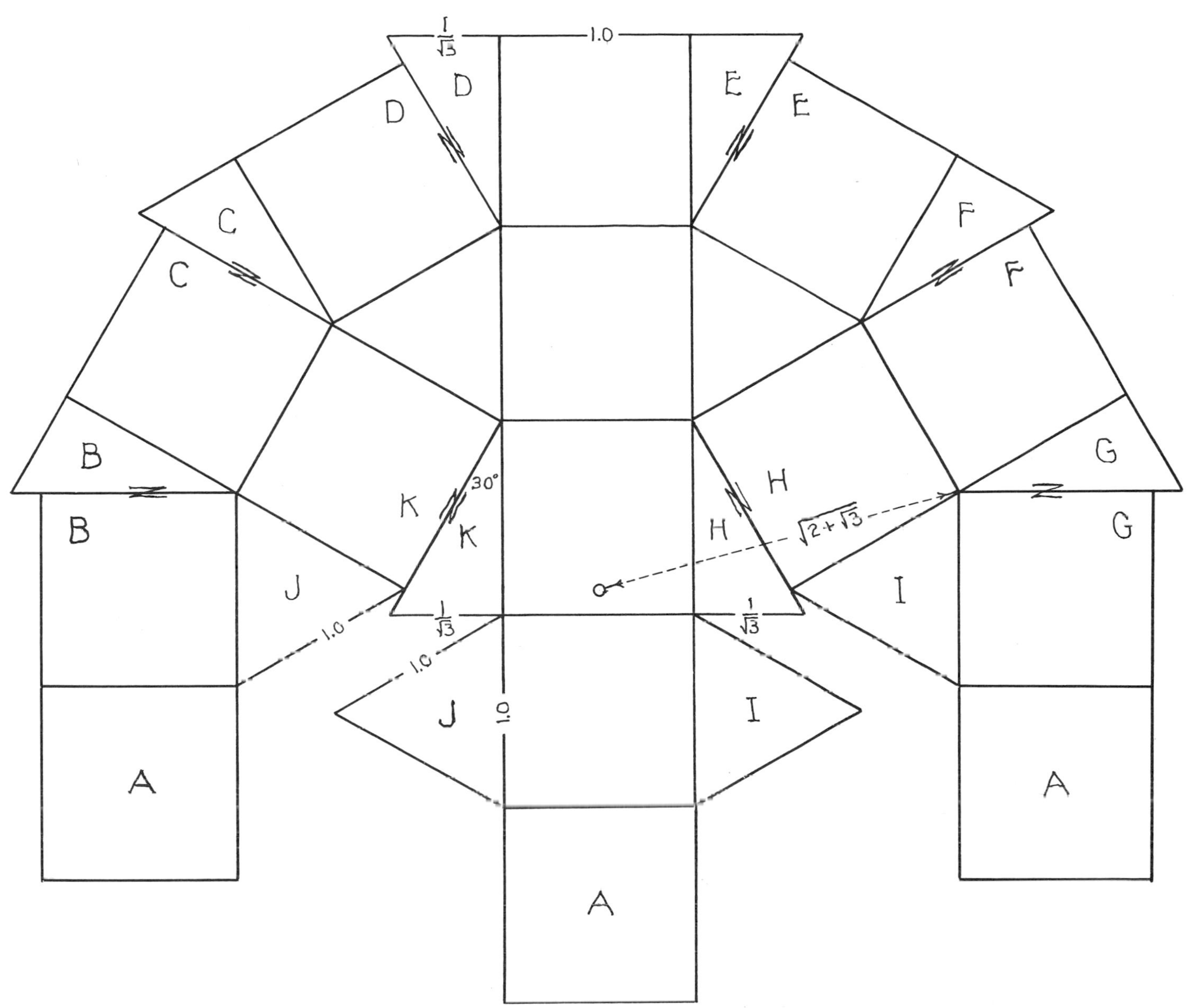

CONSTRUCTION.

Make two patterns. Omit triangles B, C, D, E, F and G from the second pattern.

In the first pattern, paste the like lettered unit areas together in their alphabetical order with their edges matching. It will then be evident how to complete the figure with the second pattern. Its case is a cube with $1+\sqrt{2}$ edges.

Code: Crease ——. Cut —z—. $1+\sqrt{2} = 2.414$ $\sqrt{2+\sqrt{3}} = 1.932$

KEPLER - POINSOT POLYHEDRA

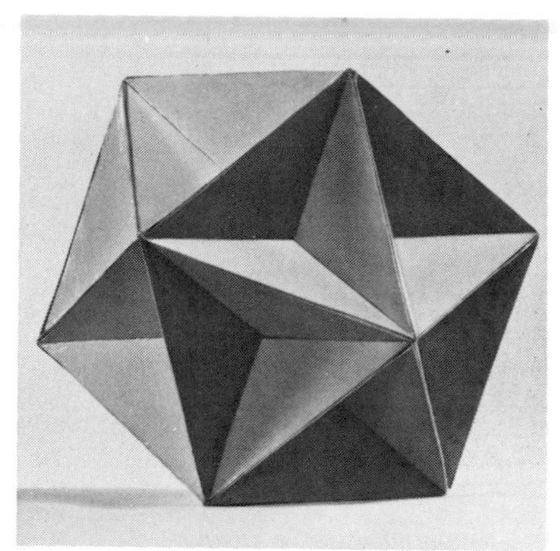

GREAT DODECAHEDRON
(STAR ICOSAHEDRON)

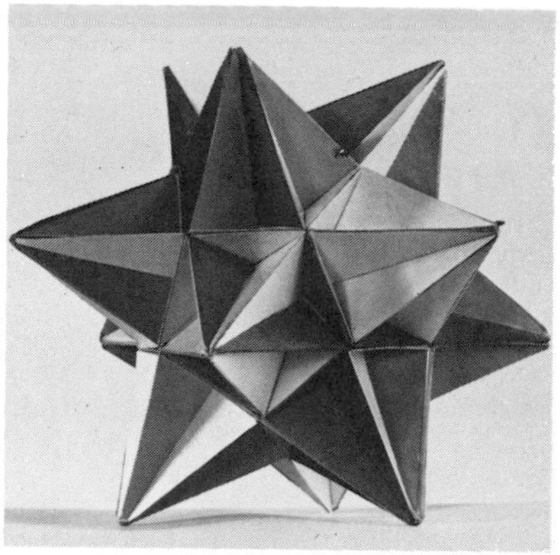

GREAT ICOSAHEDRON

SMALL STELLATED
DODECAHEDRON

GREAT STELLATED
DODECAHEDRON

THE ICOSAHEDRON STAR.

(GREAT DODECAHEDRON) PATTERN 1

The star that forms each corner of the star icosahedron is shown here in plan and elevation. Its ridges are of s length.

A pattern for this star can be made with the decagon inscribed in a circle of s radius. (Figure C.) It is subdivided into ten triangles each of types A and B as shown.

Cut the pattern along all dotted lines. Crease it along all solid lines. Paste corresponding B and B' triangles together to form the base of each star ray. The solid star can be backed with a flat star of same size as plan.

The height of the solid star is $s\sqrt{\frac{k}{\sqrt{5}}}$. Pentagons with sides of s and decagons with sides of $s\sqrt{\frac{k}{\sqrt{5}}}$ can be inscribed in the same circle.

Call width of star or diagonal of pentagon, w. $s=kw$.

$k=\frac{1}{2}\sqrt{5}-\frac{1}{2}=0.618034$. $\sqrt{\frac{k}{\sqrt{5}}}=0.525730$.

Figure A shows how to draw a star of any width, w, and figure B shows how to inscribe a decagon in any circle of radius, r. The numbers give the order of construction.

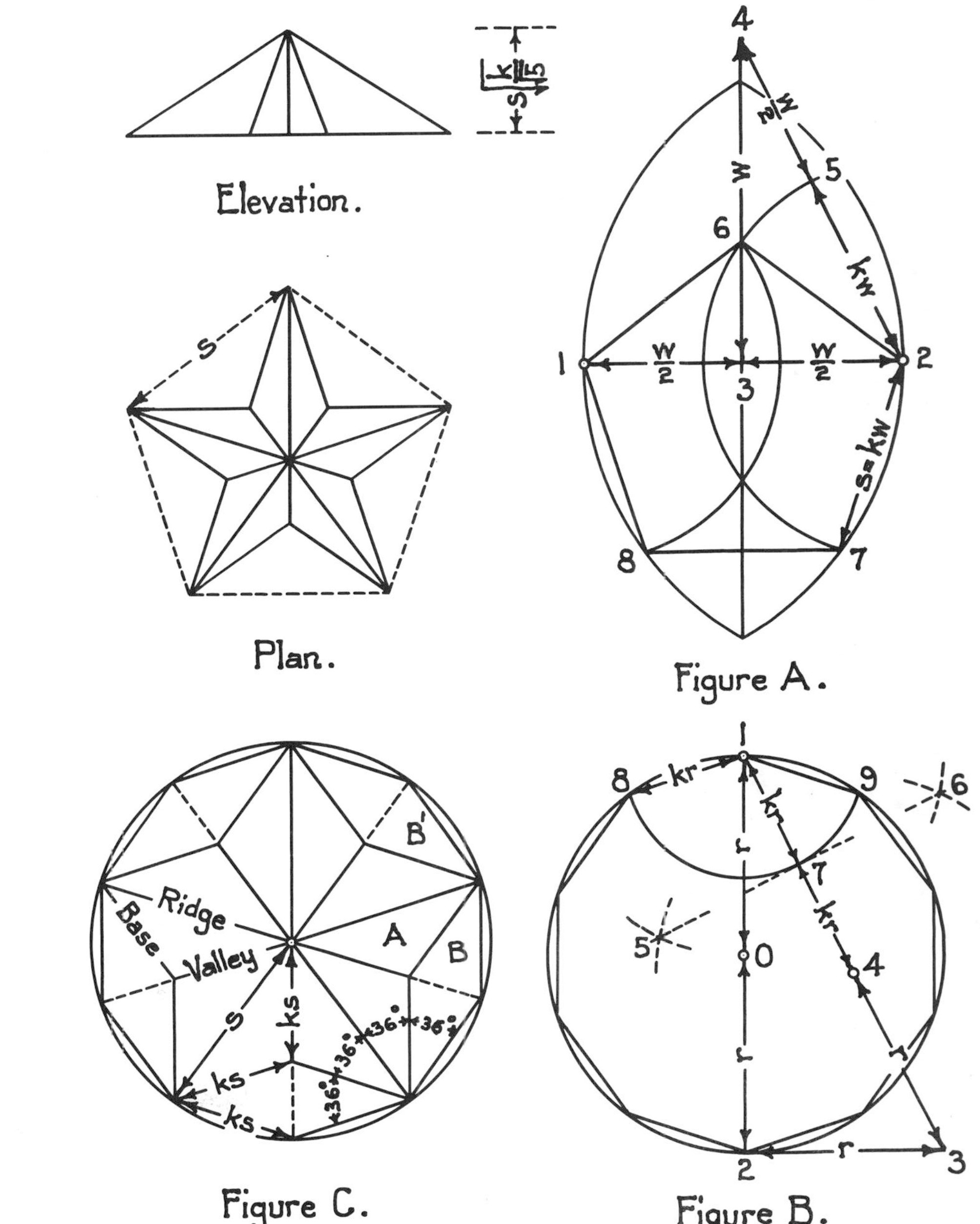

Elevation.

Plan.

Figure A.

Figure C.

Figure B.

PATTERNS FOR THE STAR ICOSAHEDRON.
(GREAT DODECAHEDRON) PATTERN 2

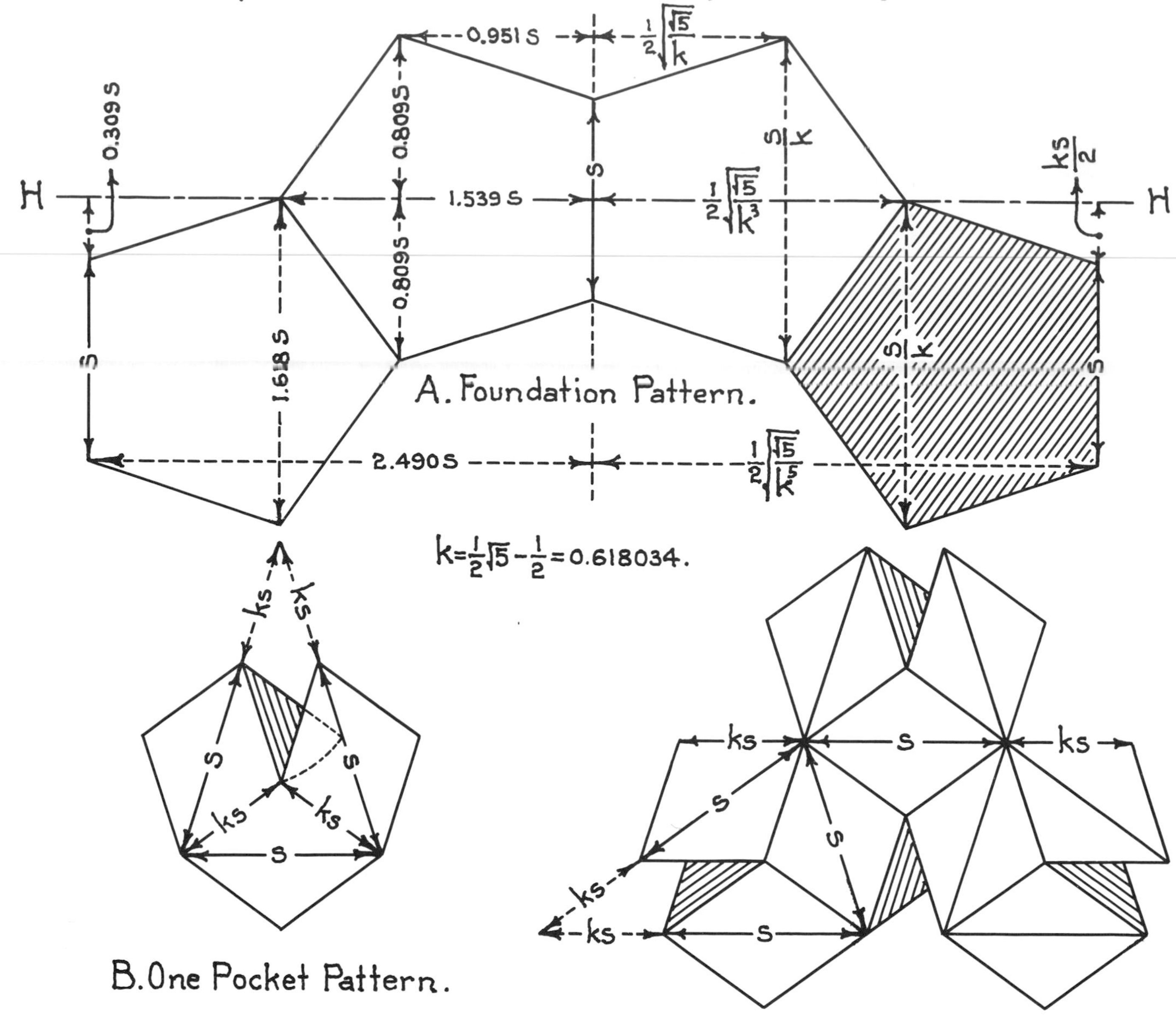

A. Foundation Pattern.

B. One Pocket Pattern.

C. Four Pocket Pattern.

CONSTRUCTION. Make three icosahedron stars and patterns A, B and C.

Pattern A. Locate vertices of pentagons on seven perpendiculars to axis H-H as shown. Crease the three sides joining the pentagons. Mount a star on each blank pentagon. Coil pattern and paste end pentagons together.

Patterns B and C. Each diamond in these patterns has a diagonal of s length and sides of ks length. Locate the s diagonals of the three diamonds forming each pocket on triangles with sides of $\frac{s}{k}$, $\frac{s}{k}$ and s. $\frac{s}{k} = s + ks = 1.618\,s$. Cut along dotted side of each crosshatched pasting tab. Crease patterns along all solid lines. All s lines are ridges and all ks lines are valleys. Form pockets by pasting tabs to backs of adjacent half diamonds.

Paste patterns B and C to fitting ends of pattern A.

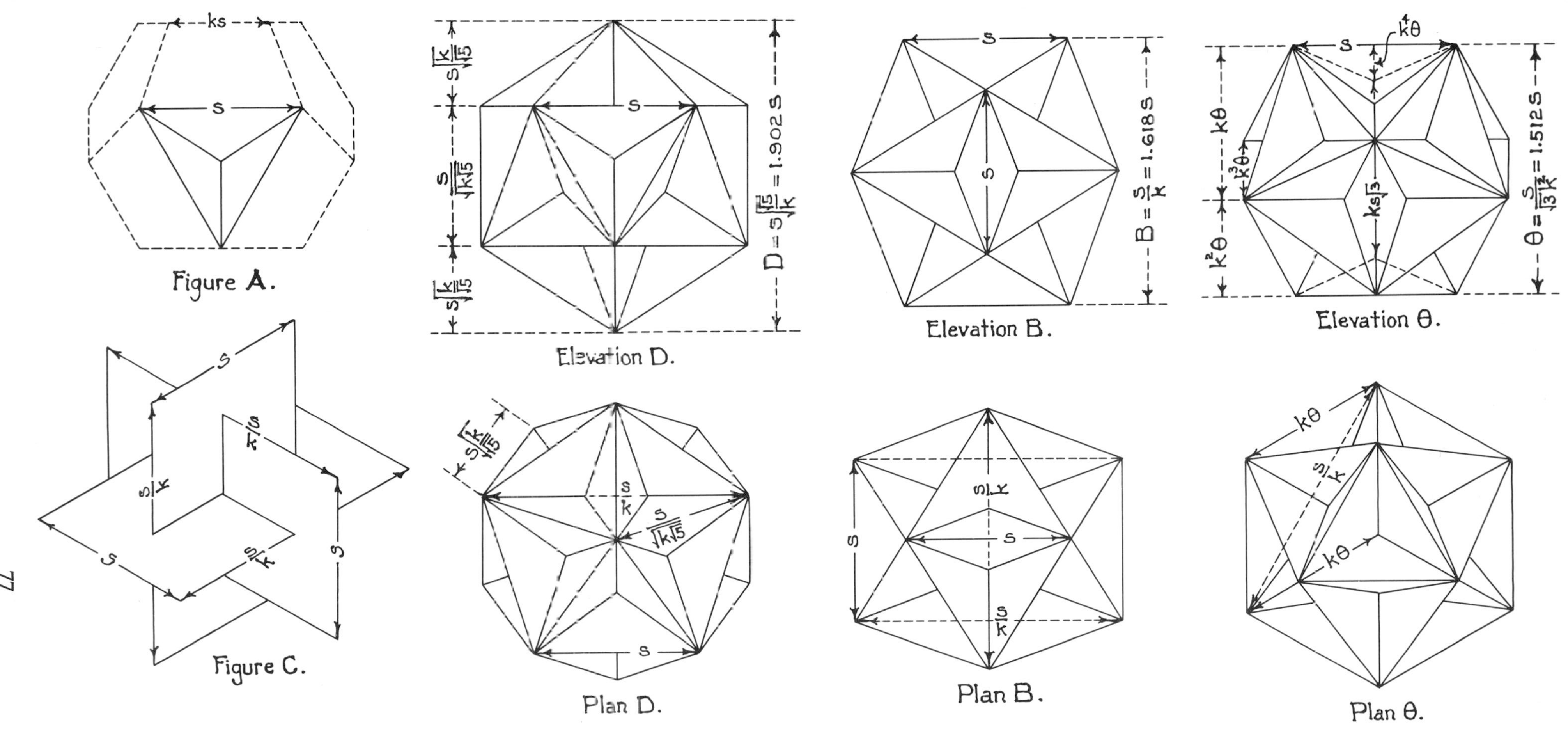

THE STAR ICOSAHEDRON. (Great dodecahedron.)

s=length of each ridge edge. $k=\frac{1}{2}\sqrt{5}-\frac{1}{2}=0.618034$, the golden mean ratio. Valley edges are ks long. Diameters of cover, blister and lining spheres are D, B and Θ respectively.

Total surface $=15s^2\sqrt{k^3\sqrt{5}}=10.89813s^2$. Volume $=\frac{5}{2}ks^3=1.545085s^3$.

Angles. Ridge-63°26'06". Valley-116°33'54". Major axis and ridge-58°16'57" $=\frac{1}{2}$ valley angle. Major axis and valley line-31°43'03" $=\frac{1}{2}$ ridge angle. Last two angles are complimentary.

Solid lines in Figure A mark pyramid with edges of s and ks on corner of regular dodecahedron.

A star icosahedron is formed by cutting such a pyramid out of each face of a regular icosahedron having edges of s length. Each corner of this cut back solid appears to be the center of a five pointed star in high relief. Projections D, B and Θ show this solid balanced on one corner, on one edge and resting on one face respectively. Its successive vertical axes in these positions are diameters of its cover, blister and lining spheres respectively.

The perimeter of plan D is a decagon with sides of $s\sqrt{\frac{k}{\sqrt{5}}}$. This decagon is insribed in a circle of $\frac{s}{\sqrt{k\sqrt{5}}}$ radius. The centers of the top and bottom stars in elevation D are raised $s\sqrt{\frac{k}{\sqrt{5}}}$ above their pentagonal bases and the distance between their bases is $\frac{s}{\sqrt{k\sqrt{5}}}$.

The perimeter of plan Θ is a hexagon inscribed in a circle of kΘ radius. Alternate corners of this hexagon form triangles with sides of $\frac{s}{k}$.

The lateral corners in elevation Θ divide the height Θ into segments of kΘ and $k^2\Theta$.

Plan B shows $s\times\frac{s}{k}$ rectangle formed by parallel edges and connecting valley lines. The three perpendicular $s\times\frac{s}{k}$ rectangles in figure C connect all outer corners of icosahedron. Each facial dent is $k^4\Theta$ deep. Dent points form dodecahedron with k^2s edges. Diameters of lining, blister and cover spheres of this core solid are $\frac{s}{\sqrt{k\sqrt{5}}}$, s and $ks\sqrt{3}$. See axes in elevations D, B and Θ.

Patterns for the Great Icosahedron.

The edge of the core icosahedron, P20, is used here as the unit of measure.

When each P20 face is extended as in Figure 1, a great icosahedron, GP20, with $\frac{1}{k^4}$ edges is formed. All lines in this figure are intersections with other faces.

Exposed segments of the GP20 face are shaded.

The GP20 vertices form a second P20 with $\frac{1}{k^3}$ edges.

<u>Construction.</u> Construct a honeycomb dodecahedron, HP12, with $\frac{1}{k}$ edges. Draw 12 patterns D. Cut and crease all interior lines as indicated. Crease ————. Reverse crease —·—·—·—. Cut - - - - - - -. Paste all like lettered triangles together.

Mount an assembled pattern D in each pocket of the HP12.

<u>Dimensions.</u>

$k = 0.618 = \frac{1}{2}\sqrt{5} - \frac{1}{2}$

$\frac{1}{k} = 1.618$

$\frac{1}{k^2} = 2.618$ $\qquad \frac{1}{k}\sqrt{\frac{2}{5}} = 1.023 = a$

$\frac{1}{k^3} = 4.236$ $\qquad \frac{1}{k^3}\sqrt{\frac{2}{5}} = 2.679 = b$

$\frac{1}{k^4} = 6.854$ $\qquad \frac{\sqrt{2}}{k^2} = 3.702 = a + b$

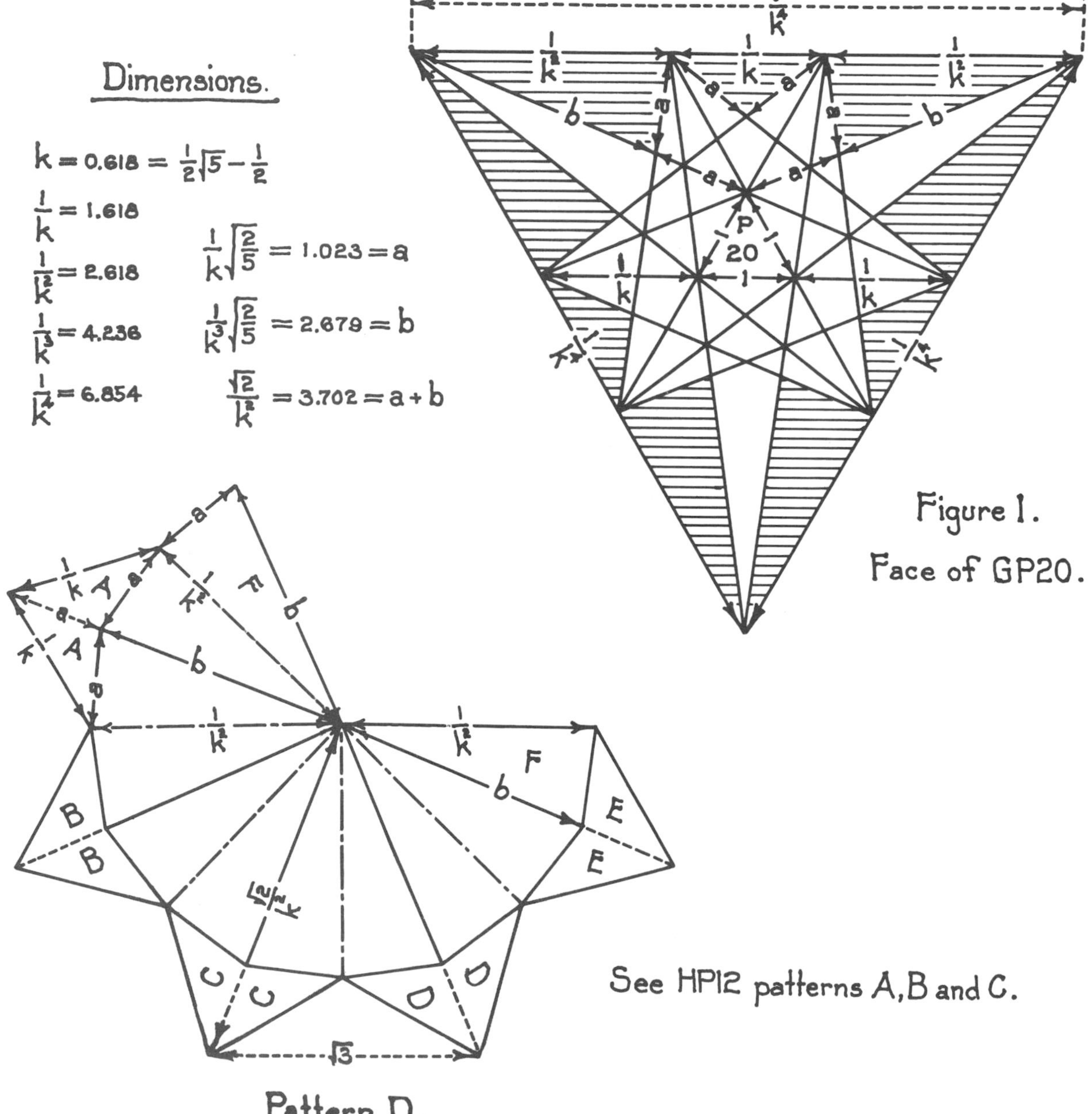

Figure 1.
Face of GP20.

Pattern D.

See HP12 patterns A, B and C.

Patterns for Small Stellated Dodecahedron.

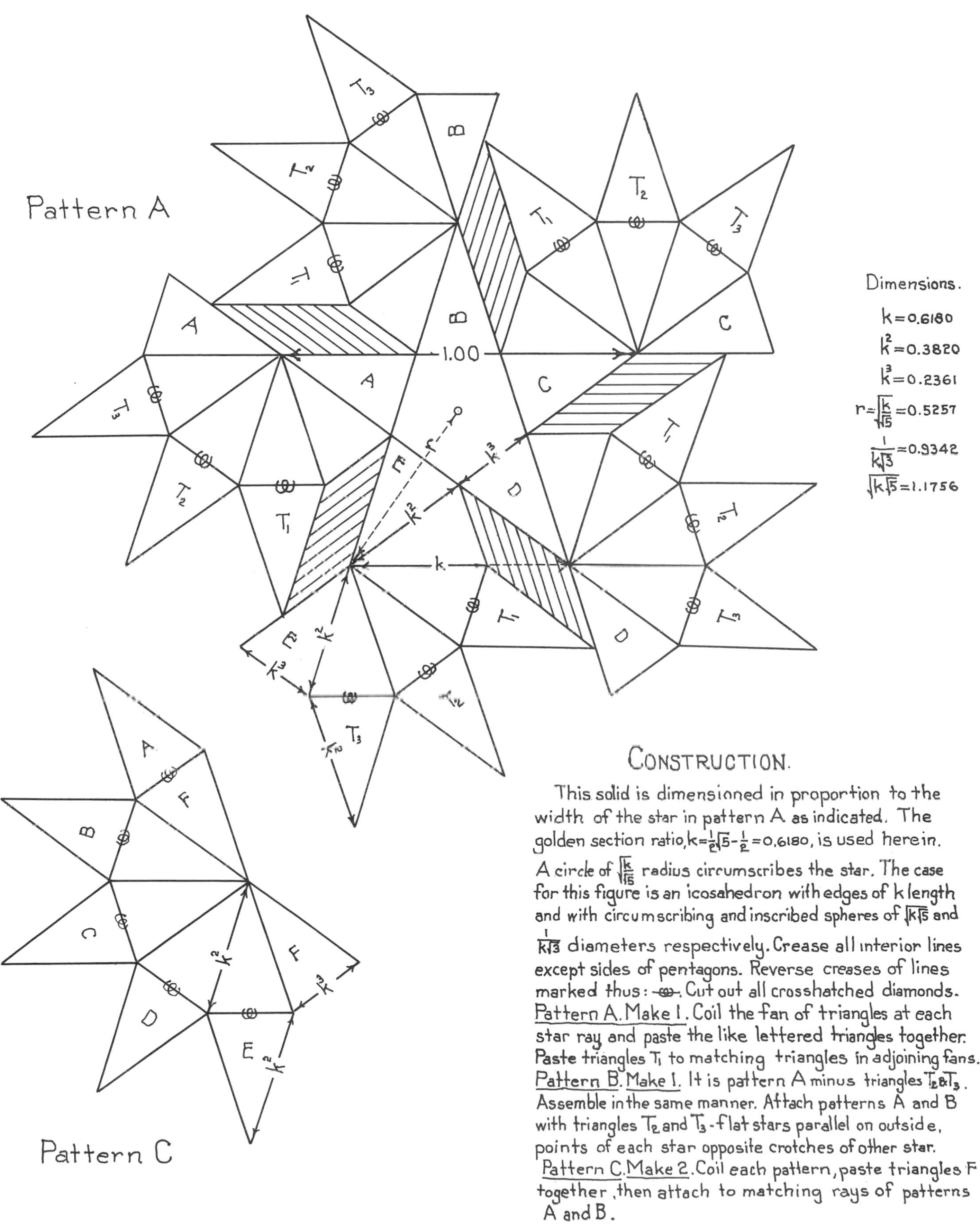

CONSTRUCTION.

This solid is dimensioned in proportion to the width of the star in pattern A as indicated. The golden section ratio, $k = \frac{1}{2}\sqrt{5} - \frac{1}{2} = 0.6180$, is used herein. A circle of $\sqrt{\frac{k}{\sqrt{5}}}$ radius circumscribes the star. The case for this figure is an icosahedron with edges of k length and with circumscribing and inscribed spheres of $\sqrt{k\sqrt{5}}$ and $\frac{1}{k\sqrt{3}}$ diameters respectively. Crease all interior lines except sides of pentagons. Reverse creases of lines marked thus: —ꝏ—. Cut out all crosshatched diamonds.

Pattern A. Make 1. Coil the fan of triangles at each star ray and paste the like lettered triangles together. Paste triangles T_1 to matching triangles in adjoining fans.

Pattern B. Make 1. It is pattern A minus triangles T_2 & T_3. Assemble in the same manner. Attach patterns A and B with triangles T_2 and T_3 - flat stars parallel on outside, points of each star opposite crotches of other star.

Pattern C. Make 2. Coil each pattern, paste triangles F together, then attach to matching rays of patterns A and B.

Patterns for Great Stellated Dodecahedron.

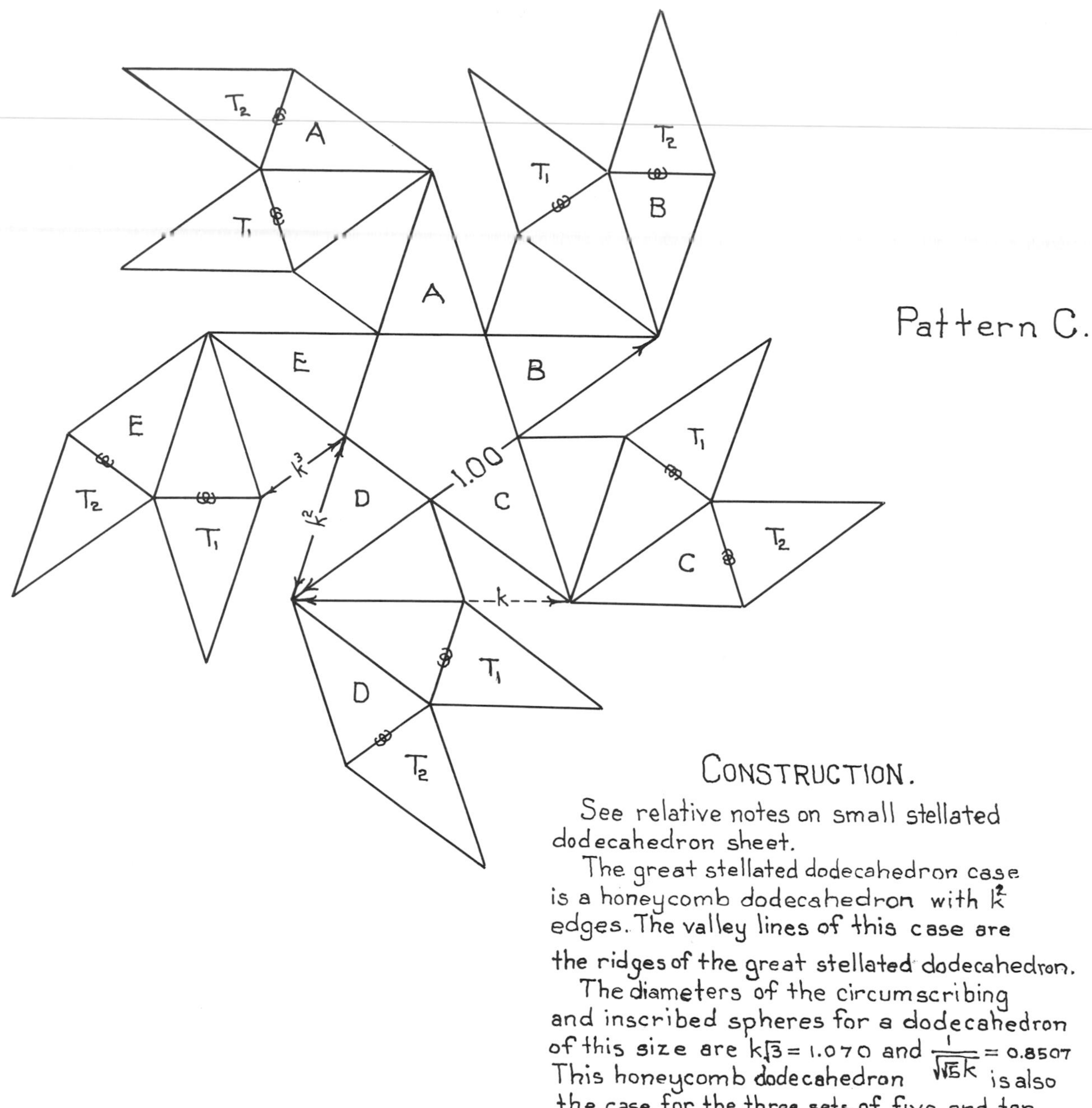

Pattern C.

CONSTRUCTION.

See relative notes on small stellated dodecahedron sheet.

The great stellated dodecahedron case is a honeycomb dodecahedron with k^2 edges. The valley lines of this case are the ridges of the great stellated dodecahedron.

The diameters of the circumscribing and inscribed spheres for a dodecahedron of this size are $k\sqrt{3} = 1.070$ and $\frac{1}{\sqrt{\sqrt{5}}\,k} = 0.8507$. This honeycomb dodecahedron is also the case for the three sets of five and ten interlocking tetrahedra.

Pattern C. Make 2 as shown with the sides of their pentagons creased. Coil the fan of triangles at each star ray and paste the like lettered triangles together with triangles T_2 outside. Paste triangles T_1 to matching triangles on adjoining fans. Attach to patterns A and B with triangles T_2. Pattern A omits triangles T_2 from pattern C. Pattern B reverses pattern A. Treat A and B as in small stellation.

MISCELLANEOUS POLYHEDRA

TWO INTERLOCKING
TETRAHEDRON

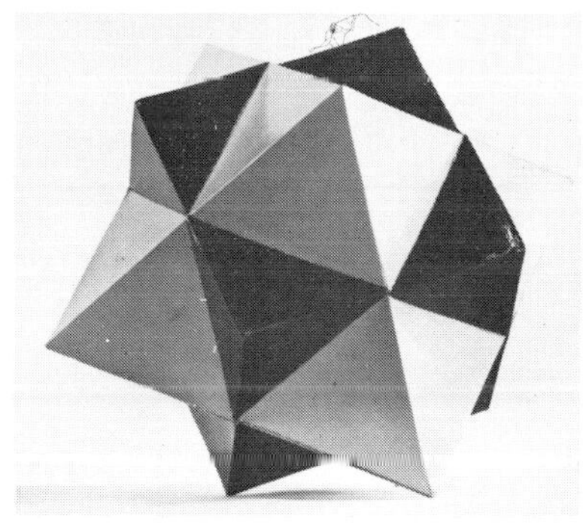

CUBE PLUS
OCTAHEDRON

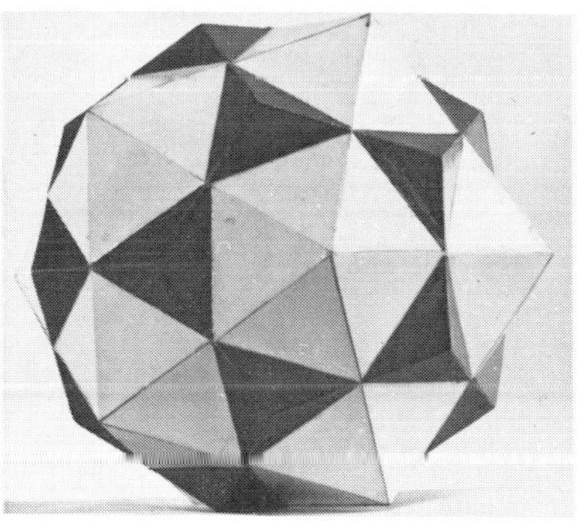

DODECAHEDRON
PLUS
ICOSAHEDRON

RHOMBIC
DODECAHEDRON

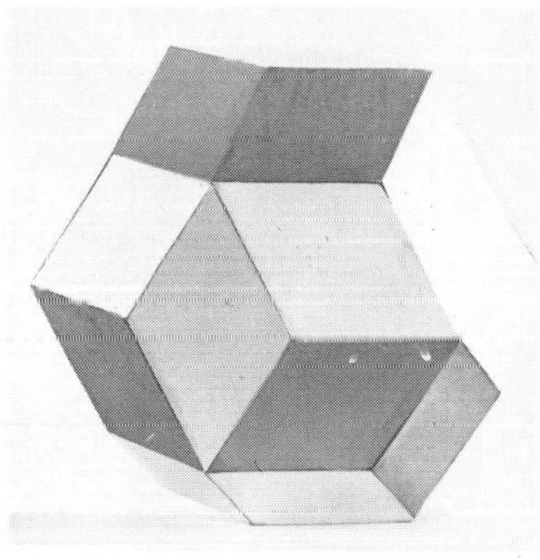

TRIACONTAHEDRON

STELLATED RHOMBIC
DODECAHEDRON

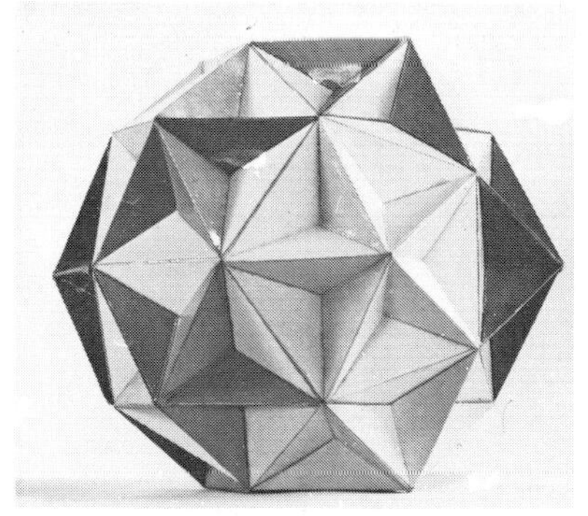

STAR LINKED
TRIACONTA–
DODECAHEDRON

STELLAR SNUB
DODECAHEDRON

Patterns for Three Compound Polyhedra.

Patterns V4, V6 and V20 are used to compound a tetrahedron, octahedron and dodecahedron with a second tetrahedron, a cube and an icosahedron respectively. In these compound solids each edge of one solid is the perpendicular bisector of an edge of the other solid. The outer edges of each pattern are half the length of the edges of its base solid. Cut V6 and V20 on lines between triangles **B**. Crease bases of outer triangles in valleys and the other interior lines in ridges. The perimeter of each pattern will match the faces of its base solid when pyramids are formed by pasting its **B** triangles together.

Four V4 patterns mounted on the faces of a tetrahedron form a second tetrahedron.

Eight V6 patterns mounted on the faces of an octahedron form a cube.

Twelve V20 patterns mounted on the faces of a dodecahedron form an icosahedron.

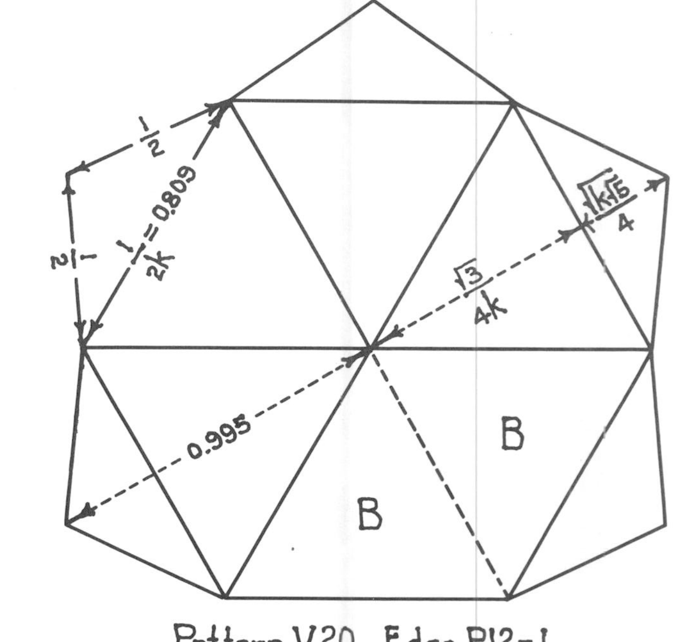

Pattern V20. Edge P12=1.

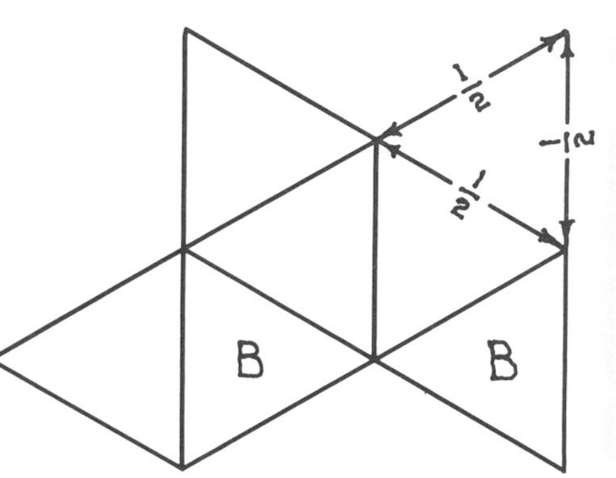

Pattern V4. Edge P4=1.

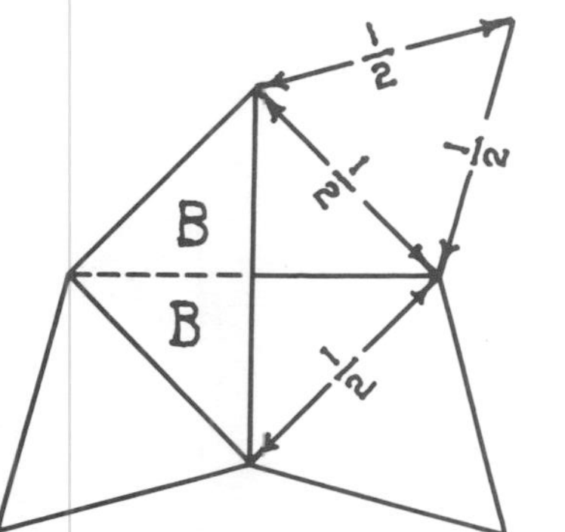

Pattern V6. Edge P8=1.

Patterns for the Rhombic Dodecahedron.

Description. The rhombic dodecahedron is a convex polyhedron faced with twelve equal diamonds. The diamonds have sides, s, and diagonals, a and b. $a = 2s\sqrt{\frac{2}{3}} = 1.633s$. $b = \frac{2s}{\sqrt{3}} = 1.155s$ $\frac{a}{b} = \sqrt{2}$. The a diagonals form an octahedron, P8. Axis $P8 = \frac{4s}{\sqrt{3}} = 2.309s$. The b diagonals form a cube, P6. Axis $P6 = 2s$.

Construction. This solid is made with one pattern A and one pattern B. Six triangles with sides of $\frac{3}{2}a, \frac{3}{2}a$ and a contain the a diagonals of all diamonds. $\frac{3}{2}a = s\sqrt{6} = 2.449s$. $a = 2s\sqrt{\frac{2}{3}} = 1.633s$. Cut division lines between areas C and areas D. Crease both patterns along their interior lines. Paste together like lettered unit areas of each pattern. Complete solid by pasting the outer diamonds of pattern A to pattern B.

Note. If the six square pyramids formed by the diagonals of a cube are mounted on its faces, a rhombic dodecahedron is formed.

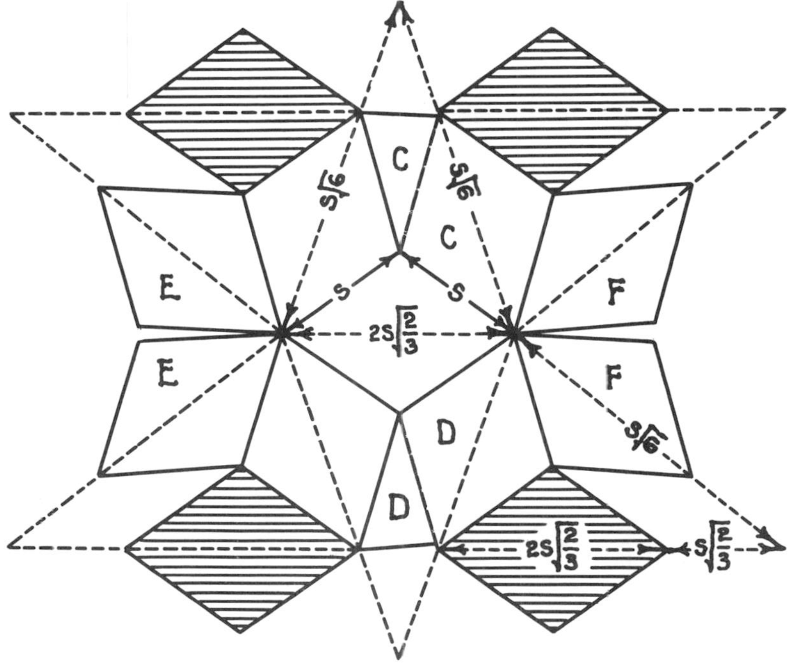

Patterns A & B.
Pattern B omits crosshatched diamonds.

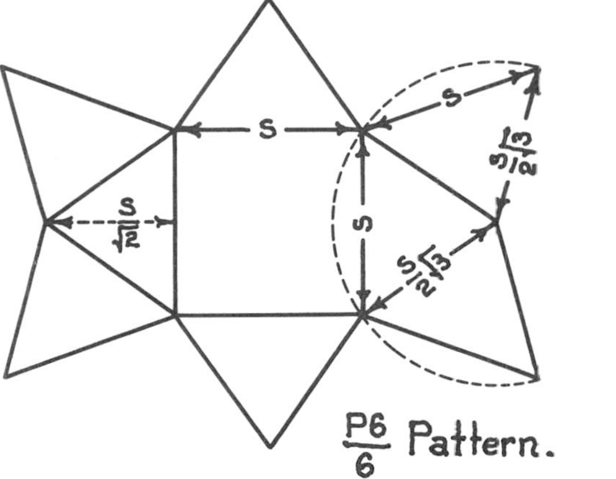

$\frac{P6}{6}$ Pattern.

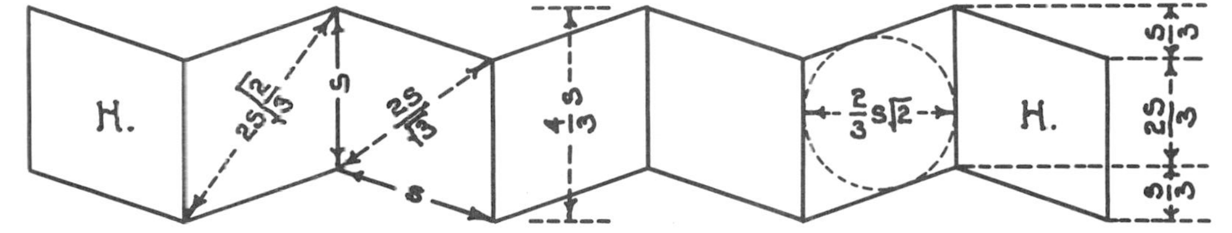

A rhombic dodecahedron can be made with this rickrack belt and two patterns B.

Patterns for the Stellated Rhombic Dodecahedron.

Description. Six square pyramids are formed by joining the vertices of a cube with its center. A flattened octahedron can be formed by joining the bases of two of these pyramids. The stellated rhombic dodecahedron is formed by three such octahedra that are concentric and have perpendicular axes.

If the diamond face of the generating rhombic dodecahedron has sides of s length, its short diagonal, b, is $\frac{2s}{\sqrt{3}}$ or 1.155s long, and the flattened octahedron has eight 2s edges and four 2b or 2.310s edges.

Construction. The stellated rhombic dodecahedron is made with one pattern A, two patterns B and four patterns C. The shaded faces have reverse folding.

First Octahedron. Paste together faces of pattern A in the order 2 to 1, 4 to 3, 5 to 6, 7 to 5 and 8 to 3.

Second Octahedron. Paste together faces of pattern B in the order 1 to 2 and 3 to 4. Paste the six other faces to matching planes of pattern A.

Third Octahedron. Paste together faces 1 and 2 of pattern C. Paste the four shaded faces to a matching plane of the first two octahedra.

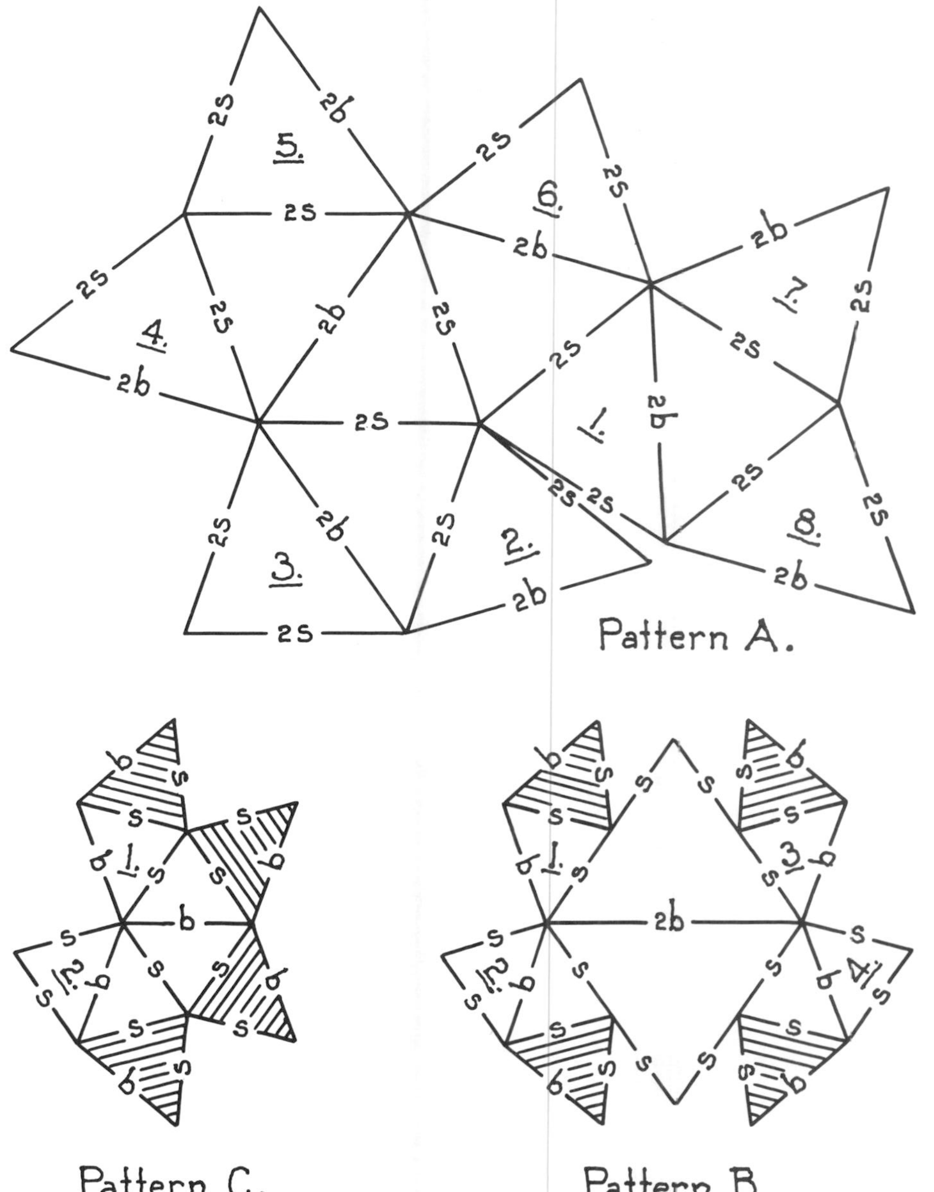

PATTERNS FOR THE TRIACONTAHEDRON.

Description. The triacontahedron is a convex polyhedron faced with thirty equal diamonds. The diamonds have sides, s, and diagonals a and b. $\frac{b}{a} = k = \frac{1}{2}\sqrt{5} - \frac{1}{2} = 0.618034.$

$$a = \frac{2S}{\sqrt{k\sqrt{5}}} = 1.701\,S. \qquad b = 2S\sqrt{\frac{k}{\sqrt{5}}} = 1.051\,S.$$

The a diagonals form an icosahedron, P20. The b diagonals form a dodecahedron, P12.

Axis $P20 = \frac{2S}{k} = 3.236\,S.$ Axis $P12 = 2S\sqrt{\frac{3}{k\sqrt{5}}} = 2.947\,S.$

Construction. Make two each of patterns A and B and one pattern C. Points 1, 2, 3, 4 and 5 of pattern B are centers of stars like pattern A. Cut pattern A on line x1. Crease all patterns along their interior lines. Paste together like lettered unit areas of each pattern. Paste the five central diamonds of each pattern B to inside of a pattern A. Complete solid by pasting the ten outer diamonds of each pattern B to pattern C.

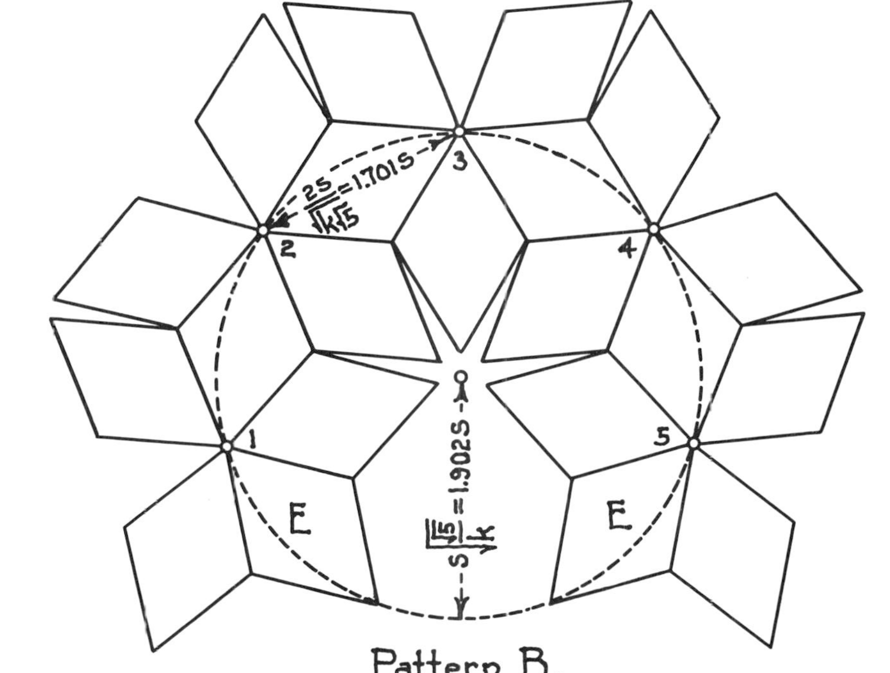

Pattern B.

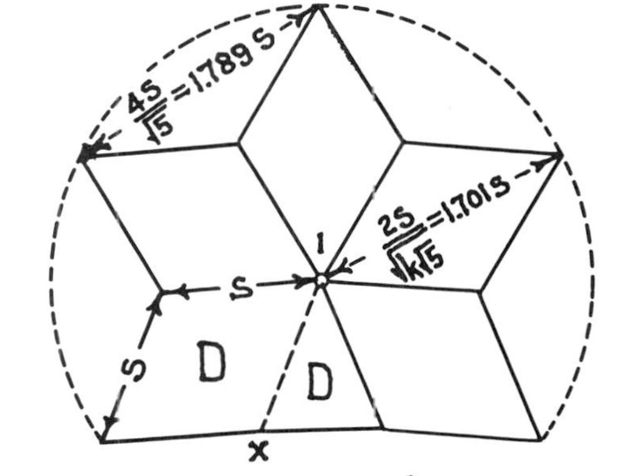

Pattern A.

Pattern C. (Eleven diamonds. $\frac{S}{\sqrt{5}} = 0.447\,S.$ $\frac{2S}{\sqrt{5}} = 0.894\,S.$ $\frac{2S}{k\sqrt{5}} = 1.447\,S.$)

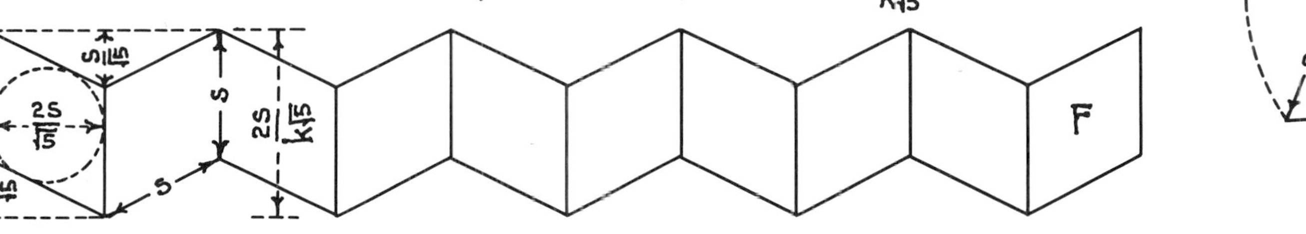

KIN OF THE TRIACONTAHEDRON

The triacontahedron is a convex polyhedron faced with thirty equal diamonds. It is the common core of the five interlocking cubes formed by the facial diagonals of a dodecahedron. Each cube is a case for the triacontahedron. The relative positions and proportions of the six diamond faces on each cube are shown on a separate model and in Figure 1 on the accompanying page on interlocking cubes from 'Patterns in Space'. The height of the cube is used herein as the unit of measure. The golden section ratio, $k = 1/2 \sqrt{5} - 1/2 = 0.6180$ is a prime factor in all of this construction.

A set of three 1 x k interlocking golden rectangles is formed by the lines connecting the ends of the long diagonals of the diamonds in the parallel faces of each cube. The k ends of these fifteen 1 x k rectangles are the edges of an inscribed icosahedron.

Corresponding sets of three 1 x k^2 rectangles are formed in each cube by the lines connecting the ends of the short diagonals of the diamond faces. The k^2 ends of these fifteen 1 x k^2 rectangles are the edges of an inscribed dodecahedron. The lines connecting the vertices of the sets of three 1 x k^2 rectangles in each cube are facial diagonals of the inscribed dodecahedron and are of the same length as the corresponding connectors of the 1 x k rectangles.

The set of five interlocking cubes formed by the diagonals of the inscribed dodecahedron also have edges of k length.

The set of five outer interlocking cubes and their triacontahedron common core, all have a common concentric inscribed sphere. Its diameter has the same length as the height of the cubes. This sphere is also the blister sphere of the compounded inscribed icosahedron and dodecahedron and is tangent to all edges of both solids at their midpoints. The circles inscribed in all faces of both solids are bases of the blisters or segments of the common sphere that protrude from the faces of both polyhedra. The spheres inscribed in the icosahedron and dodecahedron have diameters of 0.9432* and 0.8507** respectively.

My new star lined triaconta-dodecahedron is a dodecahedron with a five pointed solid star mounted on each of its faces. The base of each star is the pentagram formed by the five diagonals of each face of the dodecahedron. The elevation of the solid star is 0.1625*** times the height of the unit cube cases or 0.4472**** times one edge of the triacontahedron.

The ridges of the twelve stars are the edges of the triacontahedron. The peaks of the stars are the vertices of the inscribed icosahedron. The tips of the star rays meet at the vertices of the dodecahedron.

Strange notions keep popping up while the clock is ticking off my ninetieth year.

* $\frac{1}{k\sqrt{3}}$ ** $\frac{1}{\sqrt{k\sqrt{5}}}$ *** $\frac{1}{2}\sqrt{\frac{k3}{\sqrt{5}}}$ **** $\frac{1}{\sqrt{5}}$

New Star Linked Triaconta-Dodecahedron.

This is a dodecahedron with a solid star mounted on each of its faces.

The ridges of these twelve stars become edges of a triacontahedron. The base of each star is the pentagram formed by five facial diagonals of the dodecahedron. Height of star is 0.1625.

Star Patterns.

Crease —. Reverse crease -ω-. Cut -z-. Paste like numbered triangles together.

a = 0.4412
b = 0.2361
c = 0.3633
d = 0.2044
e = 0.1511

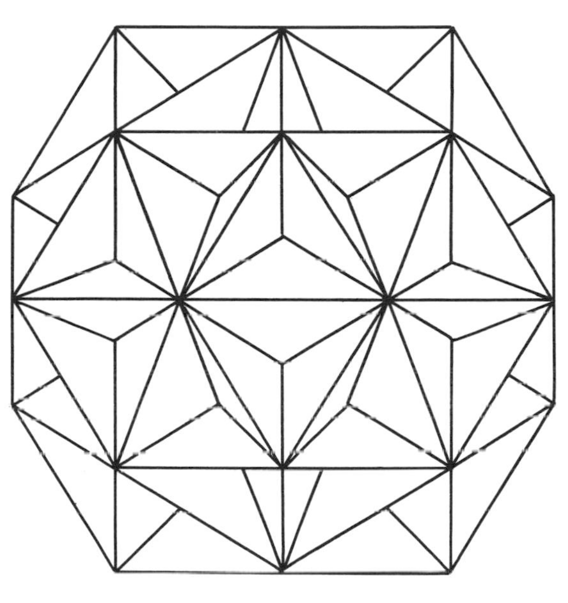

Elevation.

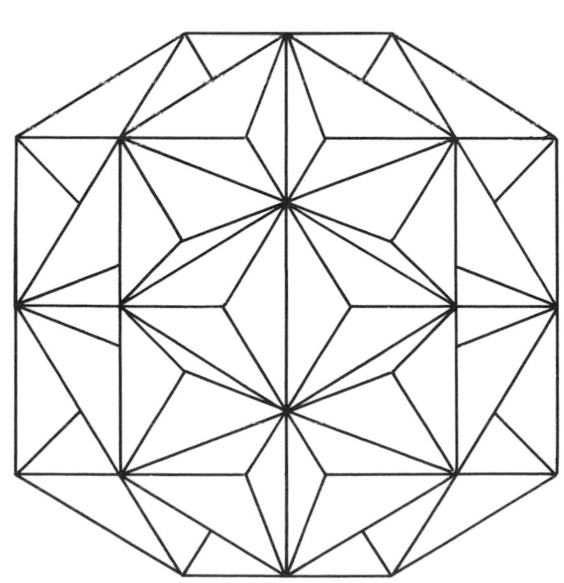

Plan.

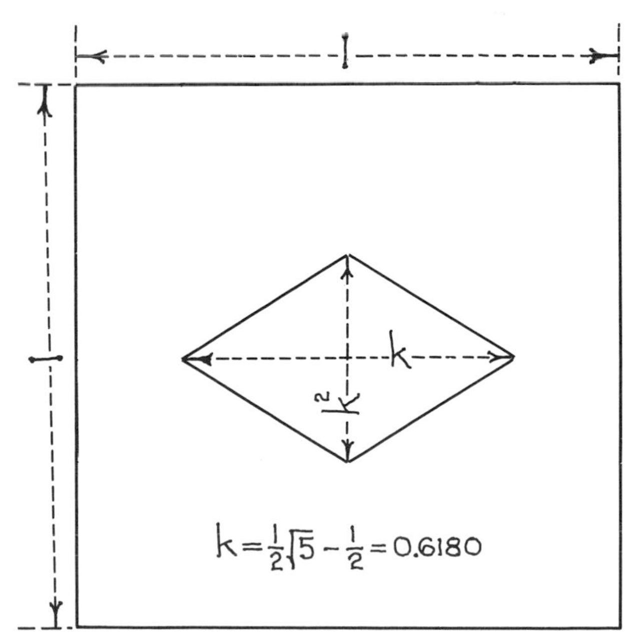

Face of bounding cube.

The Stellar Snub Dodecahedron.

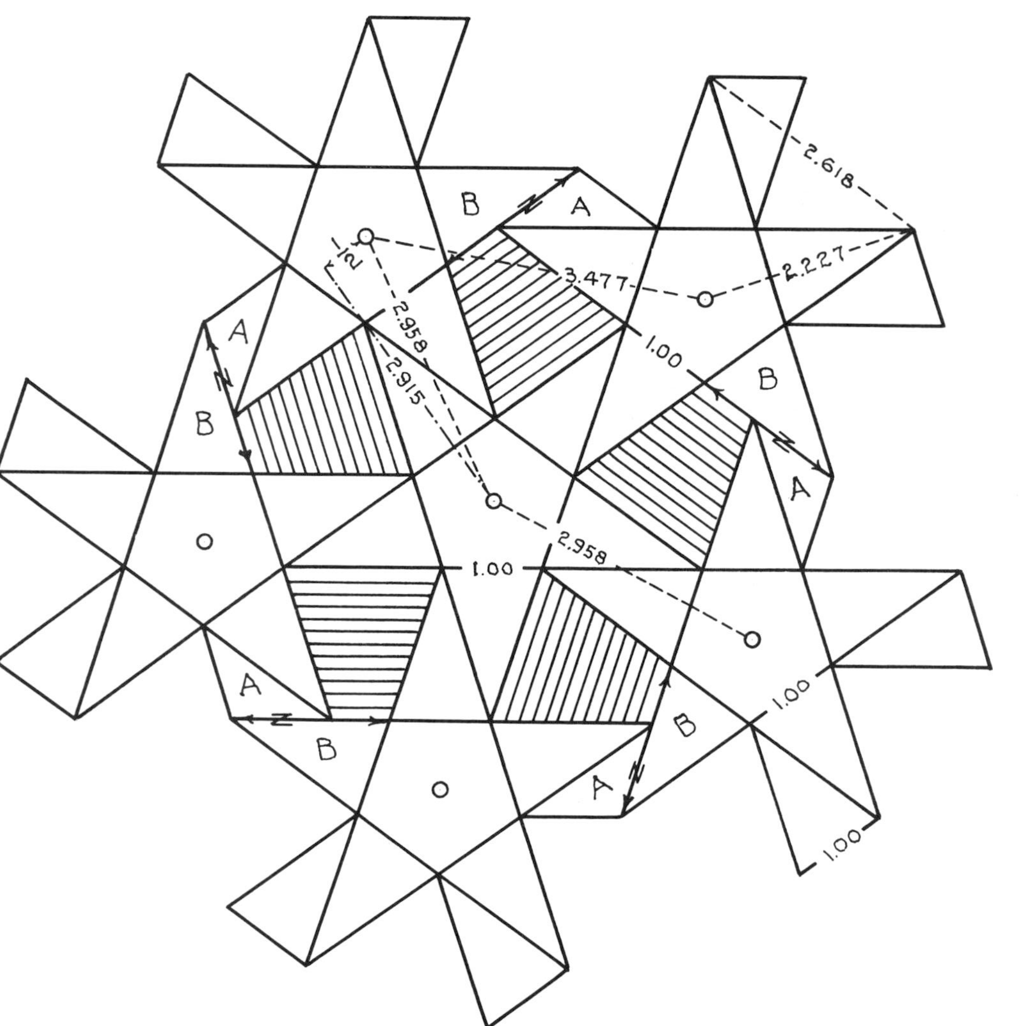

Notes.

Description. Twelve five pointed stars form a stellar snub dodecahedron when they are joined together symmetrically by one edge of each star ray.

The free edges of the star rays bound twenty triangular openings.

The extended pentagonal faces of this model form a dodecahedron with edges of 2.347 and heigt of 5.226.

The snub twist of the faces is 10°26'.

Construction. Make two patterns like the accompanying figure.

Cut the lines marked thus: —z—.

Cut out the crosshatched areas.

Crease sharply all interior lines.

Paste the A triangles to the tips of the B triangles.

Complete the model by pasting together the matching outer parallelograms of the two patterns.

INTERLOCKING POLYHEDRA

FIVE INTERLOCKING TETRAHEDRA LEFT

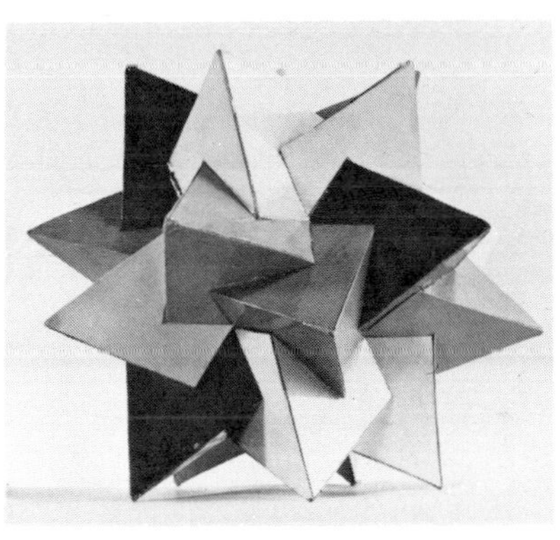

FIVE INTERLOCKING TETRAHEDRA RIGHT

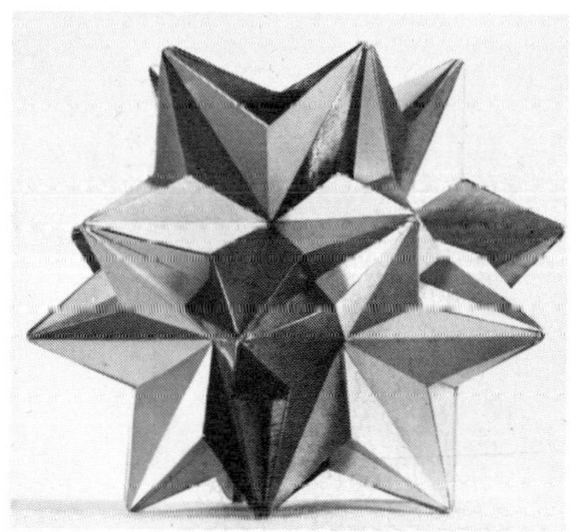

TEN INTERLOCKING TETRAHEDRA

FIVE INTERLOCKING CUBES

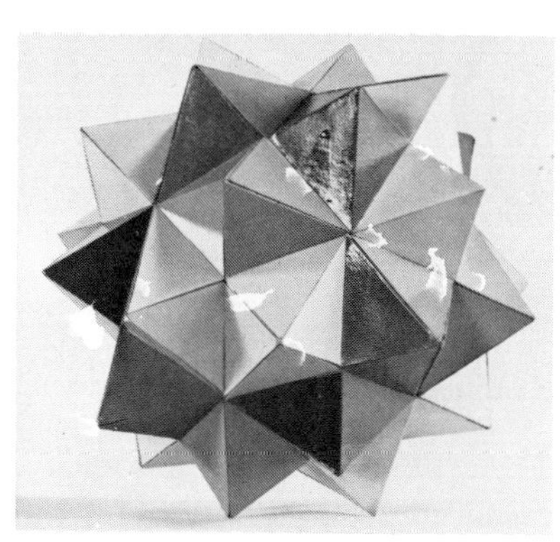

FIVE INTERLOCKING OCTAHEDRA

Interlocking Tetrahedra Patterns.

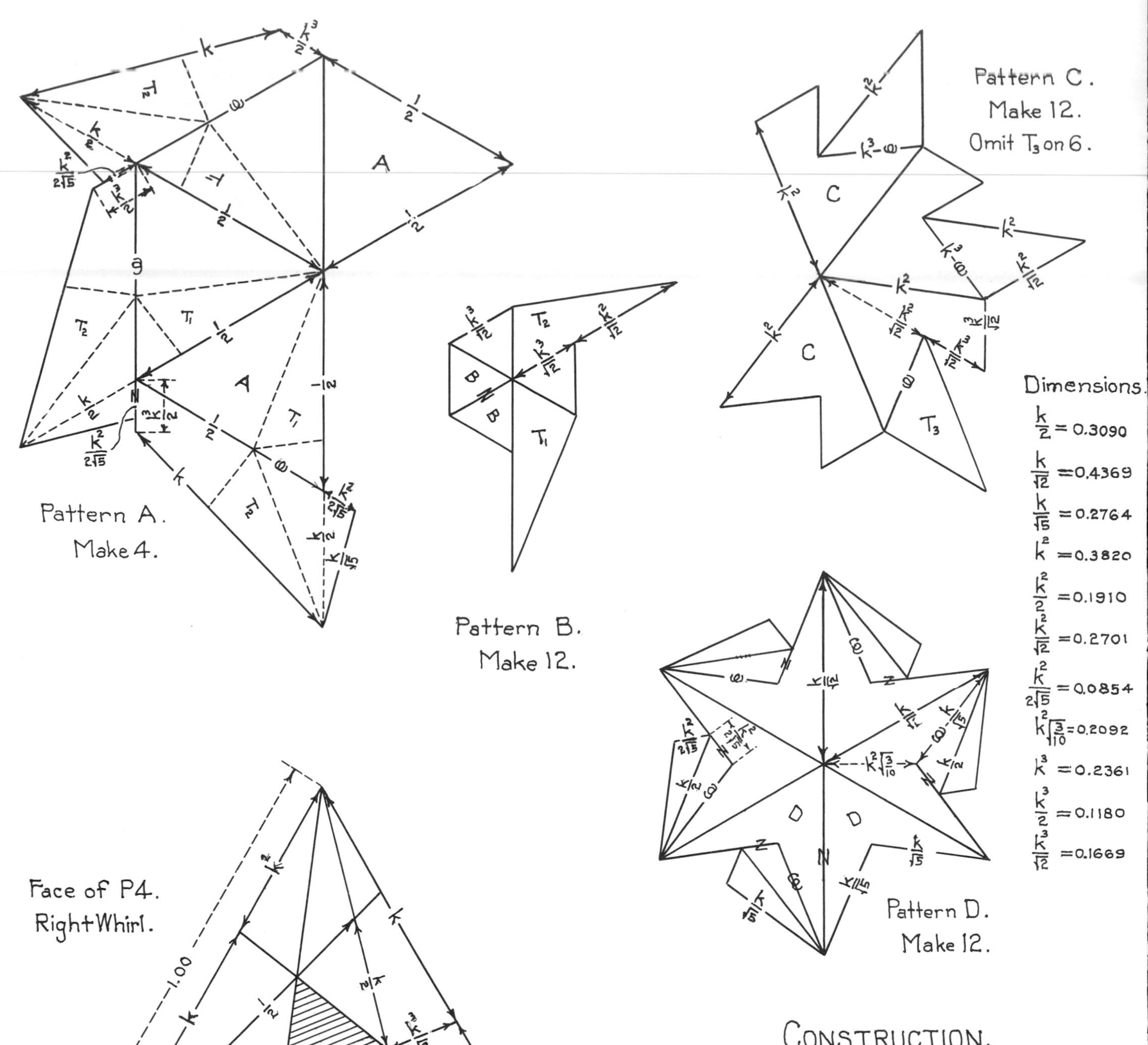

Notes. All patterns are dimensioned in their ratio to edge of unit tetrahedron or* P4. The golden section, $k = \frac{1}{2}\sqrt{5} - \frac{1}{2} = 0.6180$.

Interior Line Code. —— Crease. —ɷ— Reverse crease. —≠— Cut.

The height of each model is $\frac{k}{\sqrt{2\sqrt{5}\,k^5}} = 0.9731$.

Paste like lettered segments together. *Plato's four-sider.

CONSTRUCTION.

First make a tetrahedron or P4 of the desired size when constructing any of these models. The P4 formed by the 8.48" facial diagonals of a 6" cube is a good size.

5P4 Right Whirl Model. Mount full sets of patterns A, B and C successively on the base P4.

5P4 Left Whirl Model. Same construction as right whirl with creasing of every pattern reversed.

10P4 Model. Construct a complete right whirl 5P4 and mount a pattern D in each of its pockets.

Crosshatched triangle is a face of the core icosahedron.

Patterns for Five Interlocking Cubes.

The diagonals forming a star in each face of a dodecahedron are the edges of five interlocking cubes. Figure 1 shows one of the cube faces and its intersection lines with other faces. Exposed segments are shaded. Central diamond is face of core triacontahedron. All dimensions are ratios to edge of cube and are expressed in terms of the golden section, k. $k = \frac{1}{2}\sqrt{5} - \frac{1}{2} = 0.618$. Height of figure is $\frac{1}{\sqrt{k^3\sqrt{5}}} = 1.376$.

<u>Construction.</u> First construct a cube of size desired. Say 10 cm. to <u>15 cm</u>, or 4" to <u>6"</u>. Draw six each of patterns A, B, C and D and twelve patterns E. Reverse three each of patterns A and D. Crease all solid interior lines. Reverse creases of dot and dash lines. Cut all dotted pattern lines. Paste together all like lettered triangles in each pattern. Paste an assembled pattern A on each face of first cube to form second cube. Triangle 1-2-4 is a section of second cube. Paste patterns B, C and D in valleys 1-2, 1-4 and 2-4 respectively as indicated by numbered vertices. The end triangles of pattern D are pasted to opposite planes. Paste pattern E into fitting recesses to complete model.

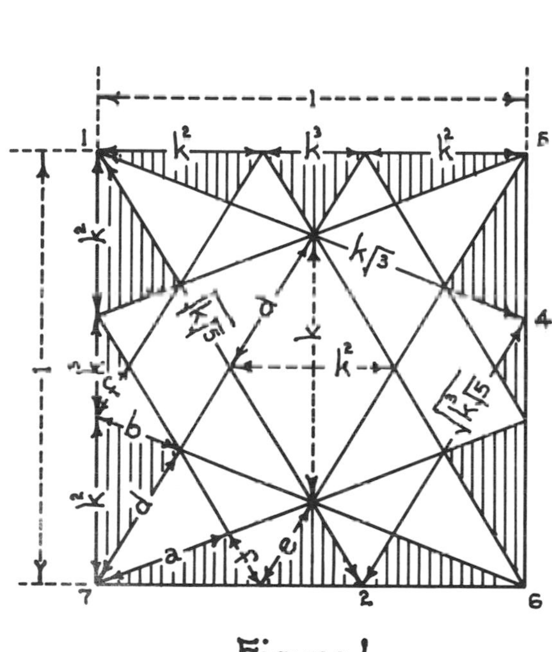

Figure 1.

<u>Dimensions.</u>

$k = 0.618$

$k^2 = 0.382$

$k^3 = 0.236$

$k\sqrt{3} = 1.070$

$a = \frac{1}{2}k^2\sqrt{3} = 0.331$

$b = \frac{1}{2}k^3\sqrt{3} = 0.204$

$c = \frac{1}{2}k^3\sqrt{5} = 0.264$

$\sqrt{k\sqrt{5}} = 1.176$

$\sqrt{k^3\sqrt{5}} = 0.727$

$d = \frac{1}{2}\sqrt{k^3\sqrt{5}} = 0.363$

$e = \frac{1}{2}\sqrt{k^5\sqrt{5}} = 0.225$

$f = \frac{1}{2}\sqrt{k^7\sqrt{5}} = 0.139$

$\frac{2k}{\sqrt{3}} = 0.714$

$\frac{8k}{3\sqrt{3}} = 0.952$

$\frac{4}{3}\sqrt{\frac{k}{\sqrt{5}}} = 0.701$

$\frac{4}{3}\sqrt{\frac{k^5}{\sqrt{5}}} = 0.268$

PATTERNS ON NEXT PAGE.

Patterns for Five Interlocking Cubes.

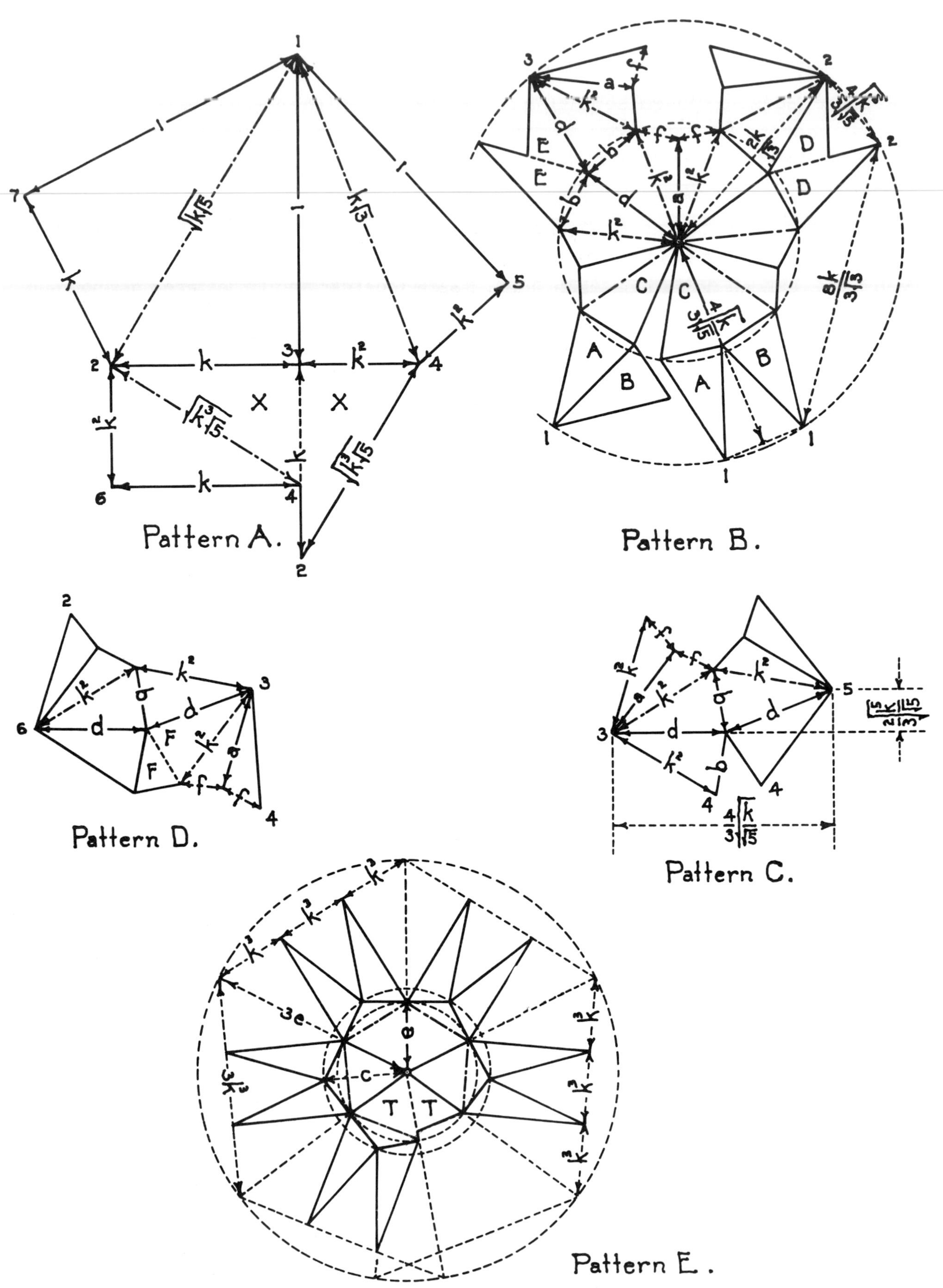

Pattern A.

Pattern B.

Pattern D.

Pattern C.

Pattern E.

Patterns for Five Interlocking Octahedra.

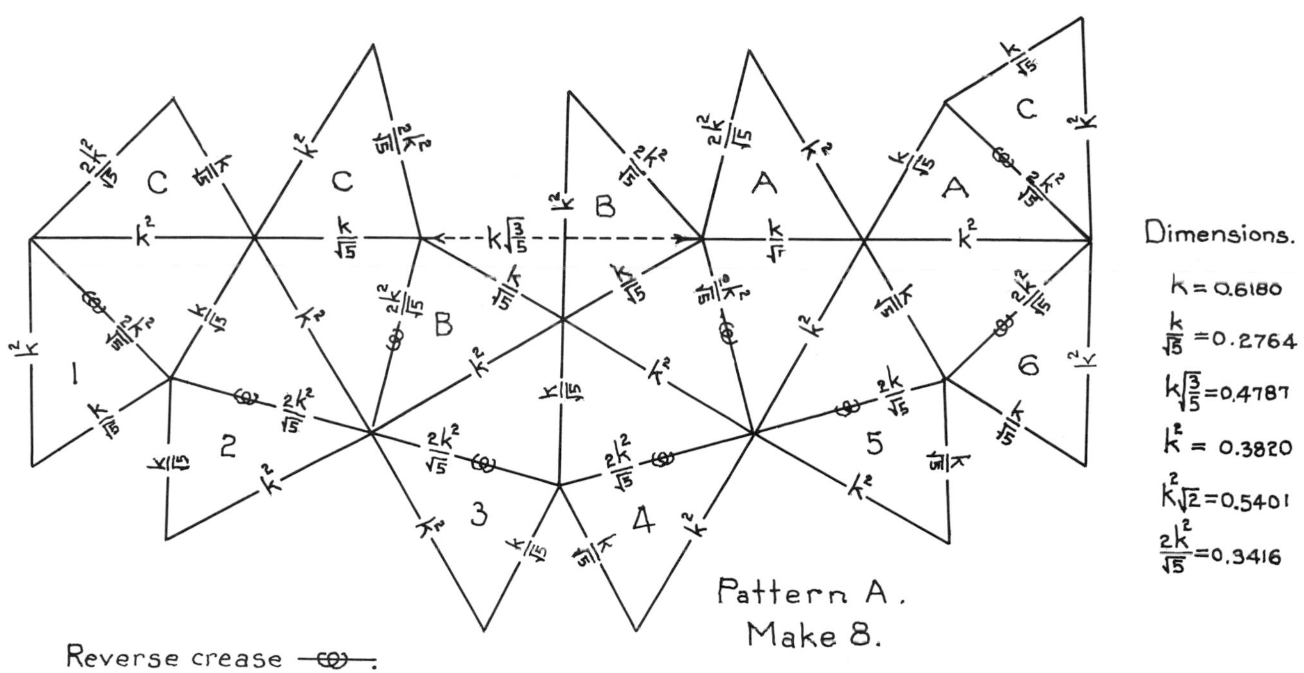

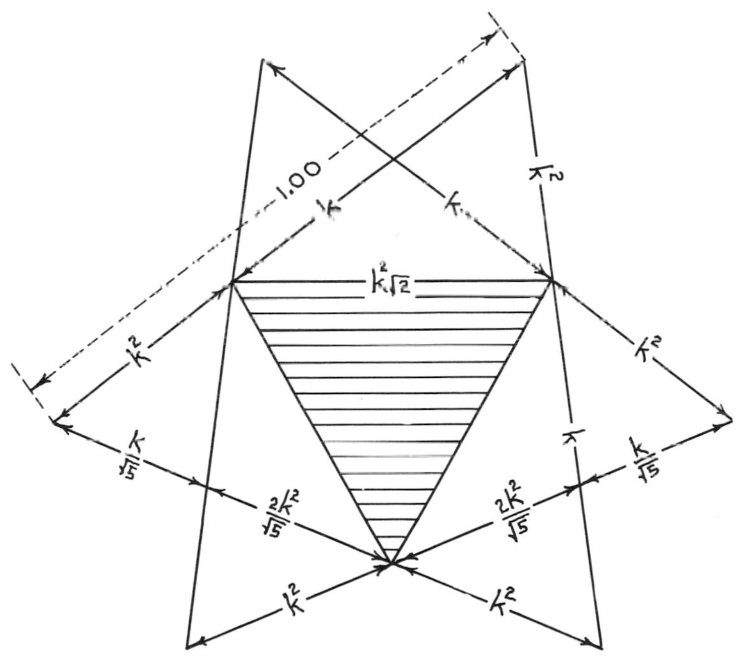

Two P8 Faces in Unit Plane.
Crosshatched triangle is face of core icosahedron.
The golden section, $k = \frac{1}{2}\sqrt{5} - \frac{1}{2} = 0.6180$.
Height of 5P8 model is $\sqrt{\frac{2}{k\sqrt{5}}} = 1.2030$.

CONSTRUCTION.

First make an octahedron or P8 of the size desired. Then construct eight patterns A. They are dimensioned in proportion to the edge of the P8 as indicated. Assemble each pattern A by pasting the like lettered triangles together. Complete the model by mounting an assembled pattern A on each face of the base P8 with either the triangles 1, 3 and 5 or the triangles 2, 4 and 6 at corners of the face of the P8. Paste the three free triangles of each pattern A to matching triangles in the same plane or to adjoining P8 faces.

Patterns for Segments of Cubes.

Cube. Edges=1. Segmental numbers, ⓝ, = Fractions of cube's volume.

Corner segment, $\left(\frac{1}{6}\right)$, contains three half faces of cube. Two $\left(\frac{1}{6}\right)$'s cut from opposing corners of cube divide the diagonal into thirds. The remaining triangular antiprism is segment $\left(\frac{2}{3}\right)$.

Four $\left(\frac{1}{6}\right)$'s cut away the entire surface of the cube. The remaining tetrahedron has $\sqrt{2}$ edges. Two such tetrahedra can be formed in a cube. These interlocking tetrahedra form a stella octangula that has half of the volume of the cube.

Twelve edge segments $\left(\frac{1}{24}\right)$, fill the spaces between the cube and the stella octangula.

Four $\left(\frac{1}{24}\right)$'s form the octahedron that connects the centers of the faces of the cube.

Three segments $\left(\frac{1}{3}\right)$ form the cube.

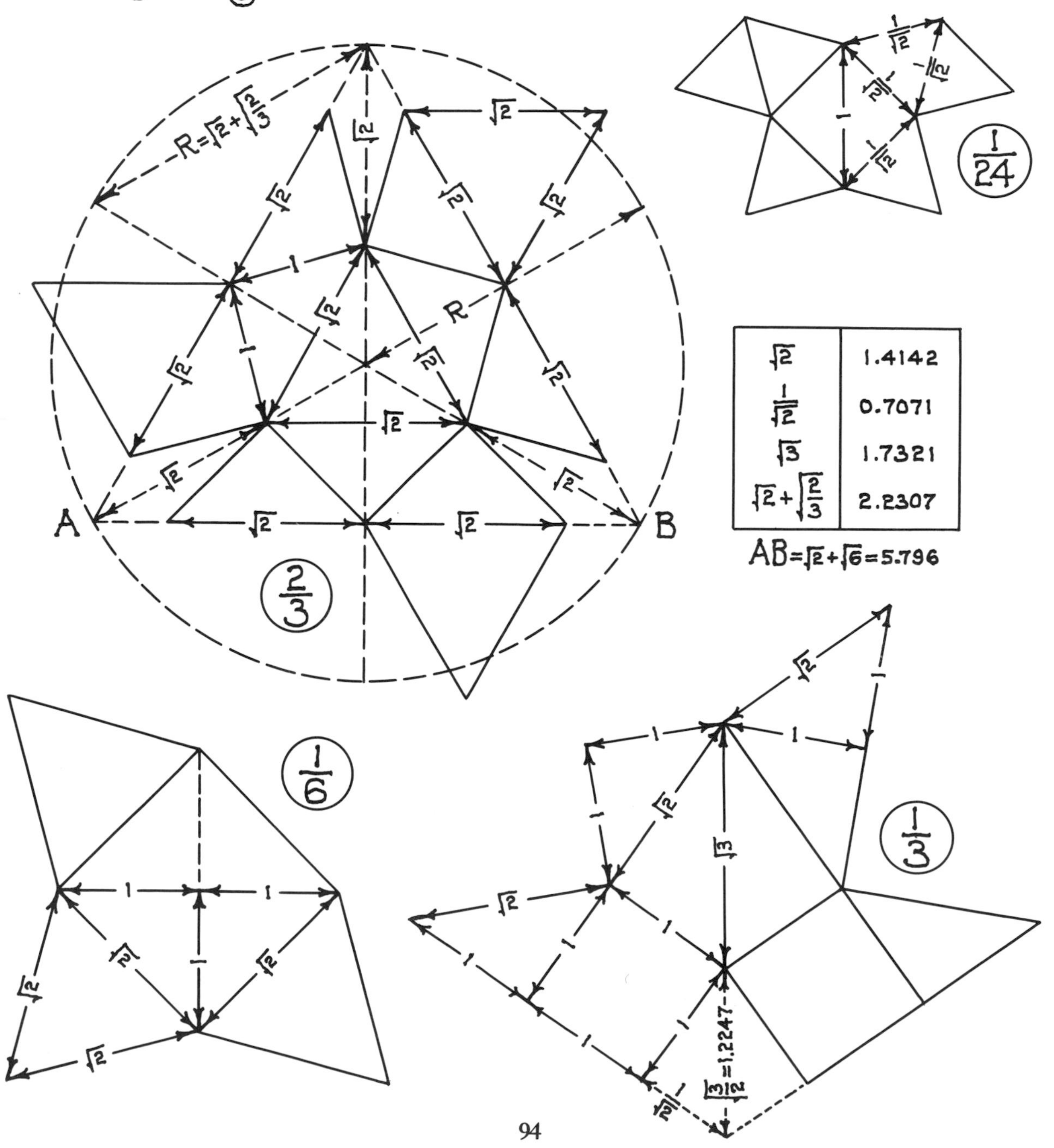

$\sqrt{2}$	1.4142
$\frac{1}{\sqrt{2}}$	0.7071
$\sqrt{3}$	1.7321
$\sqrt{2}+\sqrt{\frac{2}{3}}$	2.2307

A Quarter Tetrahedron.

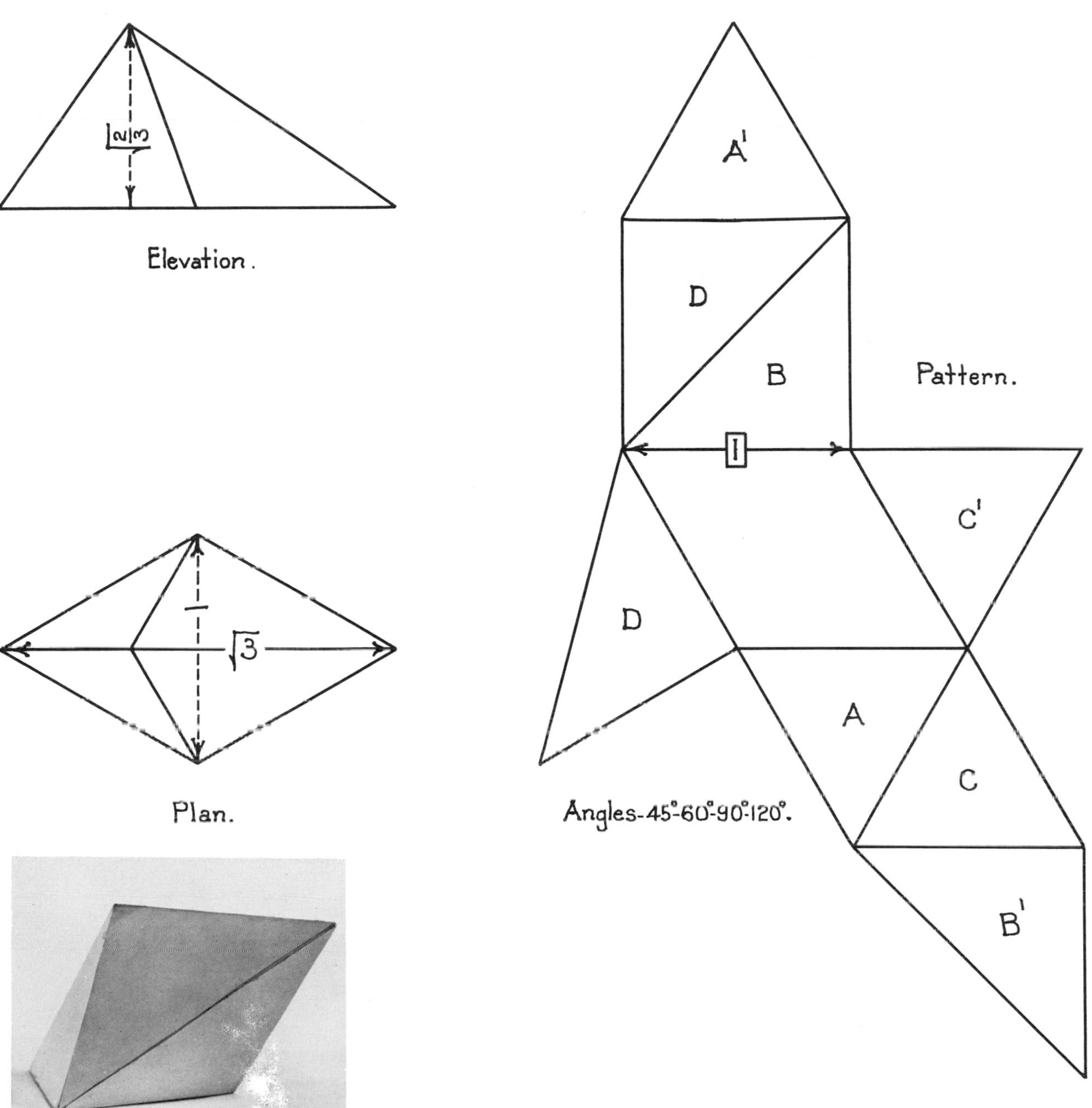

Notes.

Pattern. Paste like lettered triangles together in alphabetical order, prime letters outside.
Construction. This figure is a half size tetrahedron plus one quarter of an octahedron.
Puzzling Use. Make four quarter tetrahedra and nest them to form one large tetrahedron ----
----If you can?

Patterns for the Honeycomb Dodecahedron.

The honeycomb dodecahedron, HP12, has sixty triangular faces that form twelve inverted pentagonal pyramids. Three HP12 faces lie in each extended face of the core icosahedron, P20. See Figure 1. <u>All dimensions are ratios to the HP12 unit edges.</u>

<u>Construction.</u> Patterns A and B form the HP12. Pattern B is pattern A less the shaded triangles. Pattern C is a stiffening diaphragm. Cut all patterns on dotted lines. Crease all other interior lines. Reverse creases of dot and dash lines. Shape patterns A and B into inverted pyramids by pasting like lettered triangles together. Paste pattern C to inside of pattern B with star points at HP12 vertices and outer edges matching. Paste shaded triangles of pattern A to matching triangles of pattern B.

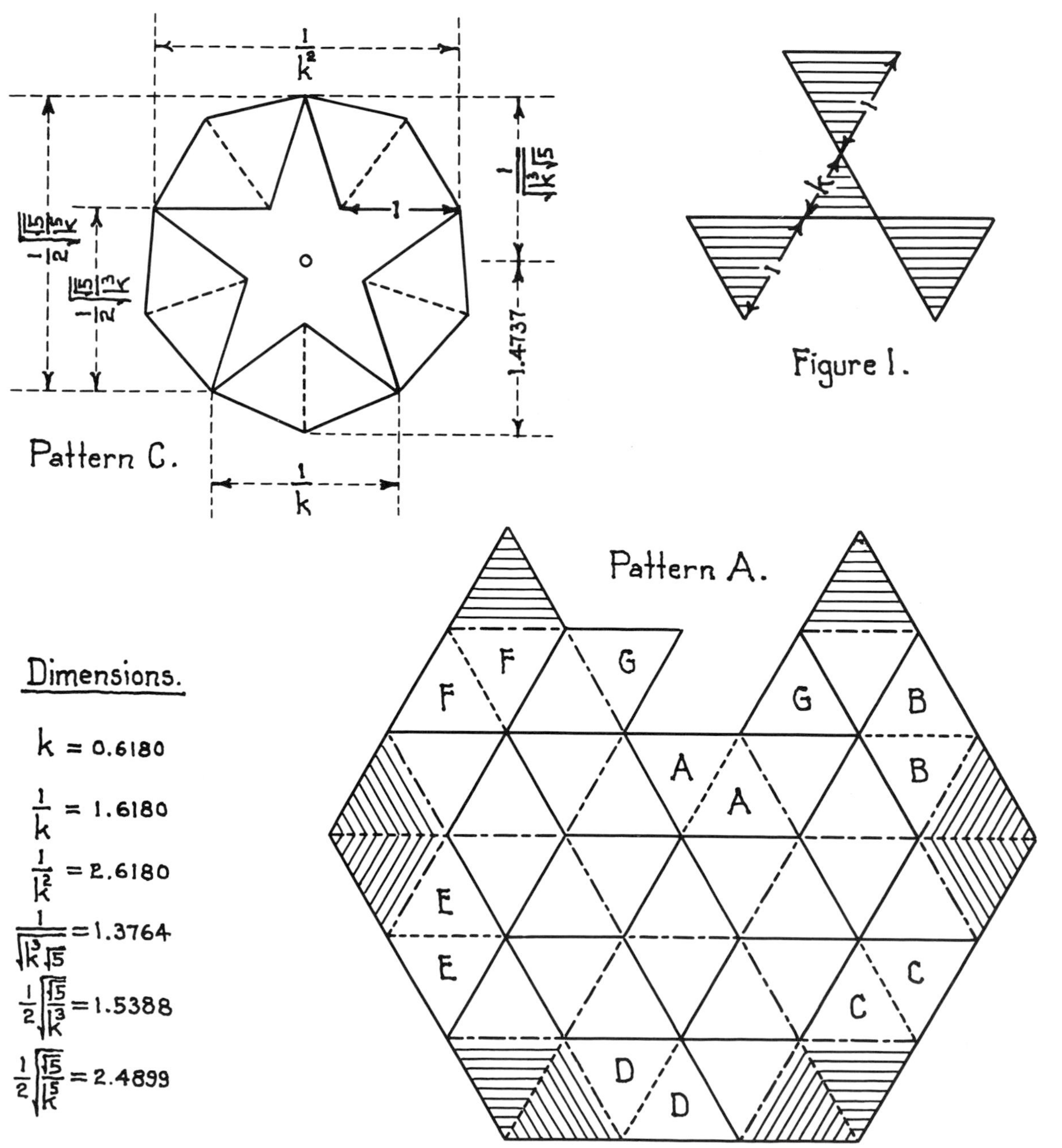

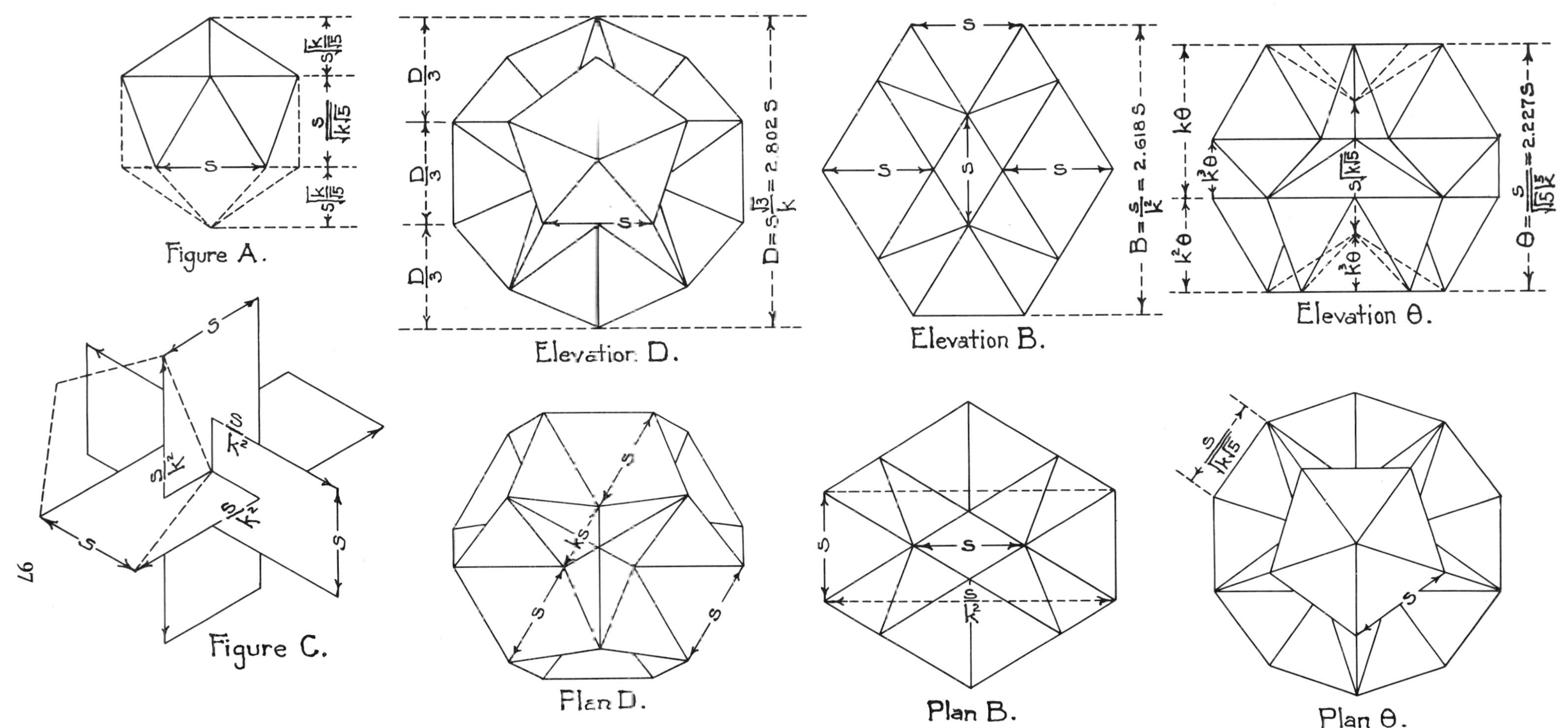

THE HONEYCOMB DODECAHEDRON.

All faces are regular triangles with sides of s length. $k = \frac{1}{2}\sqrt{5} - \frac{1}{2} = 0.618034$, the go'den mean ratio. Diameters of cover, blister and lining spheres are D, B and θ respectively. Total Surface $= 15 s^2\sqrt{3} = 25.9808 s^2$. Volume $= 2s^3\frac{\sqrt{5}}{k^2} = 11.7082 s^3$.

Angles. Ridge-41°48′37″. Valley-138°11′25″. Major axis and ridge-69°05′42″ = ½ valley angle. Major axis and valley line-20°54′19″ = ½ ridge angle. Last two angles are complimentary.

Solid lines in figure A mark pentagonal pyramid with edges of s on corner of icosahedron.

A honeycomb dodecahedron is formed by cutting such a pyramid out of each face of a regular dodecahedron having edges of s length. Projections D, B and θ show this solid balanced on one corner, on one edge and resting on one face respectively. Its successive vertical axes in these positions are diameters of its cover, bliste- and lining spheres.

The perimeter of plan θ is a decagon with sides of $\frac{s}{\sqrt{k\sqrt{5}}}$. The 'ateral corners of elevation θ divide the heigt θ into segments of $k\theta$, $k^2\theta$ and $k^3\theta$. The pyramidal dents are $k^3\theta$ deep. In elevation θ the $s\sqrt{k\sqrt{5}}$ segment of the vertical axis is a diameter of the cover sphere of the icosahedron with ks edges that connects the dent points of the dodecahedron. The s segment of the vertical axis in elevation B is a diameter of the blister sphere of the core icosahedron. In elevation D the middle third of the vertical axis is a diameter of the lining sphere of the core icosahedron. All faces of the honeycomb dodecahedron are extensions of the faces of its core icosahedron.

Plan B shows one of the $s \times \frac{s}{k^2}$ rectangles formed by each pair of opposing parallel edges and the valley lines connecting their ends. One side and the opposite corner of each pentagonal face of a dodecahedron are also sides and corners of three perpendicular $s \times \frac{s}{k^2}$ rectangles arranged as shown isometrically in figure C.

FIRST STELLATION OF ICOSAHEDRON, (P20).

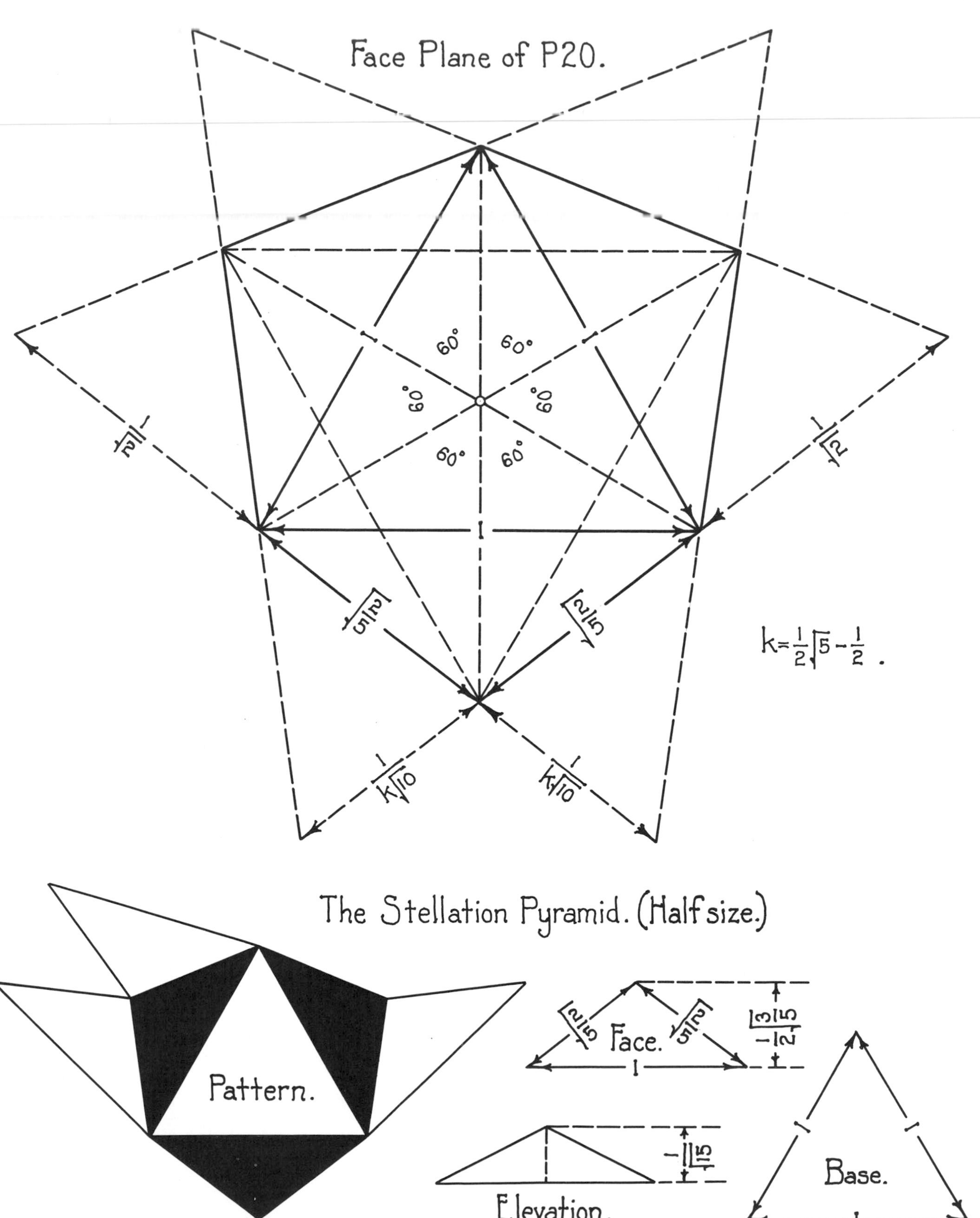

Three Pointed Solid Star.

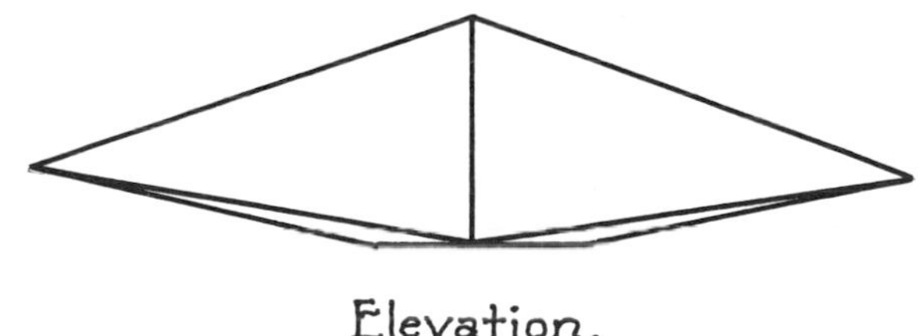

Elevation.

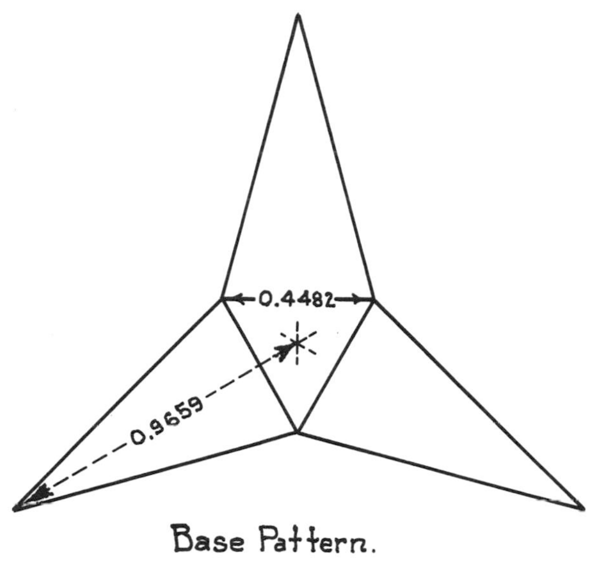

Base Pattern.

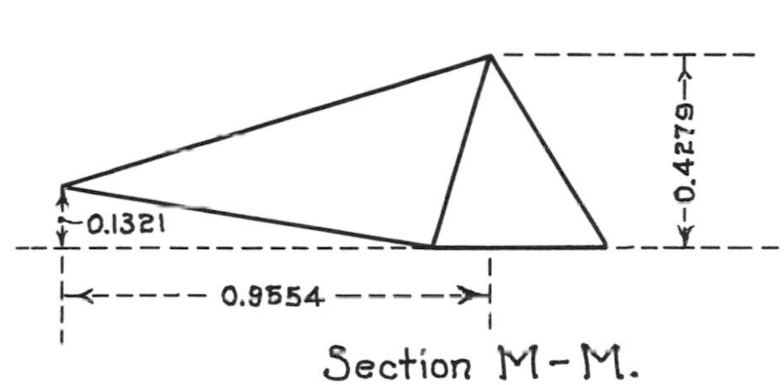

Section M-M.

Top Pattern.

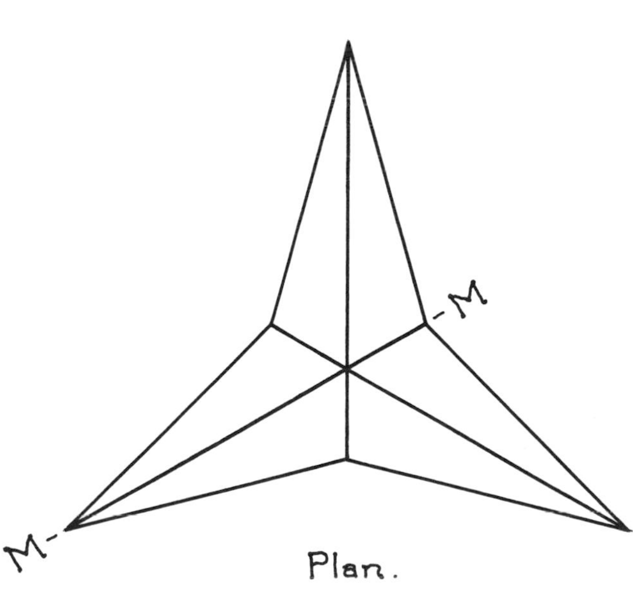

Plan.

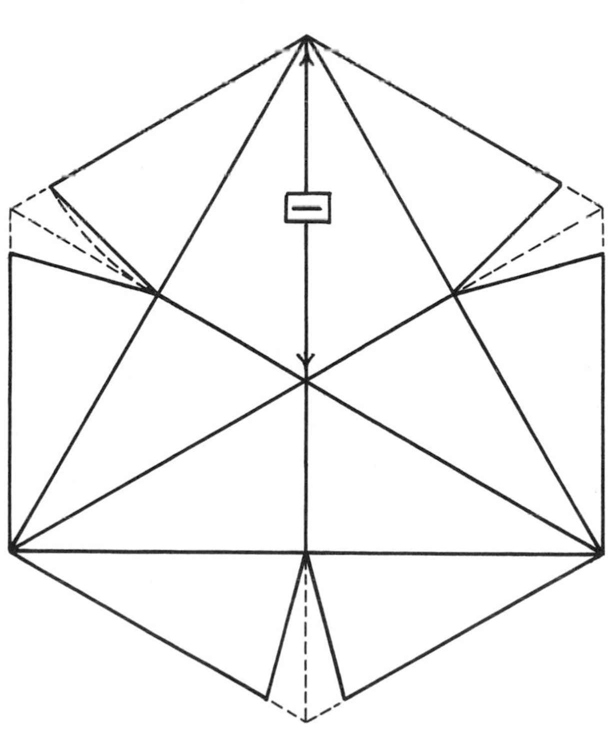

Four Pointed Solid Star.

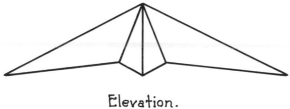

Elevation.

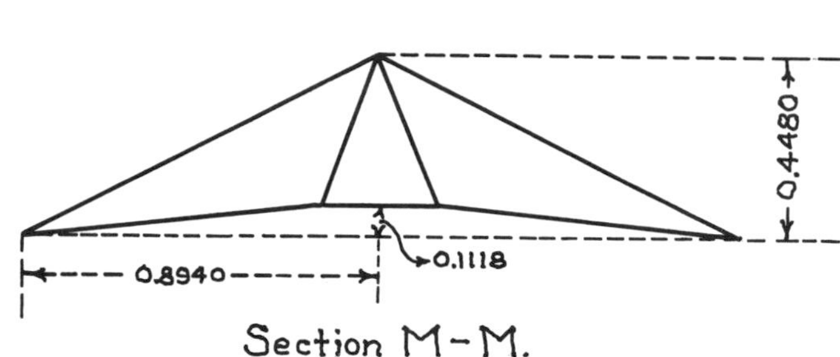

Section M-M.

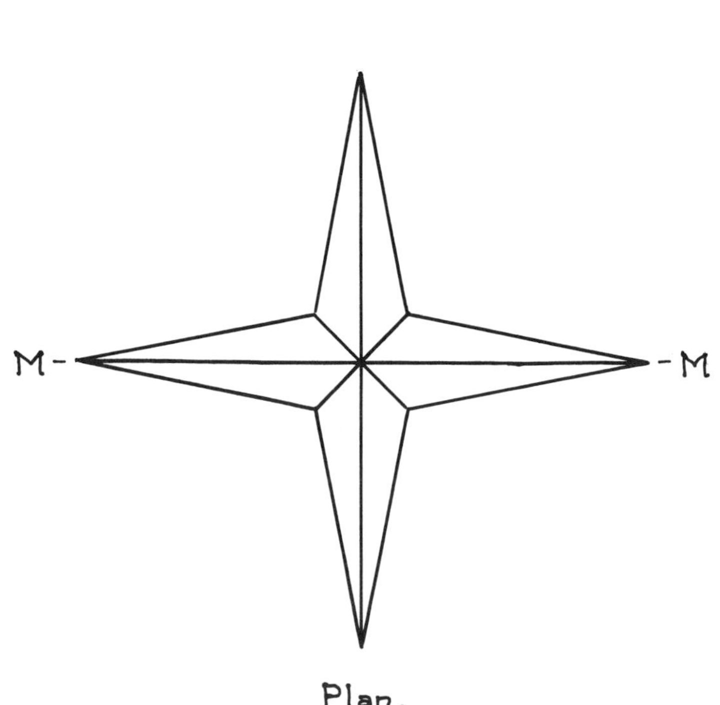

Plan.

Base Pattern.

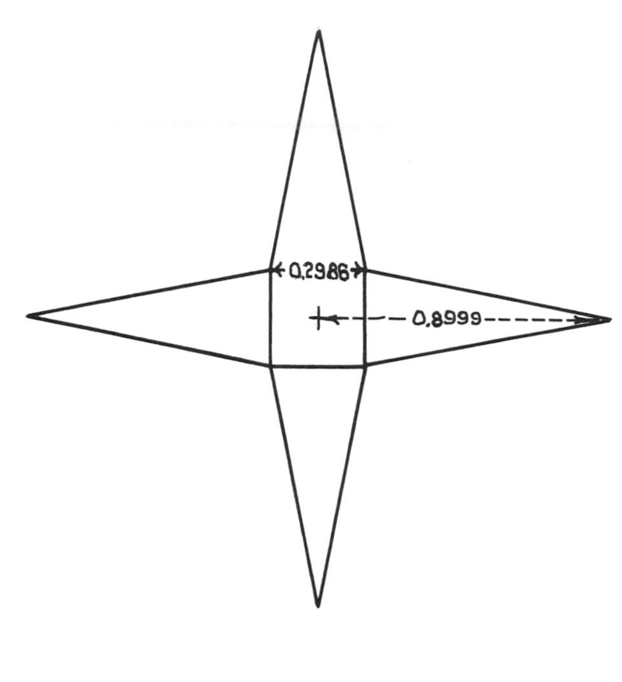

Top Pattern

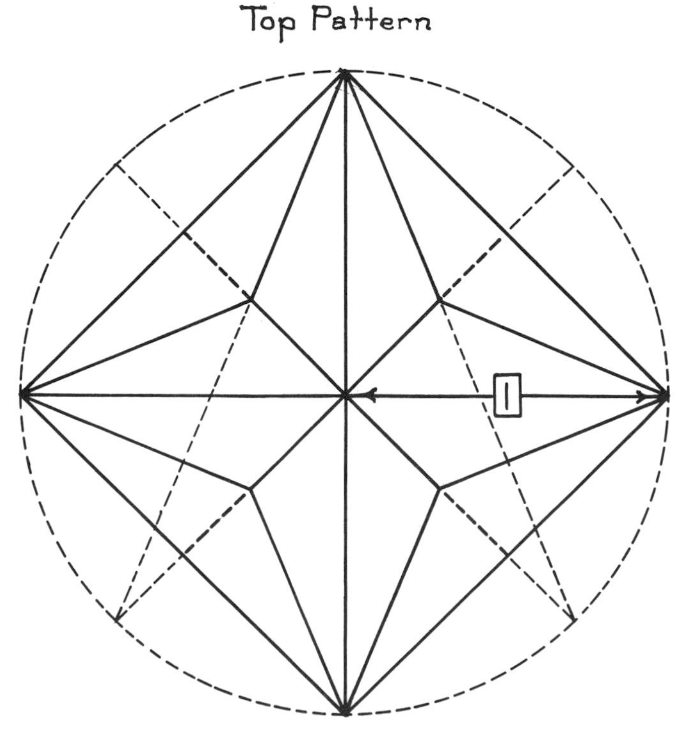

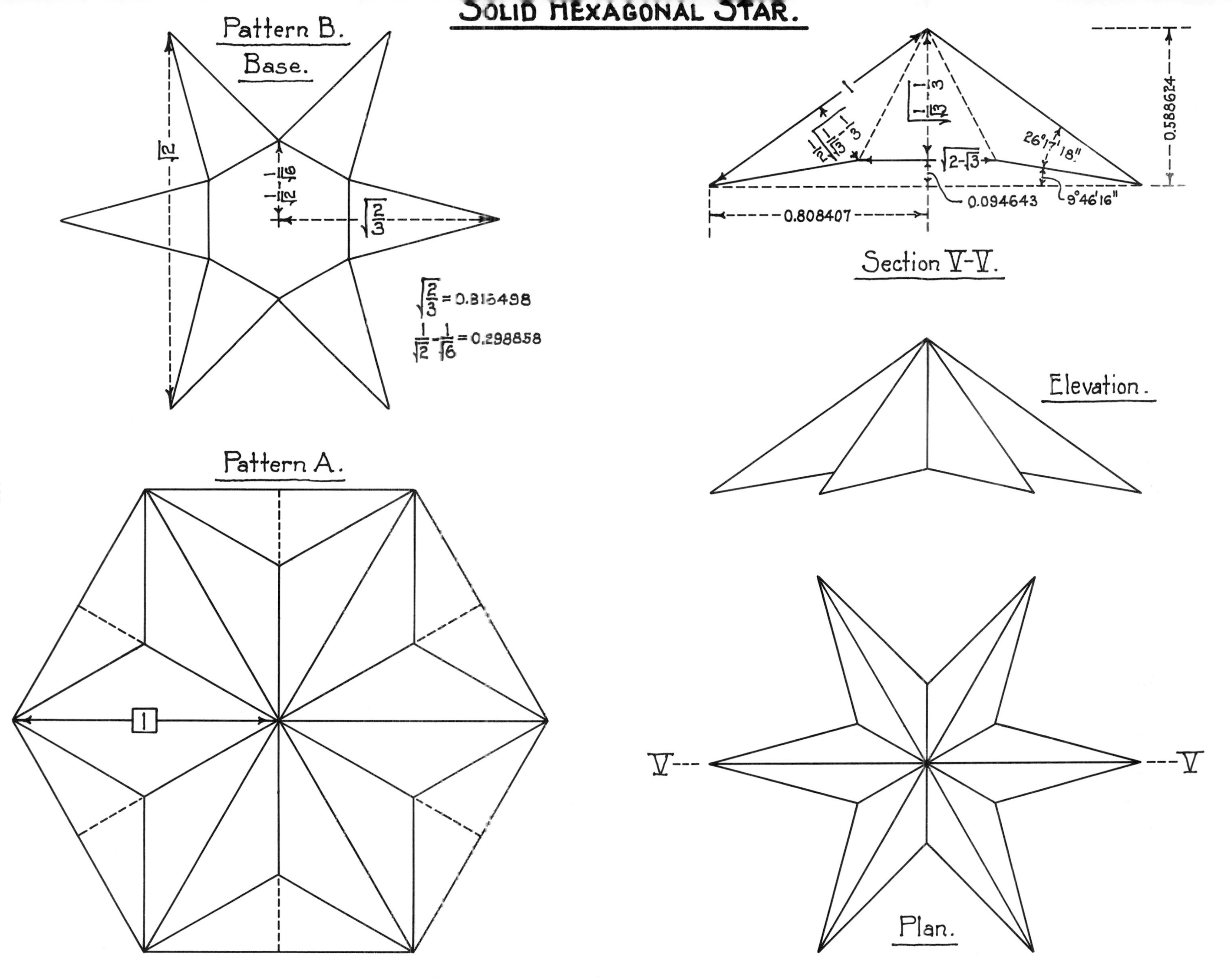

SOLID HEXAGONAL STAR.
Pattern B.
Base.
$\sqrt{2}$
$\frac{1}{\sqrt{2}}-\frac{1}{\sqrt{6}}$
$\sqrt{\frac{2}{3}}$
$\sqrt{\frac{2}{3}}=0.816498$
$\frac{1}{\sqrt{2}}-\frac{1}{\sqrt{6}}=0.298858$
Pattern A.
1
1
$\frac{1}{\sqrt{3}}$
$\frac{1}{\sqrt{2}}\sqrt{\frac{1}{\sqrt{3}}-\frac{1}{3}}$
$\sqrt{2-\sqrt{3}}$
26°17′18″
9°46′16″
0.588624
0.094643
0.808407
Section V-V.
Elevation.
V
V
Plan.

Seven Pointed Solid Star.

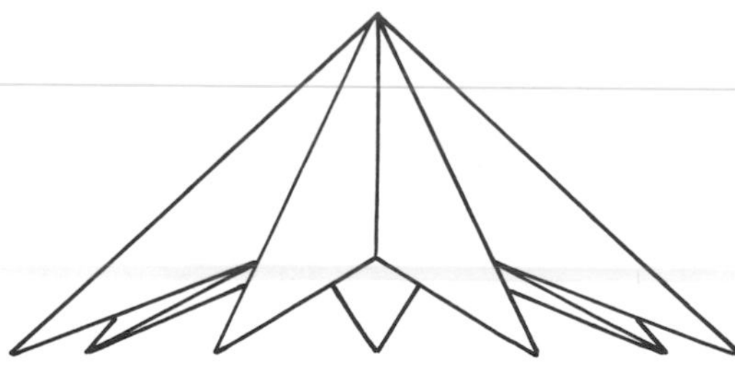

Elevation.

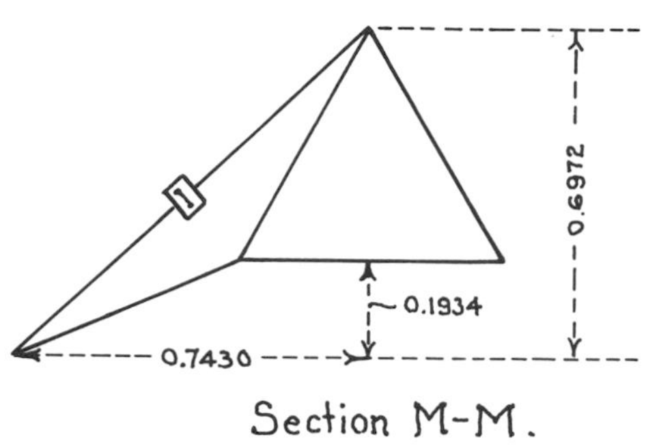

Section M-M.

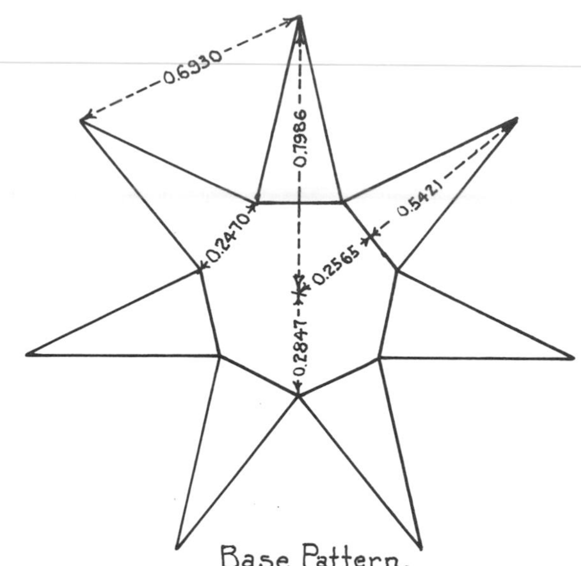

Base Pattern.

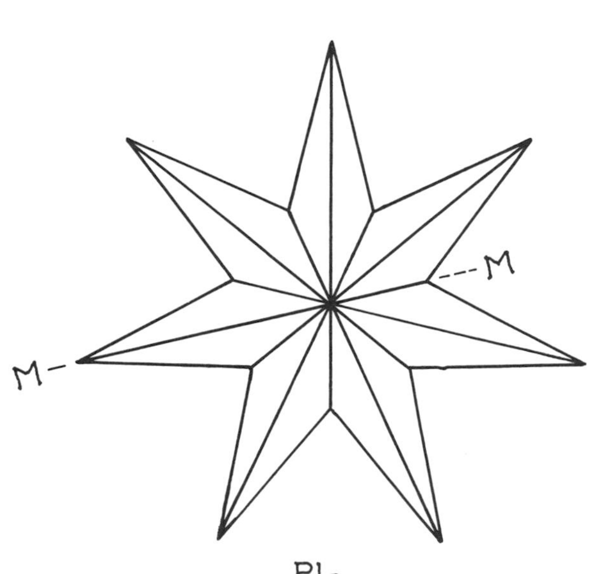

Plan.

Top Pattern.

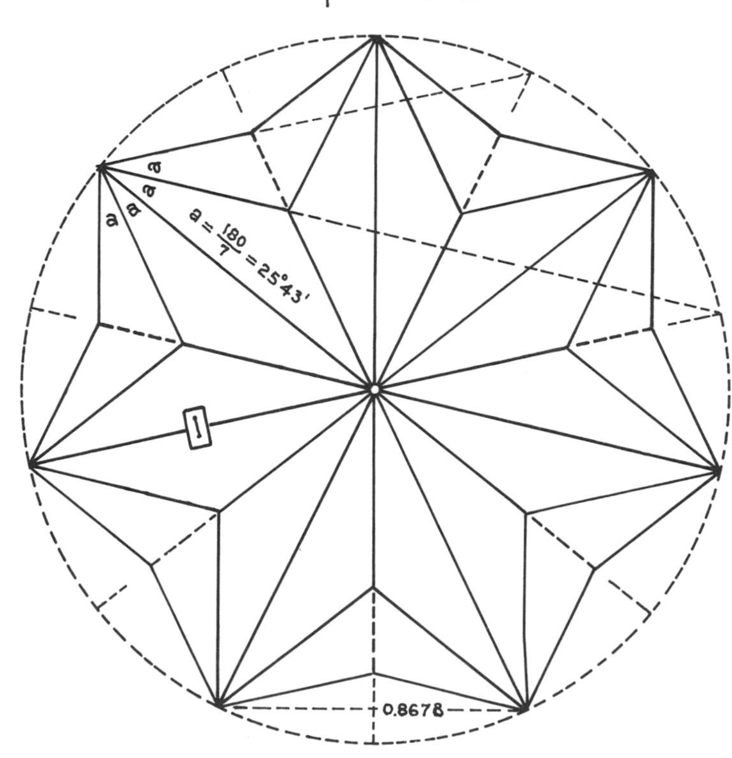

Two Hexagonal Star Pyramids.

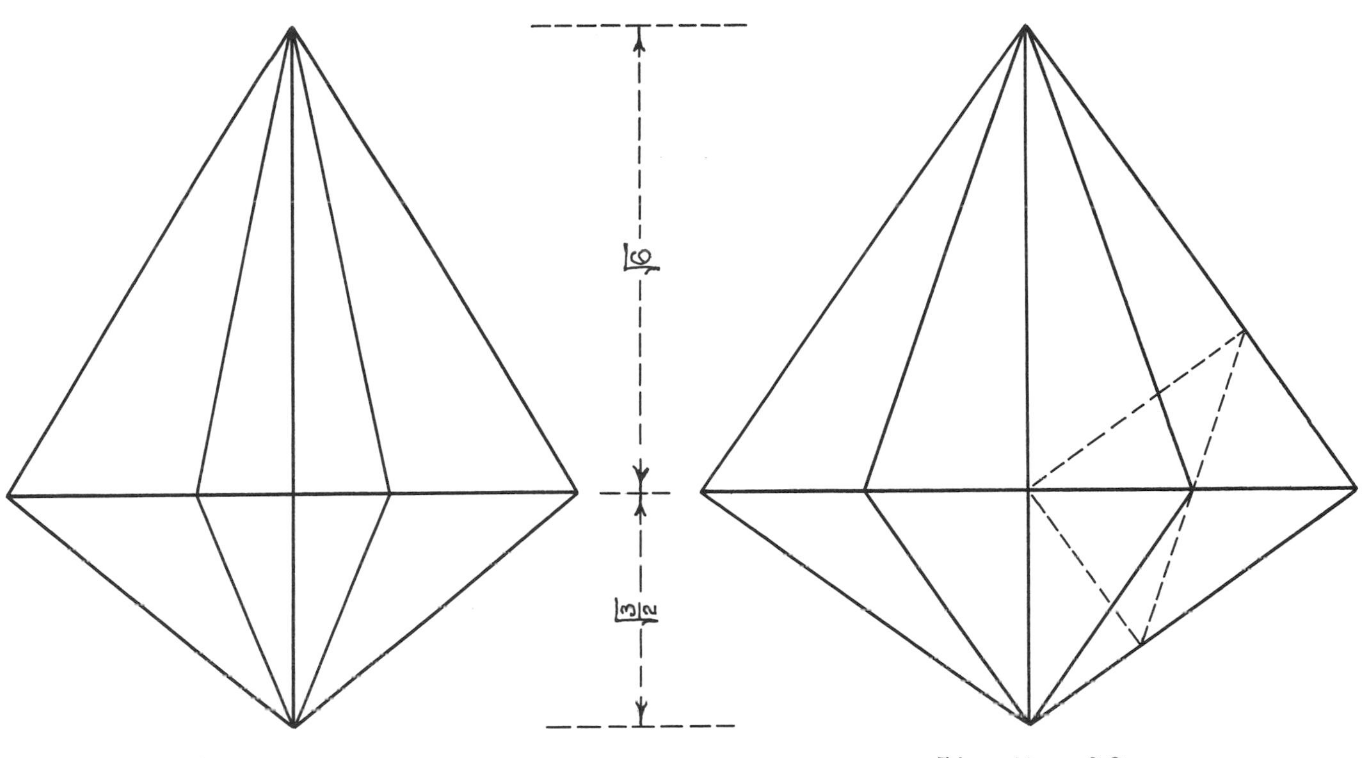

Elevation AB.

Elevation AC.

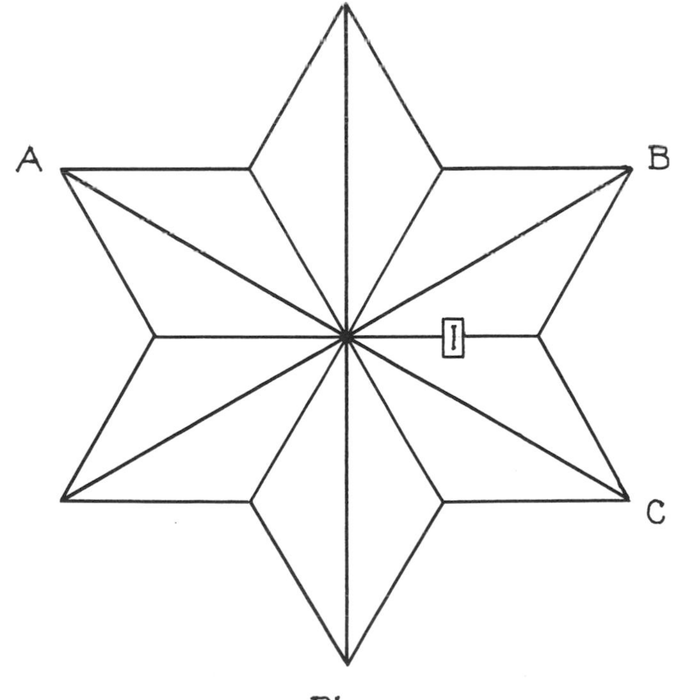

Plan.

Notes.

The quarter tetrahedron is faced with one diamond and two each equilateral and right triangles.

Six quarter tetrahedra can be nested so that their diamond faces form a hexagonal star and that each equilateral triangle face touches a tip of that star.

The extended planes of these outer triangle faces form a hexagonal star pyramid faced with six intersecting equilateral triangles. Using a side of these triangles as the unit of length, the altitude of the pyramid is $\sqrt{6}$.

When the quarter tetrahedra are revolved 180°, so that their right triangle faces touch the tips of the hexagonal star, the extended right triangles form a second hexagonal star pyramid that is faced with six intersecting right triangles. Its altitude is $\sqrt{\frac{3}{2}}$, half that of the first pyramid.

The volume of these two pyramids are 36 and 18 respectively in terms of the volume of a tetrahedron with unit edges.

Patterns for Two Hexagonal Star Pyramids.

Pyramid $\sqrt{6}$ High.

$\sqrt{7} = 2.646$

3.00

$\sqrt{7} = 2.646$

$\sqrt{3} = 1.732$

1.00

1.00

1.00

1.00

1.00

1.00

60°

60°

T

T

Pyramid $\sqrt{\frac{3}{2}}$ High.

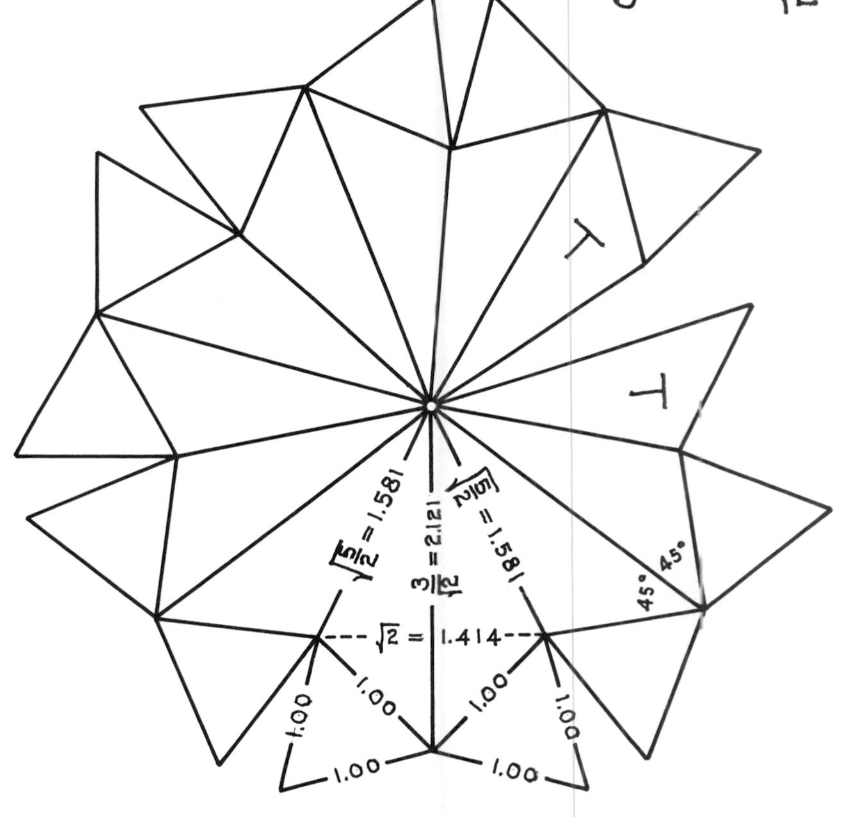

Notes.

Crease all interior lines. Give the six shorter radial lines reverse creasing.

Paste triangles T together and also the two unit triangles at each tip of the star.

Each pyramid must be mounted on a hexagonal star that can be inscribed in a circle of $\sqrt{3}$ radius.

ROTATING SECTIONS OF THE RHOMBIC DODECAHEDRON

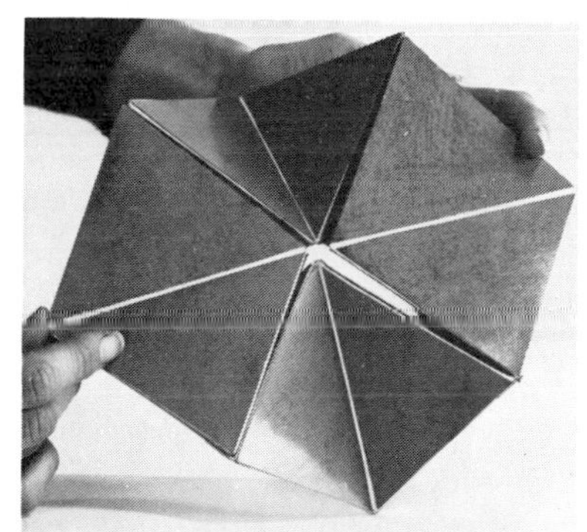

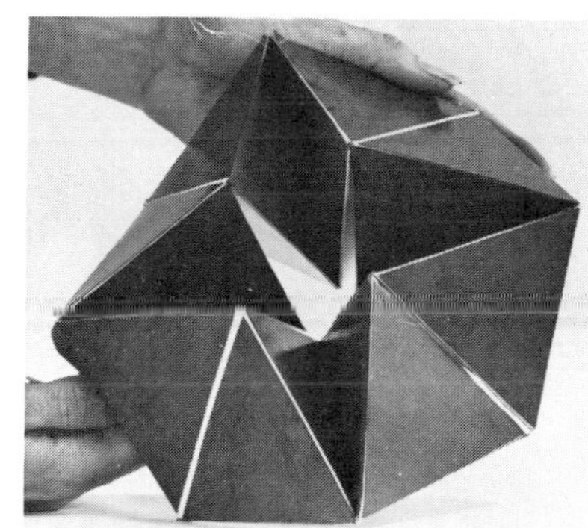

The long and short diagonals of the diamond faces of the rhombic dodecahedron are in $\sqrt{2}$ to 1 ratio. The central diagonals connecting the vertices of each pair of parallel faces are in $\sqrt{3}$ to 2 ratio. These diagonals divide the figure into twelve equal pyramids. Cut each pyramid in half on the plane passing through its vertex and the unit length diagonal of its base diamond. The half size pyramid will have two perpendicular unit length edges and four $\frac{1}{2}\sqrt{3}$ edges. A tightly rotating model can be formed by hinging together eight of these smaller pyramids along their unit length edges.

Pattern A.

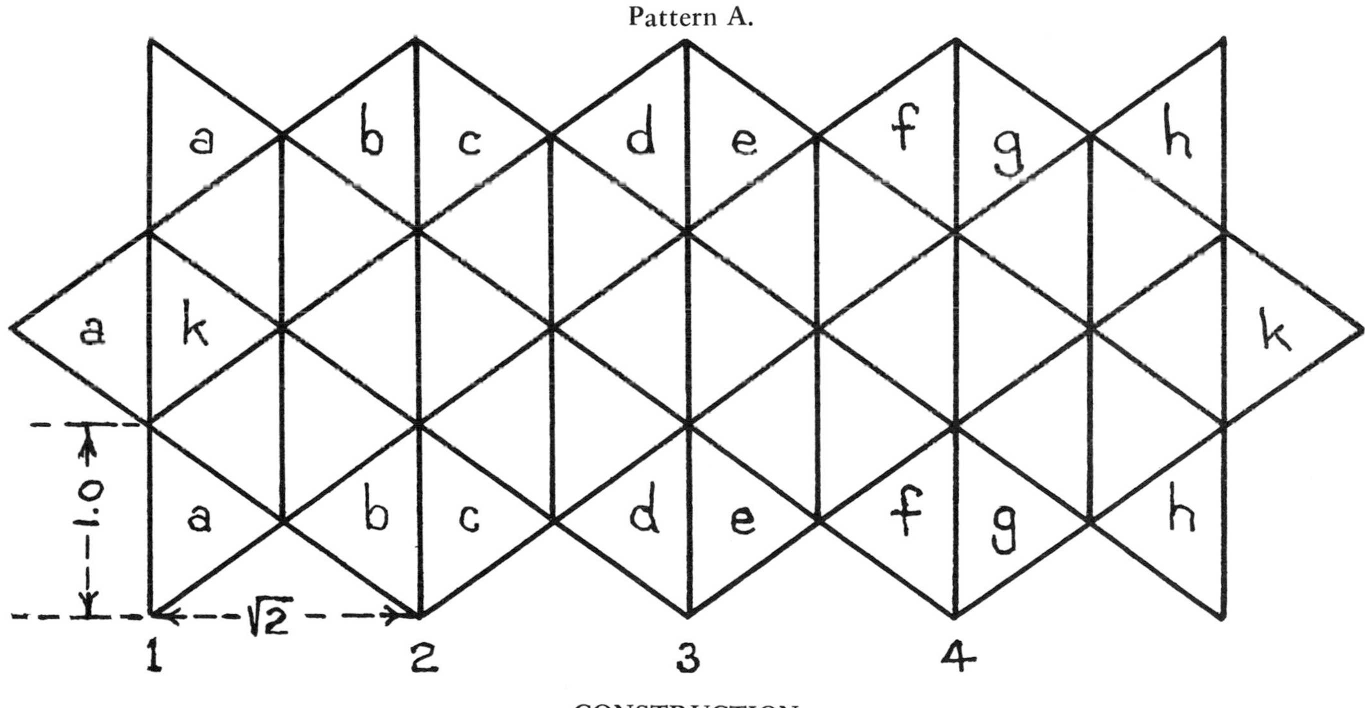

CONSTRUCTION

Make one pattern A. Crease all interior lines, reversing the creases of the vertical lines of unit length. Cut in half six outer diamonds on lines 2, 3 and 4. Paste the like lettered triangles together in alphabetical order.

Make four separate unit diamonds. Crease and mount them on matching diamonds in pattern A at joints on lines 1, 2, 3 and 4.

TWELVE ROTATING TETRAHEDRA

J. M. Andreas and R. M. Stalker

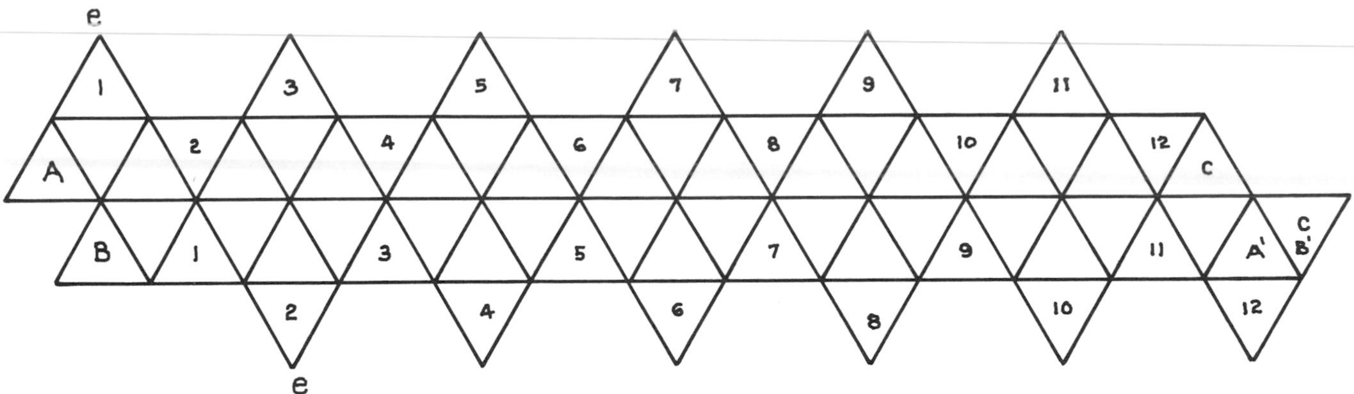

Crease all interior lines. Reverse crease of all lines parallel to line e-e. Paste all like marked triangles together. Eliminate four or two rows of interior triangles to construct eight or ten tetrahedra rings.

THE HEXAFLEXAGON

The hexaflexagon is a frustrating laminated hexagon that can eventually be flexed to change its face 6 times. The 6 triangles forming each face also keep changing their relative positions during these operations.

The figure was invented at Princeton University in 1939 by Arthur H. Stone, a British graduate student. It is essentially a multitwist variation of the mobius strip used in the study of toplogy.

It is made of 19 triangles arranged and marked as shown.

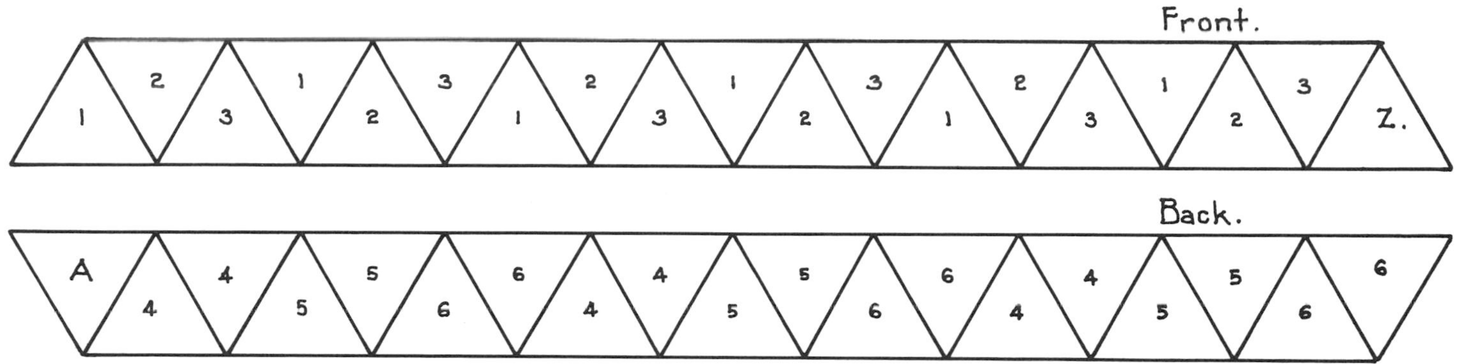

Crease accurately all of the sloping edges of the triangles keeping the 4, 5 and 6 triangles inside. Starting at end A, fold together the first two triangles 4, then the next 2 triangles 5 and so on until the whole strip is folded, leaving only triangle A free. Triangle Z is now on the same side of the folded strip as triangle A. Fold together the 2 triangles 3 near Z. Turn the figure over and fold together the 2 triangles 3 on this side by swinging the A end of the strip over the hexagon. The hexagon is now topped with 5 triangles 1 and 1 triangle 3. Now lift end Z over the hexagon and cover triangle 3 with triangle Z. Complete the hexaflexagon by pasting triangle A over triangle Z.

Think of the figure as an opened 6 rib umbrella. Fold 3 alternate ribs together under the center much as an umbrella is closed. This transforms the hexagon into the 3 dimensional figure of 3 equally spaced triangles having a common side. Restore the hexagonal shape by pulling the figure apart at the top.

It will now have a new face of 6 like numbered triangles.

Keep flexing the same ribs until balked, then shift to the alternate set of ribs. Eventually 6 different faces will appear.

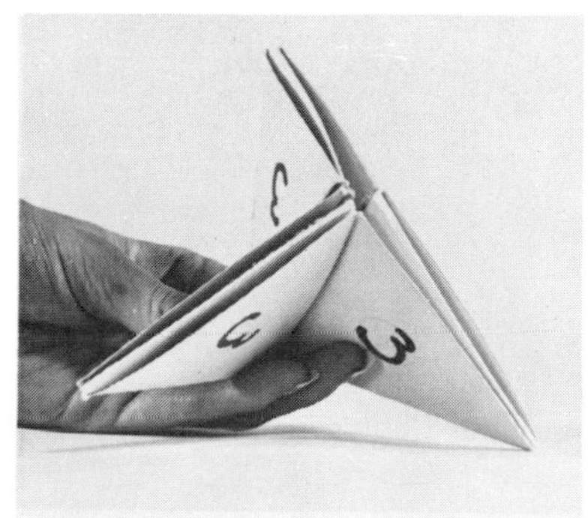

section IV

GOLDEN SECTION, FIBONACCI NUMBERS AND RELATED DRAWINGS

The Golden Rectangle.

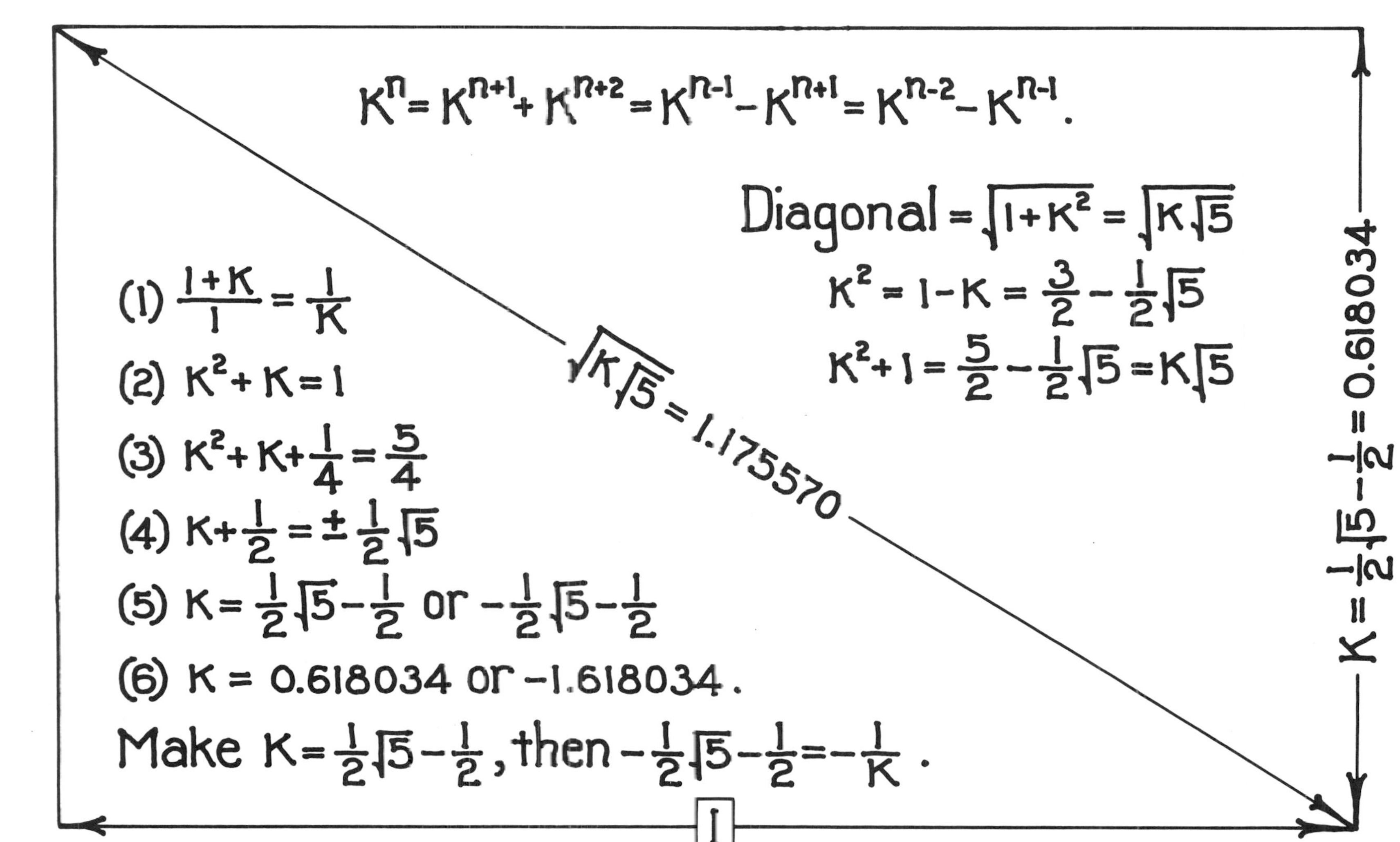

$K^n = K^{n+1} + K^{n+2} = K^{n-1} - K^{n+1} = K^{n-2} - K^{n-1}$.
Diagonal $= \sqrt{1+K^2} = \sqrt{K\sqrt{5}}$
$K^2 = 1 - K = \frac{3}{2} - \frac{1}{2}\sqrt{5}$
$K^2 + 1 = \frac{5}{2} - \frac{1}{2}\sqrt{5} = K\sqrt{5}$
(1) $\frac{1+K}{1} = \frac{1}{K}$
(2) $K^2 + K = 1$
(3) $K^2 + K + \frac{1}{4} = \frac{5}{4}$
(4) $K + \frac{1}{2} = \pm\frac{1}{2}\sqrt{5}$
(5) $K = \frac{1}{2}\sqrt{5} - \frac{1}{2}$ or $-\frac{1}{2}\sqrt{5} - \frac{1}{2}$
(6) $K = 0.618034$ or -1.618034.
Make $K = \frac{1}{2}\sqrt{5} - \frac{1}{2}$, then $-\frac{1}{2}\sqrt{5} - \frac{1}{2} = -\frac{1}{K}$.
$\sqrt{K\sqrt{5}} = 1.175570$
$K = \frac{1}{2}\sqrt{5} - \frac{1}{2} = 0.618034$
1

Regular pentagons and decagons inscribed in circles of unit radius, 1, have sides of $\sqrt{K\sqrt{5}}$ and K respectively.

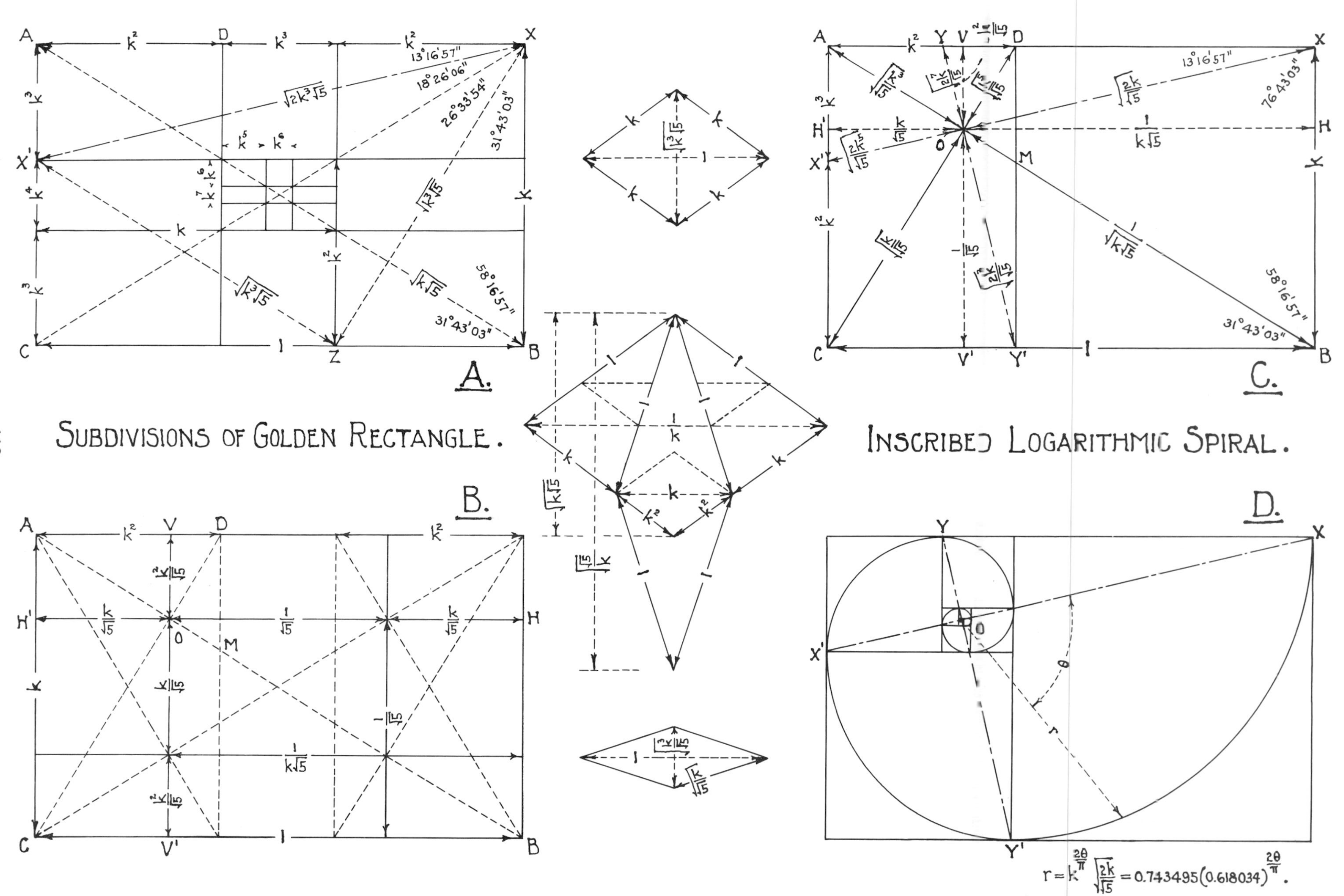

A.
13°16'57"
18°26'06"
26°33'54"
31°43'03"
58°16'57"
31°43'03"
Subdivisions of Golden Rectangle.
B.
C.
13°16'57"
76°43'03"
58°16'57"
31°43'03"
Inscribed Logarithmic Spiral.
D.
$r = k^{\frac{2\theta}{\pi}}\sqrt{\frac{2k}{\sqrt{5}}} = 0.743495(0.618034)^{\frac{2\theta}{\pi}}$.

LOGARITHMIC SPIRAL INSCRIBED IN A GOLDEN RECTANGLE.

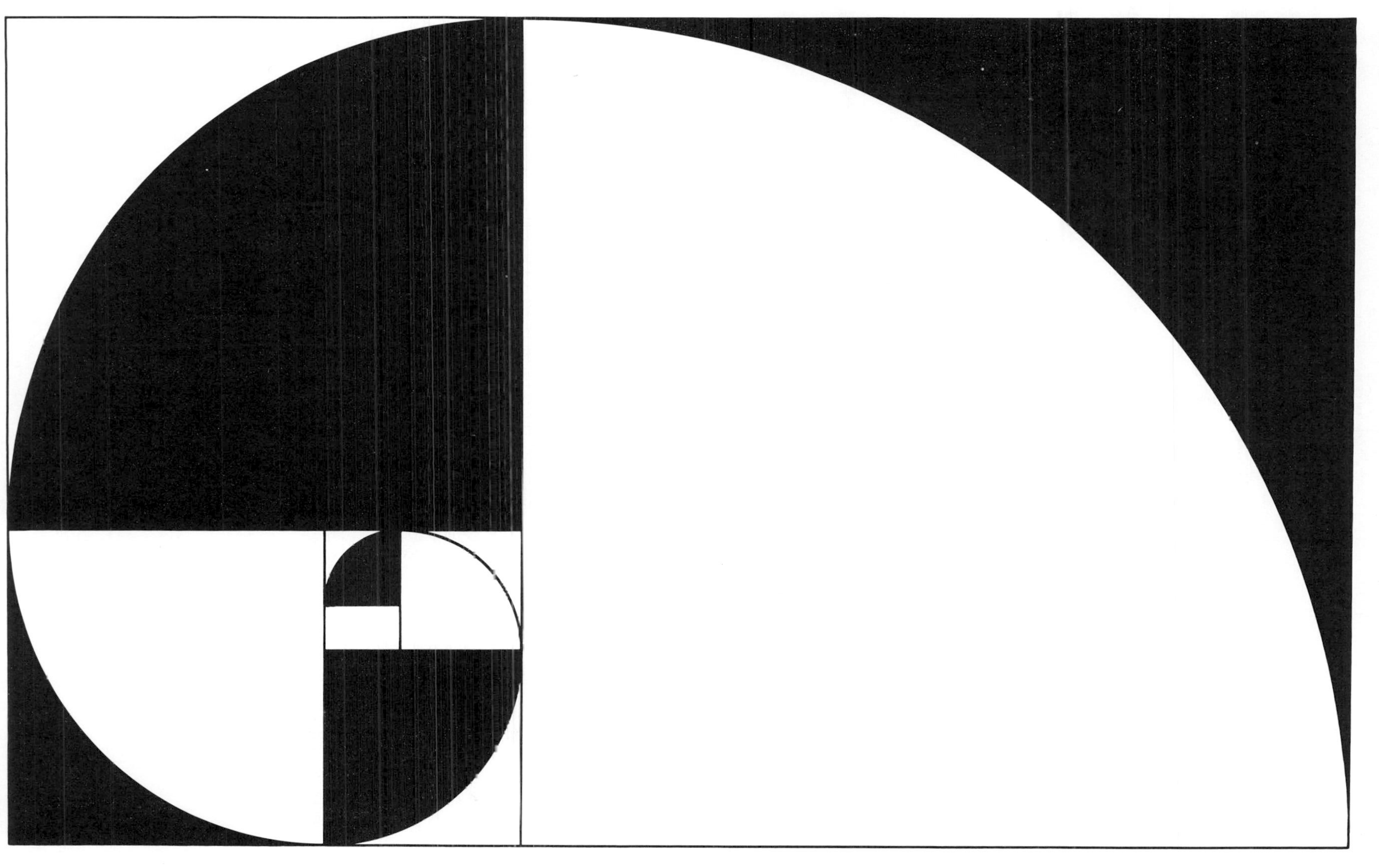

Sides of all squares are powers of k. $k = \frac{1}{2}\sqrt{5} - \frac{1}{2}$.

THE GOLDEN MEAN.—K.

$K = \cfrac{1}{1+\cfrac{1}{1+\cfrac{1}{1+\cdots}}} = \frac{1}{2}(\sqrt{5}-1) = 2\sin 18^\circ = 0.6180339887.$ $\quad K^n = K^{n+1} + K^{n+2} = K^{n-2} - K^{n-1}.$

Powers of K.	Value of Powers of K. Numerical.	Value of Powers of K. Algebraic.
$-\infty$	$+\infty$	$+\infty$
-10	122.991869	55k+89
-9	76.013156	34k+55
-8	46.978714	21k+34
-7	29.034442	13k+21
-6	17.944272	8k+13
-5	11.090170	5k+8
-4	6.854102	3k+5
-3	4.236068	2k+3
-2	2.618034	k+2
-1	1.618034	k+1
0	1.000000	0+1
1	0.618034	k+0
2	0.381966	-k+1
3	0.236068	2k-1
4	0.145898	-3k+2
5	0.090170	5k-3
6	0.055728	-8k+5
7	0.034442	13k-8
8	0.021286	-21k+13
9	0.013156	34k-21
10	0.008131	-55k+34
∞	0.000000	00.00000

K Equivalents.

$\frac{\sqrt{5}-1}{2}$; $\frac{2}{\sqrt{5}+1}$; $\frac{5-\sqrt{5}}{2\sqrt{5}}$; $\frac{2\sqrt{5}}{5+\sqrt{5}}$; $\sqrt{\frac{5-\sqrt{5}}{5+\sqrt{5}}}$; $\frac{1-k}{k}$; $\frac{1}{k+1}$; $\frac{2-k}{\sqrt{5}}$; $\frac{\sqrt{5}}{3+k}$; $\frac{1+k^2}{\sqrt{5}}$

Notes.

$\frac{\sqrt{5}}{k}=3+k$; $k\sqrt{5}=2-k$; $\sqrt{5}=2k+1$; $k^2=\frac{3-\sqrt{5}}{2}$; $k^2=\frac{2}{3+\sqrt{5}}$; $k^3=\sqrt{5}-2$; $k^3=\frac{1}{\sqrt{5}+2}$

K Trigonometry.

sin 18°	$\frac{k}{2}$
cos 18°	$\frac{1}{2}\sqrt{\frac{\sqrt{5}}{k}}$
tan 18°	$\sqrt{\frac{k^3}{\sqrt{5}}}$
cot 18°	$\sqrt{\frac{\sqrt{5}}{k^3}}$
sin 36°	$\frac{1}{2}\sqrt{k\sqrt{5}}$
cos 36°	$\frac{1}{2k}$
tan 36°	$\sqrt{k^3\sqrt{5}}$
cot 36°	$\frac{1}{\sqrt{k^3\sqrt{5}}}$
sin 54°	$\frac{1}{2k}$
cos 54°	$\frac{1}{2}\sqrt{k\sqrt{5}}$
tan 54°	$\frac{1}{\sqrt{k^3\sqrt{5}}}$
cot 54°	$\sqrt{k^3\sqrt{5}}$
sin 72°	$\frac{1}{2}\sqrt{\frac{\sqrt{5}}{k}}$
cos 72°	$\frac{k}{2}$
tan 72°	$\sqrt{\frac{\sqrt{5}}{k^3}}$
cot 72°	$\sqrt{\frac{k^3}{\sqrt{5}}}$

Recurrent Expressions.

$\sqrt{\frac{\sqrt{5}}{k}}$	1.90211	$\sqrt{\frac{k}{\sqrt{5}}}$	0.525730
$\sqrt{\frac{\sqrt{5}}{k^3}}$	3.07769	$\sqrt{\frac{k^3}{\sqrt{5}}}$	0.324920
$\sqrt{\frac{\sqrt{5}}{k^5}}$	4.97980	$\sqrt{\frac{k^5}{\sqrt{5}}}$	0.200811
$\sqrt{\frac{\sqrt{5}}{k^7}}$	8.05750	$\sqrt{\frac{k^7}{\sqrt{5}}}$	0.124108
$\sqrt{k\sqrt{5}}$	1.17557	$\frac{1}{\sqrt{k\sqrt{5}}}$	0.850651
$\sqrt{k^3\sqrt{5}}$	0.726542	$\frac{1}{\sqrt{k^3\sqrt{5}}}$	1.37639
$\sqrt{k^5\sqrt{5}}$	0.449028	$\frac{1}{\sqrt{k^5\sqrt{5}}}$	2.22704
$\sqrt{k^7\sqrt{5}}$	0.277514	$\frac{1}{\sqrt{k^7\sqrt{5}}}$	3.60342
$\sqrt{\frac{\sqrt{5}}{3k}}$	1.09819	$\sqrt{\frac{3k}{\sqrt{5}}}$	0.910592
$\sqrt{\frac{3\sqrt{5}}{k}}$	3.29455	$\sqrt{\frac{k}{3\sqrt{5}}}$	0.303531
$\sqrt{3\sqrt{5}k}$	2.03615	$\frac{1}{\sqrt{3\sqrt{5}k}}$	0.491123
$\sqrt{3\sqrt{5}k^3}$	1.25841	$\frac{1}{\sqrt{3\sqrt{5}k^3}}$	0.794656
$\sqrt{2}$	1.414214	$\frac{1}{\sqrt{2}}$	0.707107
$\sqrt{3}$	1.732051	$\frac{1}{\sqrt{3}}$	0.577350
$\sqrt{5}$	2.236068	$\frac{1}{\sqrt{5}}$	0.447213
$\sqrt{6}$	2.449490	$\frac{1}{\sqrt{6}}$	0.408248
$\sqrt{\frac{2}{3}}$	0.816498	$\sqrt{\frac{3}{2}}$	1.22474
$\sqrt{\frac{3}{5}}$	0.774598	$\sqrt{\frac{5}{3}}$	1.29099

THE FIBONACCI SERIES.—A. [Any term a_n equals term a_{n-1} + term a_{n-2}.]

A.	Order of Differences. 1st.	2nd.	3rd.	4th.	5th.
233	89	55	21	13	5
144	55	34	13	8	3
89	34	21	8	5	2
55	21	13	5	3	1
34	13	8	3	2	1
21	8	5	2	1	0
13	5	3	1	1	1
8	3	2	1	0	-1
5	2	1	0	1	2
3	1	1	1	-1	-3
2	1	0	-1	2	5
1	0	1	2	-3	-8
1	1	-1	-3	5	13
0	-1	2	5	-8	-21
1	2	-3	-8	13	34
-1	-3	5	13	-21	-55
2	5	-8	-21	34	89
-3	-8	13	34	-55	-144
5	13	-21	-55	89	233
-8	-21	34	89	-144	-377
13	34	-55	-144	233	610
-21	-55	89	233	-377	-987
34	89	-144	-377	610	1597
-55	-144	233	610	-987	-2584
89		-377		1597	

Fibonacci Fractional Series.

Odd Term Series.			Even Term Series.	
1/1	1.000000	$\frac{a_n}{a_{n+1}}$ Series. Limit=K	1/2	0.500000
2/3	0.666667		3/5	0.600000
5/8	0.625000		8/13	0.615386
13/21	0.619047		21/34	0.617647
34/55	0.618181		55/89	0.617979
89/144	0.618056		144/233	0.618026
233/377	0.618038		377/610	0.618033
610/987	0.618034		987/1597	0.618034
1/2	0.500000	$\frac{a_n}{a_{n+2}}$ Series. Limit=K^2.	1/3	0.333333
2/5	0.400000		3/8	0.375000
5/13	0.384616		8/21	0.380953
13/34	0.384118		21/55	0.381818
34/89	0.382023		55/144	0.381945
89/233	0.381974		144/377	0.381963
1/3	0.333333	$\frac{a_n}{a_{n+3}}$ Series. Limit=K^3.	1/5	0.200000
2/8	0.250000		3/13	0.230769
5/21	0.238096		8/34	0.235294
13/55	0.236363		21/89	0.235951
34/144	0.236112		55/233	0.236052
89/377	0.236074		144/610	0.236065
1/5	0.200000	$\frac{a_n}{a_{n+4}}$ Series. Limit=K^4.	1/8	0.125000
2/13	0.153846		3/21	0.142857
5/34	0.147059		8/55	0.145454
13/89	0.146067		21/144	0.145833
34/233	0.145923		55/377	0.145889
89/610	0.145902		144/987	0.145897

$K=$	$K=$	n	$K^n=$	Fibonacci Series. 0-1	1-1	2-1
$K+0$	$0+K$	1.	$\frac{1}{2}\sqrt{5}-\frac{1}{2}$	0	1	2
$-K^2+1$	K^2+K^3	2.	$-\frac{1}{2}\sqrt{5}+\frac{3}{2}$	1	1	1
$\frac{1}{2}K^3+\frac{1}{2}$	$2K^3+K^4$	3.	$\frac{2}{2}\sqrt{5}-\frac{4}{2}$	1	2	3
$-\frac{1}{3}K^4+\frac{2}{3}$	$3K^4+2K^5$	4.	$-\frac{3}{2}\sqrt{5}+\frac{7}{2}$	2	3	4
$\frac{1}{5}K^5+\frac{3}{5}$	$5K^5+3K^6$	5.	$\frac{5}{2}\sqrt{5}-\frac{11}{2}$	3	5	7
$-\frac{1}{8}K^6+\frac{5}{8}$	$8K^6+5K^7$	6.	$-\frac{8}{2}\sqrt{5}+\frac{18}{2}$	5	8	11
$\frac{1}{13}K^7+\frac{8}{13}$	$13K^7+8K^8$	7.	$\frac{13}{2}\sqrt{5}-\frac{29}{2}$	8	13	18
$-\frac{1}{21}K^8+\frac{13}{21}$	$21K^8+13K^9$	8.	$-\frac{21}{2}\sqrt{5}+\frac{47}{2}$	13	21	29
$\frac{1}{34}K^9+\frac{21}{34}$	$34K^9+21K^{10}$	9.	$\frac{34}{2}\sqrt{5}-\frac{76}{2}$	21	34	47
$-\frac{1}{55}K^{10}+\frac{34}{55}$	$55K^{10}+34K^{11}$	10.	$-\frac{55}{2}\sqrt{5}+\frac{123}{2}$	34	55	76
				55	89	123
				89	144	199
				144	233	322
				233	377	521
				377	610	843

FRACTIONAL FIBONACCI SERIES.

n	a_n	Series.	Odd Terms.		Even Terms.	
1	1	$\frac{a_n}{a_{n+1}}$ Series. Limit $= k$ $k = \frac{1}{2}\sqrt{5} - \frac{1}{2} = 0.618034$	$\frac{1}{1}$	1.000000	$\frac{1}{2}$	0.500000
2	1		$\frac{2}{3}$	0.666667	$\frac{3}{5}$	0.600000
3	2		$\frac{5}{8}$	0.625000	$\frac{8}{13}$	0.615386
4	3		$\frac{13}{21}$	0.619047	$\frac{21}{34}$	0.617647
5	5		$\frac{34}{55}$	0.618181	$\frac{55}{89}$	0.617979
6	8		$\frac{89}{144}$	0.618056	$\frac{144}{233}$	0.618026
7	13		$\frac{233}{377}$	0.618038	$\frac{377}{610}$	0.618033
8	21		$\frac{610}{987}$	0.618034	$\frac{987}{1597}$	0.618034
9	34					
10	55	$\frac{a_n}{a_{n+2}}$ Series. Limit $= k^2$ $k^2 = 0.381966$	$\frac{1}{2}$	0.500000	$\frac{1}{3}$	0.333333
11	89		$\frac{2}{5}$	0.400000	$\frac{3}{8}$	0.375000
12	144		$\frac{5}{13}$	0.384616	$\frac{8}{21}$	0.380953
13	233		$\frac{13}{34}$	0.384118	$\frac{21}{55}$	0.381818
14	377		$\frac{34}{89}$	0.382023	$\frac{55}{144}$	0.381945
15	610		$\frac{89}{233}$	0.381974	$\frac{144}{377}$	0.381963
16	987		$\frac{233}{610}$	0.381967	$\frac{377}{987}$	0.381966
17	1597					
18	2584	$\frac{a_n}{a_{n+3}}$ Series. Limit $= k^3$ $k^3 = 0.236068$	$\frac{1}{3}$	0.333333	$\frac{1}{5}$	0.200000
19	4181		$\frac{2}{8}$	0.250000	$\frac{3}{13}$	0.230769
20	6765		$\frac{5}{21}$	0.238096	$\frac{8}{34}$	0.235294
21	10946		$\frac{13}{55}$	0.236363	$\frac{21}{89}$	0.235951
22	17711		$\frac{34}{144}$	0.236112	$\frac{55}{233}$	0.236052
23	28657		$\frac{89}{377}$	0.236074	$\frac{144}{610}$	0.236065
24	46368		$\frac{233}{987}$	0.236070	$\frac{377}{1597}$	0.236068

FIBONACCI SERIES A, B & K^N.

a_n	(n.)	b_n	(n.)	k^n
-6765	(-20)	15127	(-20)	15126.999934
4181	(-19)	-9349	(-19)	9349.000107
-2584	(-18)	5778	(-18)	5777.999827
1597	(-17)	-3571	(-17)	3571.000280
-987	(-16)	2207	(-16)	2206.999547
610	(-15)	-1364	(-15)	1364.000733
-377	(-14)	843	(-14)	842.998814
233	(-13)	-521	(-13)	521.001919
-144	(-12)	322	(-12)	321.996894
89	(-11)	-199	(-11)	199.005025
-55	(-10)	123	(-10)	122.991869
34	(-9)	-76	(-9)	76.013156
-21	(-8)	47	(-8)	46.978714
13	(-7)	-29	(-7)	29.034442
-8	(-6)	18	(-6)	17.944272
5	(-5)	-11	(-5)	11.090170
-3	(-4)	7	(-4)	6.854102
2	(-3)	-4	(-3)	4.236068
-1	(-2)	3	(-2)	2.618034
1	(-1)	-1	(-1)	1.618034
0	(0)	2	(0)	1.000000
1	(1)	1	(1)	0.618034
1	(2)	3	(2)	0.381966
2	(3)	4	(3)	0.236068
3	(4)	7	(4)	0.145898
5	(5)	11	(5)	0.090170
8	(6)	18	(6)	0.055728
13	(7)	29	(7)	0.034442
21	(8)	47	(8)	0.021286
34	(9)	76	(9)	0.013156
55	(10)	123	(10)	0.008130
89	(11)	199	(11)	0.005025
144	(12)	322	(12)	0.003106
233	(13)	521	(13)	0.001919
377	(14)	843	(14)	0.001186
610	(15)	1364	(15)	0.000733
987	(16)	2207	(16)	0.000453
1597	(17)	3571	(17)	0.000280
2584	(18)	5778	(18)	0.000173
4181	(19)	9349	(19)	0.000107
6765	(20)	15127	(20)	0.000066

n and p are symbols for any number.
a_n and b_n are the values of the nth terms of series A and B. k^n is the nth power of k.
k is $\frac{1}{2}\sqrt{5}-\frac{1}{2}$, the golden mean ratio.

$$a_n = a_{n-1} + a_{n-2}, \quad b_n = b_{n-1} + b_{n-2}.$$

$$k^n = k^{n-2} - k^{n-1} = k^{n+1} + k^{n+2} = k^{n-1} - k^{n+1}.$$

$$a_n = \frac{k^{-n} - (-k)^n}{\sqrt{5}} = \frac{b_{n+1} + b_{n-1}}{5} = \frac{b_{n+2} - b_{n-2}}{5}$$

$$a_n = \frac{b_{n+3} + b_{n-3}}{10} = \frac{b_{n+p} - (-1)^p b_{n-p}}{5a_p}$$

$$b_n = k^{-n} + (-k)^n = \frac{a_{2n}}{a_n} = a_{n+1} + a_{n-1} = a_{n+2} - a_{n-2}$$

$$b_n = \frac{a_{n+3} + a_{n-3}}{2} = \frac{a_{n+p} - (-1)^p a_{n-p}}{a_p}$$

$$k^n = \frac{-a_n k + a_{n-1}}{(-1)^n a_{-1}} = \frac{-a_n k^2 + a_{n-2}}{(-1)^n a_{-2}} = \frac{-a_n k^3 + a_{n-3}}{(-1)^n a_{-3}}$$

$$k^n = \frac{-a_n k^p + a_{n-p}}{(-1)^n a_{-p}}$$

Alternate terms of each of the expressions $\frac{a_n}{a_{n+p}}$ and $\frac{b_n}{b_{n+p}}$ form two series that approach the value of k^p as a limit.

$\frac{a_{19}}{a_{20}} = 0.6180339985$ $\quad \frac{b_{19}}{b_{20}} = 0.618033978$

$k = 0.6180339887$

$\frac{a_{18}}{a_{20}} = 0.381966002$ $\quad \frac{b_{18}}{b_{20}} = 0.381966021$

$k^2 = 0.381966011$

$\frac{a_{17}}{a_{20}} = 0.236067997$ $\quad \frac{b_{17}}{b_{20}} = 0.236067958$

$k^3 = 0.236067977.$

RSB.

THE GOLDEN SECTION AND FIBONACCI NUMBERS

BY COLONEL ROBERT S. BEARD

1. The Golden Section is the positive root k of the quadratic equation: $x^2 = -x + 1$; that is, $k = {}^1/_2(\sqrt{5} - 1)$.

Higher powers of k are reducible to the form $Ak + B$, where A and B are Fibonacci numbers. Thus,

$$\begin{aligned} k^2 &= -k + 1 \\ k^3 &= k^2 \cdot k = -k^2 + k = -(-k+1) + k = 2k - 1 \\ k^4 &= 2k^2 - k = -3k + 2 \\ k^5 &= 3k^2 + 2k = 5k - 3. \end{aligned}$$

In general, $k^n = (-1)^{n+1}(a_n k - a_{n-1})$, which may be written in the form

$$\frac{-a_n k + a_{n-1}}{(-1)^n a_{-1}}$$

Proof. Suppose (1) is valid for k^s, that is $k^s = (-1)^{s+1}(a_s k - a_{s-1})$. Then:

$k^{s+1} = (-1)^{s+1}(a_s k^2 - a_{s-1}k) = (-1)^{s+1}[a_s(-k+1) - a_{s-1}k] =$
$(-1)^{s+1}[-a_s k - a_{s-1}k + a_s] = (-1)^{s+1}(-a_{s+1}k + a_s) = (-1)^{s+2}(a_{s+1}k - a_s)$

Hence, the validity of (1) for k^s implies its validity for k^{s+1}. But (1) it is true for $s = 2, 3, 4$; hence, it is true for any integral positive value of s.

The formula for negative powers of k is

$$k^{-n} = a_n k + a_{n+1}. \tag{1a}$$

Thus

$$\begin{aligned} k^{-1} &= \frac{2}{\sqrt{5} - 1} = \frac{\sqrt{5} + 1}{2} = k + 1, \\ k^{-2} &= (k+1)k^{-1} = 1 + k^{-1} = k + 2, \\ k^{-3} &= (k+2)k^{-1} = 1 + 2k^{-1} = 2k + 3, \\ k^{-4} &= (2k+3)k^{-1} = 2 + 3k^{-1} = 3k + 5, \text{ etc.} \end{aligned}$$

Proof, as above, by induction.

2. We shall now show how to express powers of k in the form of $Ak^2 + B$, where A and B are Fibonacci numbers.

From $k^2 = -k + 1$, we get

$$\begin{aligned} k &= -k^2 + 1 \\ k^3 &= k^2 k = (-k+1)k = -k^2 + k = -2k^2 + 1 \\ k^4 &= -2k^3 + k = 3k^2 - 1 \\ k^5 &= 3k^3 - k = -5k^2 + 2 \\ k^n &= (-1)^n(a_n k^2 - a_{n-2}). \end{aligned} \tag{2}$$

In a similar way, we find that

$$k^{-n} = a_{n+2} - a_n k^2. \tag{2a}$$

The proof of (2) and (2a) by induction presents no difficulty.

3. A different situation arises when we try to express k^n or k^{-n} in terms of k^p, where $p > 2$. For $p = 3$ we start with the formula $k^3 = 2k - 1$ (1) and obtain:

$$\begin{aligned} k &= {}^1/_2 k^3 + {}^1/_2, \\ k^2 &= -k + 1 = -{}^1/_2 k^3 + {}^1/_2 k^3 - {}^1/_2 + 1 = -{}^1/_2 k^3 + {}^1/_2, \\ k^4 &= -3k + 2 = -{}^3/_2 k^3 + {}^1/_2. \end{aligned}$$

In general

$$k^n = {}^1/_2(-1)^{n+1}(a_n k^3 - a_{n-3})$$

or

$$k^n = (-1)^{n+1}\frac{a_n k^3 - a_{n-3}}{a_3}. \tag{3}$$

In a somewhat similar way we find

$$k^{-n} = \frac{a_n k^3 + a_{n+3}}{a_3}. \tag{3}$$

4. The process may be continued indefinitely. In the appended table the reader will find expressions of k^n in terms of k^p for $n = -10, -9 \ldots -1, 0, 1, 2 \ldots 10$ and $p = -5, -4, -3, -2, -1, 0, 1, 2, 3, 4, 5$.

EDITOR'S NOTE.—Colonel Beards' numerical results lead to the following formulae, in which $i = (-1)^{n+p}$

$$k^n = \frac{i(a_n k^p - a_{n-p})}{a_p} = \frac{i(a_n k^{-p} + a_{n+p})}{a_p} \tag{A}$$

$$k^{-n} = \frac{(-1)^{p+1}a_n k^p + a_{n+p}}{a_p} = \frac{a_n k^{-p} + (-1)^{p+1}a_{n-p}}{a_p}. \tag{B}$$

Thus

$$k^n = (-1)^{n+1}(a_n k - a_{n-1}) = (-1)^n(a_n k^2 - a^{n-2}) = \frac{(-1)^{n+1}(a_n k^3 - a_{n-3})}{a_3},$$

etc.

$$k^{-n} = a_n k + a_{n+1} = -a_n k^2 + a_{n+2} = \frac{a_n k^3 + a_{n+3}}{a_3} = -\frac{a_n k^4 + a_{n+4}}{a_4}, \text{ etc.}$$

Formulae (A) and (B) seem to be a useful tool for the derivation or rediscovery of some well-known theorems and identities in the theory of Fibonacci numbers. The possibilities they offer for the discovery of new theorems are still to be explored.

Examples: Since $k^n \cdot k^{-n} = 1$, we may write

$$(-1)^{n+1}(a_n k - a_{n-1})(a_n k + a_{n+1}) = 1 \quad (C)$$

$$(-1)^n(a_n k^2 - a_{n-2})(-a_n k^2 + a_{n+2}) = 1 \quad (D)$$

$$(-1)^{n+1}(a_n k^3 - a_{n-3})(a_n k^3 + a_{n+3}) = 1. \quad (E)$$

From (C) we get

$$a_n^2 k^2 + k(a_n a_{n+1} - a_n a_{n-1}) - a_{n-1}a_{n+1} = (-1)^{n+1}.$$

Replacing k^2 by its value, $-k + 1$, and observing that the coefficient of k must be $=0$, we obtain the well-known formula

$$a_n^2 - a_{n+1}a_{n-1} = (-1)^{n+1}.$$

Multiplying out the terms in (D) and replacing k^4 by its value in terms of k^2, we obtain

$$a_n^2 - a_{n+2}a_{n-2} = (-1)^n.$$

From (E) we get

$$a_n^2 - a_{n+3}a_{n-3} = 4(-1)^{n+1}.$$

Continuing in the same way we get the curious string of identities

$$a_n^2 - a_{n+4}a_{n-4} = 9(-1)_n$$

$$a_n^2 - a_{n+5}a_{n-5} = 25(-1)^{n+1}, \text{ etc.}$$

or in general

$$a_n^2 - a_{n+p}a_{n-p} = a_p^2(-1)^p.$$

This formula may or may not be new but the ease with which it is obtained by this method is suggestive of other possibilities.

Notes.

The following two tables for the transformation of powers k are an expansion of the missing page 117 of the original article.

Complex expressions involving various powers of k can often be very much simplified with the aid of these transformation tables and of the recurrent k expressions on the pentagon sheet.

This was done in dimensioning the patterns for the five interlocking cubes, the great icosahedron, the triacontahedron and many of the other polyhedra.

Scripta Mathematica
Volume 16. March–June 1950.
Jekuthiel Ginsburg, Editor

The Fibonacci Quarterly

VOLUME 4 NUMBER 2 1966

POWERS OF THE GOLDEN SECTION

Robert S. Beard
Berkeley, Calif.

The Golden Section is the positive root k of the equation $x^2 + x = 1$,

$$k = (\sqrt{5} - 1)/2 = 0.618034.$$

The negative root, $(-\sqrt{5} - 1)/2$, is $-1/k$, the negative reciprocal of k. From the above equation,

$$k^n = k^{n+1} + k^{n+2} = k^{n-2} - k^{n-1},$$

That is, any power of k is the sum of the next two higher powers or the difference between the next two lower powers.

If the powers of k are listed serially as in the box tabulation with the accompanying diagram, the ascending and descending ratios of the successive powers are k and 1/k respectively.

Each power of k can be expressed in terms of its first power and a Fibonacci number as indicated in the right column of the box tabulation. Starting with the successive powers k^0 and k^1, this column can be completed by repeated application of the k^n formula. It is evident from this tabulation and the k^n formula that the powers of k form a Fibonacci series which can be separated into two component Fibonacci series.

Continuing further, all power of k can be expressed in terms of any other power and a number as shown on the accompanying transformation tables. The box tabulation on the diagram can be used to determine the values given in the transformation table. For example, the value $k = \frac{1}{8}k^6 - \frac{5}{8}$ is obtained from $k^6 = 5 - 8k$. This value for k, coupled with the value $k^0 = 0 + \frac{8}{8}$, can be used to determine all of the values listed in the vertical k^6 column with the aid of the k^n formulas.

It is interesting to note the recurrence of the Fibonacci sequence in the numerators in the vertical columns and in the denominators in the horizontal columns.

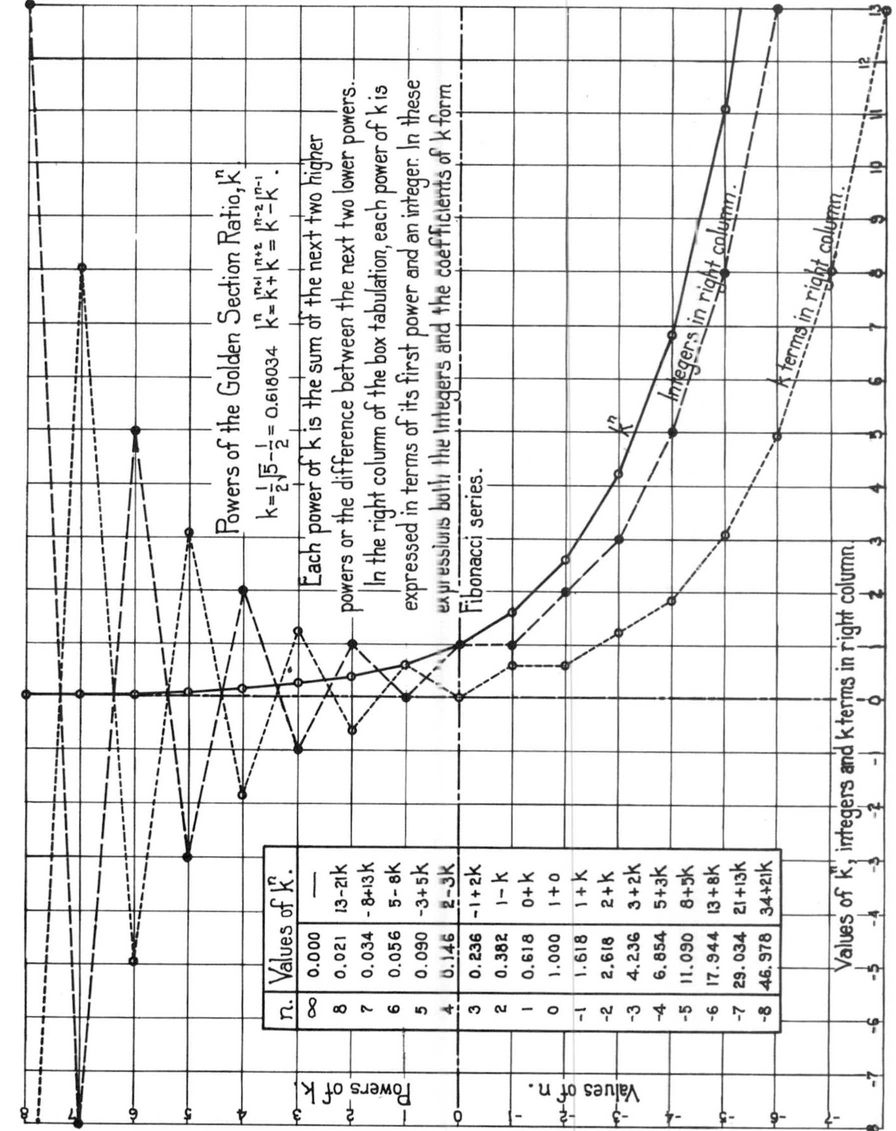
Powers of the Golden Section Ratio, K^n.
$k = \frac{1}{2}\sqrt{5} - \frac{1}{2} = 0.618034$ $K^n = K^{n+1} + K^{n+2} = K^{n-2} - K^{n-1}$.
Each power of k is the sum of the next two higher powers or the difference between the next two lower powers.
In the right column of the box tabulation, each power of k is expressed in terms of its first power and an integer. In these expressions both the integers and the coefficients of k form Fibonacci series.
K^n
Integers in right column.
k terms in right column.
Powers of k.
Values of n.
Values of K^n, integers and k terms in right column.

n.	Values of K^n.	
∞	0.000	—
8	0.021	13-21k
7	0.034	-8+13k
6	0.056	5-8k
5	0.090	-3+5k
4	0.146	2-3k
3	0.236	-1+2k
2	0.382	1-k
1	0.618	0+k
0	1.000	1+0
-1	1.618	1+k
-2	2.618	2+k
-3	4.236	3+2k
-4	6.854	5+3k
-5	11.090	8+5k
-6	17.944	13+8k
-7	29.034	21+13k
-8	46.978	34+21k

TRANSFORMATION OF POWERS OF K. (Equivalents in Other Powers.)

Powers of K.	K^{0}	K^{-1}	K^{-2}	K^{-3}	K^{-4}	K^{-5}	K^{-6}	K^{-7}	K^{-8}	K^{-9}	K^{-10}	Powers of K.
-10	$\frac{55}{2}\sqrt{5}+\frac{123}{2}$	$55K^{-1}+34$	$55K^{-2}-21$	$\frac{55}{2}K^{-3}+\frac{13}{2}$	$\frac{55}{3}K^{-4}-\frac{8}{3}$	$\frac{55}{5}K^{-5}+\frac{5}{5}$	$\frac{55}{8}K^{-6}-\frac{3}{8}$	$\frac{55}{13}K^{-7}+\frac{2}{13}$	$\frac{55}{21}K^{-8}-\frac{1}{21}$	$\frac{55}{34}K^{-9}+\frac{1}{34}$	$\frac{55}{55}K^{-10}+0$	-10
-9	$\frac{34}{2}\sqrt{5}+\frac{76}{2}$	$34K^{-1}+21$	$34K^{-2}-13$	$\frac{34}{2}K^{-3}+\frac{8}{2}$	$\frac{34}{3}K^{-4}-\frac{5}{3}$	$\frac{34}{5}K^{-5}+\frac{3}{5}$	$\frac{34}{8}K^{-6}-\frac{2}{8}$	$\frac{34}{13}K^{-7}+\frac{1}{13}$	$\frac{34}{21}K^{-8}-\frac{1}{21}$	$\frac{34}{34}K^{-9}+0$	$\frac{34}{55}K^{-10}-\frac{1}{55}$	-9
-8	$\frac{21}{2}\sqrt{5}+\frac{47}{2}$	$21K^{-1}+13$	$21K^{-2}-8$	$\frac{21}{2}K^{-3}+\frac{5}{2}$	$\frac{21}{3}K^{-4}-\frac{3}{3}$	$\frac{21}{5}K^{-5}+\frac{2}{5}$	$\frac{21}{8}K^{-6}-\frac{1}{8}$	$\frac{21}{13}K^{-7}+\frac{1}{13}$	$\frac{21}{21}K^{-8}+0$	$\frac{21}{34}K^{-9}+\frac{1}{34}$	$\frac{21}{55}K^{-10}+\frac{1}{55}$	-8
-7	$\frac{13}{2}\sqrt{5}+\frac{29}{2}$	$13K^{-1}+8$	$13K^{-2}-5$	$\frac{13}{2}K^{-3}+\frac{3}{2}$	$\frac{13}{3}K^{-4}-\frac{2}{3}$	$\frac{13}{5}K^{-5}+\frac{1}{5}$	$\frac{13}{8}K^{-6}-\frac{1}{8}$	$\frac{13}{13}K^{-7}+0$	$\frac{13}{21}K^{-8}-\frac{1}{21}$	$\frac{13}{34}K^{-9}-\frac{1}{34}$	$\frac{13}{55}K^{-10}-\frac{2}{55}$	-7
-6	$\frac{8}{2}\sqrt{5}+\frac{18}{2}$	$8K^{-1}+5$	$8K^{-2}-3$	$\frac{8}{2}K^{-3}+\frac{2}{2}$	$\frac{8}{3}K^{-4}-\frac{1}{3}$	$\frac{8}{5}K^{-5}+\frac{1}{5}$	$\frac{8}{8}K^{-6}+0$	$\frac{8}{13}K^{-7}+\frac{1}{13}$	$\frac{8}{21}K^{-8}+\frac{1}{21}$	$\frac{8}{34}K^{-9}+\frac{2}{34}$	$\frac{8}{55}K^{-10}+\frac{3}{55}$	-6
-5	$\frac{5}{2}\sqrt{5}+\frac{11}{2}$	$5K^{-1}+3$	$5K^{-2}-2$	$\frac{5}{2}K^{-3}+\frac{1}{2}$	$\frac{5}{3}K^{-4}-\frac{1}{3}$	$\frac{5}{5}K^{-5}+0$	$\frac{5}{8}K^{-6}-\frac{1}{8}$	$\frac{5}{13}K^{-7}-\frac{1}{13}$	$\frac{5}{21}K^{-8}-\frac{2}{21}$	$\frac{5}{34}K^{-9}-\frac{3}{34}$	$\frac{5}{55}K^{-10}-\frac{5}{55}$	-5
-4	$\frac{3}{2}\sqrt{5}+\frac{7}{2}$	$3K^{-1}+2$	$3K^{-2}-1$	$\frac{3}{2}K^{-3}+\frac{1}{2}$	$\frac{3}{3}K^{-4}+0$	$\frac{3}{5}K^{-5}+\frac{1}{5}$	$\frac{3}{8}K^{-6}+\frac{1}{8}$	$\frac{3}{13}K^{-7}+\frac{2}{13}$	$\frac{3}{21}K^{-8}+\frac{3}{21}$	$\frac{3}{34}K^{-9}+\frac{5}{34}$	$\frac{3}{55}K^{-10}+\frac{8}{55}$	-4
-3	$\frac{2}{2}\sqrt{5}+\frac{4}{2}$	$2K^{-1}+1$	$2K^{-2}-1$	$\frac{2}{2}K^{-3}+0$	$\frac{2}{3}K^{-4}-\frac{1}{3}$	$\frac{2}{5}K^{-5}-\frac{1}{5}$	$\frac{2}{8}K^{-6}-\frac{2}{8}$	$\frac{2}{13}K^{-7}-\frac{3}{13}$	$\frac{2}{21}K^{-8}-\frac{5}{21}$	$\frac{2}{34}K^{-9}-\frac{8}{34}$	$\frac{2}{55}K^{-10}-\frac{13}{55}$	-3
-2	$\frac{1}{2}\sqrt{5}+\frac{3}{2}$	$K^{-1}+1$	$K^{-2}+0$	$\frac{1}{2}K^{-3}+\frac{1}{2}$	$\frac{1}{3}K^{-4}+\frac{1}{3}$	$\frac{1}{5}K^{-5}+\frac{2}{5}$	$\frac{1}{8}K^{-6}+\frac{3}{8}$	$\frac{1}{13}K^{-7}+\frac{5}{13}$	$\frac{1}{21}K^{-8}+\frac{8}{21}$	$\frac{1}{34}K^{-9}+\frac{13}{34}$	$\frac{1}{55}K^{-10}+\frac{21}{55}$	-2
-1	$\frac{1}{2}\sqrt{5}+\frac{1}{2}$	$K^{-1}+0$	$K^{-2}-1$	$\frac{1}{2}K^{-3}-\frac{1}{2}$	$\frac{1}{3}K^{-4}-\frac{2}{3}$	$\frac{1}{5}K^{-5}-\frac{3}{5}$	$\frac{1}{8}K^{-6}-\frac{5}{8}$	$\frac{1}{13}K^{-7}-\frac{8}{13}$	$\frac{1}{21}K^{-8}-\frac{13}{21}$	$\frac{1}{34}K^{-9}-\frac{21}{34}$	$\frac{1}{55}K^{-10}-\frac{34}{55}$	-1
0	$0+1$	$0+1$	$0+1$	$0+\frac{2}{2}$	$0+\frac{3}{3}$	$0+\frac{5}{5}$	$0+\frac{8}{8}$	$0+\frac{13}{13}$	$0+\frac{21}{21}$	$0+\frac{34}{34}$	$0+\frac{55}{55}$	0
1	$\frac{1}{2}\sqrt{5}-\frac{1}{2}$	$K^{-1}-1$	$K^{-2}-2$	$\frac{1}{2}K^{-3}-\frac{3}{2}$	$\frac{1}{3}K^{-4}-\frac{5}{3}$	$\frac{1}{5}K^{-5}-\frac{8}{5}$	$\frac{1}{8}K^{-6}-\frac{13}{8}$	$\frac{1}{13}K^{-7}-\frac{21}{13}$	$\frac{1}{21}K^{-8}-\frac{34}{21}$	$\frac{1}{34}K^{-9}-\frac{55}{34}$	$\frac{1}{55}K^{-10}-\frac{89}{55}$	1
2	$-\frac{1}{2}\sqrt{5}+\frac{3}{2}$	$-K^{-1}+2$	$-K^{-2}+3$	$-\frac{1}{2}K^{-3}+\frac{5}{2}$	$-\frac{1}{3}K^{-4}+\frac{8}{3}$	$-\frac{1}{5}K^{-5}+\frac{13}{5}$	$-\frac{1}{8}K^{-6}+\frac{21}{8}$	$-\frac{1}{13}K^{-7}+\frac{34}{13}$	$-\frac{1}{21}K^{-8}+\frac{55}{21}$	$-\frac{1}{34}K^{-9}+\frac{89}{34}$	$-\frac{1}{55}K^{-10}+\frac{144}{55}$	2
3	$\frac{2}{2}\sqrt{5}-\frac{4}{2}$	$2K^{-1}-3$	$2K^{-2}-5$	$\frac{2}{2}K^{-3}-\frac{8}{2}$	$\frac{2}{3}K^{-4}-\frac{13}{3}$	$\frac{2}{5}K^{-5}-\frac{21}{5}$	$\frac{2}{8}K^{-6}-\frac{34}{8}$	$\frac{2}{13}K^{-7}-\frac{55}{13}$	$\frac{2}{21}K^{-8}-\frac{89}{21}$	$\frac{2}{34}K^{-9}-\frac{144}{34}$	$\frac{2}{55}K^{-10}-\frac{233}{55}$	3
4	$-\frac{3}{2}\sqrt{5}+\frac{7}{2}$	$-3K^{-1}+5$	$-3K^{-2}+8$	$-\frac{3}{2}K^{-3}+\frac{13}{2}$	$-\frac{3}{3}K^{-4}+\frac{21}{3}$	$-\frac{3}{5}K^{-5}+\frac{34}{5}$	$-\frac{3}{8}K^{-6}+\frac{55}{8}$	$-\frac{3}{13}K^{-7}+\frac{89}{13}$	$-\frac{3}{21}K^{-8}+\frac{144}{21}$	$-\frac{3}{34}K^{-9}+\frac{233}{34}$	$-\frac{3}{55}K^{-10}+\frac{377}{55}$	4
5	$\frac{5}{2}\sqrt{5}-\frac{11}{2}$	$5K^{-1}-8$	$5K^{-2}-13$	$\frac{5}{2}K^{-3}-\frac{21}{2}$	$\frac{5}{3}K^{-4}-\frac{34}{3}$	$\frac{5}{5}K^{-5}-\frac{55}{5}$	$\frac{5}{8}K^{-6}-\frac{89}{8}$	$\frac{5}{13}K^{-7}-\frac{144}{13}$	$\frac{5}{21}K^{-8}-\frac{233}{21}$	$\frac{5}{34}K^{-9}-\frac{377}{34}$	$\frac{5}{55}K^{-10}-\frac{610}{55}$	5
6	$-\frac{8}{2}\sqrt{5}+\frac{18}{2}$	$-8K^{-1}+13$	$-8K^{-2}+21$	$-\frac{8}{2}K^{-3}+\frac{34}{2}$	$-\frac{8}{3}K^{-4}+\frac{55}{3}$	$-\frac{8}{5}K^{-5}+\frac{89}{5}$	$-\frac{8}{8}K^{-6}+\frac{144}{8}$	$-\frac{8}{13}K^{-7}+\frac{233}{13}$	$-\frac{8}{21}K^{-8}+\frac{377}{21}$	$-\frac{8}{34}K^{-9}+\frac{610}{34}$	$-\frac{8}{55}K^{-10}+\frac{987}{55}$	6
7	$\frac{13}{2}\sqrt{5}-\frac{29}{2}$	$13K^{-1}-21$	$13K^{-2}-34$	$\frac{13}{2}K^{-3}-\frac{55}{2}$	$\frac{13}{3}K^{-4}-\frac{89}{3}$	$\frac{13}{5}K^{-5}-\frac{144}{5}$	$\frac{13}{8}K^{-6}-\frac{233}{8}$	$\frac{13}{13}K^{-7}-\frac{377}{13}$	$\frac{13}{21}K^{-8}-\frac{610}{21}$	$\frac{13}{34}K^{-9}-\frac{987}{34}$	$\frac{13}{55}K^{-10}-\frac{1597}{55}$	7
8	$-\frac{21}{2}\sqrt{5}+\frac{47}{2}$	$-21K^{-1}+34$	$-21K^{-2}+55$	$-\frac{21}{2}K^{-3}+\frac{89}{2}$	$-\frac{21}{3}K^{-4}+\frac{144}{3}$	$-\frac{21}{5}K^{-5}+\frac{233}{5}$	$-\frac{21}{8}K^{-6}+\frac{377}{8}$	$-\frac{21}{13}K^{-7}+\frac{610}{13}$	$-\frac{21}{21}K^{-8}+\frac{987}{21}$	$-\frac{21}{34}K^{-9}+\frac{1597}{34}$	$-\frac{21}{55}K^{-10}+\frac{2584}{55}$	8
9	$\frac{34}{2}\sqrt{5}-\frac{76}{2}$	$34K^{-1}-55$	$34K^{-2}-89$	$\frac{34}{2}K^{-3}-\frac{144}{2}$	$\frac{34}{3}K^{-4}-\frac{233}{3}$	$\frac{34}{5}K^{-5}-\frac{377}{5}$	$\frac{34}{8}K^{-6}-\frac{610}{8}$	$\frac{34}{13}K^{-7}-\frac{987}{13}$	$\frac{34}{21}K^{-8}-\frac{1597}{21}$	$\frac{34}{34}K^{-9}-\frac{2584}{34}$	$\frac{34}{55}K^{-10}-\frac{4181}{55}$	9
10	$-\frac{55}{2}\sqrt{5}+\frac{123}{2}$	$-55K^{-1}+34$	$-55K^{-2}+144$	$-\frac{55}{2}K^{-3}+\frac{233}{2}$	$-\frac{55}{3}K^{-4}+\frac{377}{3}$	$-\frac{55}{5}K^{-5}+\frac{610}{5}$	$-\frac{55}{8}K^{-6}+\frac{987}{8}$	$-\frac{55}{13}K^{-7}+\frac{1597}{13}$	$-\frac{55}{21}K^{-8}+\frac{2584}{21}$	$-\frac{55}{34}K^{-9}+\frac{4181}{34}$	$-\frac{55}{55}K^{-10}+\frac{6765}{55}$	10

TRANSFORMATION OF POWERS OF K. (Equivalents in Other Powers.)

Powers of K.	K^0	K	K^2	K^3	K^4	K^5	K^6	K^7	K^8	K^9	K^{10}	Powers of K.
-10	122.991870	$55k+89$	$-55k^2+144$	$\frac{55}{2}k^3+\frac{233}{2}$	$-\frac{55}{3}k^4+\frac{377}{3}$	$\frac{55}{5}k^5+\frac{610}{5}$	$-\frac{55}{8}k^6+\frac{987}{8}$	$\frac{55}{13}k^7+\frac{1597}{13}$	$-\frac{55}{21}k^8+\frac{2584}{21}$	$\frac{55}{34}k^9+\frac{4181}{34}$	$-\frac{55}{55}k^{10}+\frac{6765}{55}$	-10
-9	76.013156	$34k+55$	$-34k^2+89$	$\frac{34}{2}k^3+\frac{144}{2}$	$-\frac{34}{3}k^4+\frac{233}{3}$	$\frac{34}{5}k^5+\frac{377}{5}$	$-\frac{34}{8}k^6+\frac{610}{8}$	$\frac{34}{13}k^7+\frac{987}{13}$	$-\frac{34}{21}k^8+\frac{1597}{21}$	$\frac{34}{34}k^9+\frac{2584}{34}$	$-\frac{34}{55}k^{10}+\frac{4181}{55}$	-9
-8	46.978714	$21k+34$	$-21k^2+55$	$\frac{21}{2}k^3+\frac{89}{2}$	$-\frac{21}{3}k^4+\frac{144}{3}$	$\frac{21}{5}k^5+\frac{233}{5}$	$-\frac{21}{8}k^6+\frac{377}{8}$	$\frac{21}{13}k^7+\frac{610}{13}$	$-\frac{21}{21}k^8+\frac{987}{21}$	$\frac{21}{34}k^9+\frac{1597}{34}$	$-\frac{21}{55}k^{10}+\frac{2584}{55}$	-8
-7	29.034442	$13k+21$	$-13k^2+34$	$\frac{13}{2}k^3+\frac{55}{2}$	$-\frac{13}{3}k^4+\frac{89}{3}$	$\frac{13}{5}k^5+\frac{144}{5}$	$-\frac{13}{8}k^6+\frac{233}{8}$	$\frac{13}{13}k^7+\frac{377}{13}$	$-\frac{13}{21}k^8+\frac{610}{21}$	$\frac{13}{34}k^9+\frac{987}{34}$	$-\frac{13}{55}k^{10}+\frac{1597}{55}$	-7
-6	17.944272	$8k+13$	$-8k^2+21$	$\frac{8}{2}k^3+\frac{34}{2}$	$-\frac{8}{3}k^4+\frac{55}{3}$	$\frac{8}{5}k^5+\frac{89}{5}$	$-\frac{8}{8}k^6+\frac{144}{8}$	$\frac{8}{13}k^7+\frac{233}{13}$	$-\frac{8}{21}k^8+\frac{377}{21}$	$\frac{8}{34}k^9+\frac{610}{34}$	$-\frac{8}{55}k^{10}+\frac{987}{55}$	-6
-5	11.090170	$5k+8$	$-5k^2+13$	$\frac{5}{2}k^3+\frac{21}{2}$	$-\frac{5}{3}k^4+\frac{34}{3}$	$\frac{5}{5}k^5+\frac{55}{5}$	$-\frac{5}{8}k^6+\frac{89}{8}$	$\frac{5}{13}k^7+\frac{144}{13}$	$-\frac{5}{21}k^8+\frac{233}{21}$	$\frac{5}{34}k^9+\frac{377}{34}$	$-\frac{5}{55}k^{10}+\frac{610}{55}$	-5
-4	6.854102	$3k+5$	$-3k^2+8$	$\frac{3}{2}k^3+\frac{13}{2}$	$-\frac{3}{3}k^4+\frac{21}{3}$	$\frac{3}{5}k^5+\frac{34}{5}$	$-\frac{3}{8}k^6+\frac{55}{8}$	$\frac{3}{13}k^7+\frac{89}{13}$	$-\frac{3}{21}k^8+\frac{144}{21}$	$\frac{3}{34}k^9+\frac{233}{34}$	$-\frac{3}{55}k^{10}+\frac{377}{55}$	-4
-3	4.236068	$2k+3$	$-2k^2+5$	$\frac{2}{2}k^3+\frac{8}{2}$	$-\frac{2}{3}k^4+\frac{13}{3}$	$\frac{2}{5}k^5+\frac{21}{5}$	$-\frac{2}{8}k^6+\frac{34}{8}$	$\frac{2}{13}k^7+\frac{55}{13}$	$-\frac{2}{21}k^8+\frac{89}{21}$	$\frac{2}{34}k^9+\frac{144}{34}$	$-\frac{2}{55}k^{10}+\frac{233}{55}$	-3
-2	2.618034	$k+2$	$-k^2+3$	$\frac{1}{2}k^3+\frac{5}{2}$	$-\frac{1}{3}k^4+\frac{8}{3}$	$\frac{1}{5}k^5+\frac{13}{5}$	$-\frac{1}{8}k^6+\frac{21}{8}$	$\frac{1}{13}k^7+\frac{34}{13}$	$-\frac{1}{21}k^8+\frac{55}{21}$	$\frac{1}{34}k^9+\frac{89}{34}$	$-\frac{1}{55}k^{10}+\frac{144}{55}$	-2
-1	1.618034	$k+1$	$-k^2+2$	$\frac{1}{2}k^3+\frac{3}{2}$	$-\frac{1}{3}k^4+\frac{5}{3}$	$\frac{1}{5}k^5+\frac{8}{5}$	$-\frac{1}{8}k^6+\frac{13}{8}$	$\frac{1}{13}k^7+\frac{21}{13}$	$-\frac{1}{21}k^8+\frac{34}{21}$	$\frac{1}{34}k^9+\frac{55}{34}$	$-\frac{1}{55}k^{10}+\frac{89}{55}$	-1
0	1.000000	$0+1$	$0+1$	$0+\frac{2}{2}$	$0+\frac{3}{3}$	$0+\frac{5}{5}$	$0+\frac{8}{8}$	$0+\frac{13}{13}$	$0+\frac{21}{21}$	$0+\frac{34}{34}$	$0+\frac{55}{55}$	0
1	0.618034	$k+0$	$-k^2+1$	$\frac{1}{2}k^3+\frac{1}{2}$	$-\frac{1}{3}k^4+\frac{2}{3}$	$\frac{1}{5}k^5+\frac{3}{5}$	$-\frac{1}{8}k^6+\frac{5}{8}$	$\frac{1}{13}k^7+\frac{8}{13}$	$-\frac{1}{21}k^8+\frac{13}{21}$	$\frac{1}{34}k^9+\frac{21}{34}$	$-\frac{1}{55}k^{10}+\frac{34}{55}$	1
2	0.381966	$-k+1$	k^2+0	$-\frac{1}{2}k^3+\frac{1}{2}$	$\frac{1}{3}k^4+\frac{1}{3}$	$-\frac{1}{5}k^5+\frac{2}{5}$	$\frac{1}{8}k^6+\frac{3}{8}$	$-\frac{1}{13}k^7+\frac{5}{13}$	$\frac{1}{21}k^8+\frac{8}{21}$	$-\frac{1}{34}k^9+\frac{13}{34}$	$\frac{1}{55}k^{10}+\frac{21}{55}$	2
3	0.236068	$2k-1$	$-2k^2+1$	$\frac{2}{2}k^3+0$	$-\frac{2}{3}k^4+\frac{1}{3}$	$\frac{2}{5}k^5+\frac{1}{5}$	$-\frac{2}{8}k^6+\frac{2}{8}$	$\frac{2}{13}k^7+\frac{3}{13}$	$-\frac{2}{21}k^8+\frac{5}{21}$	$\frac{2}{34}k^9+\frac{8}{34}$	$-\frac{2}{55}k^{10}+\frac{13}{55}$	3
4	0.145898	$-3k+2$	$3k^2-1$	$-\frac{3}{2}k^3+\frac{1}{2}$	$\frac{3}{3}k^4+0$	$-\frac{3}{5}k^5+\frac{1}{5}$	$\frac{3}{8}k^6+\frac{1}{8}$	$-\frac{3}{13}k^7+\frac{2}{13}$	$\frac{3}{21}k^8+\frac{3}{21}$	$-\frac{3}{34}k^9+\frac{5}{34}$	$\frac{3}{55}k^{10}+\frac{8}{55}$	4
5	0.090170	$5k-3$	$-5k^2+2$	$\frac{5}{2}k^3-\frac{1}{2}$	$-\frac{5}{3}k^4+\frac{1}{3}$	$\frac{5}{5}k^5+0$	$-\frac{5}{8}k^6+\frac{1}{8}$	$\frac{5}{13}k^7+\frac{1}{13}$	$-\frac{5}{21}k^8+\frac{2}{21}$	$\frac{5}{34}k^9+\frac{3}{34}$	$-\frac{5}{55}k^{10}+\frac{5}{55}$	5
6	0.055728	$-8k+5$	$8k^2-3$	$-\frac{8}{2}k^3+\frac{2}{2}$	$\frac{8}{3}k^4-\frac{1}{3}$	$-\frac{8}{5}k^5+\frac{1}{5}$	$\frac{8}{8}k^6+0$	$-\frac{8}{13}k^7+\frac{1}{13}$	$\frac{3}{21}k^8+\frac{1}{21}$	$-\frac{8}{34}k^9+\frac{2}{34}$	$\frac{8}{55}k^{10}+\frac{3}{55}$	6
7	0.034442	$13k-8$	$-13k^2+5$	$\frac{13}{2}k^3-\frac{3}{2}$	$-\frac{13}{3}k^4+\frac{2}{3}$	$\frac{13}{5}k^5-\frac{1}{5}$	$-\frac{13}{8}k^6+\frac{1}{8}$	$\frac{13}{13}k^7+0$	$-\frac{13}{21}k^8+\frac{1}{21}$	$\frac{13}{34}k^9+\frac{1}{34}$	$-\frac{13}{55}k^{10}+\frac{2}{55}$	7
8	0.021286	$-21k+13$	$21k^2-8$	$-\frac{21}{2}k^3+\frac{5}{2}$	$\frac{21}{3}k^4-\frac{3}{3}$	$-\frac{21}{5}k^5+\frac{2}{5}$	$\frac{21}{8}k^6-\frac{1}{8}$	$-\frac{21}{13}k^7+\frac{1}{13}$	$\frac{21}{21}k^8+0$	$-\frac{21}{34}k^9+\frac{1}{34}$	$\frac{21}{55}k^{10}+\frac{1}{55}$	8
9	0.013156	$34k-21$	$-34k^2+13$	$\frac{34}{2}k^3-\frac{8}{2}$	$-\frac{34}{3}k^4+\frac{5}{3}$	$\frac{34}{5}k^5-\frac{3}{5}$	$-\frac{34}{8}k^6+\frac{2}{8}$	$\frac{34}{13}k^7-\frac{1}{13}$	$-\frac{34}{21}k^8+\frac{1}{21}$	$\frac{34}{34}k^9+0$	$-\frac{34}{55}k^{10}+\frac{1}{55}$	9
10	0.008130	$-55k+34$	$55k^2-21$	$-\frac{55}{2}k^3+\frac{13}{2}$	$\frac{55}{3}k^4-\frac{8}{3}$	$-\frac{55}{5}k^5+\frac{5}{5}$	$\frac{55}{8}k^6-\frac{3}{8}$	$-\frac{55}{13}k^7+\frac{2}{13}$	$\frac{55}{21}k^8-\frac{1}{21}$	$-\frac{55}{34}k^9+\frac{1}{34}$	$\frac{55}{55}k^{10}+0$	10

THE FIVE POINTED STAR.

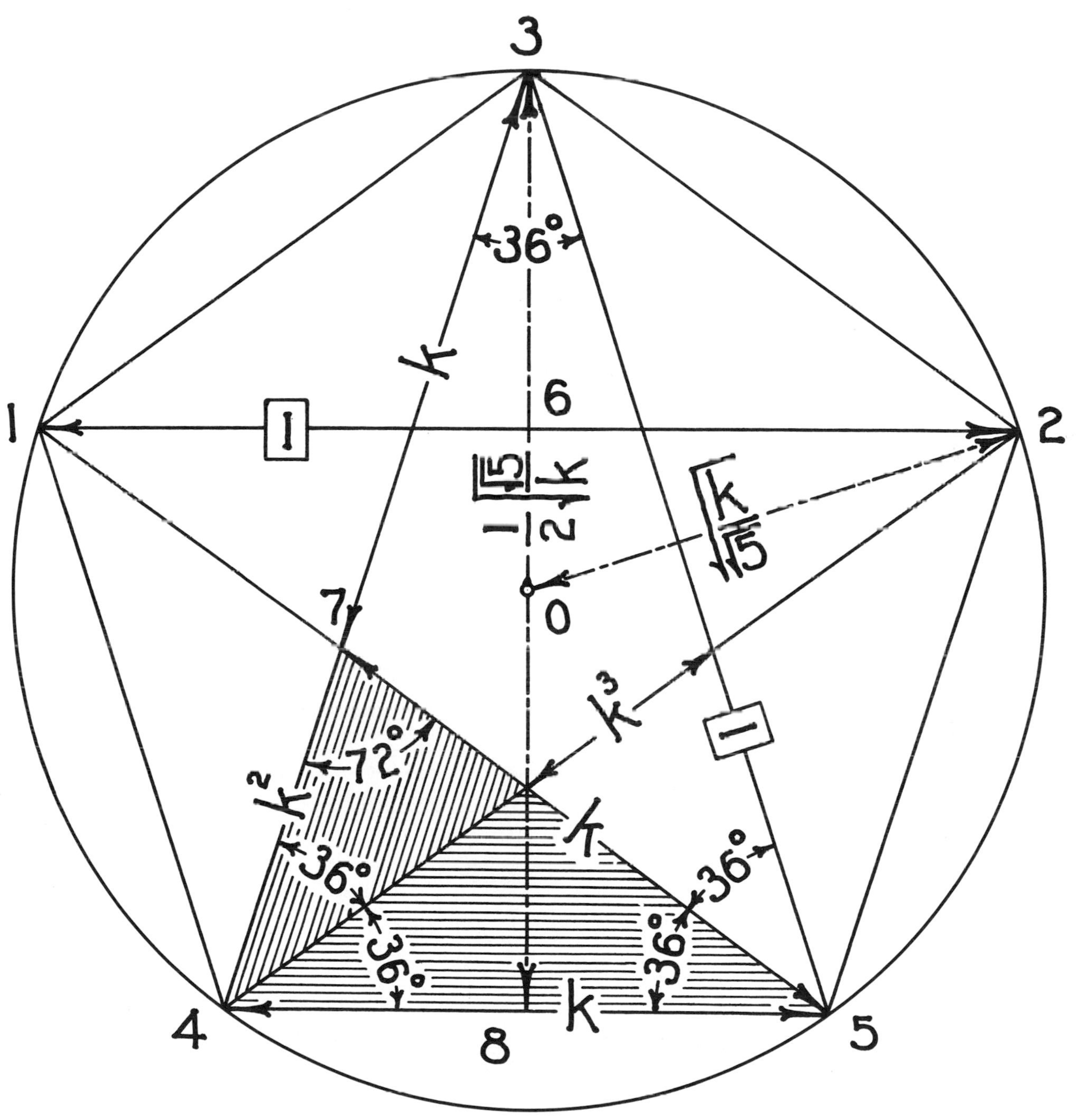

The Pentagon. (Fifteen dimensions in five different units.)

Unit.	1	2	3	4	5	6	7	8	9	10	11	12	13	14	15
① Side.	1	$\frac{1}{k}$	$\frac{1}{\sqrt{k\sqrt5}}$	$\frac{1}{2\sqrt{k^3\sqrt5}}$	$\frac12\sqrt{\frac{\sqrt5}{k^3}}$	$\frac12\sqrt{\frac{\sqrt5}{k}}$	$\frac12\sqrt{k\sqrt5}$	k	k^2	$\frac12\sqrt{k^3\sqrt5}$	$\frac12\sqrt{\frac{k}{\sqrt5}}$	$\sqrt{\frac{k}{\sqrt5}}$	$\frac12\sqrt{\frac{k^3}{\sqrt5}}$	$\frac12\sqrt{\frac{\sqrt5}{k^5}}$	$\sqrt{\frac{\sqrt5}{k^3}}$
② Diagonal.	k	1	$\sqrt{\frac{k}{\sqrt5}}$	$\frac{1}{2\sqrt{k\sqrt5}}$	$\frac12\sqrt{\frac{\sqrt5}{k}}$	$\frac12\sqrt{k\sqrt5}$	$\frac12\sqrt{k^3\sqrt5}$	k^2	k^3	$\frac12\sqrt{k^5\sqrt5}$	$\frac12\sqrt{\frac{k^3}{\sqrt5}}$	$\sqrt{\frac{k^3}{\sqrt5}}$	$\frac12\sqrt{\frac{k^5}{\sqrt5}}$	$\frac12\sqrt{\frac{\sqrt5}{k^3}}$	$\sqrt{\frac{\sqrt5}{k}}$
③ Out Radius.	$\sqrt{k\sqrt5}$	$\sqrt{\frac{\sqrt5}{k}}$	1	$\frac{1}{2k}$	$\frac{\sqrt5}{2k}$	$\frac{\sqrt5}{2}$	$\frac12 k\sqrt5$	$\sqrt{k^3\sqrt5}$	$\sqrt{k^5\sqrt5}$	$\frac12 k^2\sqrt5$	$\frac{k}{2}$	k	$\frac{k^2}{2}$	$\frac{\sqrt5}{2k^2}$	$\frac{\sqrt5}{k}$
④ In Radius.	$2\sqrt{k^3\sqrt5}$	$2\sqrt{k\sqrt5}$	$2k$	1	$\sqrt5$	$k\sqrt5$	$k^2\sqrt5$	$2\sqrt{k^5\sqrt5}$	$2\sqrt{k^7\sqrt5}$	$k^3\sqrt5$	k^2	$2k^2$	k^3	$\frac{\sqrt5}{k}$	$2\sqrt5$
⑤ Altitude.	$2\sqrt{\frac{k^3}{\sqrt5}}$	$2\sqrt{\frac{k}{\sqrt5}}$	$\frac{2k}{\sqrt5}$	$\frac{1}{\sqrt5}$	1	k	k^2	$2\sqrt{\frac{k^5}{\sqrt5}}$	$2\sqrt{\frac{k^7}{\sqrt5}}$	k^3	$\frac{k^2}{\sqrt5}$	$\frac{2k^2}{\sqrt5}$	$\frac{k^3}{\sqrt5}$	$\frac{1}{k}$	2

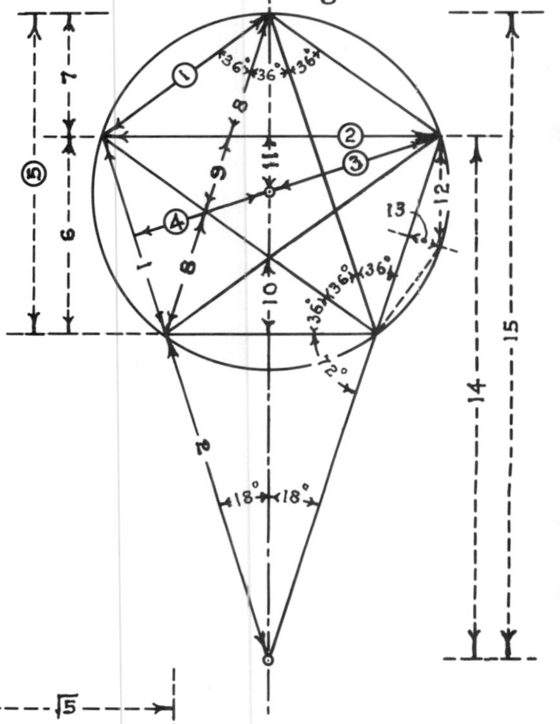

Recurrent K Expressions et al. $K=\frac12\sqrt5-\frac12=0.6180339887498948482045 87.$

$\frac{\sqrt5}{k}$	3.618034	$\frac{k}{\sqrt5}$	0.276393	$\sqrt{\frac{\sqrt5}{k}}$	1.90211	$\sqrt{\frac{k}{\sqrt5}}$	0.525730
$\frac{\sqrt5}{k^2}$	5.85411	$\frac{k^2}{\sqrt5}$	0.170820	$\sqrt{\frac{\sqrt5}{k^3}}$	3.07769	$\sqrt{\frac{k^3}{\sqrt5}}$	0.324920
$\frac{\sqrt5}{k^3}$	9.47214	$\frac{k^3}{\sqrt5}$	0.105573	$\sqrt{\frac{\sqrt5}{k^5}}$	4.97980	$\sqrt{\frac{k^5}{\sqrt5}}$	0.200811
$\frac{\sqrt5}{k^4}$	15.3263	$\frac{k^4}{\sqrt5}$	0.065247	$\sqrt{\frac{\sqrt5}{k^7}}$	8.05750	$\sqrt{\frac{k^7}{\sqrt5}}$	0.124108
$\frac{\sqrt5}{k^5}$	24.7985	$\frac{k^5}{\sqrt5}$	0.040325	$\sqrt{k\sqrt5}$	1.17557	$\frac{1}{\sqrt{k\sqrt5}}$	0.850651
$\frac{\sqrt5}{k^6}$	40.1248	$\frac{k^6}{\sqrt5}$	0.024922	$\sqrt{k^3\sqrt5}$	0.726542	$\frac{1}{\sqrt{k^3\sqrt5}}$	1.37639
$k\sqrt5$	1.381966	$\frac{1}{k\sqrt5}$	0.723607	$\sqrt{k^5\sqrt5}$	0.449028	$\frac{1}{\sqrt{k^5\sqrt5}}$	2.22704
$k^2\sqrt5$	0.854100	$\frac{1}{k^2\sqrt5}$	1.17082	$\sqrt{k^7\sqrt5}$	0.277514	$\frac{1}{\sqrt{k^7\sqrt5}}$	3.60342
$k^3\sqrt5$	0.527872	$\frac{1}{k^3\sqrt5}$	1.89445	$\sqrt{\frac{\sqrt5}{3k}}$	1.09819	$\sqrt{\frac{3k}{\sqrt5}}$	0.910592
$k^4\sqrt5$	0.326237	$\frac{1}{k^4\sqrt5}$	3.06526	$\sqrt{\frac{3\sqrt5}{k}}$	3.29455	$\sqrt{\frac{k}{3\sqrt5}}$	0.303531
$k^5\sqrt5$	0.201625	$\frac{1}{k^5\sqrt5}$	4.95969	$\sqrt{3\sqrt5 k}$	2.03615	$\frac{1}{\sqrt{3\sqrt5 k}}$	0.491123
$k^6\sqrt5$	0.124611	$\frac{1}{k^6\sqrt5}$	8.02496	$\sqrt{3\sqrt5 k^3}$	1.25841	$\frac{1}{\sqrt{3\sqrt5 k^3}}$	0.794656
1 cm.	0.3937"	1"	2.540 cm.	$\sqrt{k}$	0.786151	$1/\sqrt{k}$	1.27202

k	0.618034	k^{-1}	1.618034
k^2	0.381966	k^{-2}	2.618034
k^3	0.236068	k^{-3}	4.236068
k^4	0.145898	k^{-4}	6.854102
k^5	0.090170	k^{-5}	11.090170
k^6	0.055728	k^{-6}	17.944272
k^7	0.034442	k^{-7}	29.034442
k^8	0.021286	k^{-8}	46.978714
k^9	0.013156	k^{-9}	76.013156
k^{10}	0.008130	k^{-10}	122.991870
$\sqrt2$	1.414214	$\frac{1}{\sqrt2}$	0.707107
$\sqrt3$	1.732051	$\frac{1}{\sqrt3}$	0.577350
$\sqrt5$	2.236068	$\frac{1}{\sqrt5}$	0.447213
$\sqrt6$	2.449490	$\frac{1}{\sqrt6}$	0.408248
$\sqrt{2/3}$	0.816498	$\sqrt{3/2}$	1.22474
$\sqrt{3/5}$	0.774598	$\sqrt{5/3}$	1.29099

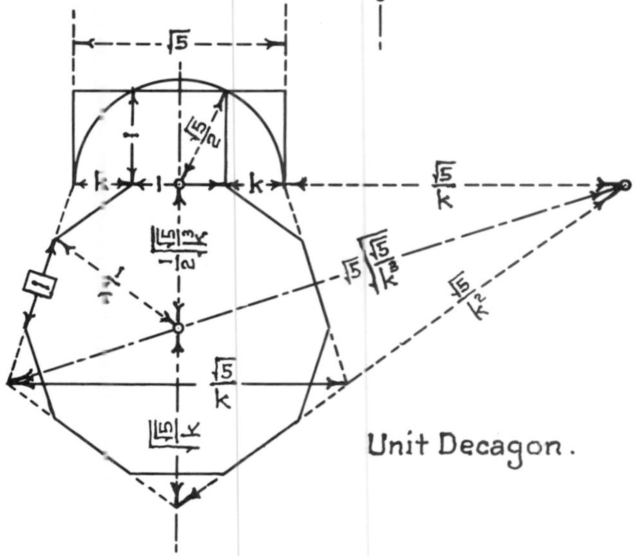

Unit Pentagon.

Unit Decagon.

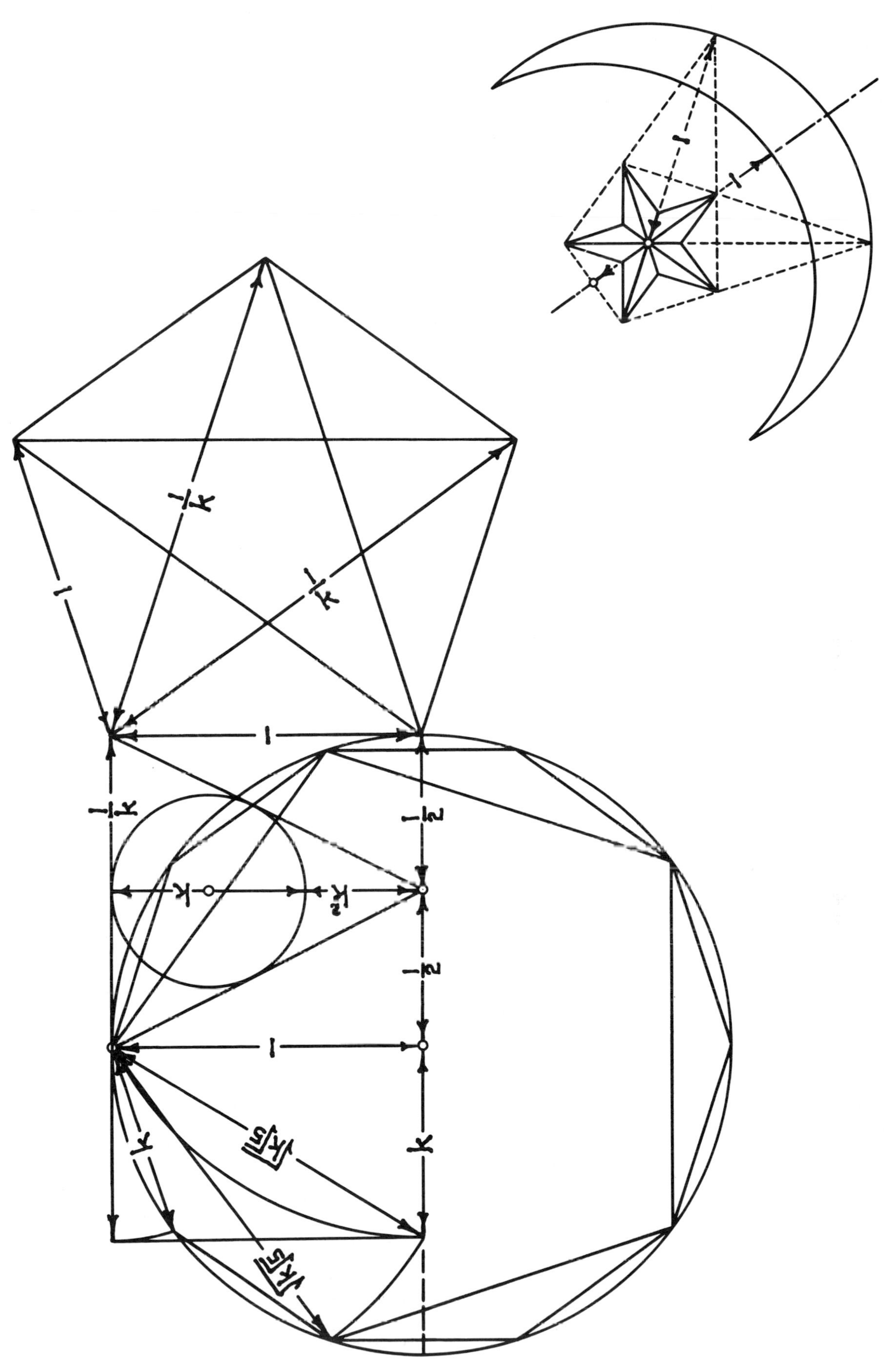

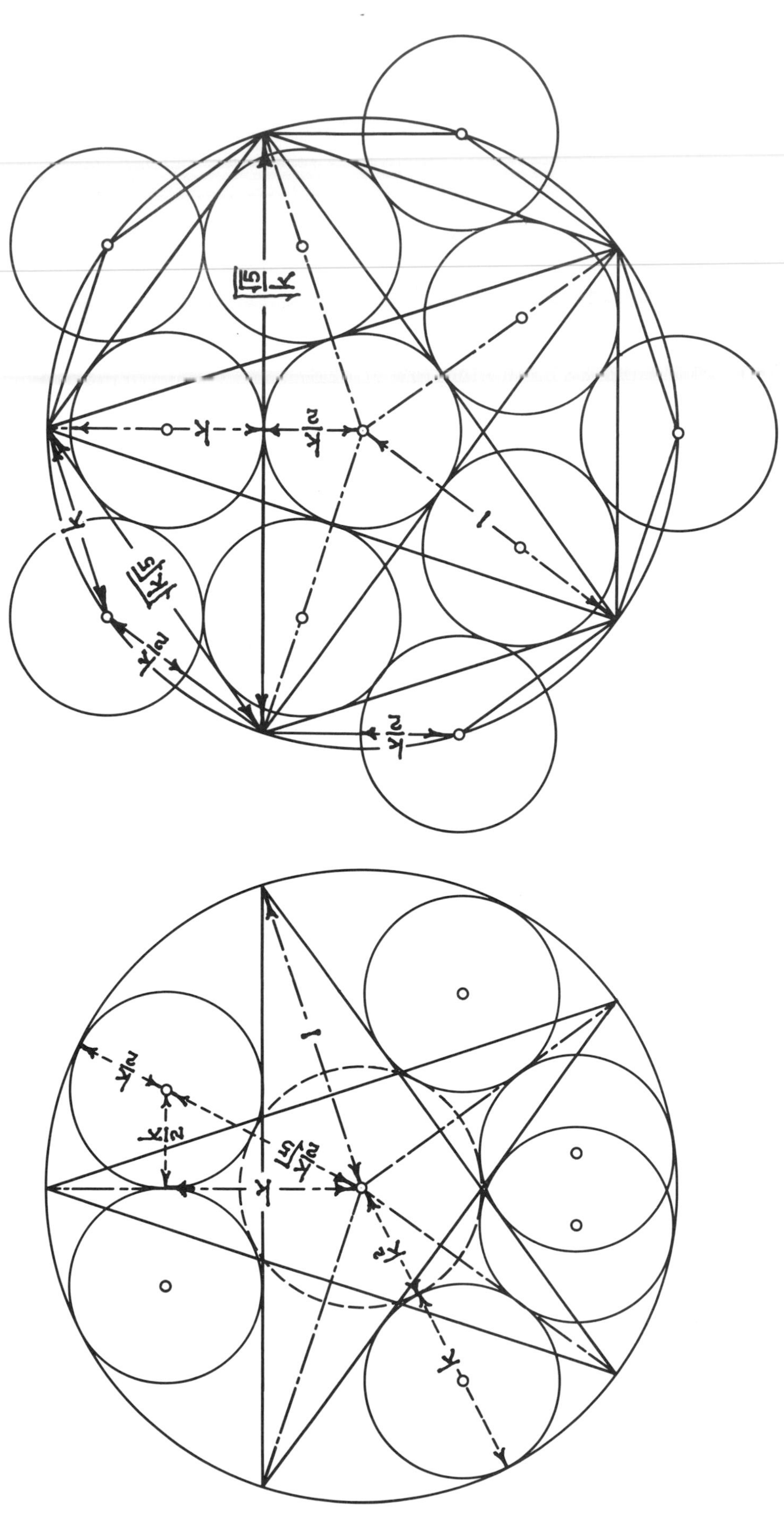

The Decagon.

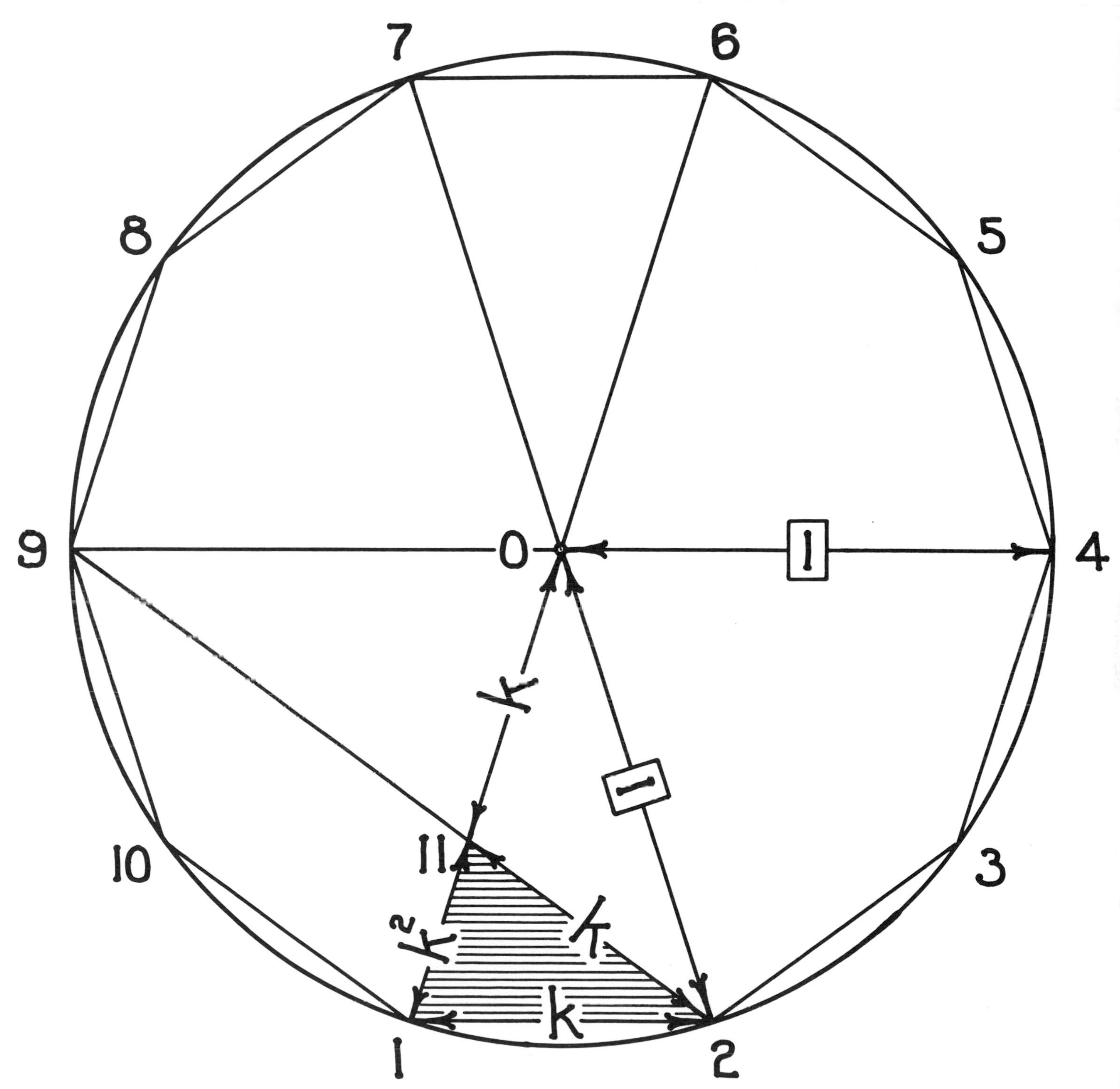

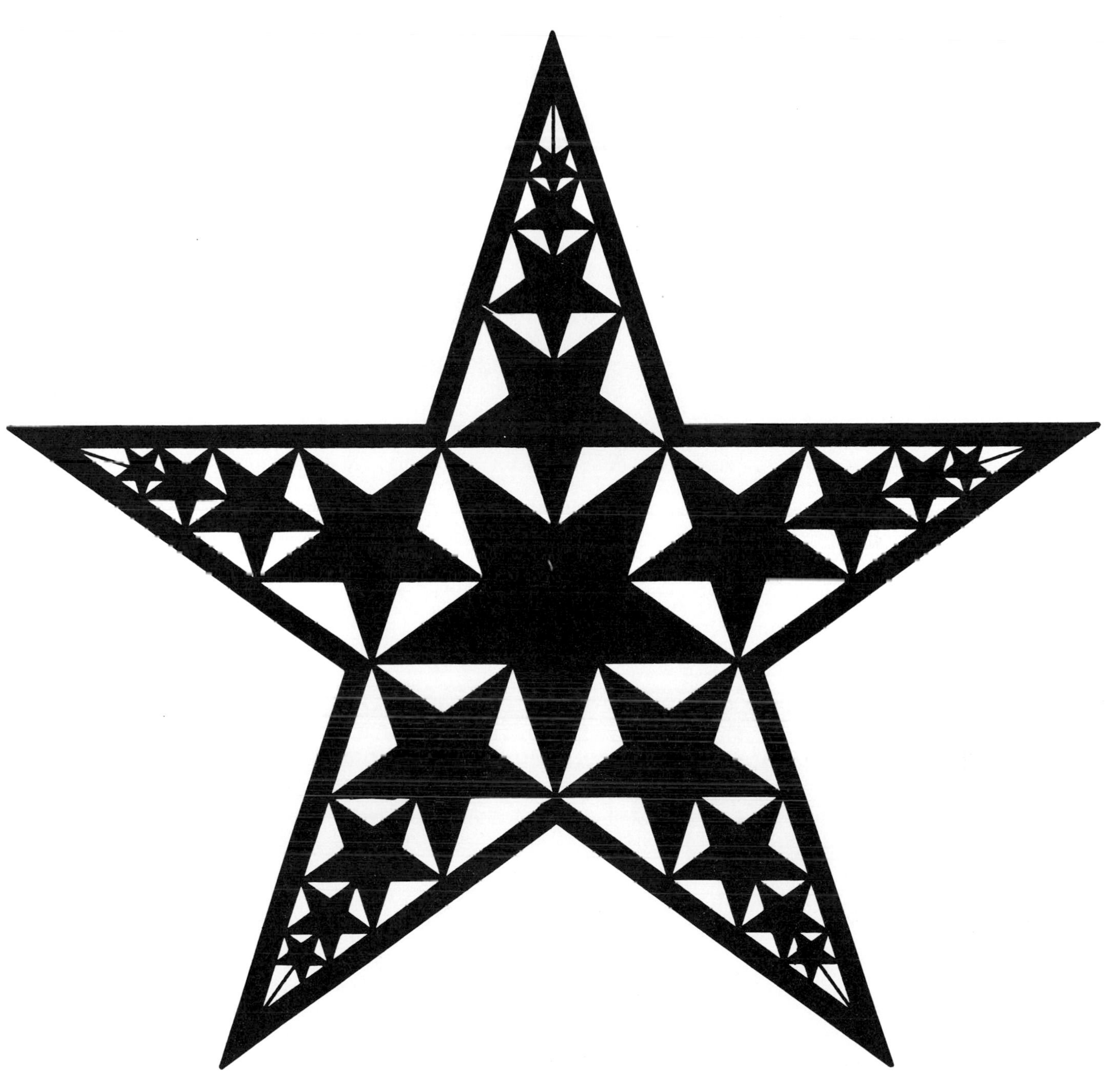

THE FIBONACCI QUARTERLY

FIBONACCI DRAWING BOARD

COLONEL ROBERT S. BEARD

It is in order to preface the work of the Fibonacci Drawing Board with something of the story of our emblem, The Fibonacci Star.

This star of 21 stars is a refinement of the beautiful star-pentagram commonly used to represent the heavenly bodies.

That star formed by the five diagonals of the regular pentagon was the emblem of the Pythagorean school of philosophy and mathematics. It was discovered by that organization somewhere around 500 B.C. It was probably the first emblem of any mathematical organization.

In time the pentagram or pentacle became credited with the magic power of warding off witches and demons and of insuring good health and good fortune somewhat akin to the power of the hex marks of the Pennsylvania Dutch.

Here are some pertinent quotations:

"They had their crystals I do know and rings and virgin parchment and their deadman's skulls. Their raven's wings, their lights and pentacles with characters," B. Johnson, Devil is an Ass.

"His shoes were marked with cross and shell. Upon his breast a pentacle," Scott Marmion.

"Sketching with slender pointed foot some figure like a wizard pentagram on garden gravel," Tennyson, The Brook.

The universal appeal of the pentagram to the imagination is demonstrated by its use in the design of the flags of many nations and also in its wide use as a symbol for hope, excellence, outstanding performance, rank and authority.

My United Nations flag design encircled a red cross with a wreath of pentagrams on a white field to symbolize world hope united around our willingness to help each other. No comment on how things are going.

The rank of our top military commanders has been designated by pentagram insignia ever since the American Revolution.

"In 1780 Major Generals were ordered to wear two epaulettes with two stars each,' while Brigadier Generals had one star, and later when the rank of Lieutenant General was established for the Commander-in-Chief, Washington, three stars were prescribed for him. This was the commencement of our rank insignia." Orders, Decorations and Insignia, Military and Civil, Colonel Robert E. Wyllie, G. P. Putnam's Sons.

World War I produced our first four-star general, while World War II furnished our top admirals and generals with clusters of five pentagrams.

No doubt the foreign devils are being kept away from our shores by the pentacles flashing on the uniforms of our military leaders as they circulate around our great Pentagon Building on the banks of the Potomac.

The mathematics of the Fibonacci Star will be discussed in proper order at a later date. However, it might be mentioned here that it is proportioned in 10 successive terms of a Fibonacci series, the powers of the golden section or golden mean.

Perhaps you'll tolerate the winding up of this story with the second verse of Cowper's poem, "The Golden Mean," which is a translation from the Latin of Horace.

"He that holds fast the golden mean
And lives contentedly between
The little and the great,
Feels not the wants that pinch the poor
Nor plagues that haunt the rich man's door
Embittering all his state."

Have your pencils sharpened next time and get ready to go to work.

STAR GEOMETRY

Pythagoras, Fibonacci and Beard
R.S. Beard

The diagonal of the pentagon is made the unit of length in the upper left circle of the accompanying drawings. K is the ratio of the side of the pentagon to its diagonal.

Line 4.3 is the short side of triangle 1-4-3 and the long side of triangle 3-4-6.

Line 4.6 is the short side of triangle 3-4-6 and the long side of triangle 4-6-7.

Therefore the sides of these three similar isosceles triangles are respectively 1 and K, K and K^2, K^2 and K^3. Lines 1-6 and 3-6 have the same length, K, as they are the equal sides of the isosceles triangle 1-3-6. Diagonal 1-4 of unit length is thus divided into segments K and K^2, that is $K^2 + K = 1$.

It follows from this equation that

$$K = \frac{1}{2}\sqrt{5} - \frac{1}{2} = 0.618034$$

and that $K^n = K^{n+1} + K^{n+2}$.

Since each power of K is the sum of its next two higher powers, these powers form a Fibonacci series when arranged in their descending order.

The radius is made the unit of length in the upper right circle. Similar triangles divide radius O-1 into segments K and K^2. This construction demonstrates that each side of a regular decagon has the golden section ratio to the radius of its circumscribing circle.

The right triangle in the lower circle has sides of 1, 1/2 and $1/2\sqrt{5}$. The dimension K with the value of $1/2\sqrt{5} - 1/2$ is the length of the side of the inscribed decagon.

The leaf shaped figure shows one simple way to construct a five pointed star of a given width.

The Fibonacci star of stars is proportioned in the ten successive powers of the golden section from K^0 to K^9.

AB is made the unit of length or K^0.

AC, the side of the bounding pentagon has the length of K.

The side of each ray of the master star is K^2 long.

The bounding pentagon of the central star has sides of K^3 length.

Since one diagonal of each of the smaller stars is a side of the bounding pentagon of the next larger star all of the corresponding dimensions of these successive stars are in golden section ratio.

The bounding pentagons of the successive stars have sides of K^4, K^5, K^6 and K^7 respectively.

The rays of the smallest stars have K^8 edges and base widths of K^9.

This figure can be used to demonstrate that any power of the golden section K^n, is the sum of all of its higher powers from K^{n+2} to K^∞.

The lines connecting the tips of the central star and the centers of the five next smaller stars form a decagon.

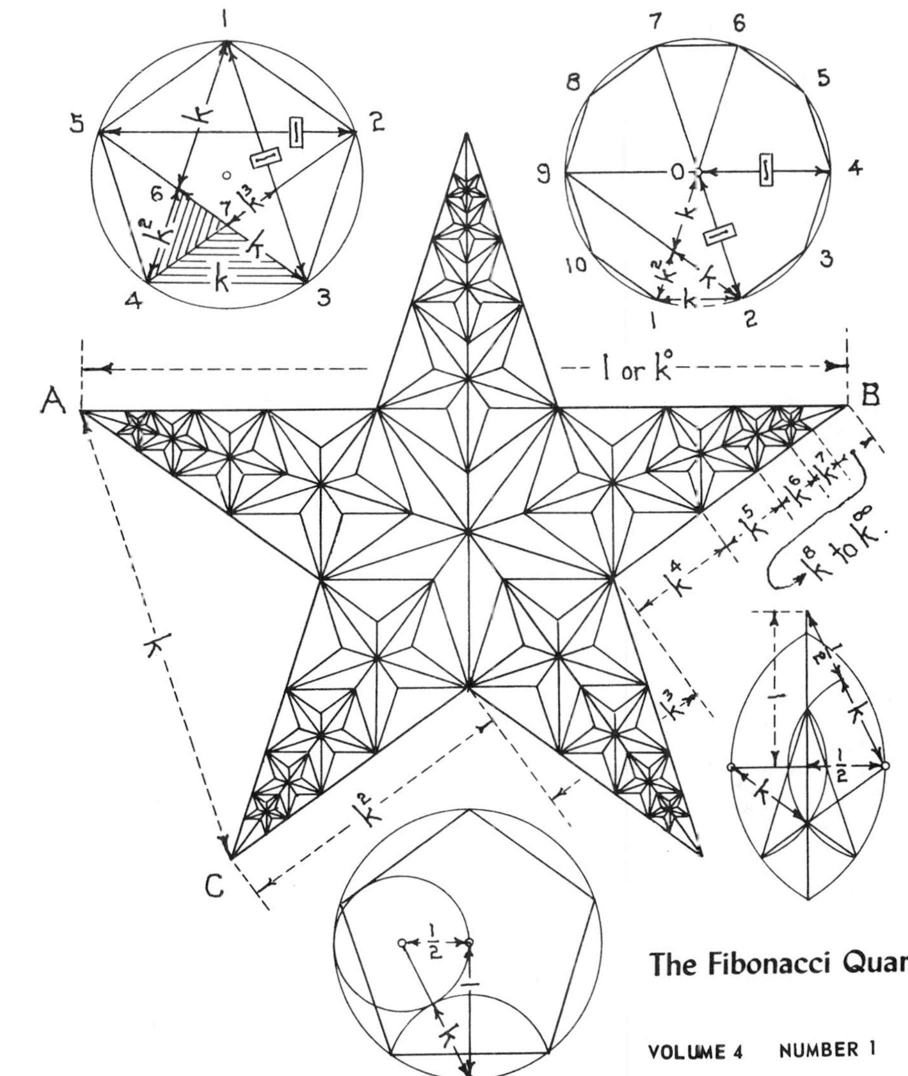

THE FIVE STAR INSIGNE.

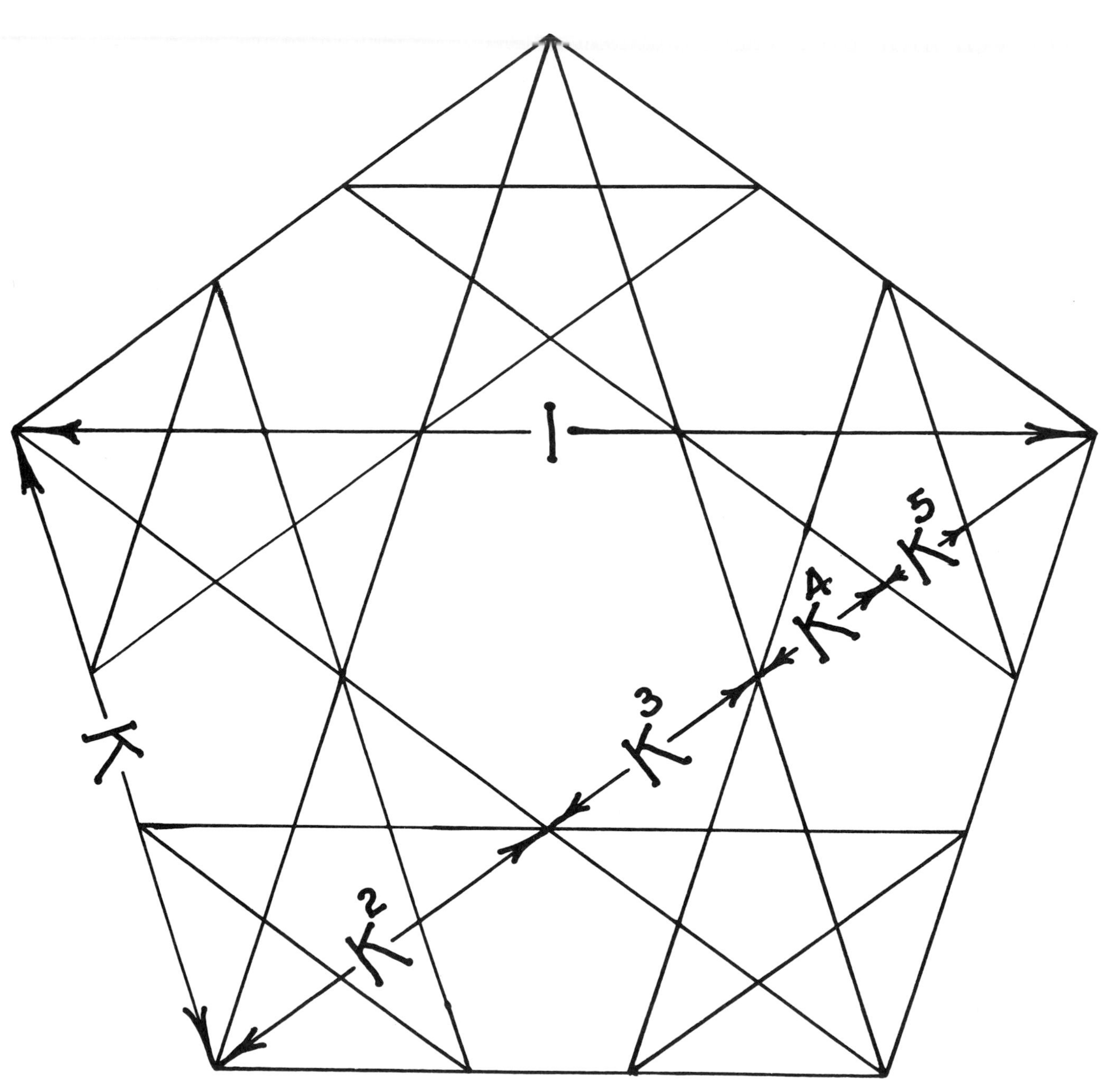

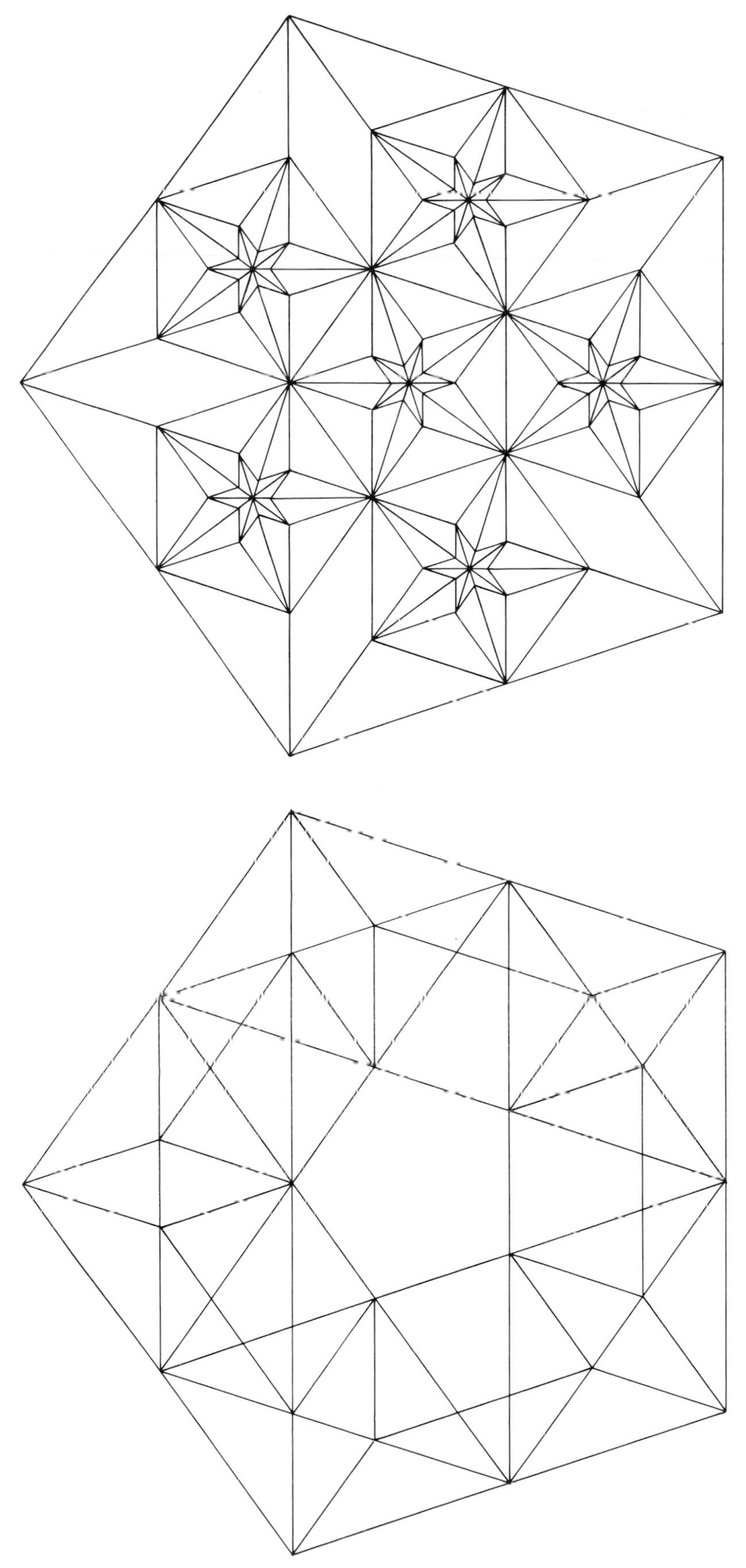

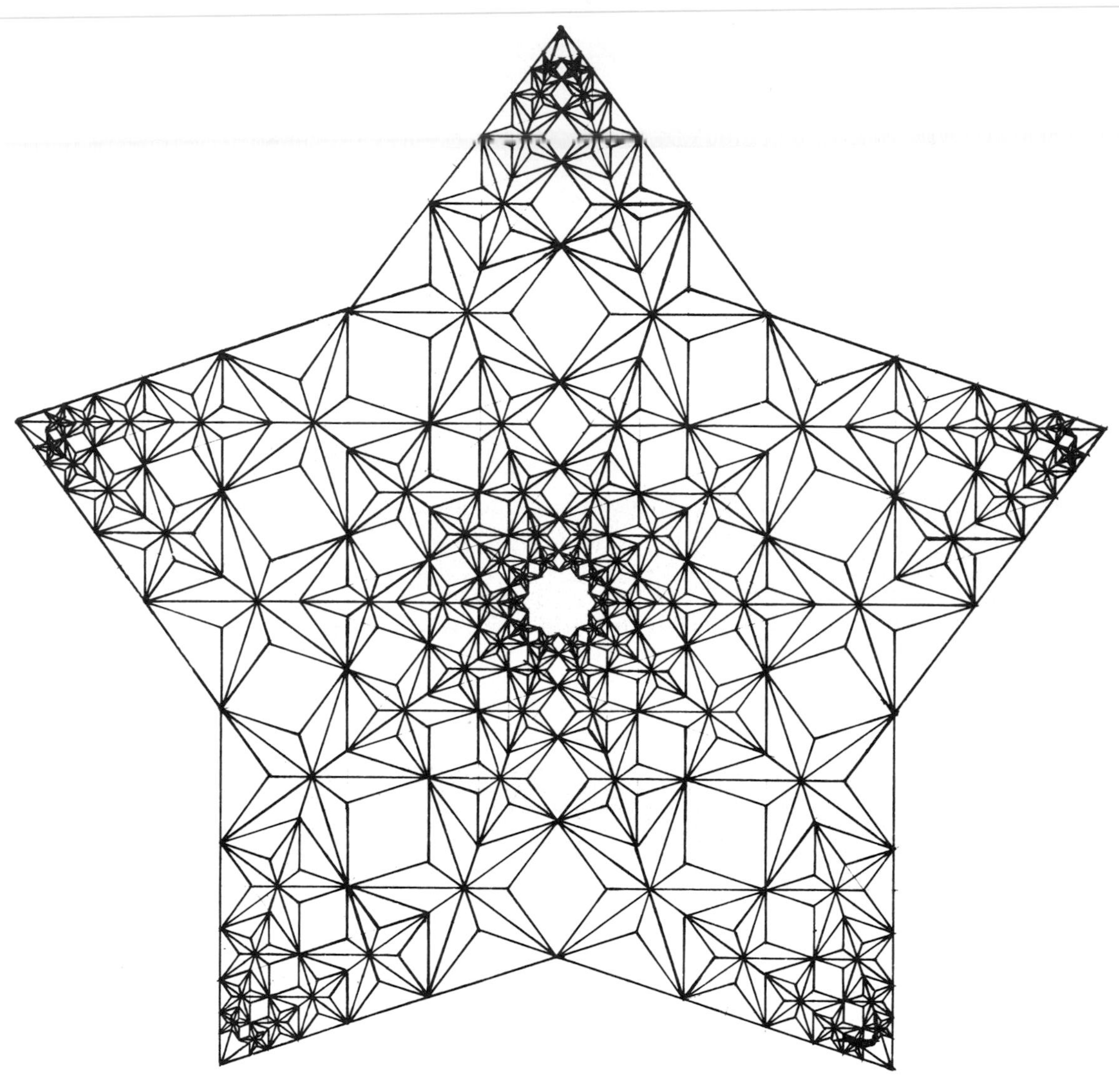

STAR OF TWIN STARS.

Robert S. Beard. April 14, 1947.

Circumscribing circle has radius of Wk^{-2} or 2.618034 W, where W is width of largest of unit stars. Chord for arc of $\frac{1}{10}$ of this circle is Wk^{-1} or 1.618034 W.

Crotch points of star are located in circle with radius of Wk^{-1} or 1.618034W.

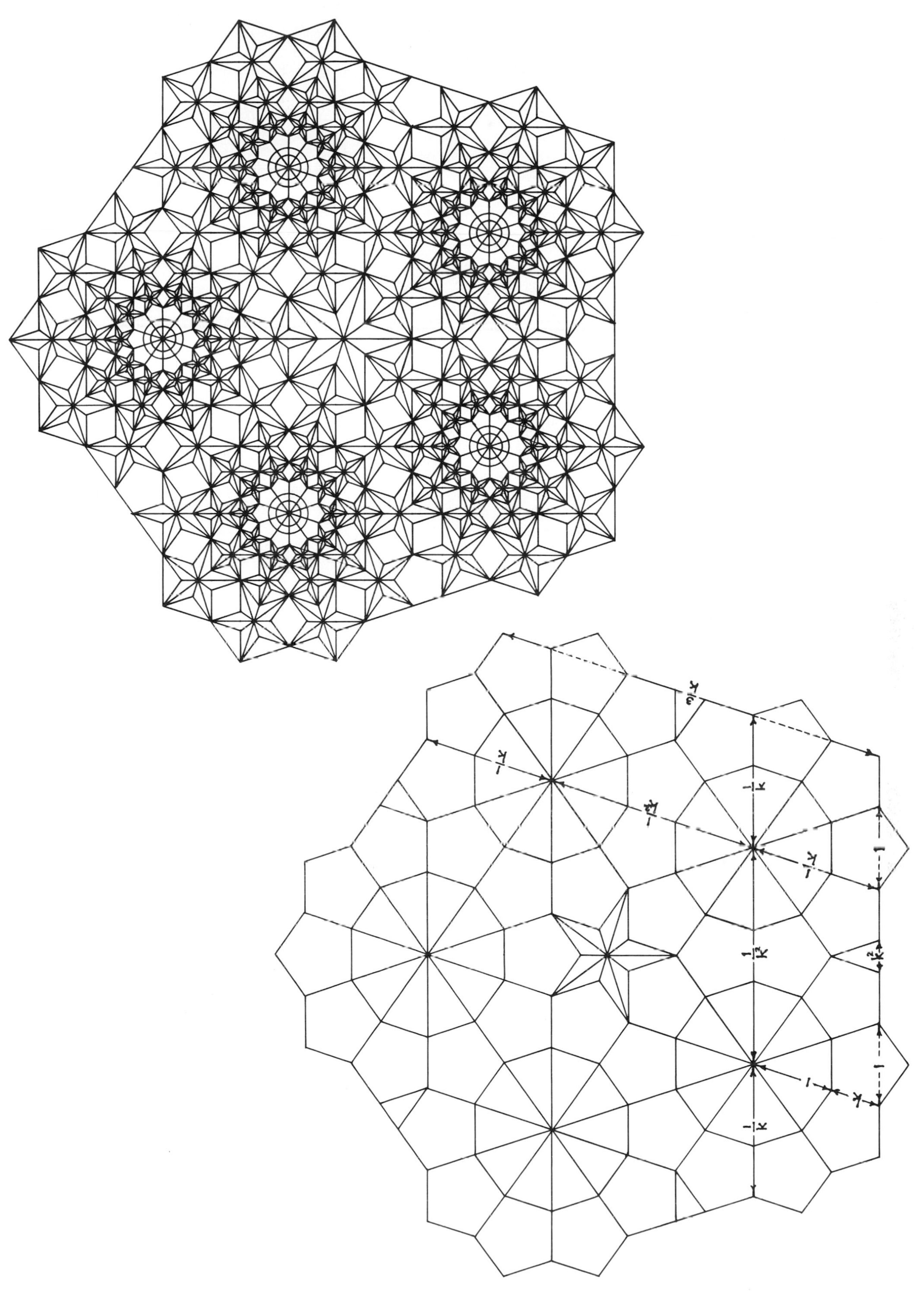

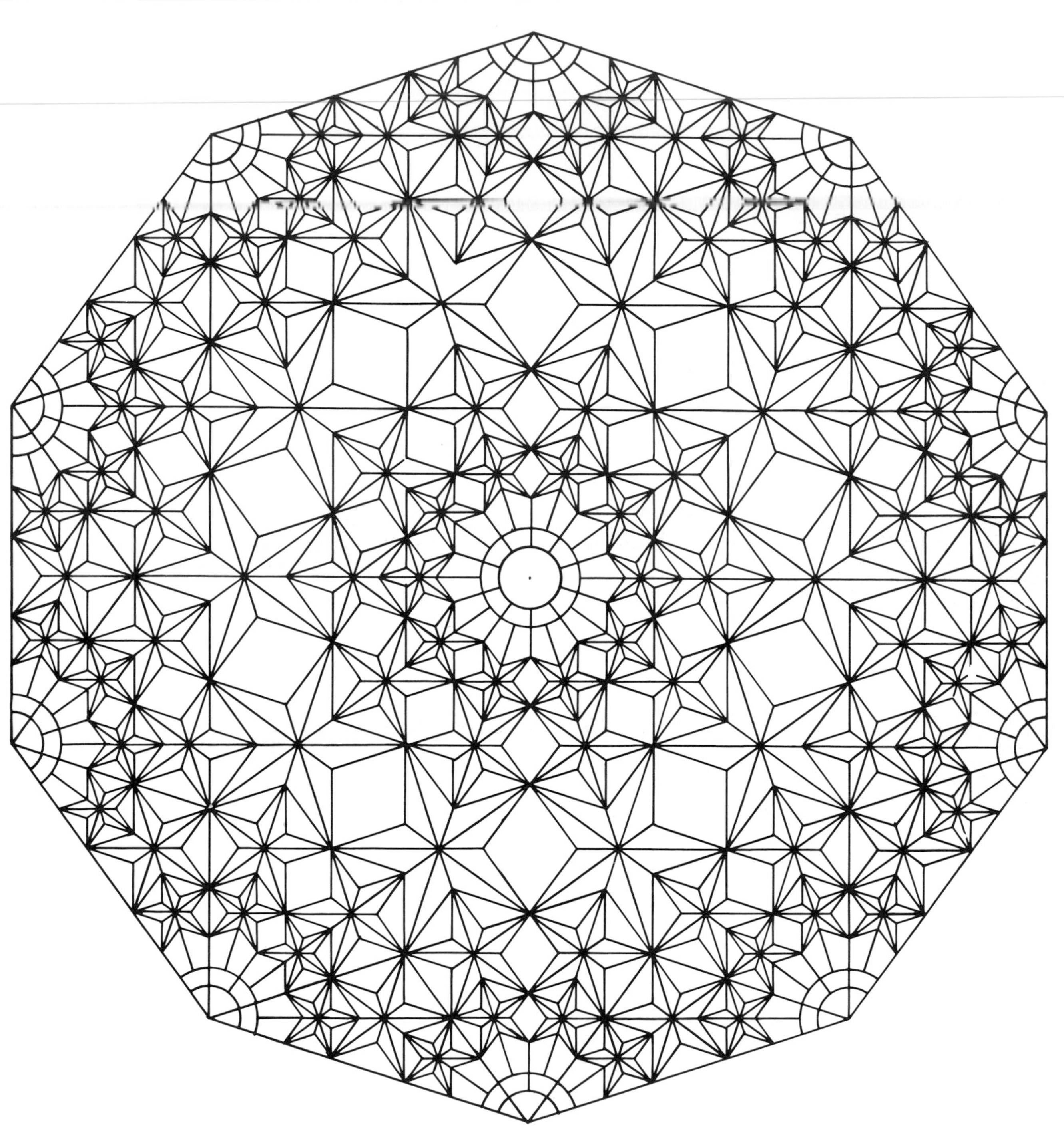

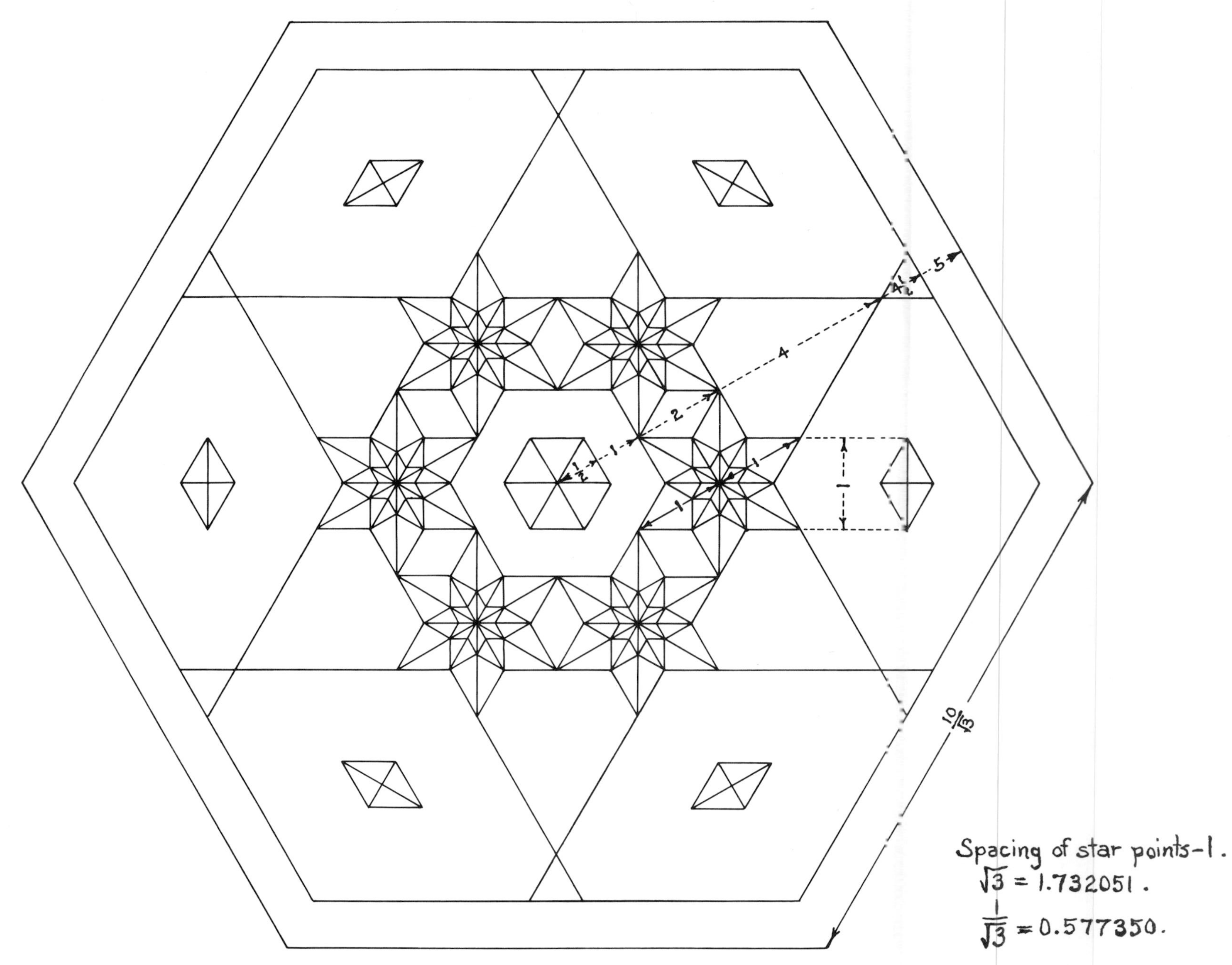
Spacing of star points-1.
√3 = 1.732051.
1/√3 = 0.577350.

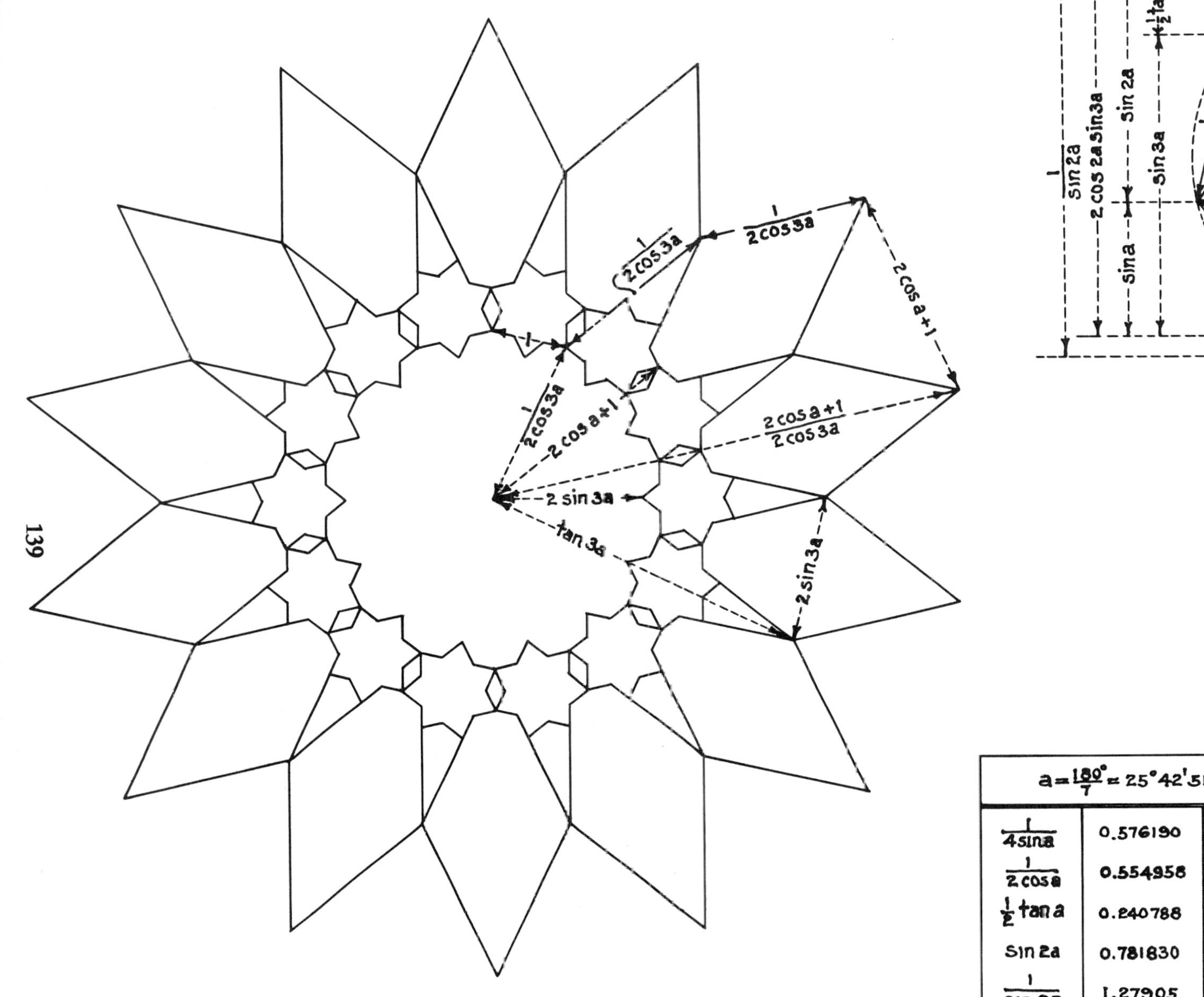

$a=\frac{180°}{7}=25°42'51\frac{3}{7}''$.		$2a=51°25'42\frac{6}{7}''$.		$3a=77°08'34\frac{2}{7}''$.	
$\frac{1}{4\sin a}$	0.576190	$2\cos 2a$	1.246980	$\frac{1}{2}\tan 3a$	2.190645
$\frac{1}{2\cos a}$	0.554958	$\frac{1}{2\cos 2a}$	0.801939	$2\cos 2a\sin 3a$	1.21571
$\frac{1}{2}\tan a$	0.240788	$\sin 3a$	0.974929	$4\cos 2a\sin 3a$	2.43142
$\sin 2a$	0.781830	$2\sin 3a$	1.949858	$2\cos a+1$	2.801944
$\frac{1}{\sin 2a}$	1.27905	$\frac{1}{2\cos 3a}$	2.246980	$\frac{2\cos a+1}{2\cos 3a}$	6.29590
$\frac{1}{2\sin 2a}$	0.639525	$\tan 3a$	4.38129	$\frac{\tan 3a-\tan a}{2}$	1.949858

$\sin a = 0.433884$.

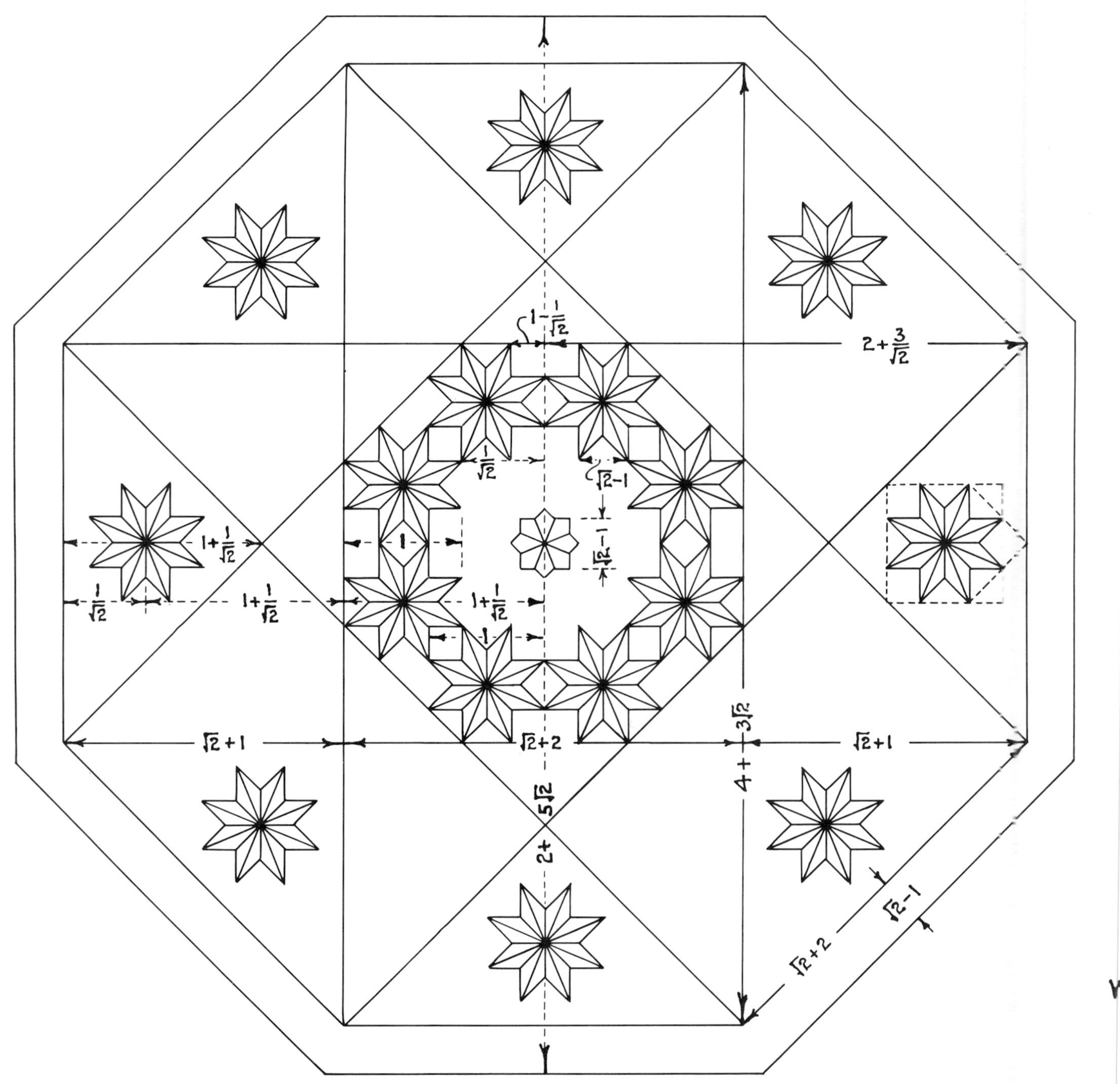

Width of stars – 1.

$\sqrt{2} = 1.4\,4214.$

$\frac{1}{\sqrt{2}} = 0.707107.$

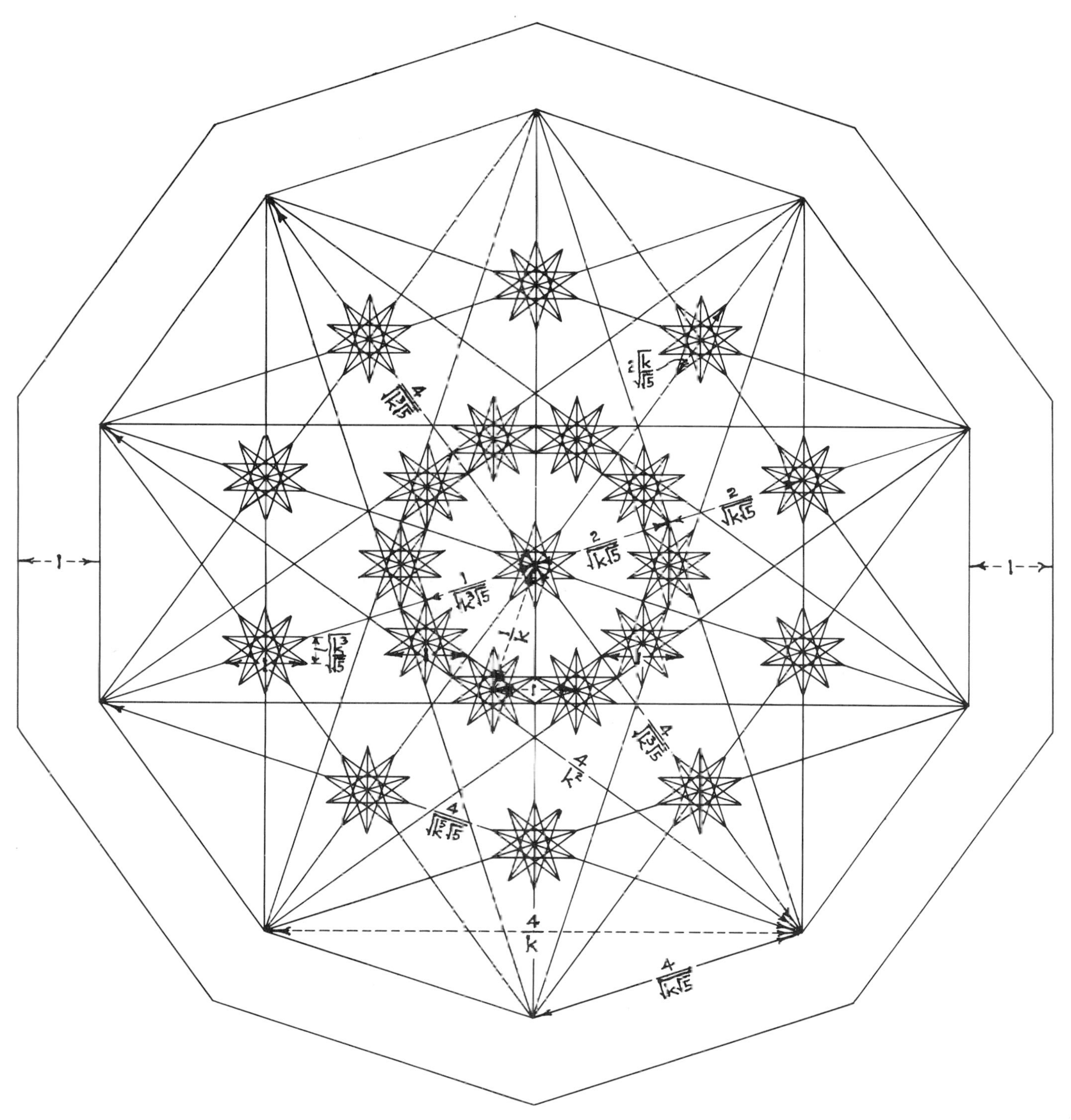

DIMENSIONS.	
k	0.618034
$\frac{1}{k}$	1.618034
$\frac{4}{k}$	6.472136
$\frac{4}{k^2}$	10.472136
$\sqrt{\frac{k}{\sqrt{5}}}$	0.525730
$\sqrt{\frac{k^3}{\sqrt{5}}}$	0.324920
$\frac{1}{2}\sqrt{k\sqrt{5}}$	0.58778
$\frac{2}{\sqrt{k\sqrt{5}}}$	1.701302
$\frac{4}{\sqrt{k\sqrt{5}}}$	3.402604
$\frac{1}{\sqrt{k^3\sqrt{5}}}$	1.37639
$\frac{4}{\sqrt{k^3\sqrt{5}}}$	5.50556
$\frac{4}{\sqrt{k^5\sqrt{5}}}$	8.90816

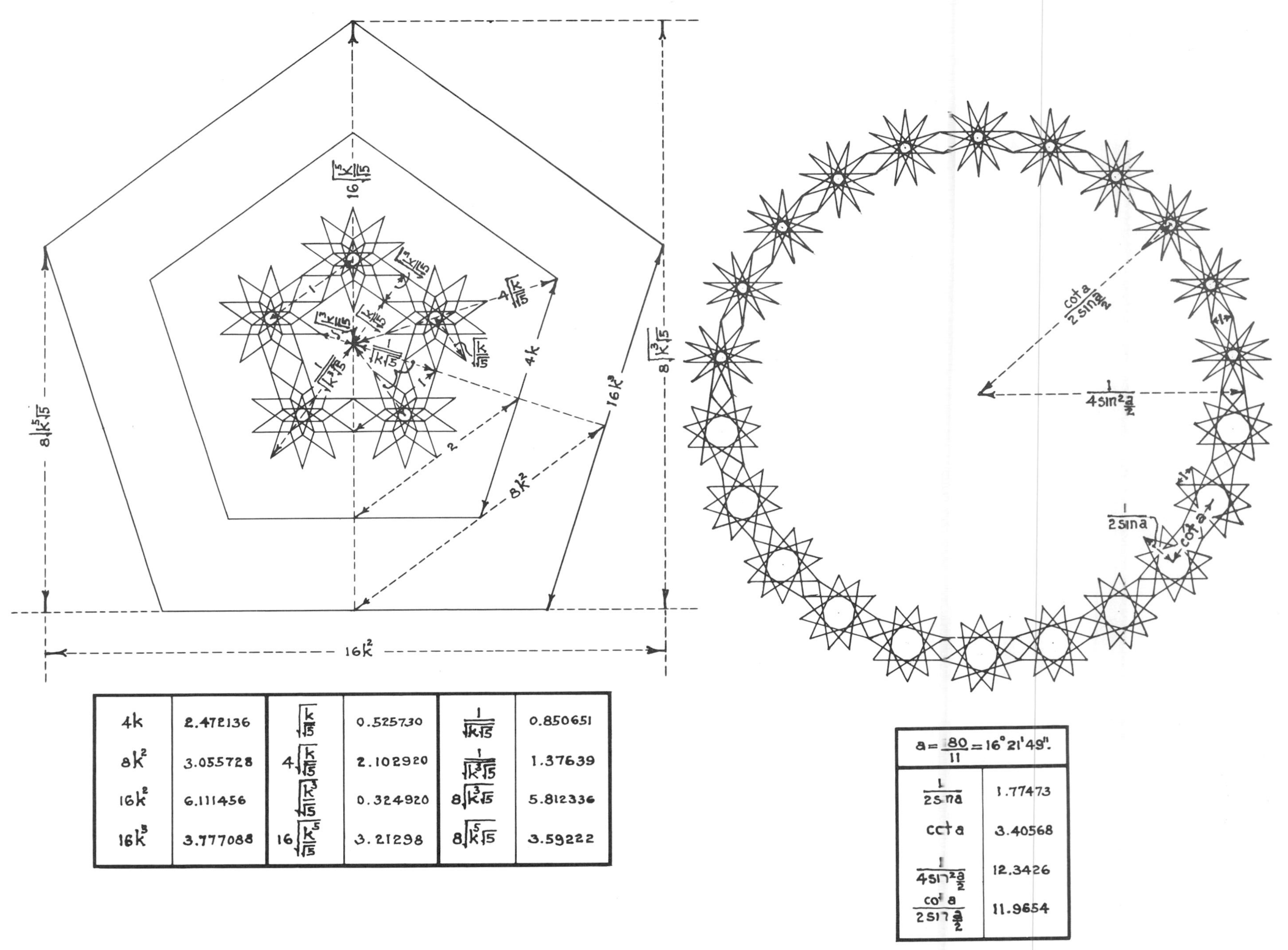

$4k$	2.472136	$\sqrt{\frac{k}{\sqrt5}}$	0.525730	$\frac{1}{\sqrt{k\sqrt5}}$	0.850651
$8k^2$	3.055728	$4\sqrt{\frac{k}{\sqrt5}}$	2.102920	$\frac{1}{\sqrt{k^3\sqrt5}}$	1.37639
$16k^2$	6.111456	$\sqrt{\frac{k^3}{\sqrt5}}$	0.324920	$8\sqrt{k^3\sqrt5}$	5.812336
$16k^3$	3.777088	$16\sqrt{\frac{k^5}{\sqrt5}}$	3.21298	$8\sqrt{k^5\sqrt5}$	3.59222

$a = \frac{180}{11} = 16°21'49''$.	
$\frac{1}{2\sin a}$	1.77473
$\cot a$	3.40568
$\frac{1}{4\sin^2\frac{a}{2}}$	12.3426
$\frac{\cot a}{2\sin\frac{a}{2}}$	11.9654

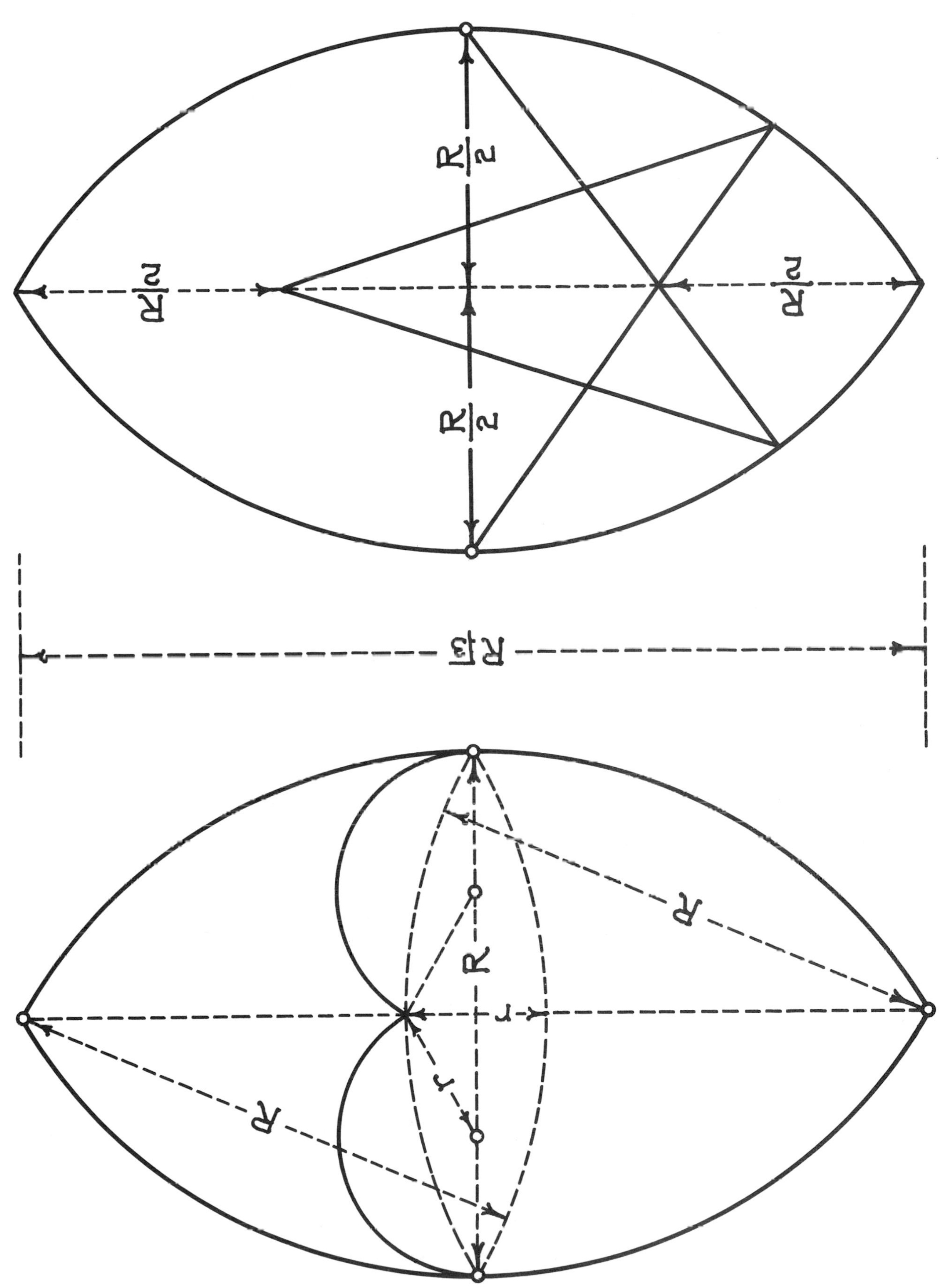

R/2
R/2
R/2
R/2
R√3
R
R
R
r
r

THE STAR SPANGLED HEART.

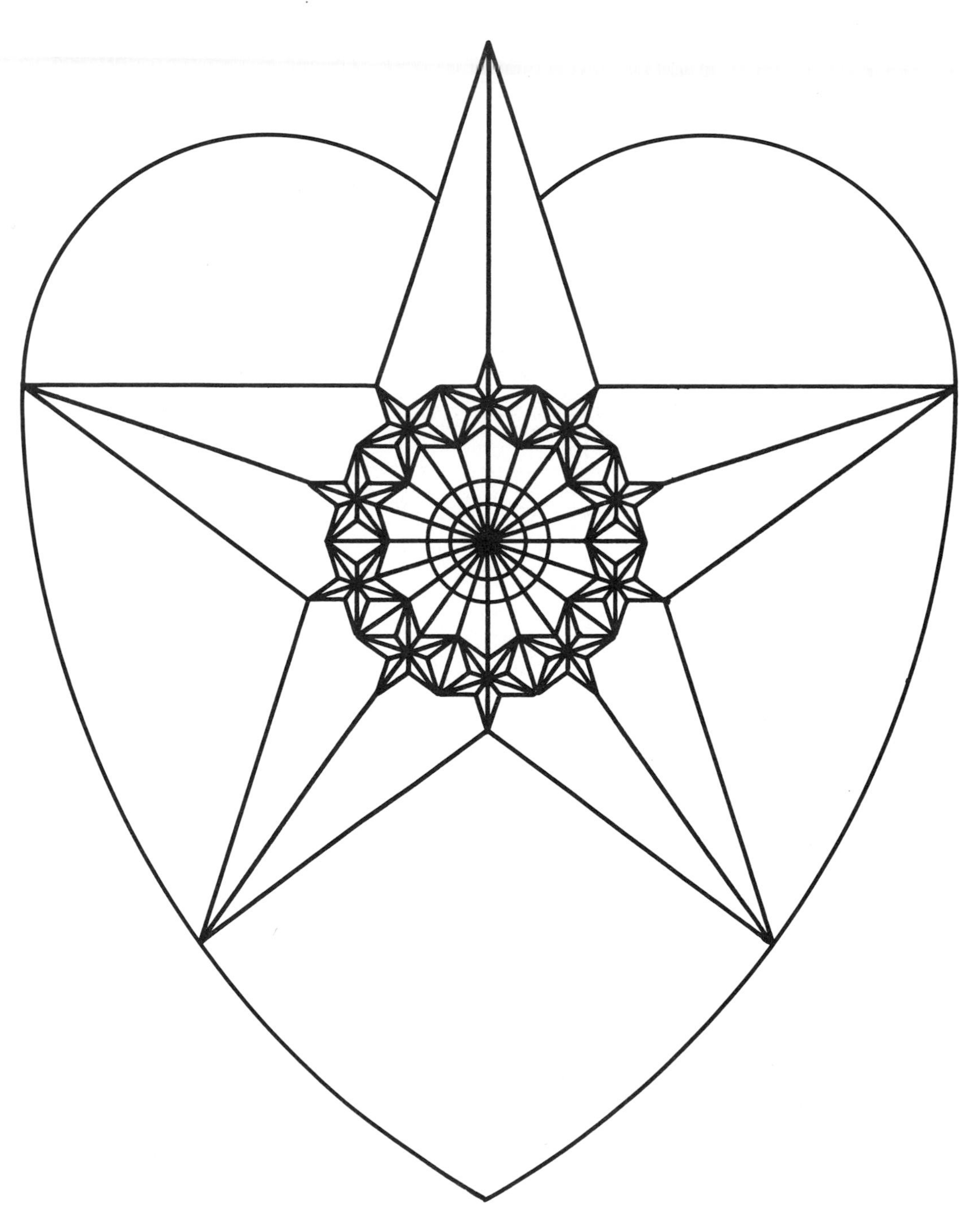

THE FIBONACCI DRAWING BOARD
DESIGN OF THE GREAT PYRAMID OF GIZEH

Col. R. S. Beard
Berkeley, Calif.

The comments on the Great Pyramid of Gizeh by Herodotus (484 to 424 B.C.) contained the statement that "The base was a square. The base side was 800 feet. The height was equal."

Apparently some student of the dimensions of this pyramid has interpreted this 'obscure' statement to mean that the square of the vertical height of the pyramid is equal to the area of each of its triangular faces.

Such an imaginative interpretation is not acceptable evidence. It also credits the Egyptians of 3000 B.C. with familiarity with the golden section. However, the facts fit the theory remarkably well.

The elevation of the face triangles of the pyramid is made the unit of measure in the accompanying cross section of the pyramid. Let k symbolize the golden section ratio of $\frac{1}{2}\sqrt{5} - \frac{1}{2}$.

If the square of the vertical height of the pyramid equals the area of one triangular face, each such face is a golden rectangle that has been halved on one diagonal and rejoined on its long sides. The base of the pyramid is then a 2k x 2k square and it has an altitude of $\sqrt{k}$. Each quarter section of the 2 x 2k golden rectangle in the sketch has the area of one triangular face. The inscribed ellipse has one focus at the apex of the pyramid. A circle of radius 1 is centered on the base. The inscribed regular decagon has sides of k length. The sides of the inscribed regular pentagon has sides of the same length as the sloping edges of the pyramid.

Such relationships would certainly have appealed to these Egyptian masters of practical geometry.

The Great Pyramid is now about 750 ft. square at the base. It is 451 ft. high and has a small flat deck on top. Sir William Mathew Flanders Petrie made an exceptionally accurate survey of the pyramid in the early 1880's. On the basis of his painstaking studies, he concluded that the original base of the pyramid was 755.73 ft. square and that its original height was 481.33 ft.

Under the Herodotus design, a base of 755.73 ft. would correspond to the 2k dimension in the drawing. This would make the height of the pyramid

$$\frac{755.73}{2\sqrt{k}}$$

or 480.65 ft.

Surprisingly the dimensions of the pyramid conform equally well to a second and a third theory as to its design.

A widely held second theory makes the height of the pyramid equal to the radius of the circle that has a circumference equal to the perimeter of the base of the pyramid.

$$\frac{4 \times 755.73}{2\pi} = 481.11$$

Sir William Petrie himself was thoroughly convinced that the Egyptians constructed the pyramid with a height-to-width-of-base ratio of seven to eleven.

$$\frac{7}{11} \times 755.73 = 480.92 .$$

Herodotus reports that 100,000 men labored for 30 years to construct this gigantic exhibit of personal egotism. This massive structure has probably settled more than the variations in these computed heights. Nobody will ever know its true original height and early Egyptian knowledge of the golden section remains unconfirmed So roll the dice and choose your own theory.

REFERENCES

1. J. E. Powell, A Lexicon to Herodotus, Cambridge (England) 1938, x + 392.
2. James R. Newman, The World of Mathematics, Vol. 1, p. 10, Simon and Schuster, N. Y., 1956.
3. "The Geometry of the Pentagon and the Golden Section," The Mathematics Teacher, Jan. 1948.
4. Sir William M. F. Petrie, Seventy Years in Archeology.

* * * * *

THE GREAT PYRAMID.

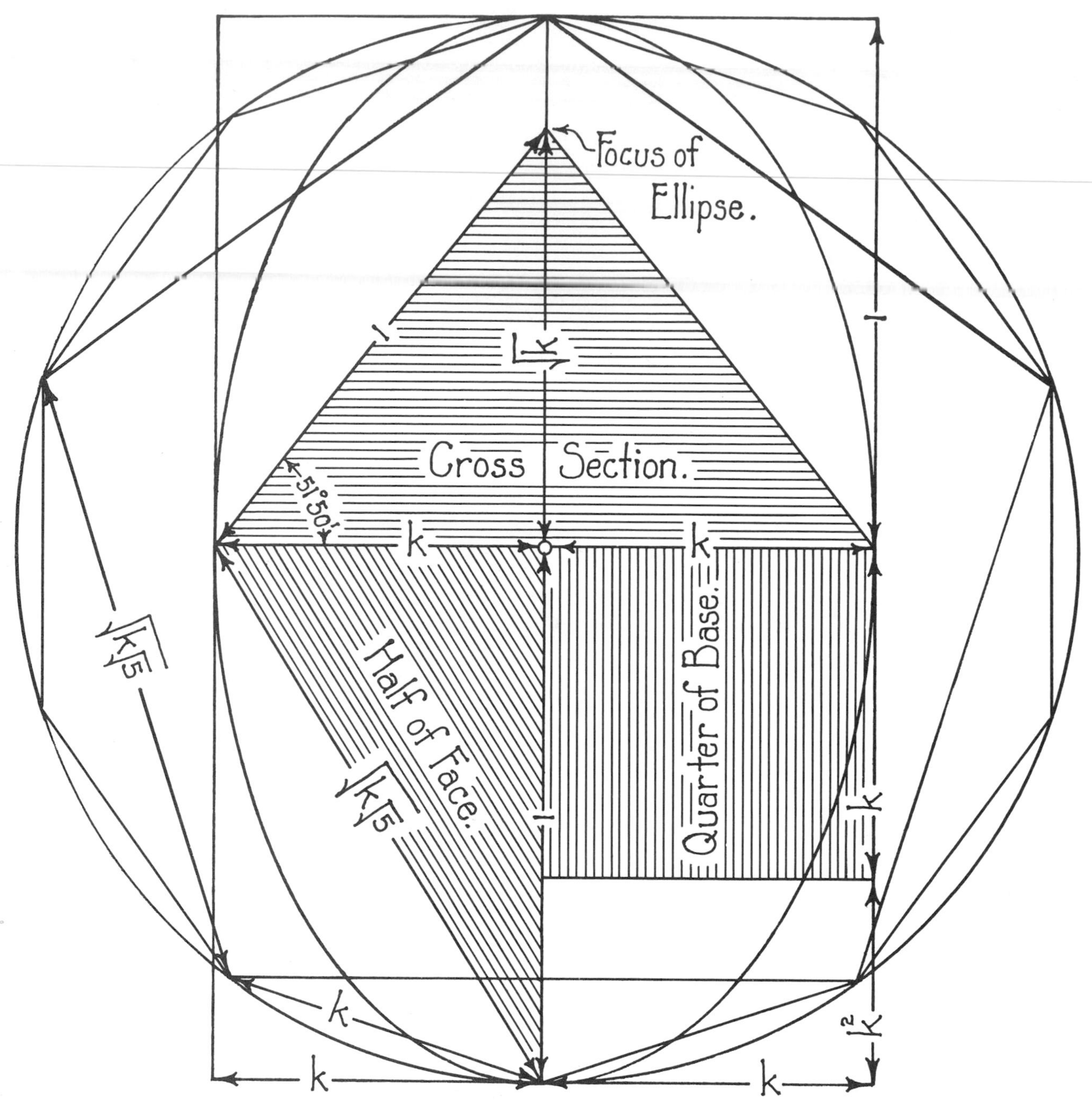

Item Intact.- Feet.		Slant Height Ratio.
Height. –	481.33	$\sqrt{k} = 0.786151$
* Base. –	$(755.73)^2$	$(2k)^2 = (1.236068)^2$
* Slant Height. –	611.93	$\sqrt{k\sqrt{5}} = 1.175570$

$k = \frac{1}{2}\sqrt{5} - \frac{1}{2} = 0.618034$ *

Square of Height $= (481.33)^2 =$ 231679.

Face Triangle $= \frac{1}{2} \times 611.93 \times 755.73 =$ 231229.

* $\frac{377.87}{611.93} = 0.6175$ $\frac{377.87}{481.33} = 0.7851$

THE K CIRCLE GRID.

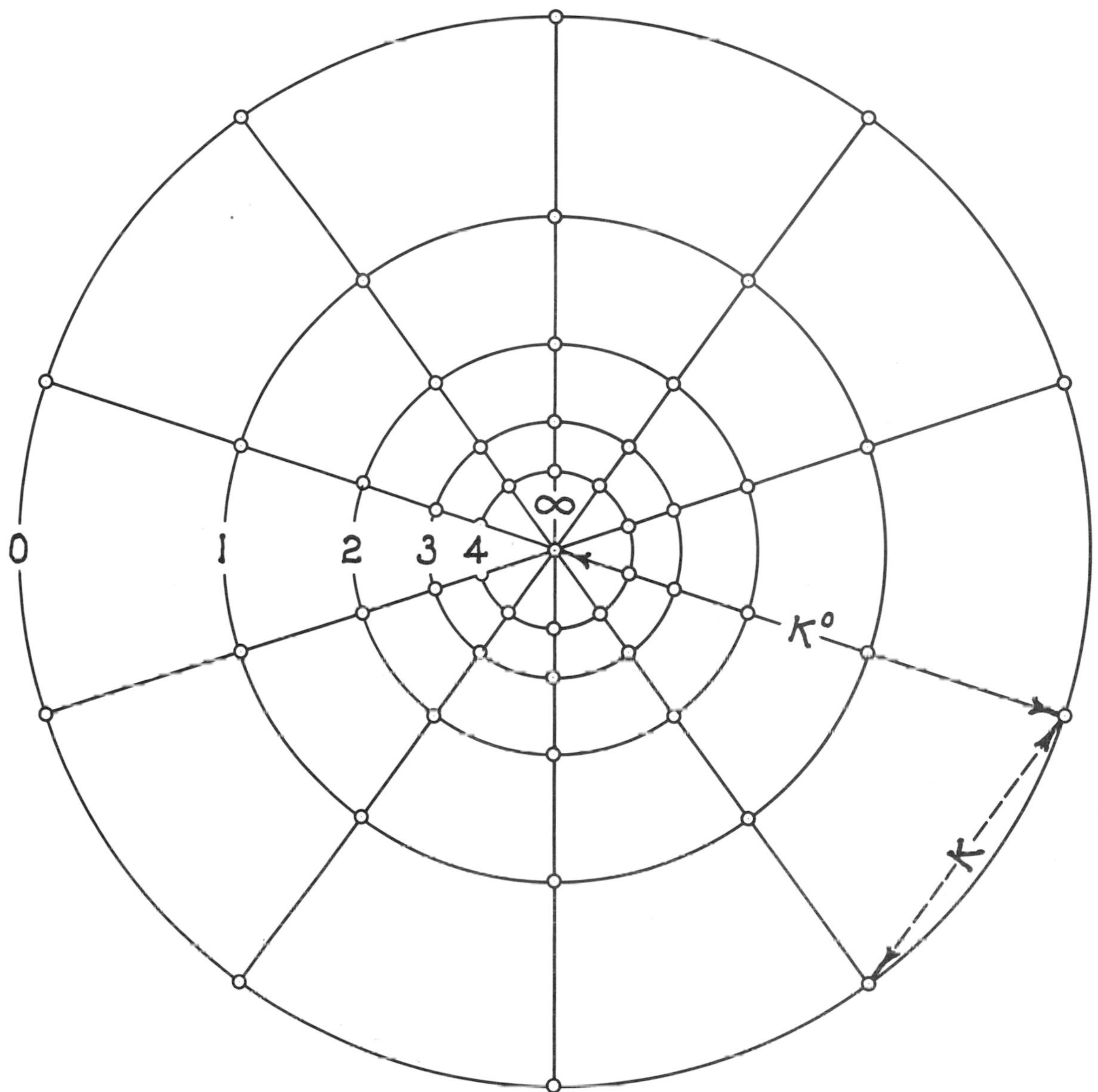

Circle 0 has a radius of k^0 or unity. Circles 1,2,3 and 4 have radii of k^1, k^2, k^3 and k^4 respectively. $k = \frac{1}{2}\sqrt{5} - \frac{1}{2} = 0.618034$.

All arcs in the k circle designs are centered on the intersections of the ten equally spaced radii with the numbered circles. A two figure number, np, on a k circle design means that ten arcs having the p circle radius are centered on circle n.

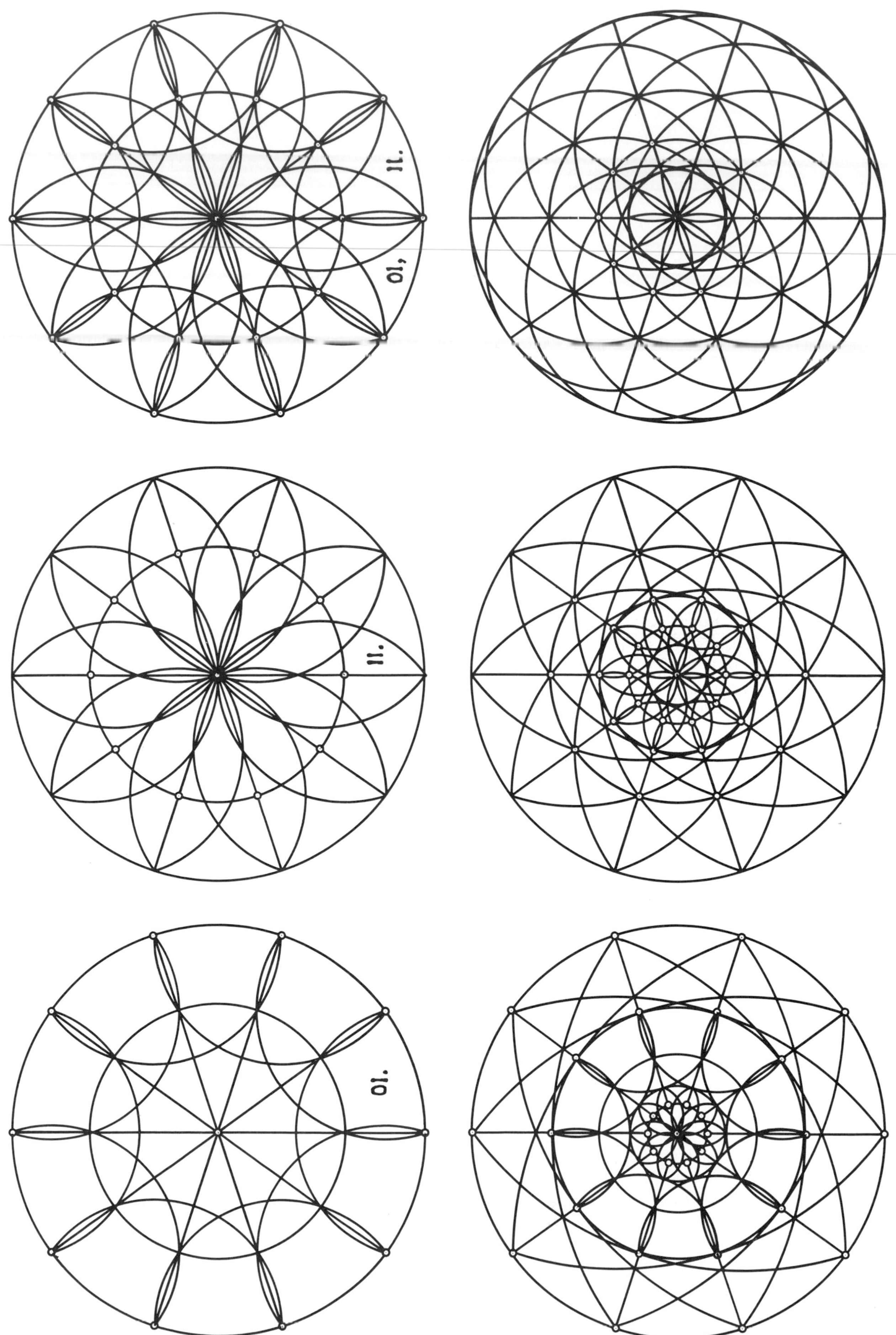
11.
10.
11.
10.

section v

CONICS & CURVES

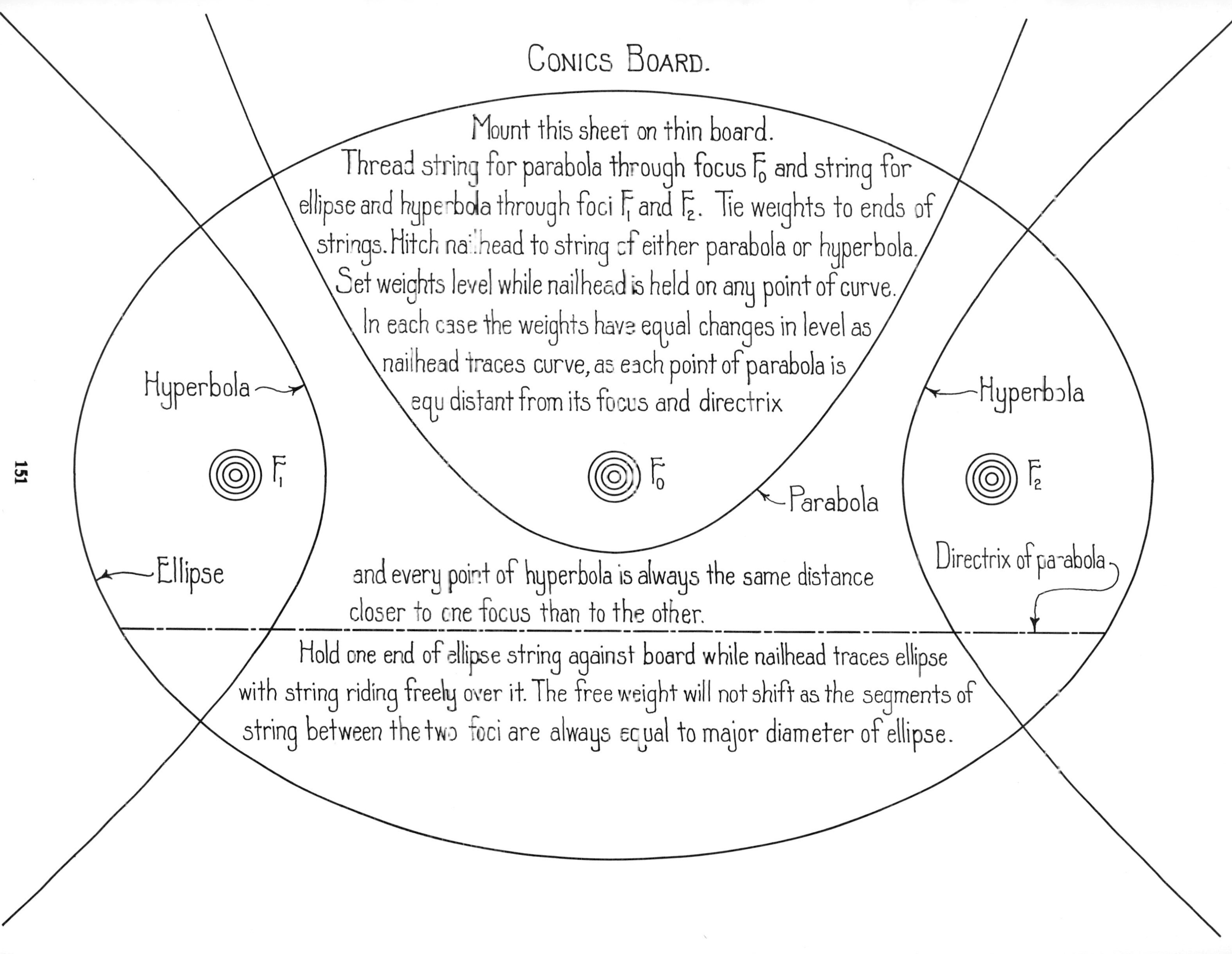
Conics Board.
Mount this sheet on thin board.
Thread string for parabola through focus F_0 and string for ellipse and hyperbola through foci F_1 and F_2. Tie weights to ends of strings. Hitch nailhead to string of either parabola or hyperbola.
Set weights level while nailhead is held on any point of curve.
In each case the weights have equal changes in level as nailhead traces curve, as each point of parabola is equidistant from its focus and directrix
and every point of hyperbola is always the same distance closer to one focus than to the other.
Hold one end of ellipse string against board while nailhead traces ellipse with string riding freely over it. The free weight will not shift as the segments of string between the two foci are always equal to major diameter of ellipse.
Hyperbola
F_1
Ellipse
F_0
Parabola
Hyperbola
F_2
Directrix of parabola

The Parabola.

Any point of a parabola $P(x,y)$ is equidistant from the focus $F(p,o)$ and the directrix $x=-p$.

A circle of radius x centered on point $P(x,y)$ is tangent to the Y-axis and to the circle of radius p centered on the focus $F(p,o)$.

Since a light ray emanating from the focus is reflected parallel to the axis, the normal $P'N$ bisects $FP'Z$ and intersects the X-axis $2p+x$ from the origin. The tangent intersects the X-axis at $T(-x,o)$.

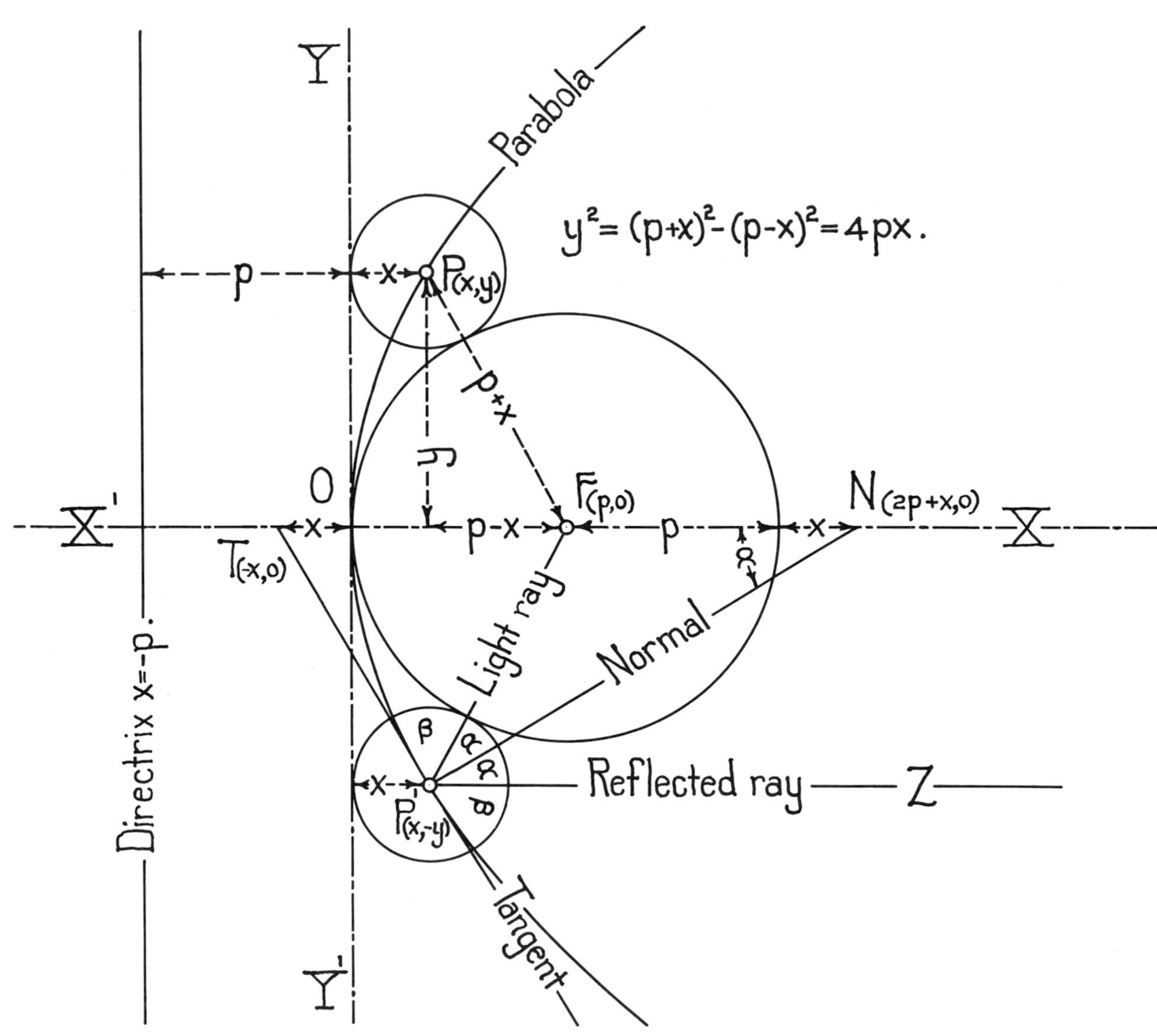

Constructing the Parabola.

A parabola can be constructed in a set of concentric circles.

The difference between the radii of the inner or focal circle and of each larger circle is the x abscissa of the two points of the parabola that are located in the larger circle.

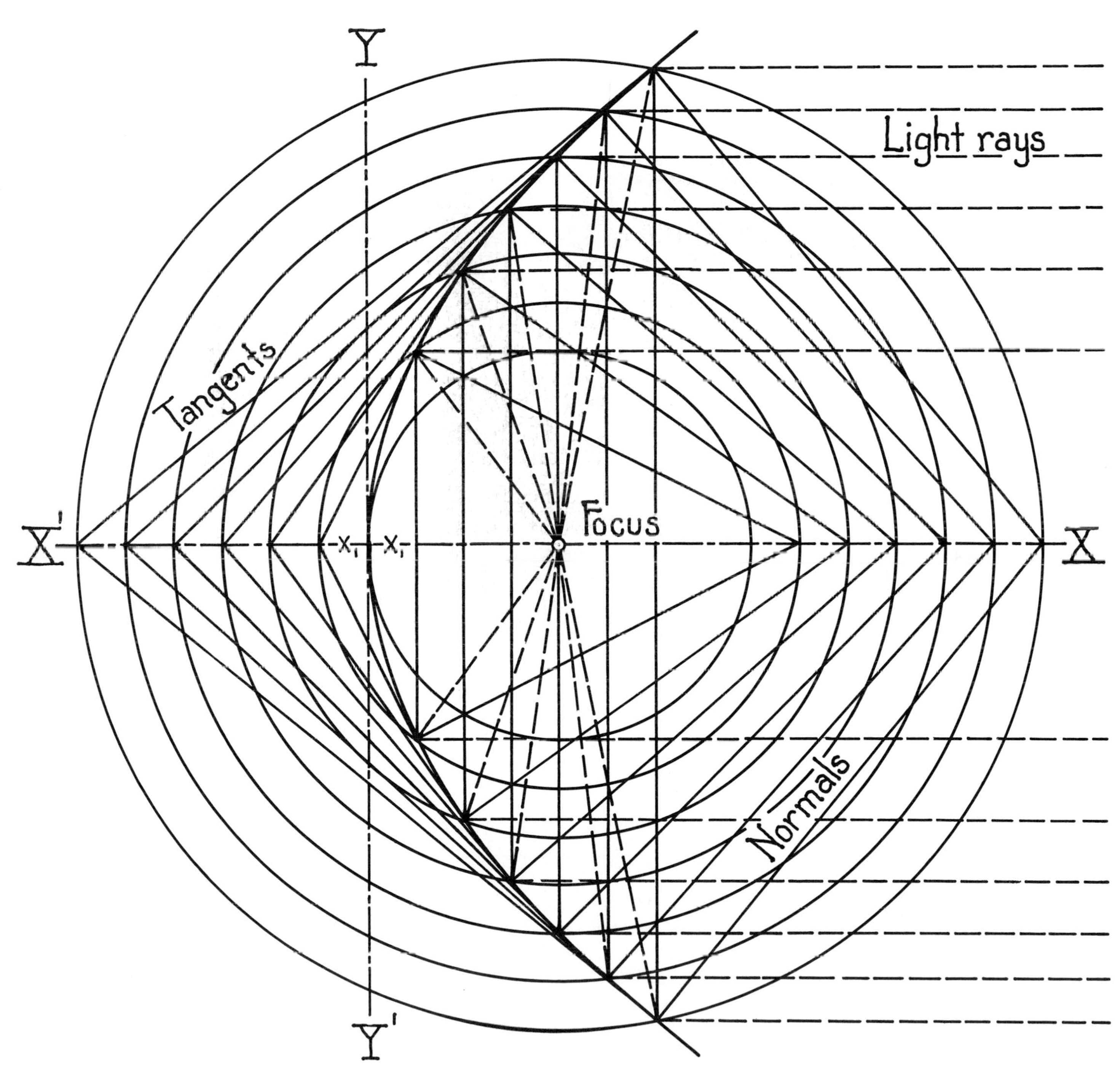

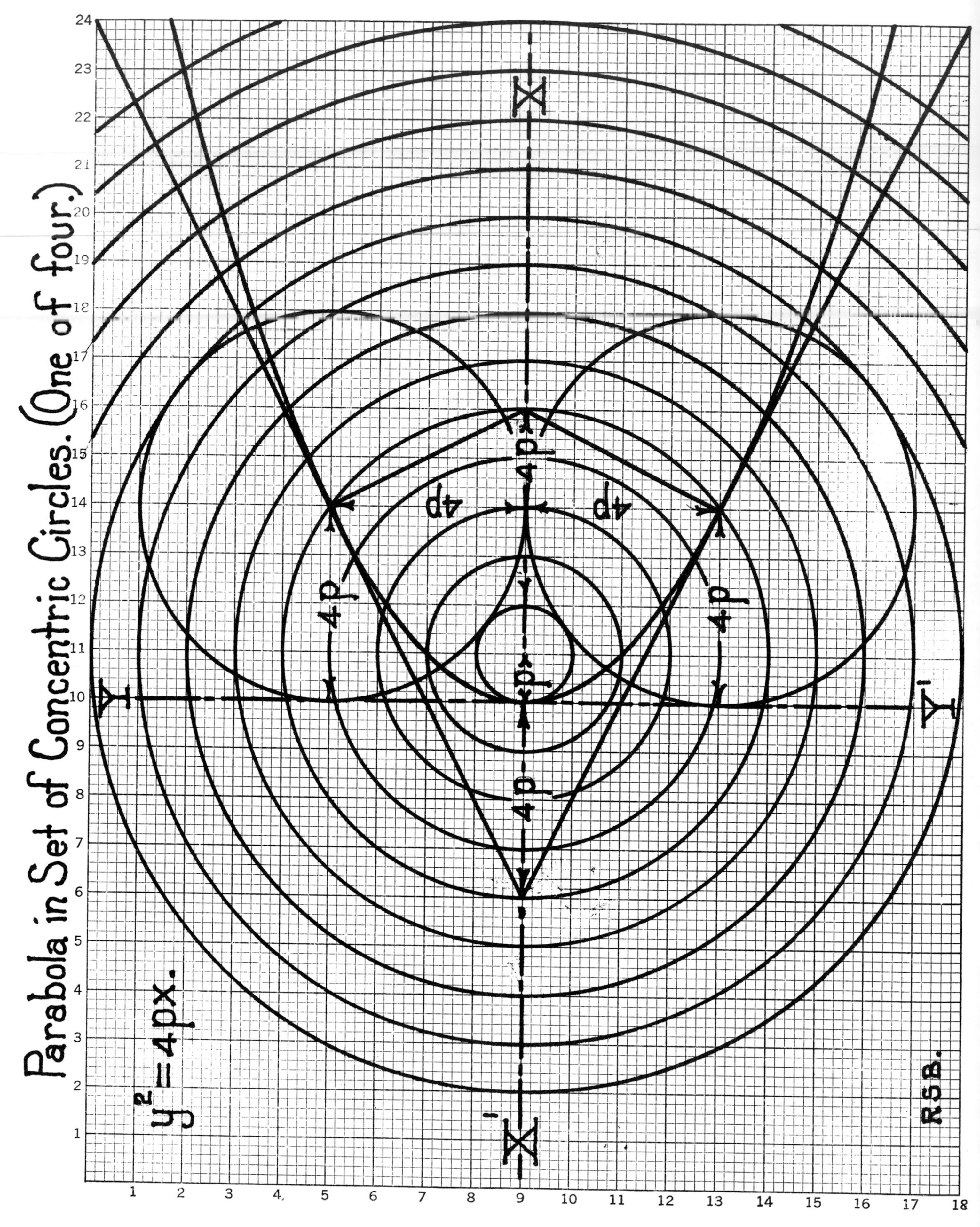
Parabola in Set of Concentric Circles. (One of four.)
$y^2 = 4px$.
RSB.
X
X'
Y
Y'
4p
4p
4p
4p
4p
4p
p
1
2
3
4
5
6
7
8
9
10
11
12
13
14
15
16
17
18
19
20
21
22
23
24

THE ELLIPSE.

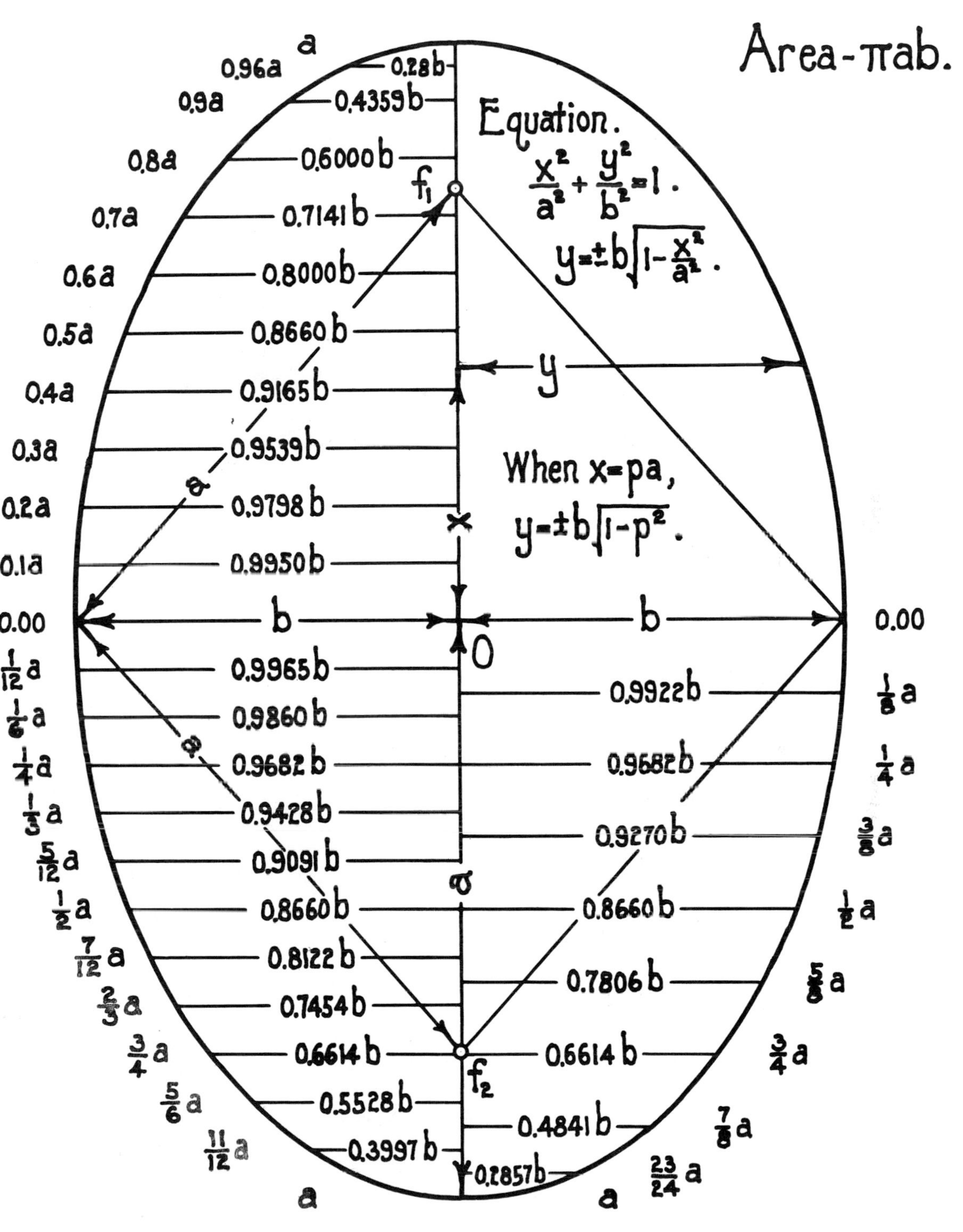

$$f_1o=f_2o=\sqrt{a^2-b^2}.$$

THE HYPERBOLA.

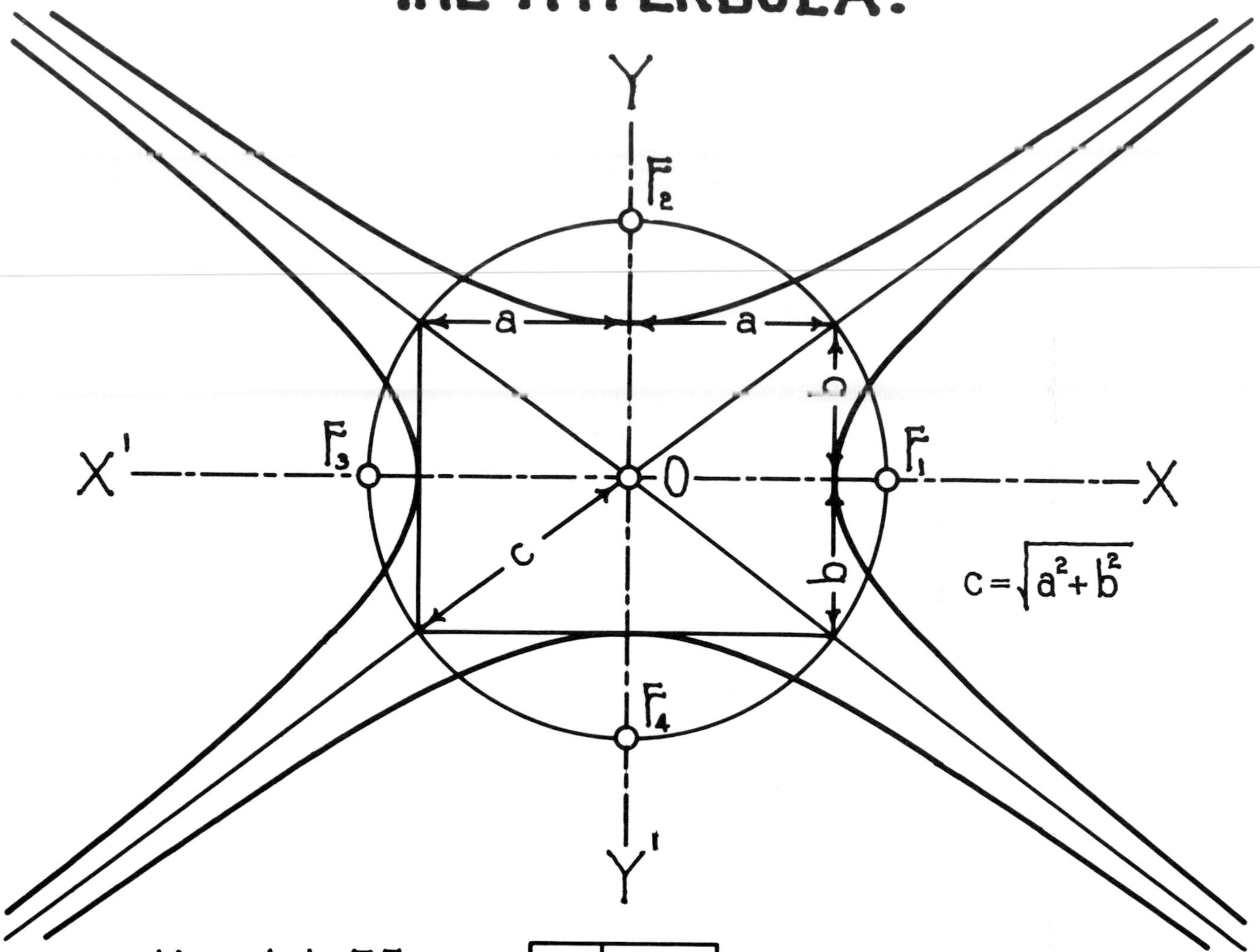

<table>
<tr><td>

Hyperbola F_1F_3.

$$\frac{x^2}{a^2}-\frac{y^2}{b^2}=1$$

When $x=na$,

$y=\pm b\sqrt{n^2-1}$.

Examples. $a=2$ $b=1.50$

$n=2$

$x=2\times 2.00=4.00$

$y=\pm 1.50\times 1.732=\pm 2.598$

$n=3$

$x=na=3\times 2.00=6.00$

$y=\pm 1.50\times 2.828=\pm 4.242$

</td></tr>
</table>

n.	$\sqrt{n^2-1}$.
1.0	0.000
1.1	0.458
1.2	0.663
1.3	0.831
1.4	0.980
1.5	1.118
1.6	1.249
1.7	1.375
1.8	1.497
1.9	1.616
2.0	1.732
2.2	1.960
2.4	2.182
2.6	2.400
2.8	2.615
3.0	2.828

Hyperbola F_2F_4.

$$\frac{y^2}{b^2}-\frac{x^2}{a^2}=1$$

When $y=nb$,

$x=\pm a\sqrt{n^2-1}$.

Examples. $b=1.50$ $a=2$

$n=2$

$y=2\times 1.50=3.00$

$x=\pm 2\times 1.732=3.464$

$n=3$

$y=3\times 1.50=4.50$

$x=\pm 2\times 2.828=\pm 5.656$

Tangent Circle Parabolas.

Both f_1 and line, $x=-\phi$, are $\phi+r$ from any center, C.

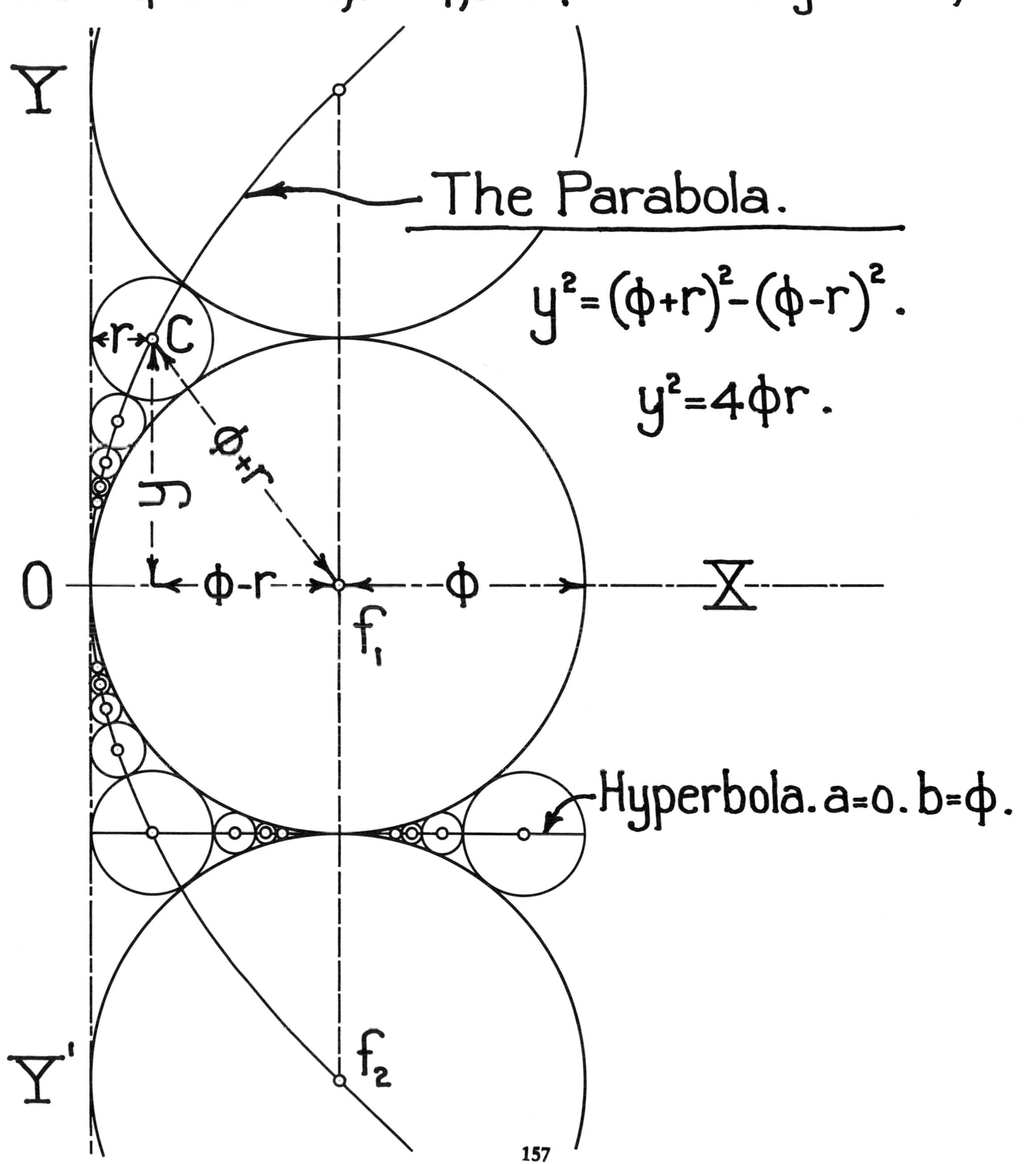

Tangent Circle Ellipses.

$F_1 + F_2$ for any center, C, $= \phi + \theta$. $x^2/a^2 + y^2/b^2 = 1$.

$a = \frac{1}{2}(\phi + \theta)$. $e = \frac{\phi - \theta}{\phi + \theta}$. $b = \sqrt{a^2 - a^2e^2}$.

$ae = \frac{1}{2}(\phi - \theta)$. $\frac{a}{e} = \frac{(\phi + \theta)^2}{2(\phi - \theta)}$. $b = \sqrt{\phi\theta}$.

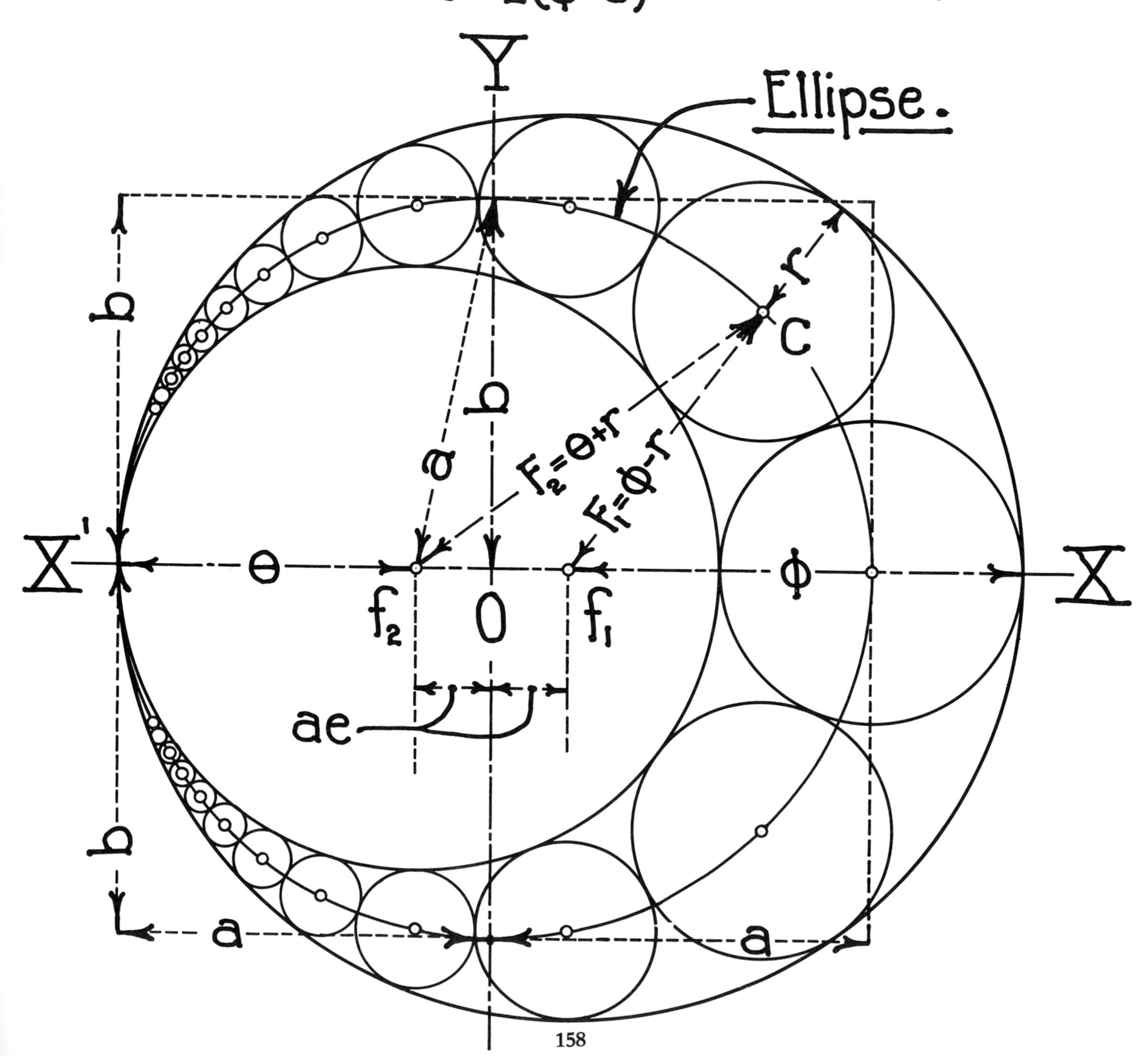

Tangent Circle Hyperbolas.

The circles that are tangent to both shaded circles have their centers on hyperbola AB. The shaded circles are externally tangent to circles centered on branch A and internally tangent to circles centered on branch B.

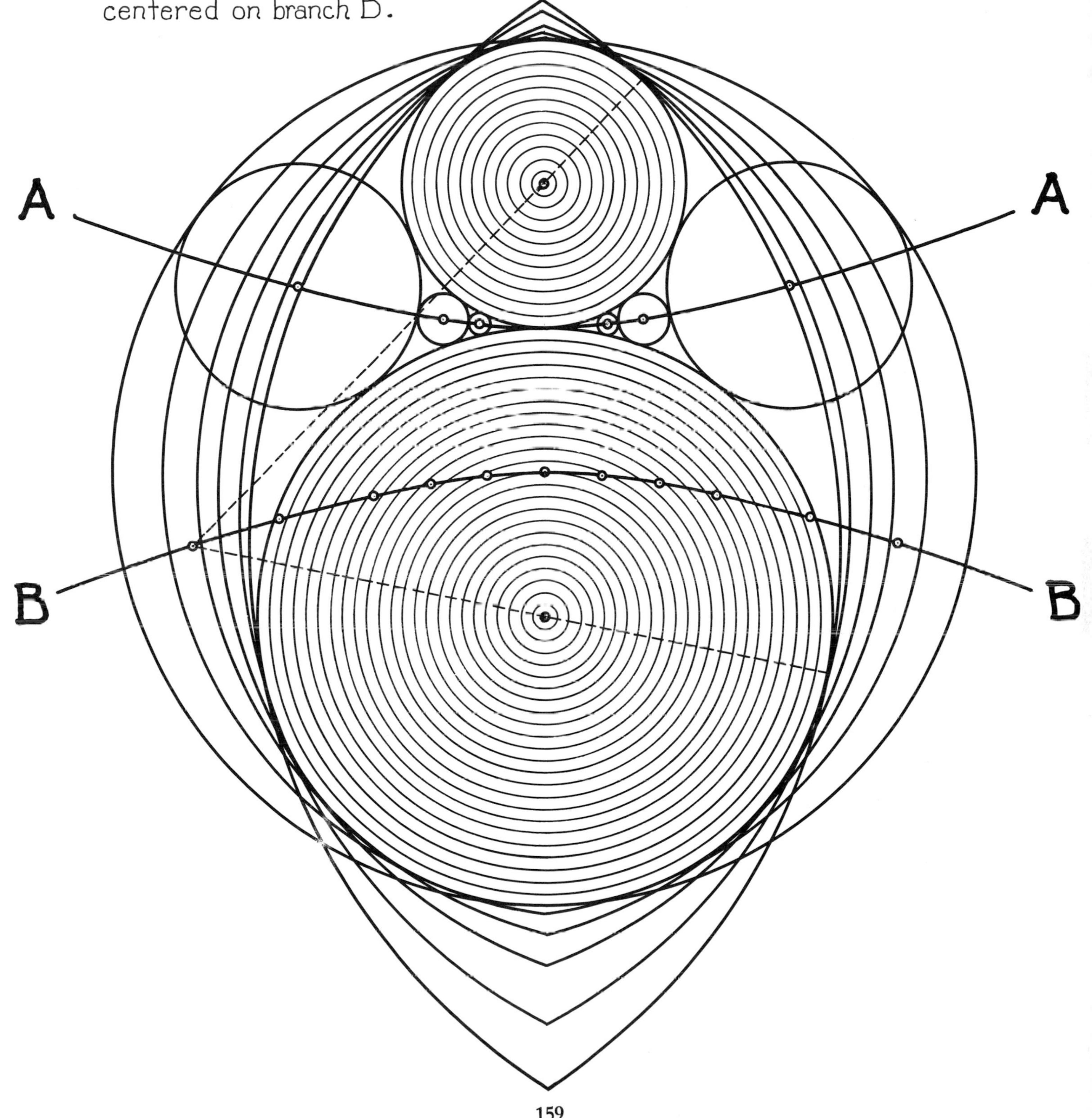

The Three Hyperbolas Based on Any Triangle.

The mutually tangent circles centered at vertices 1,2 and 3 are also tangent to the circles centered at points 4 and 5.

Three hyperbolas with foci at vertices 1,2 and 3 and axes 1-2, 1-3 and 2-3 intersect at centers 4 and 5.

The difference between the radii of the tangent circles centered on the foci of each hyperbola is also the difference between the focal radii of any point in that hyperbola.

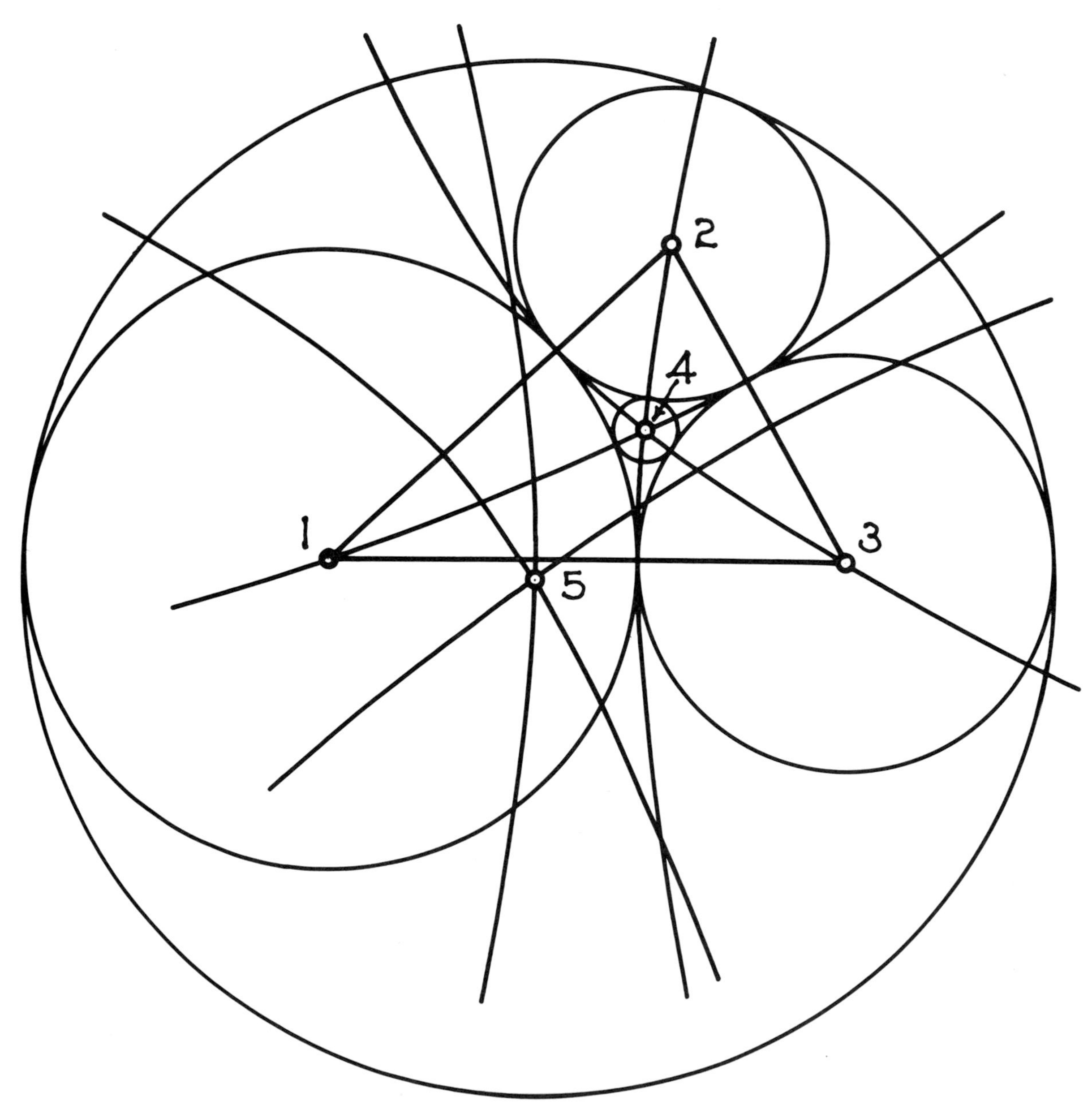

Hyperbolic Paraboloid.

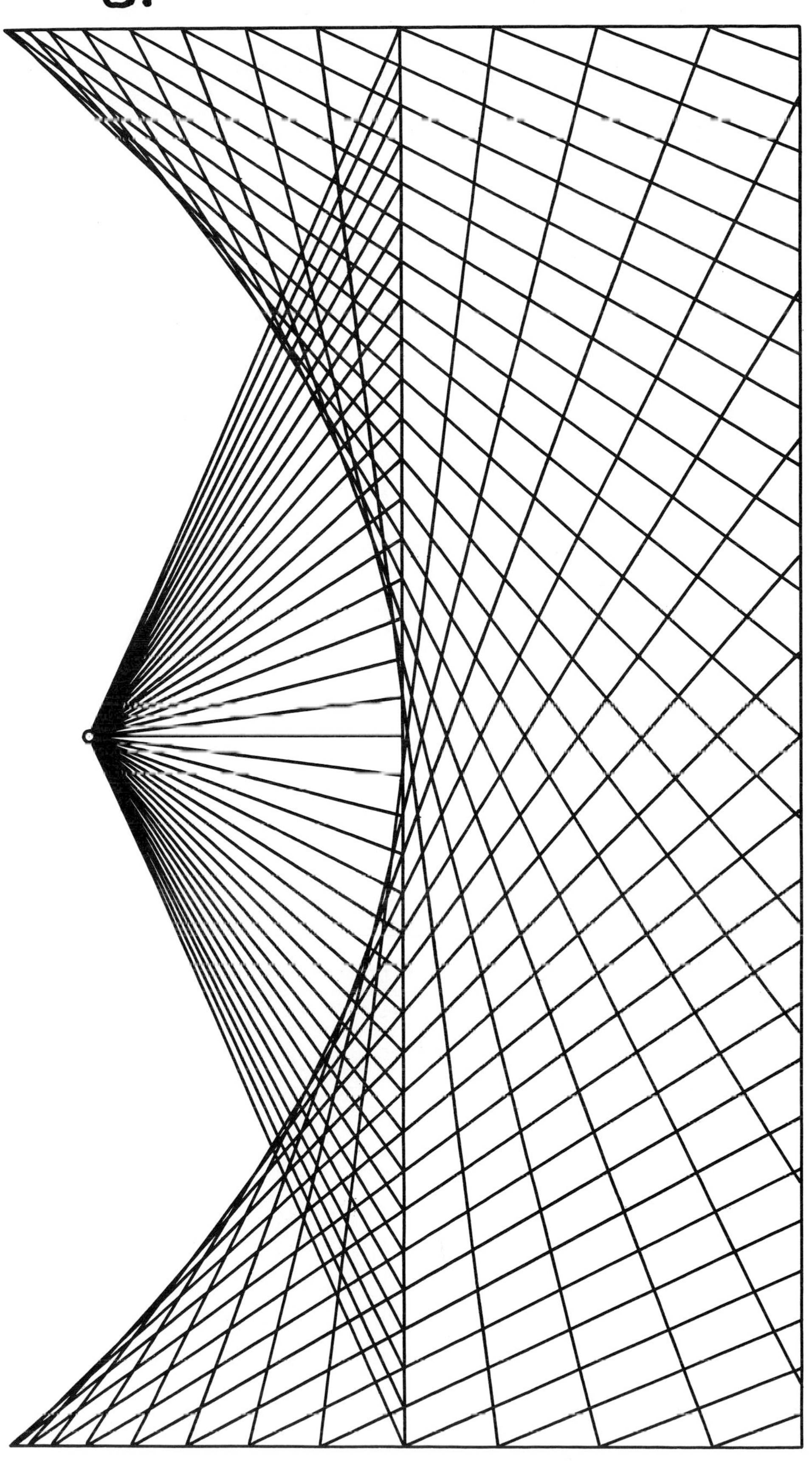

Draw perpendiculars to rays at intersections with base line.

Elliptical Envelope.

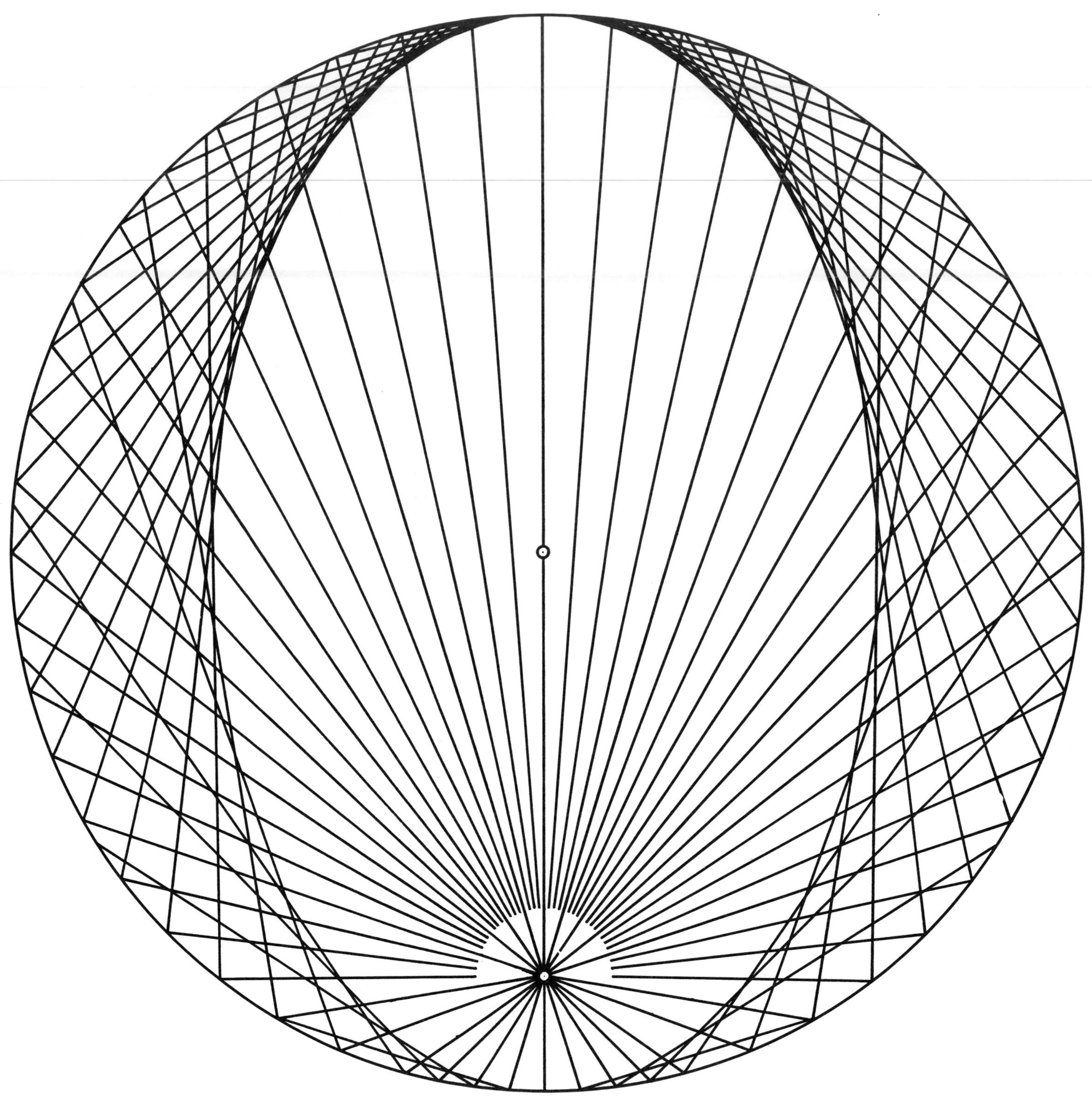

Draw rays from any point in a circle. Erect a perpendicular to each ray where it meets the circle. The envelope of these perpendiculars is an ellipse.

Hyperboloid.

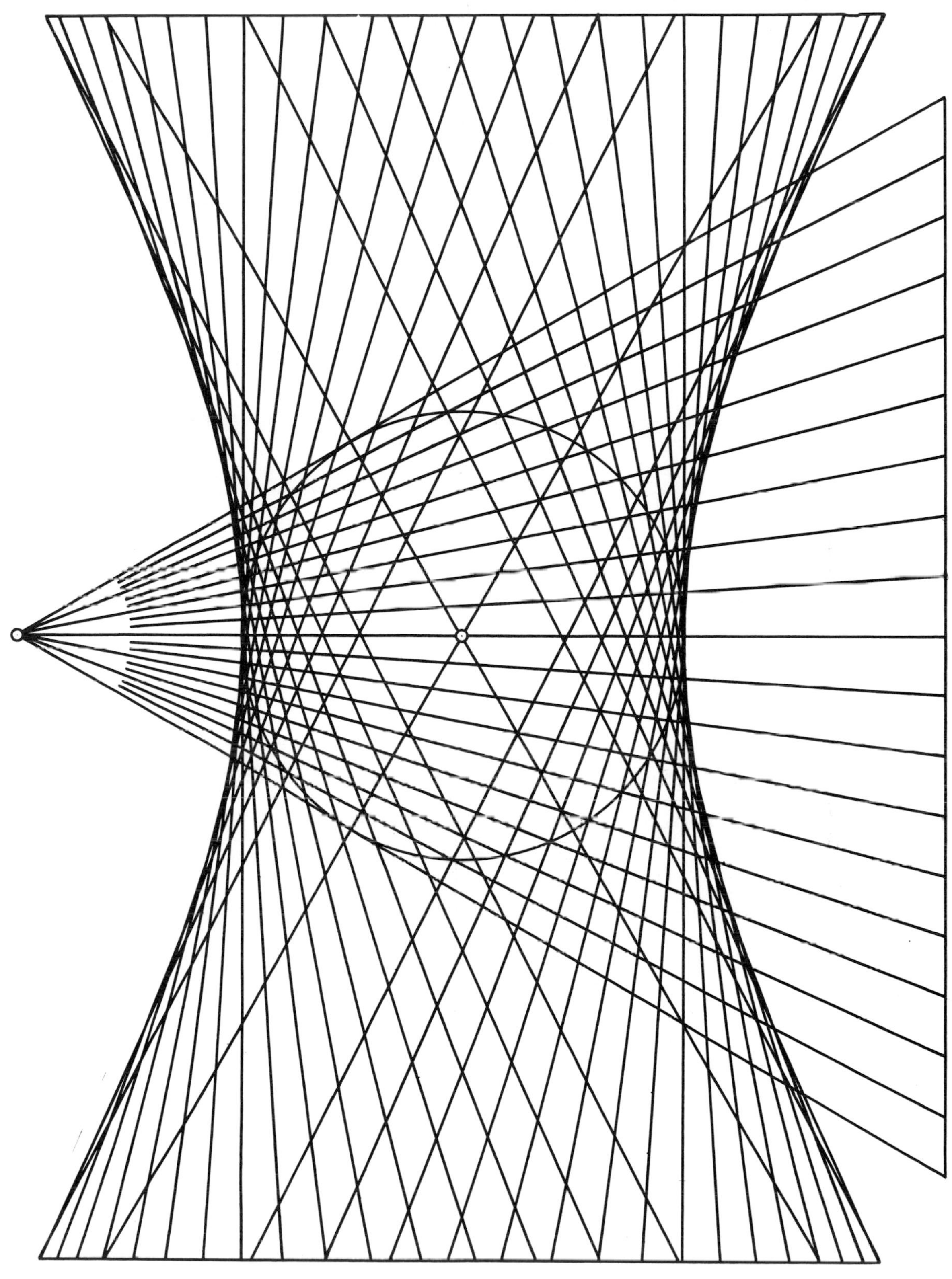

Draw perpendiculars to rays at intersections with circle.

Conics Creased in Wax Paper.

Fold paper with fixed point F held on any point N of line or circle.

The creases or perpendicular bisectors of lines FN envelop conics.

Loci of midpoints of lines FN marked thus :- ——————

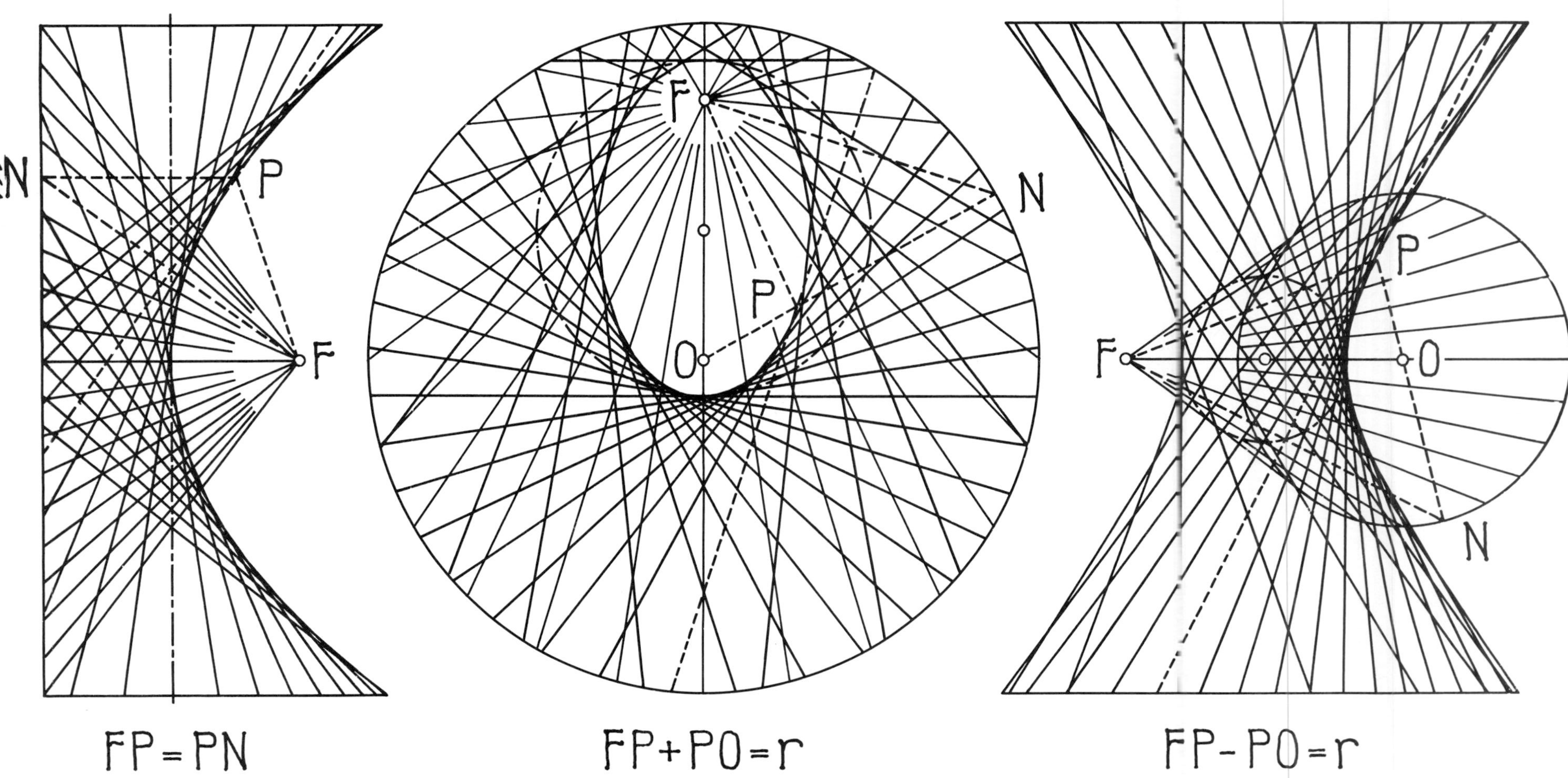

Two Foci for a Circle.

A point travels in a circle when it moves so that its distance from one fixed point bears a constant ratio to its distance from a second fixed point.

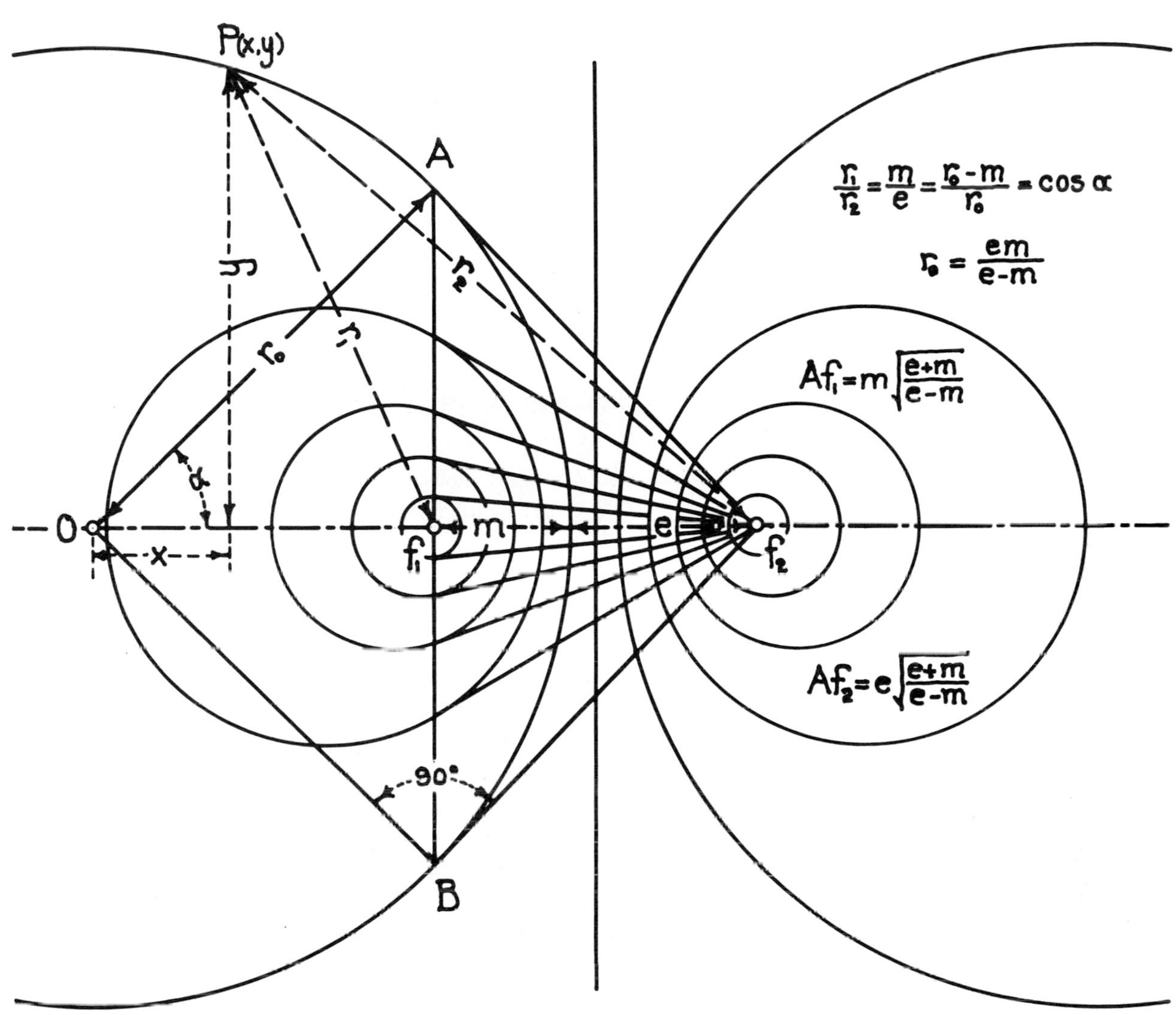

f_1 and f_2 are fixed points or foci for all circles shown in the diagram.

The circles divide axis $f_1 f_2$ into twelve equal units.

In circle PAB, $m = 5$, $e = 7$, $r_0 = \frac{7 \times 5}{7-5} = 17.5$, $Af_1 = 5\sqrt{\frac{7+5}{7-5}} = 12.25$, $Af_2 = 7\sqrt{\frac{7+5}{7-5}} = 17.15$ and the ratio of the focal radii, $\frac{r_1}{r_2}$, is $\frac{5}{7}$ for every point in the circle.

The corresponding values for the smallest circle are, $m = 1$, $e = 11$, $r_0 = \frac{11 \times 1}{11-1} = 1.10$, $Af_1 = 1\sqrt{\frac{11+1}{11-1}} = 1.095$, $Af_2 = 11\sqrt{\frac{11+1}{11-1}} = 12.05$ and $\frac{r_1}{r_2} = \frac{1}{11}$.

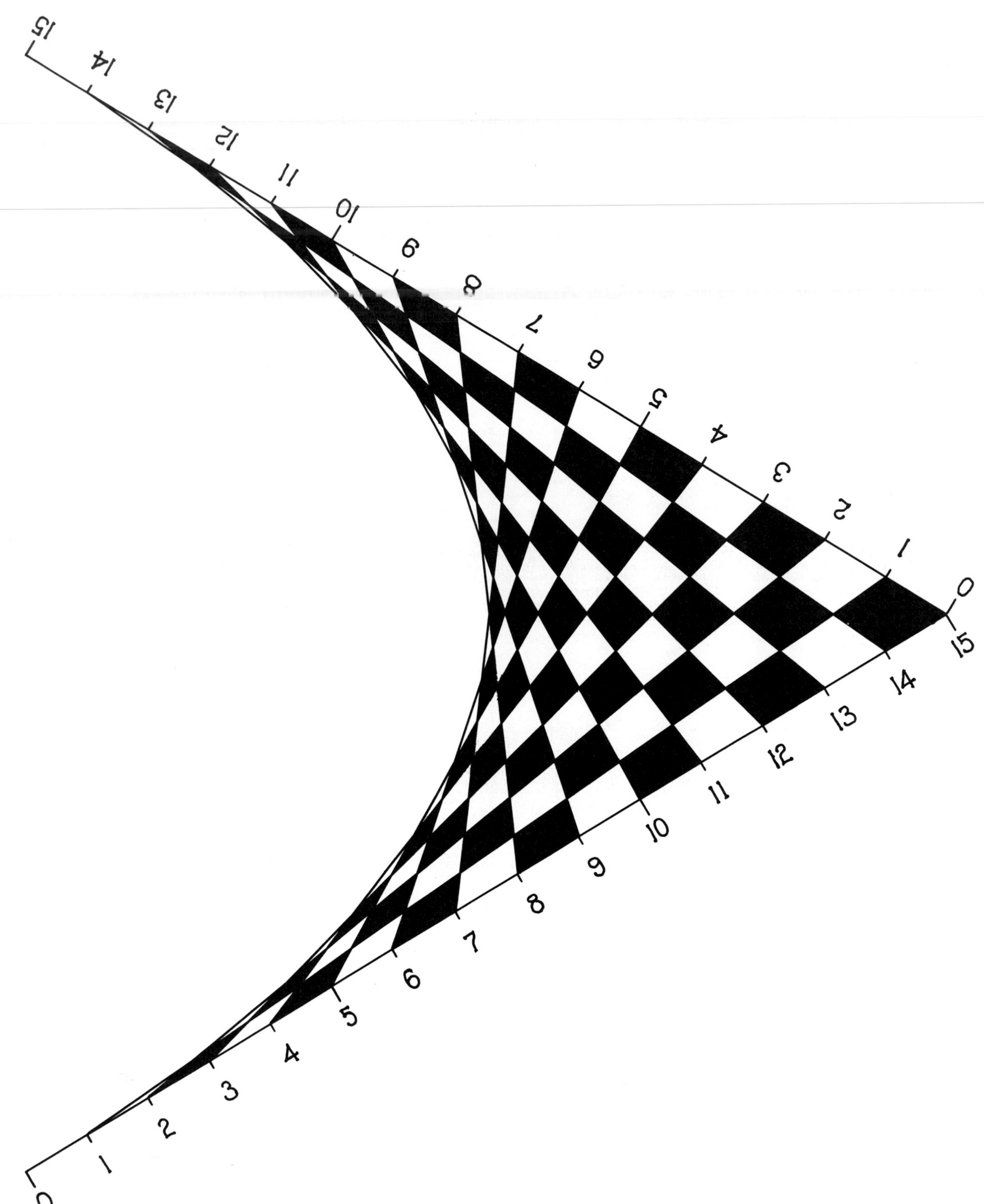

0
1
2
3
4
5
6
7
8
9
10
11
12
13
14
15
0
1
2
3
4
5
6
7
8
9
10
11
12
13
14
15

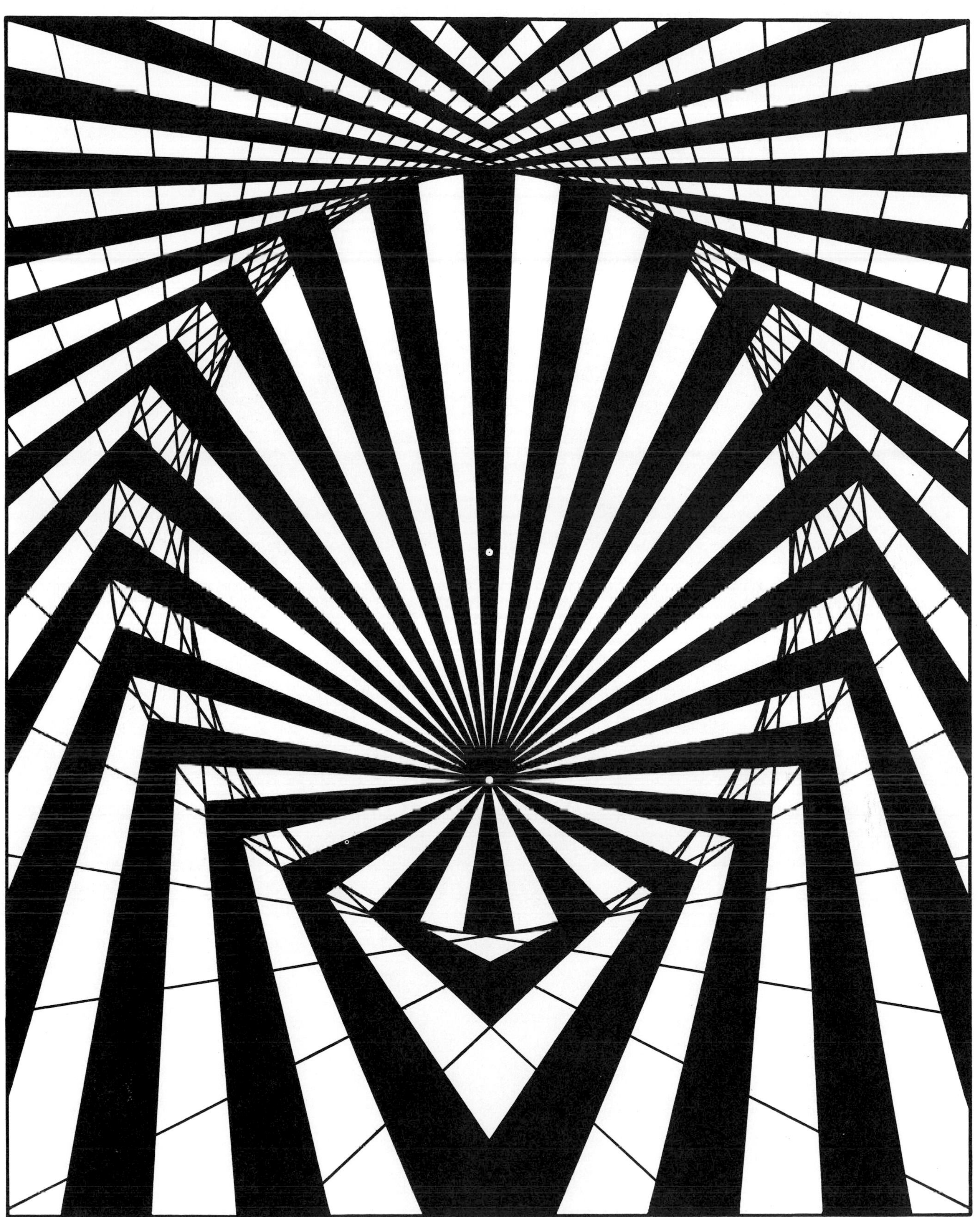

Circles with Radii in Arithmetical Progression.

Intersections with parallel tangents are loci of parabolas.

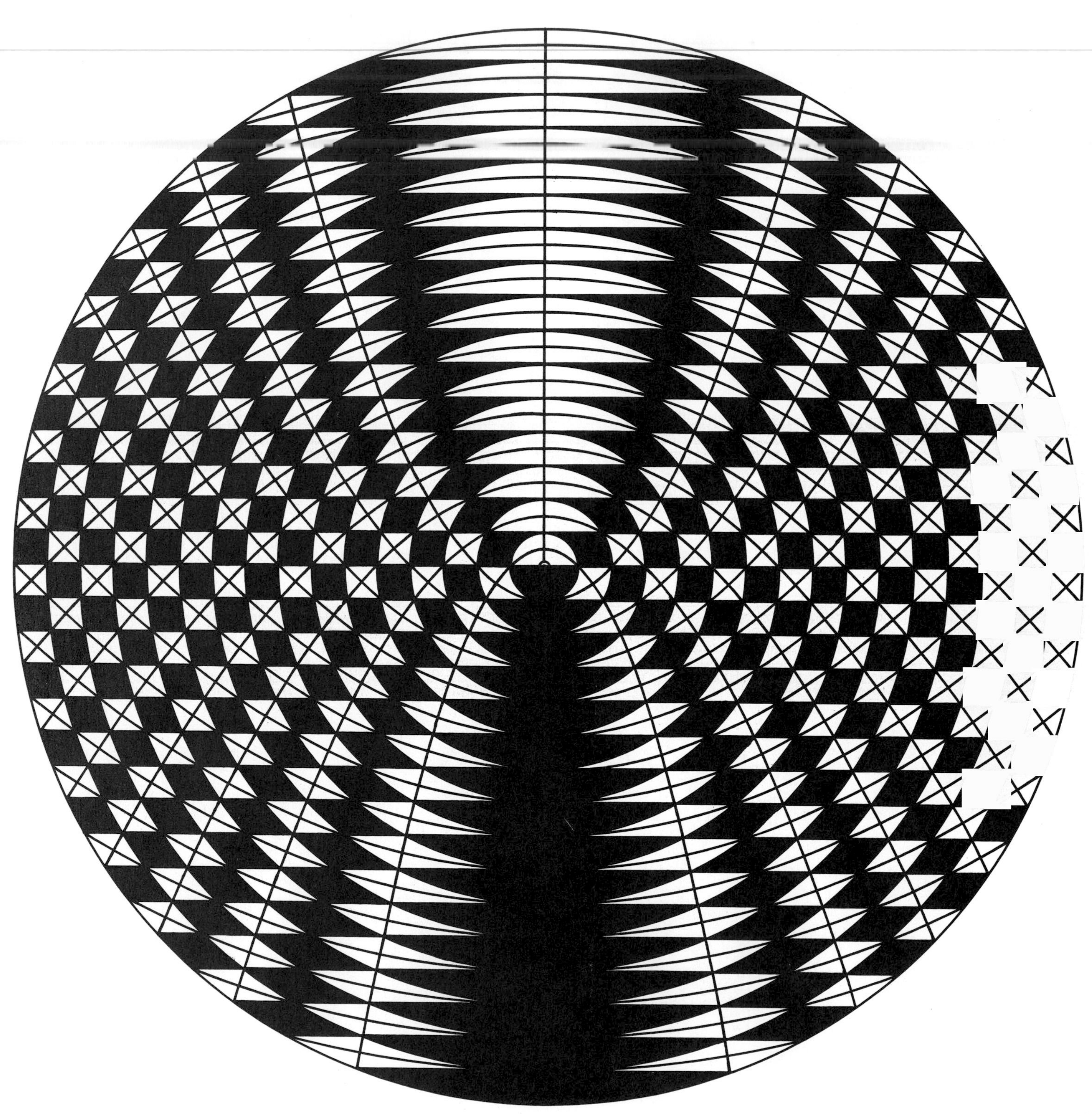

Circles in Arithmetic Progression.

Successive radii at each center lengthen equal amounts.
Loops of diamonds in intersection pattern are ellipses. $r_1 + r_2 = k$.
Cross chains of diamonds are hyperbolas. $r_1 - r_2 = k$.

Circles in Geometric Progression.

Radii at each center lengthen ten percent consecutively.
Loops of diamonds in intersection pattern are Cassini curves. $r_1 r_2 = k.$
Cross chains of diamonds are arcs of circles. $\frac{r_1}{r_2} = k.$

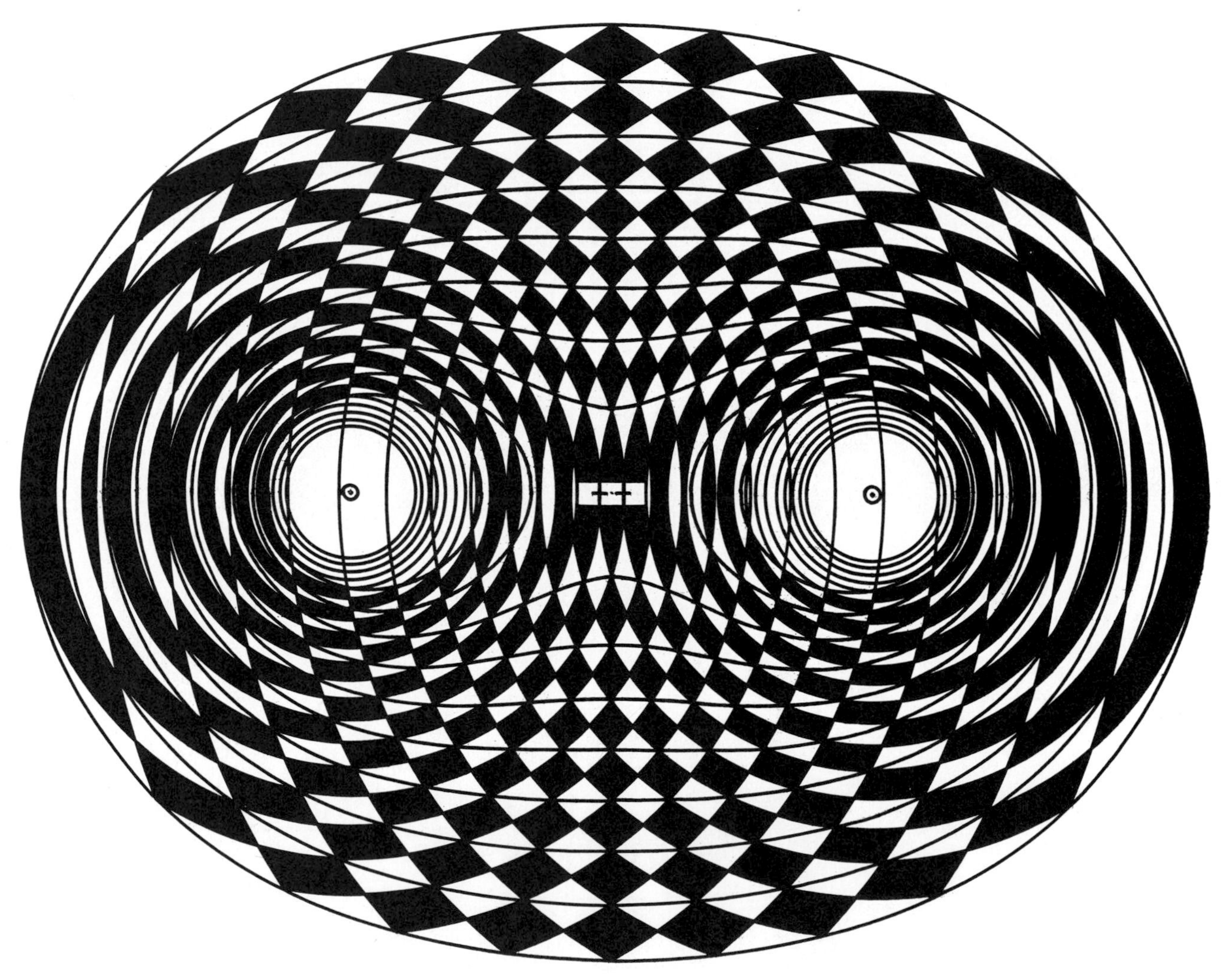

Circles in Geometric Progression.

Radii of concentric circles lengthen 21% consecutively. $r^n = (1.10)^{2n}$.
Loops of diamonds form Cassini curves. Focal radii, $r_1 \times r_2 = k'$.
Double loop Cassini curve is a Lemniscate.
Cross chains of diamonds form circles. Focal radii, $\frac{r_1}{r_2} = k''$.
Centers of concentric circles are spaced 2×9th radius = e+m on 'Two Foci for a Circle' sheet. $\frac{r_1}{r_2} = \frac{m}{e}$ for any point on chain circle. Solve for e and m.
Radius of chain circle, $r_0 = \frac{em}{e-m}$.

Cycloidal Curves.

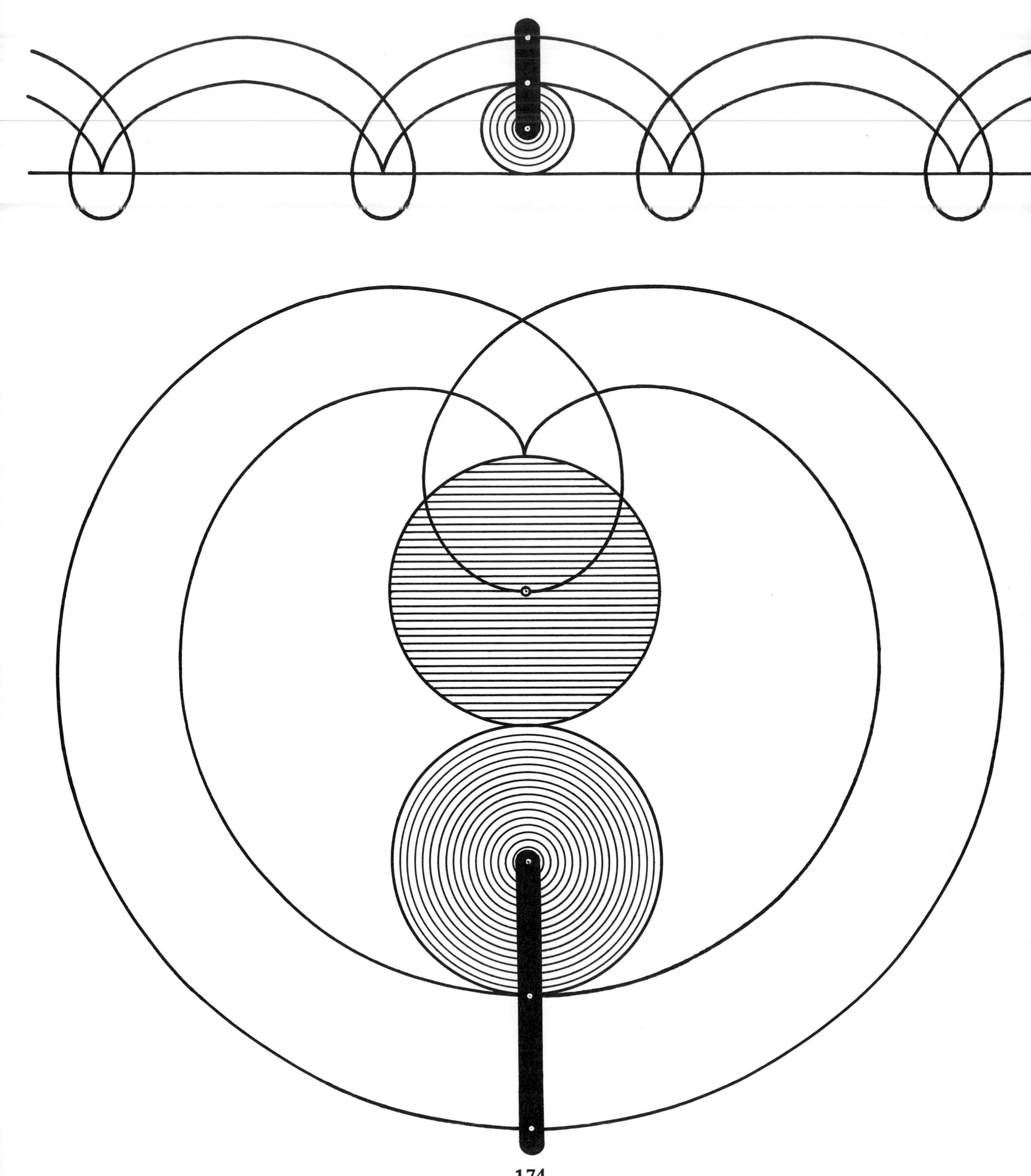

Cycloidal Curves.

A point on a circle traces a three cusp epicycloid as the circle rolls twice around the outside of a base circle of $\frac{3}{2}$ its radius.

When this circle rolls twice around the inside of the base circle a three cusp hypocycloid or deltoid is traced by the point.

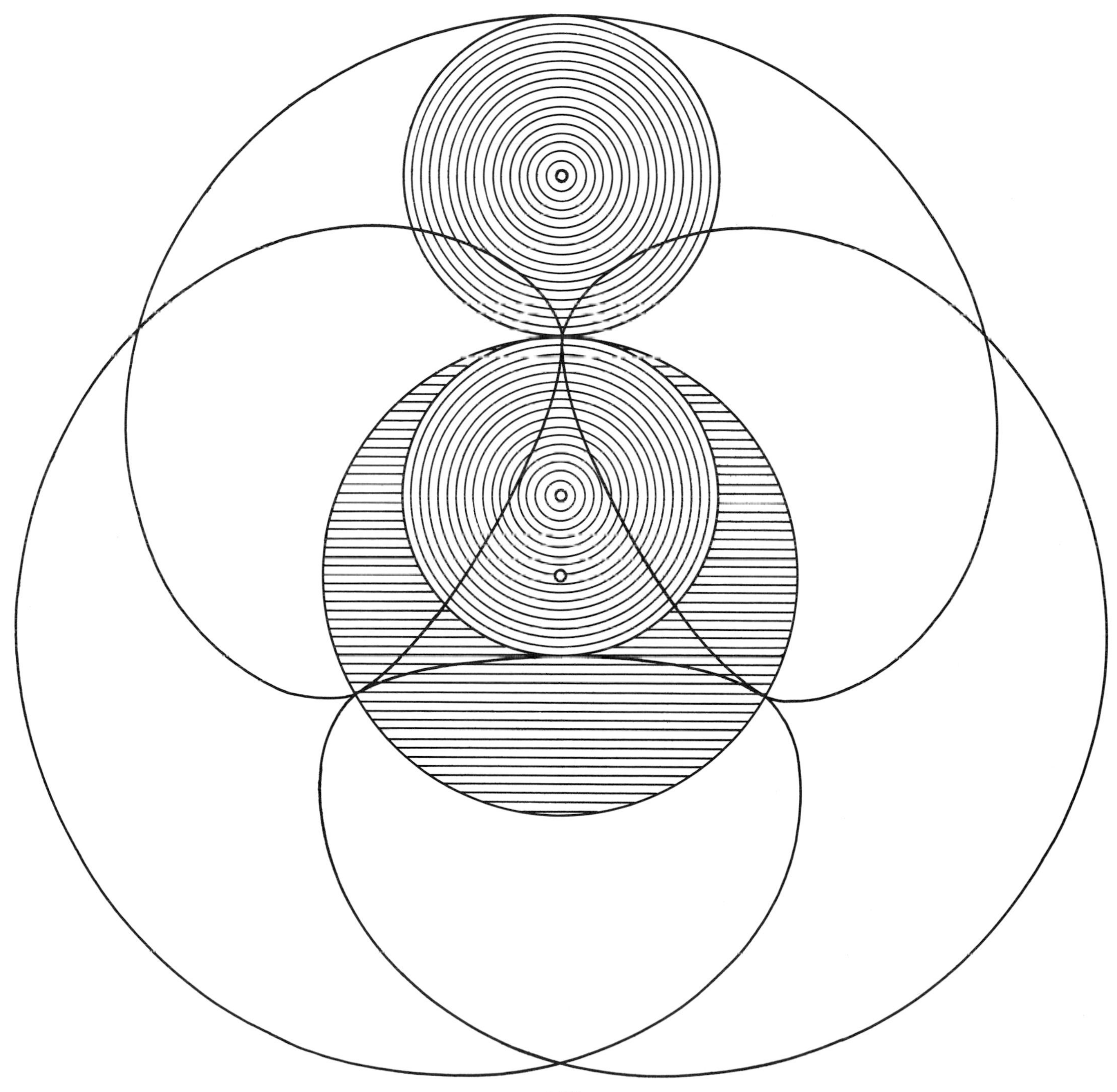

Straight Line Hypocycloids.

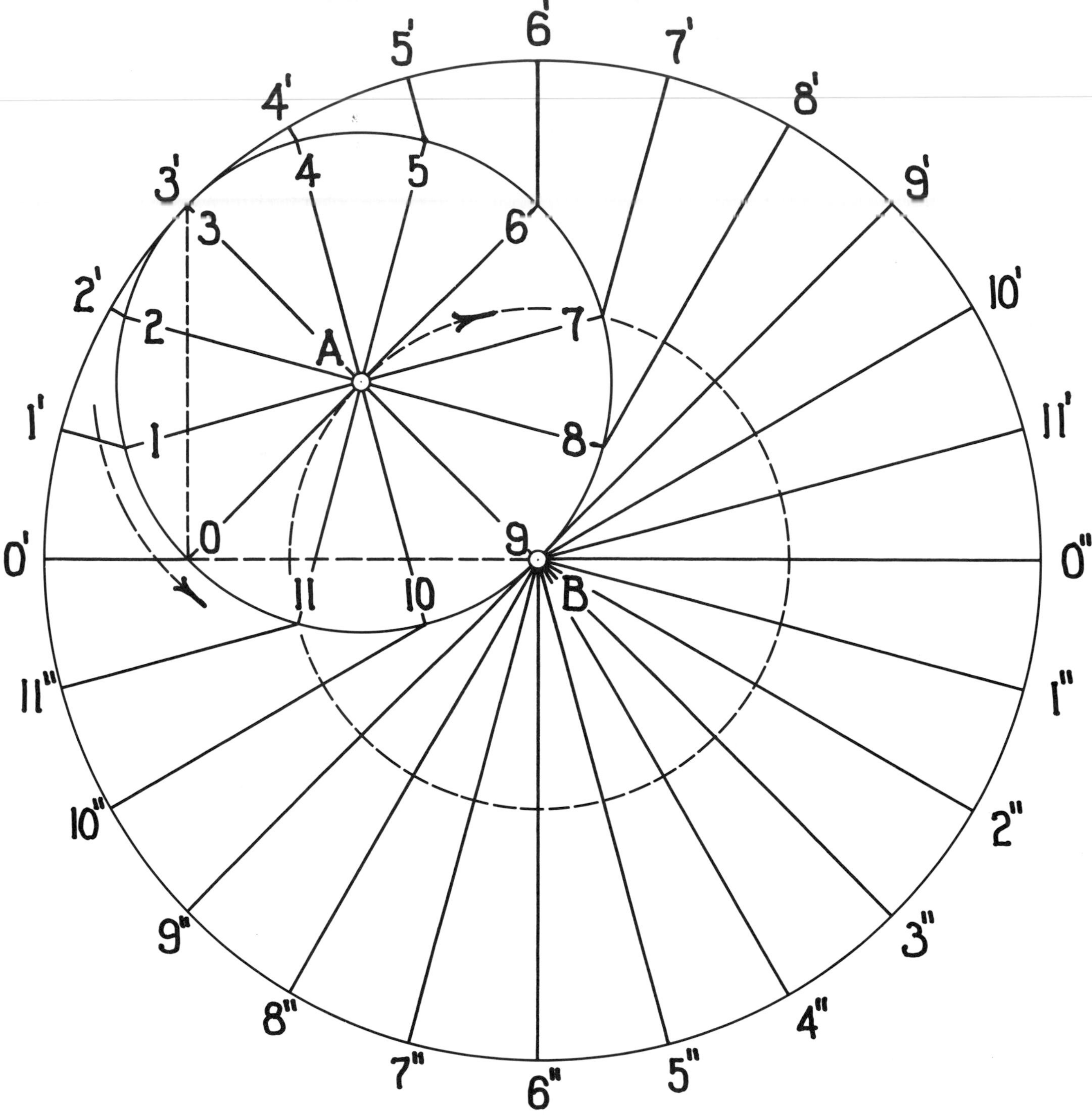

Each marked point on wheel A travels on the like numbered diameter of wheel B, as A rolls on rim of B.

Cycloidal Curves.

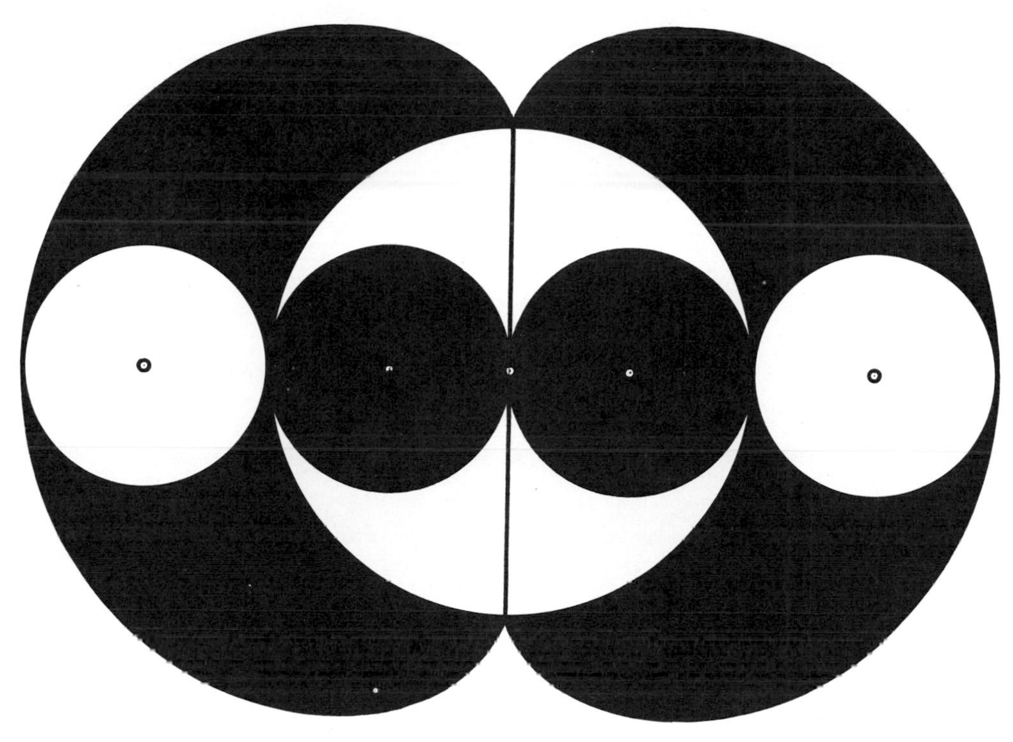

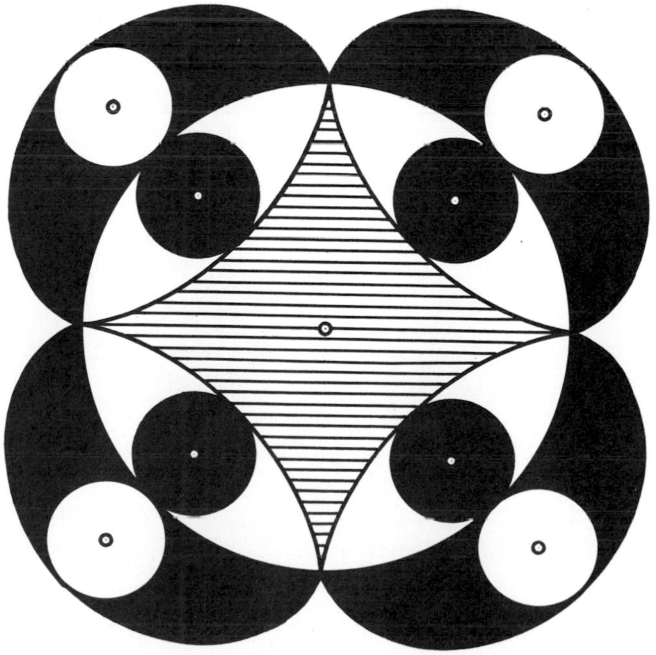

Cycloidal Curves.

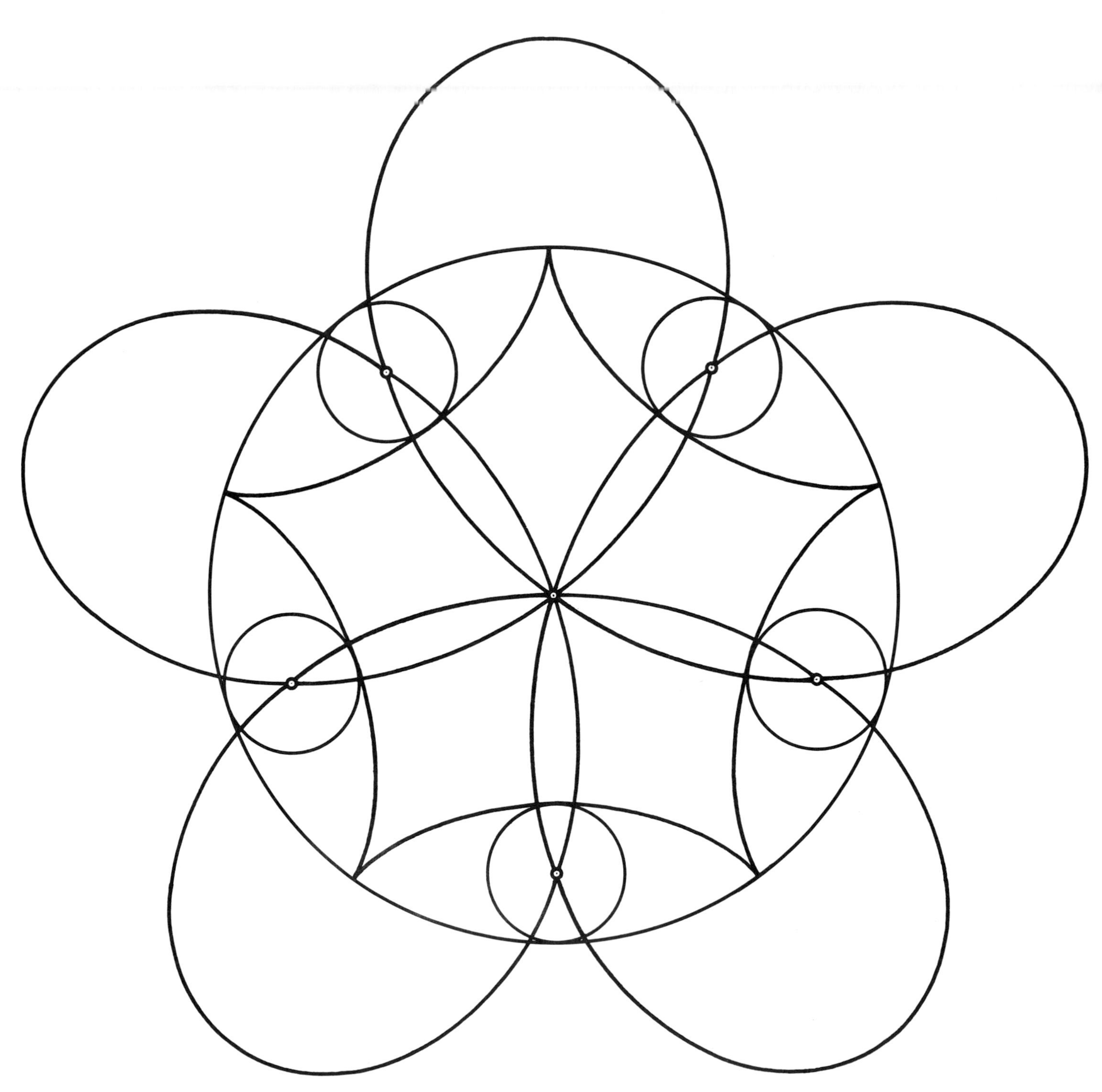

Cardioid.

The circle is cut into an even number of equal parts. Successive chords rotate two parts at one end and one part at the other end.

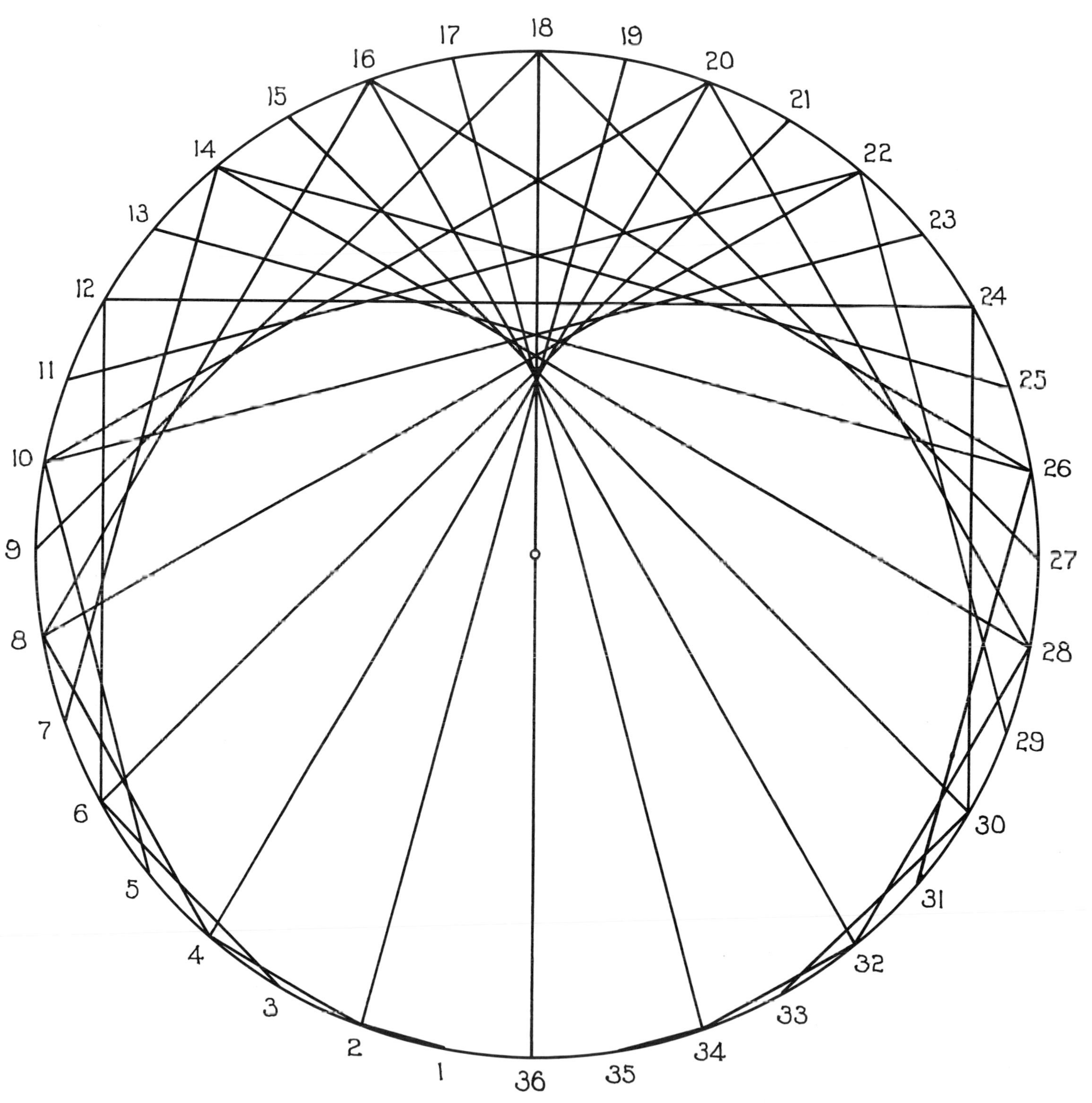

Cardioid.

A cardioid or one cusp epicycloid is formed by each point of a circle as the circle rolls around a base circle of same size. Rolling circle is shown in thirty six positions.

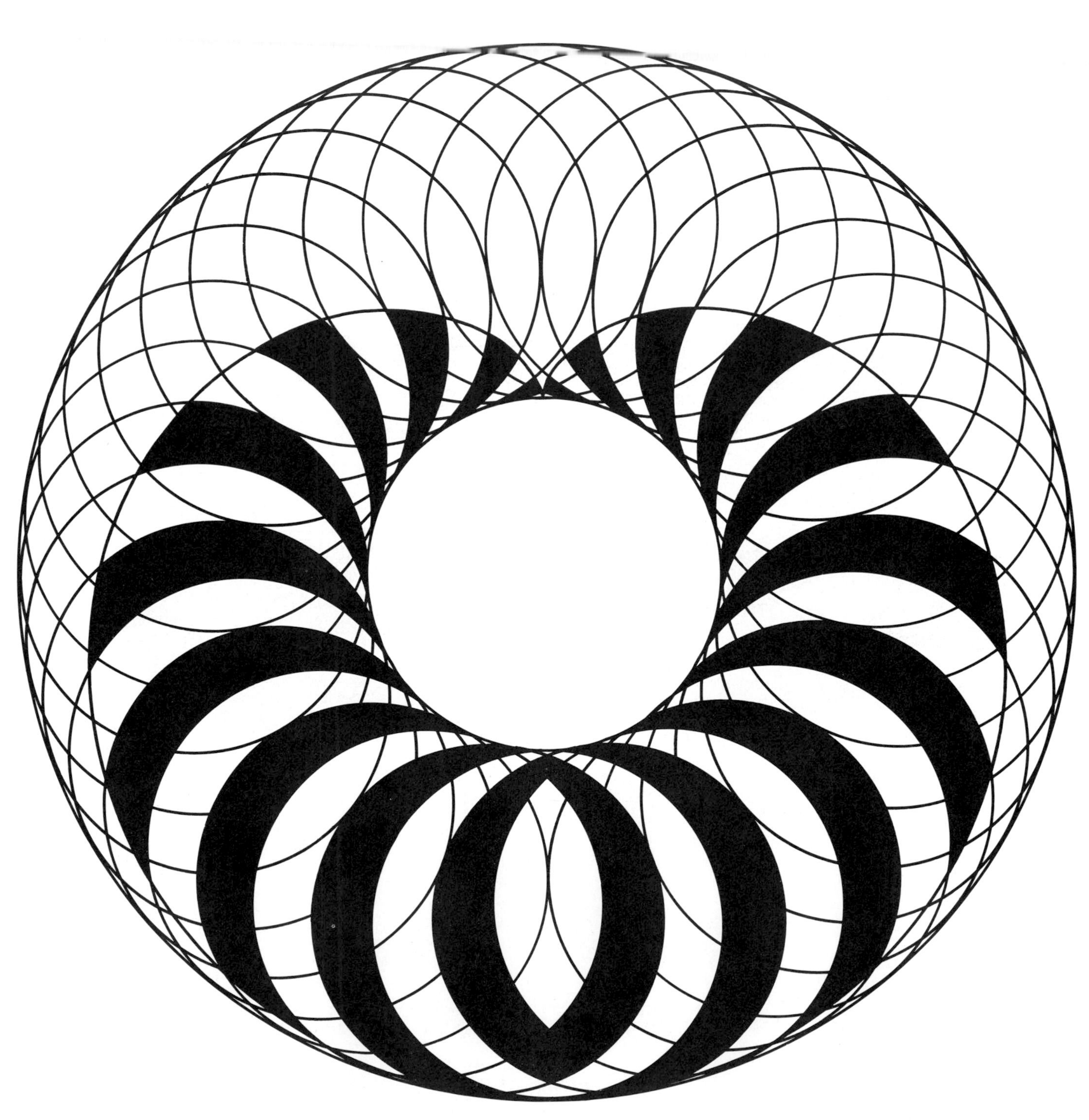

Cardioid.

A cardioid is the envelope of all circles that are centered on a base circle and pass through a fixed point on that circle.

In this drawing the centers of the outer circles divide the base circle into ten degree arcs.

Nephroid.

A nephroid is the envelope of all circles that are centered on a base circle and are tangent to one diameter of that circle. This curve is a two cusp epicycloid.

In this drawing the centers of the outer circles divide the base circle into forty-eight equal arcs.

Cycloidal Envelopes.

The base circle for matching epicycloids and hypocycloids is the locus of the centers of the circles that are tangent to both curves. Either curve is the envelope of such circles tangent to the other curve.

In this drawing the tangent circles are centered on the base circle at 5° intervals.

Conchoidal Transformation of a Line.

When all points of line abc advance toward point p at the same rate, they will form the cusp a_1pc_1 when point b reaches position p. The moving points will form loop pb_2 when points a and c meet at p. Arc $a_3b_3c_3$ is a later stage in the continued uniform advance. Curve $a_{-1}b_{-1}c_{-1}$ is a stage in the corresponding reverse movement.

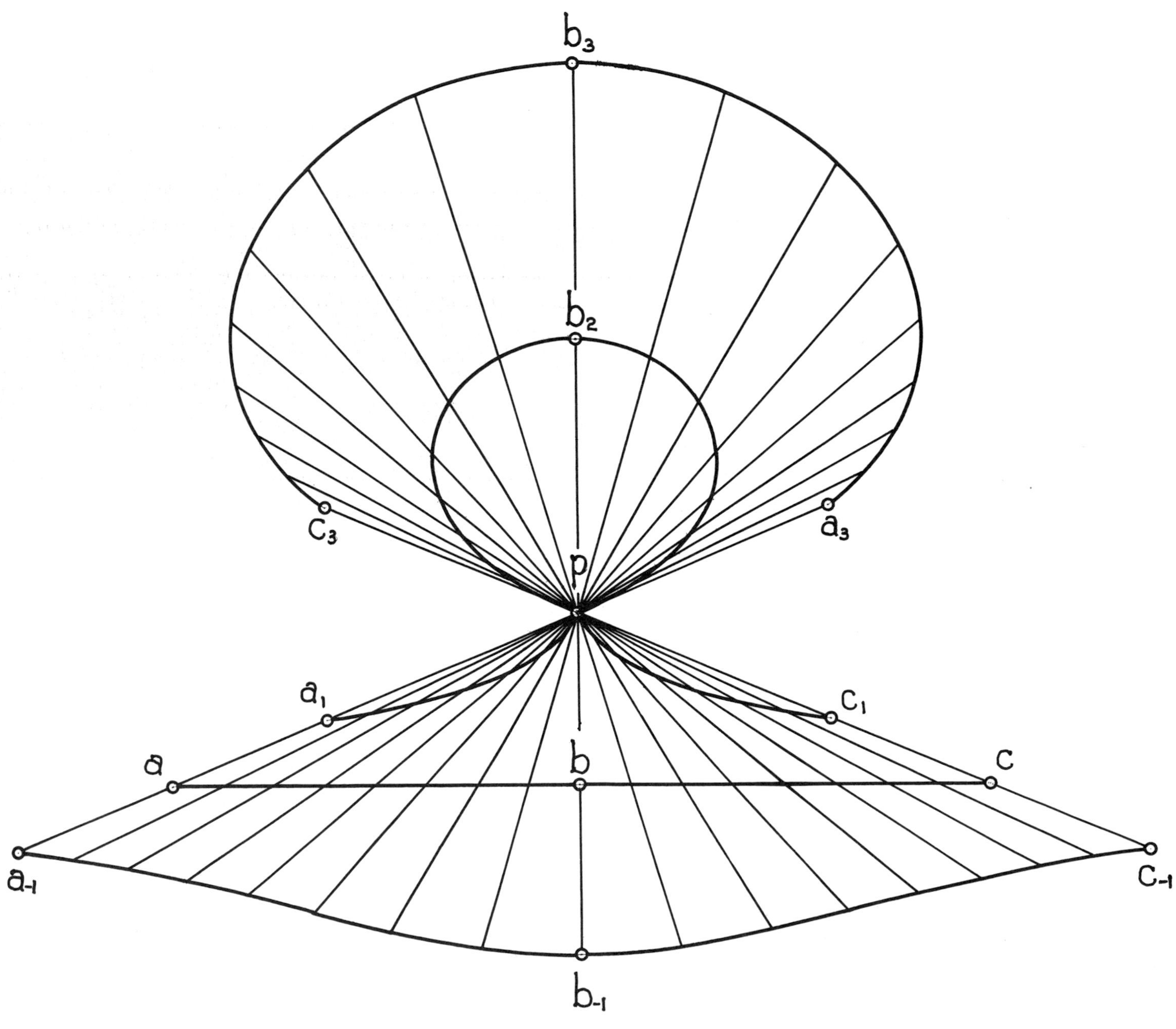

Conchoidal Transformation of a Circle.

When all points of the circle advance at the same rate along their lines through internal point p, they will form curves 1-1, 2_1-2_2-2_3-2_4, 3-3 and 4-4 at half radius intervals.

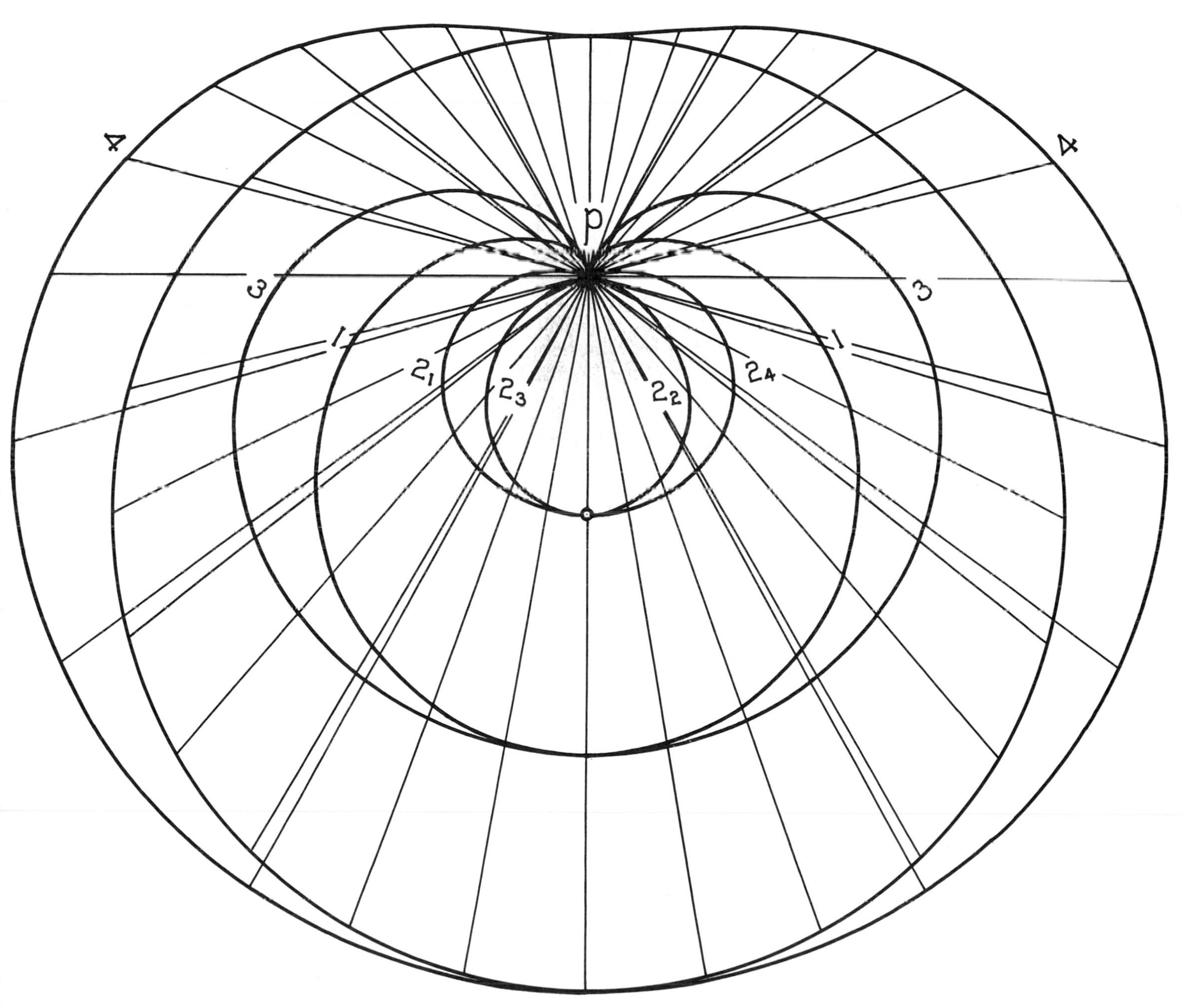

Conchoidal Transformation of a Circle.

When all points of the circle advance at the same rate along their lines through circumferential point p, they will form curves 1, 2, 3 and 4-p-4 at half radius intervals.

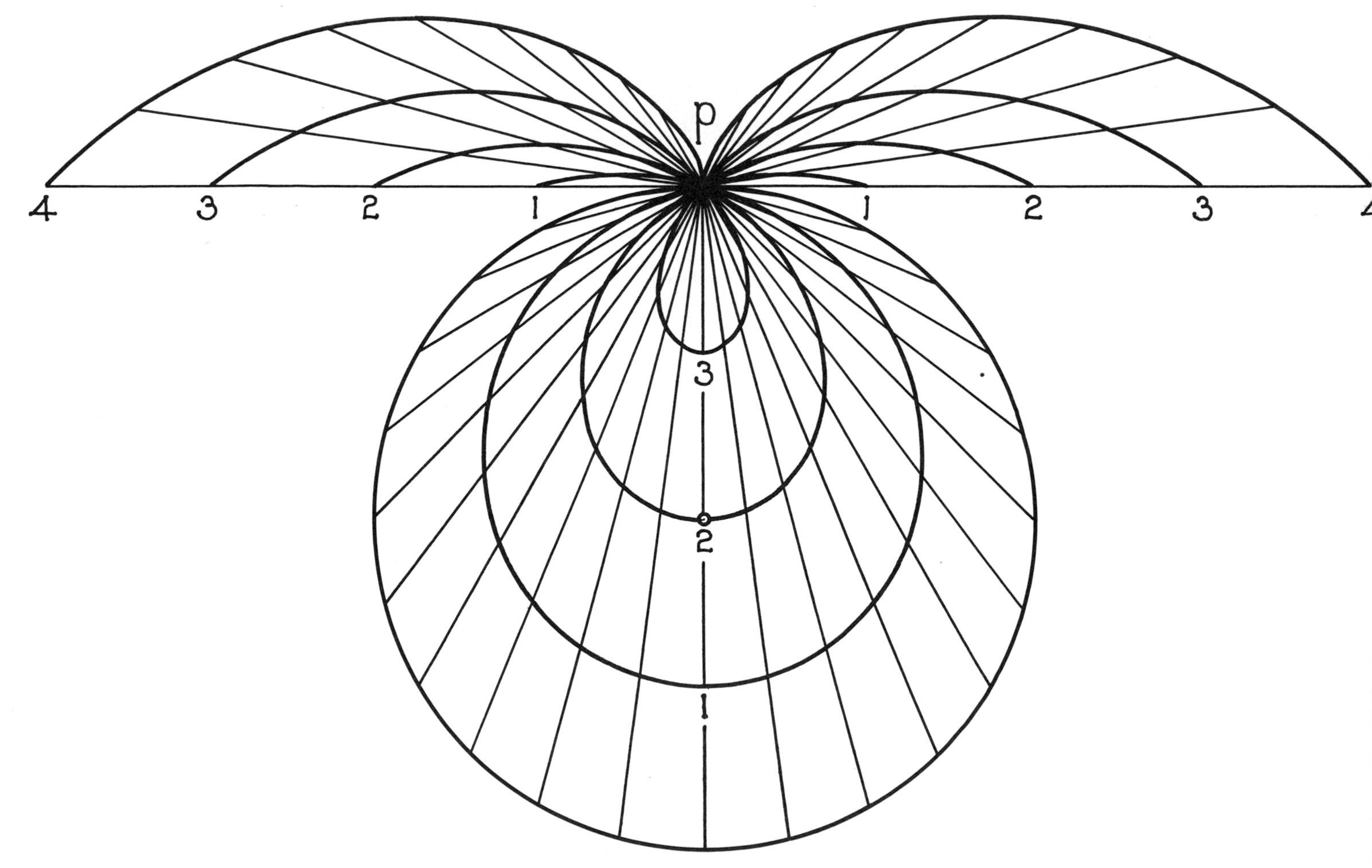

Conchoidal Transformation of a Circle.

When all points of the circle advance at the same rate along their lines through external point p, they will form curves 1-1, 2-p, 3-3 and 4-4 at half radius intervals.

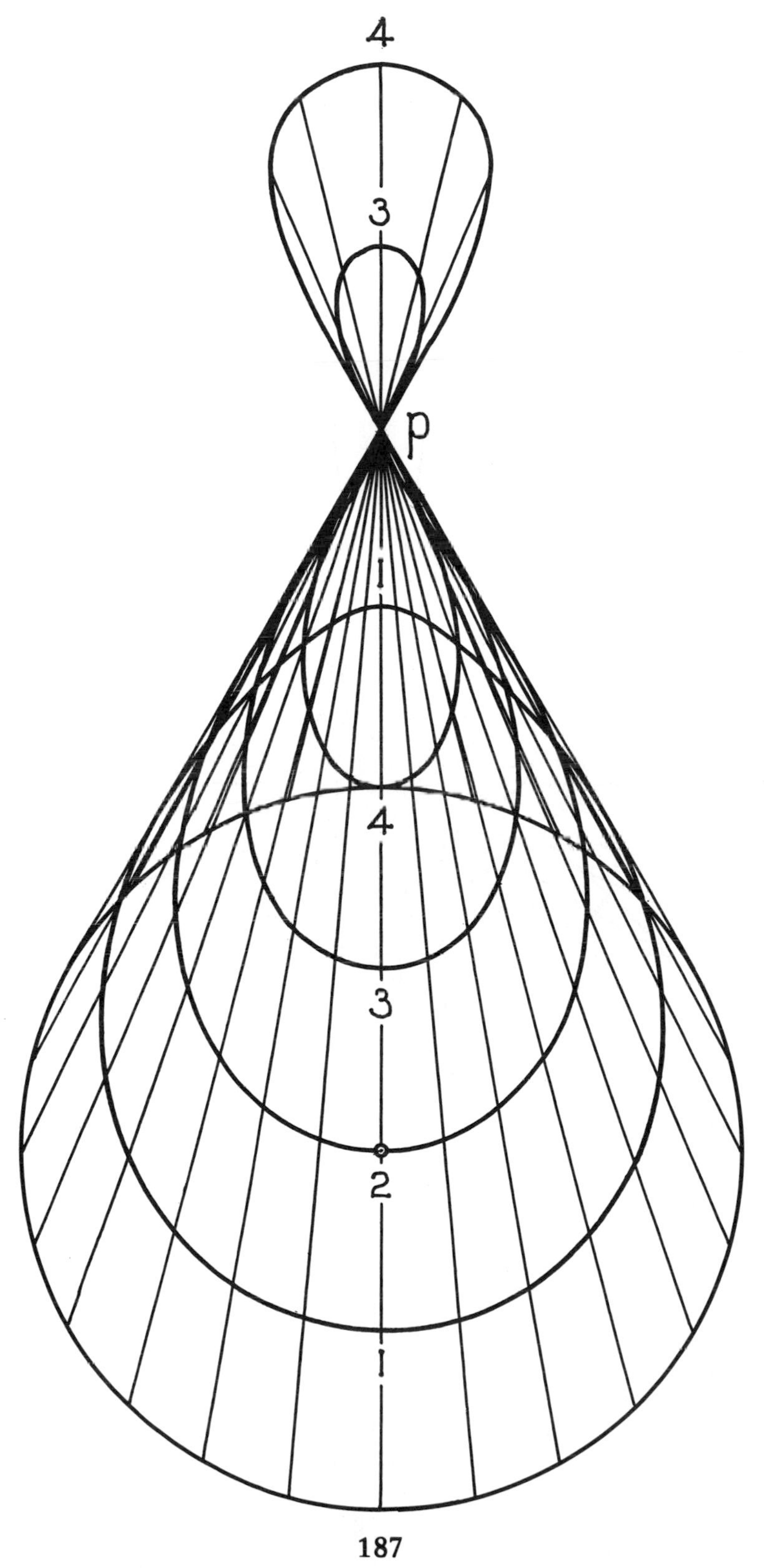

Conchoidal Transformation of Triangles.

When all points in sides of the three triangles move in at the same rate on their lines through center, they will form the floral pattern when midpoints of outer sides meet at the center.

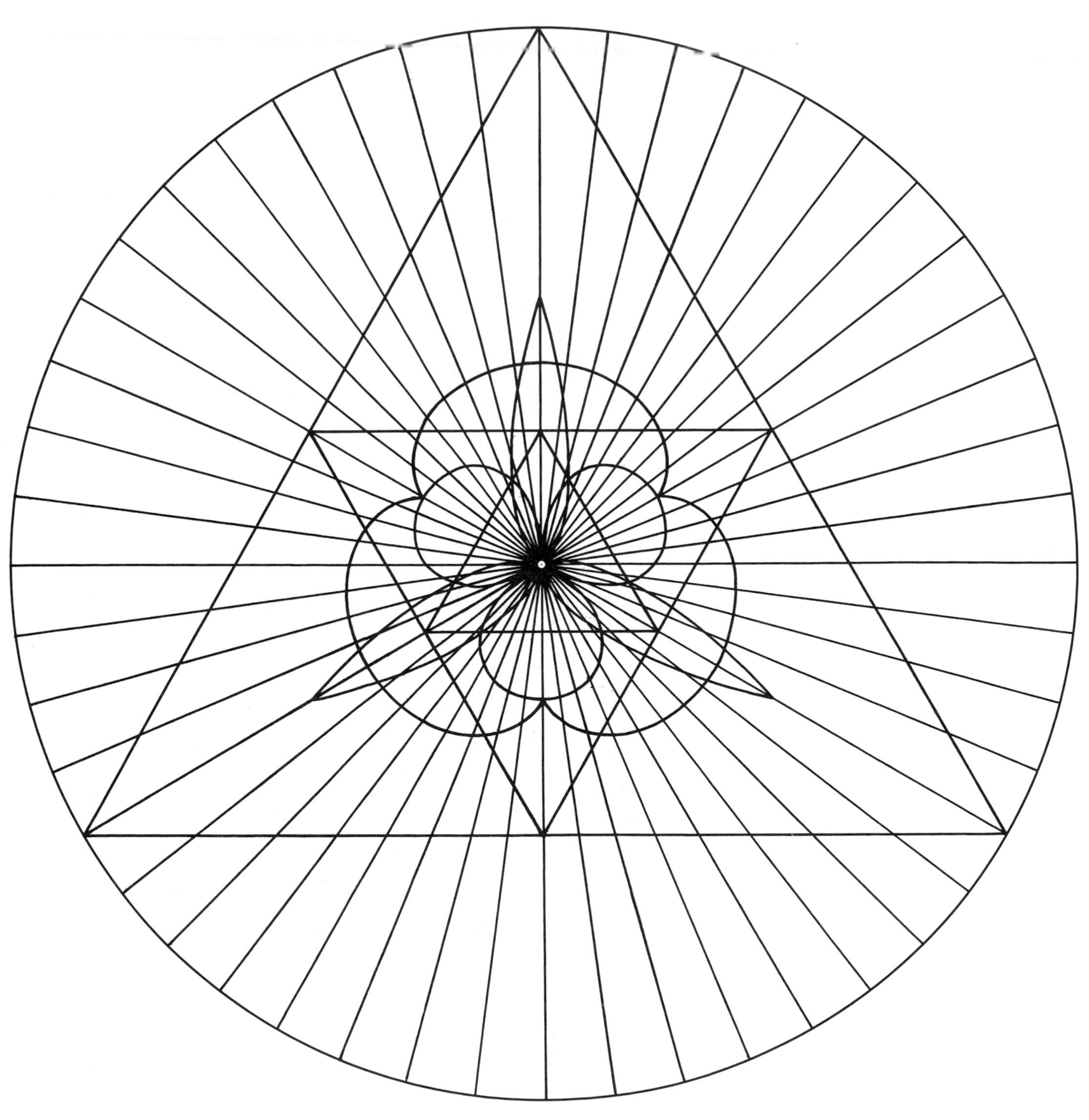

Dynamic Circle.

Twenty positions of a circle as the circle revolves around a point in its circumference.

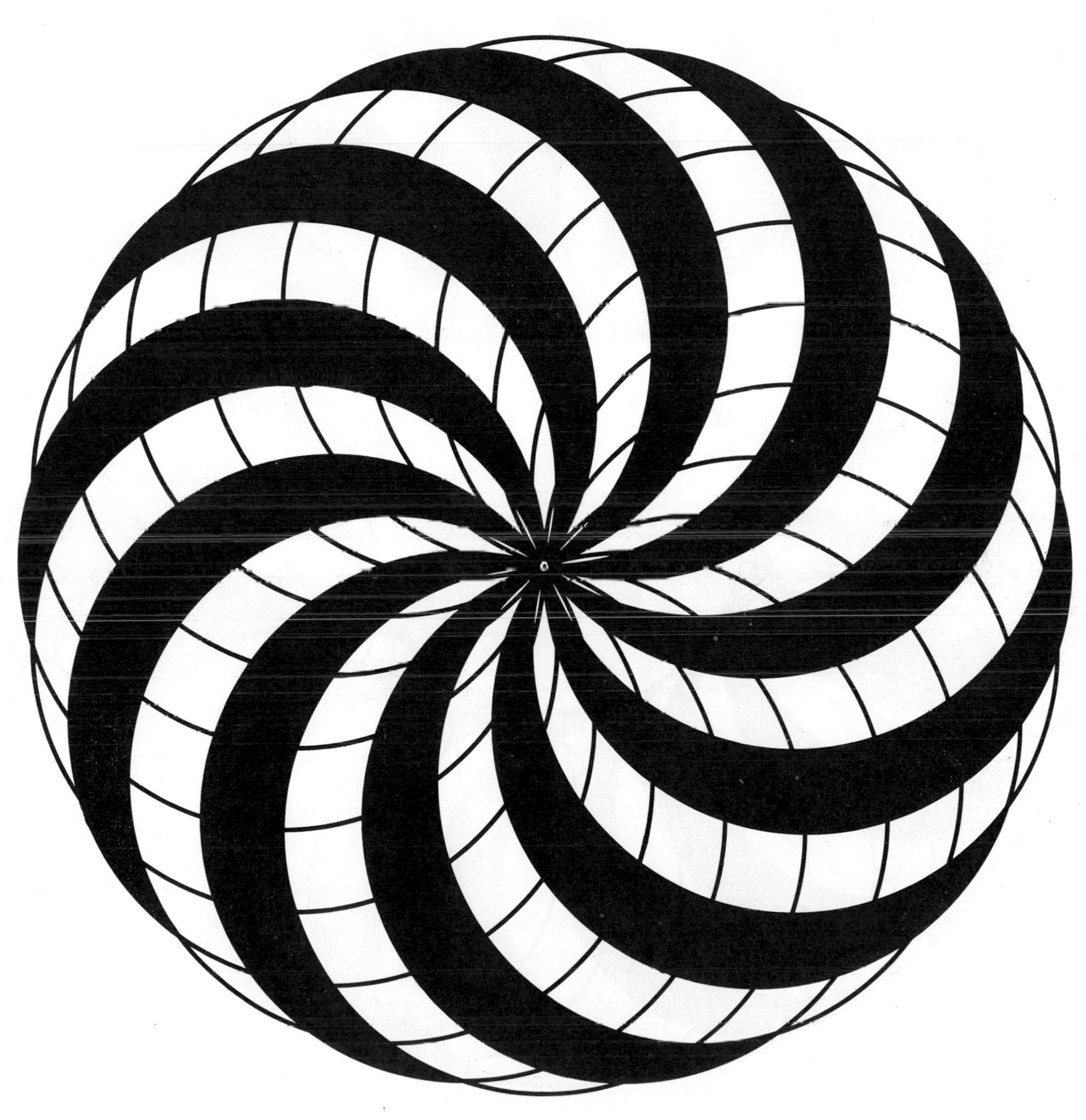

Dynamic Circle.

Thirty six positions of a circle as the circle rolls around a base circle of the same size.

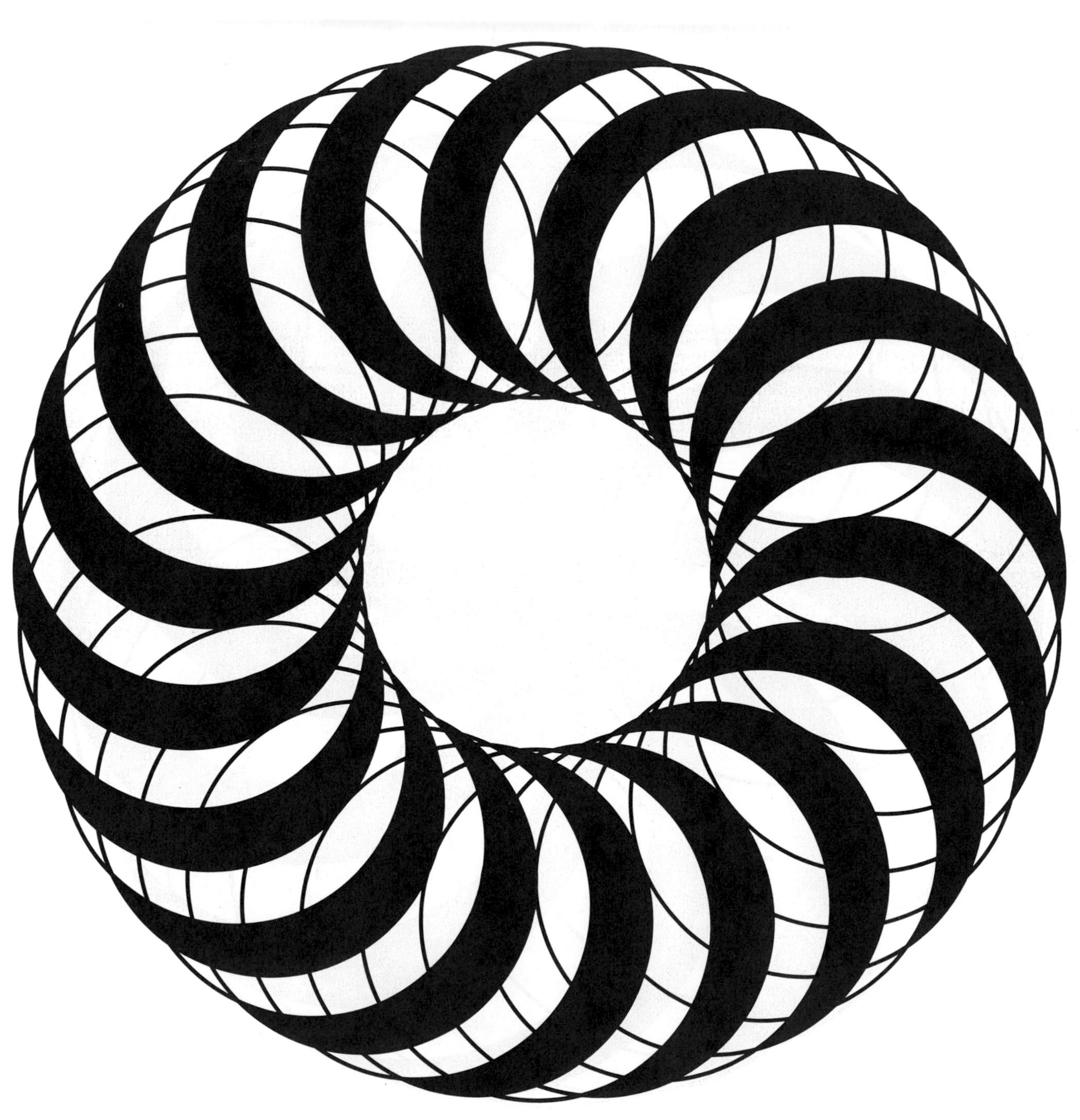

Tangent Circles in $\sqrt{3}$ Ratios.

Circles are centered on crotches of concentric six pointed stars.

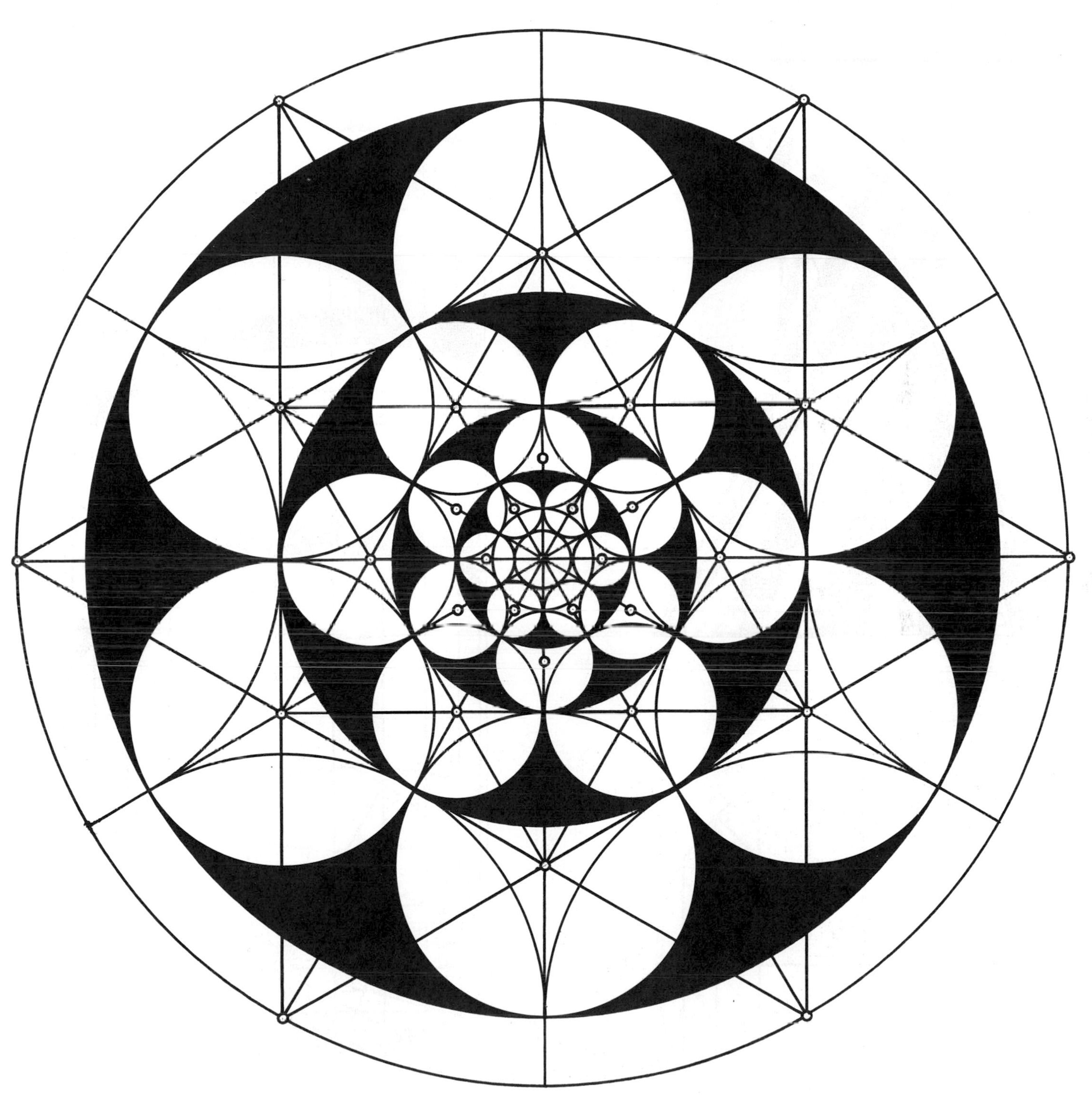

Hyperboloid.

Twist – 135°.

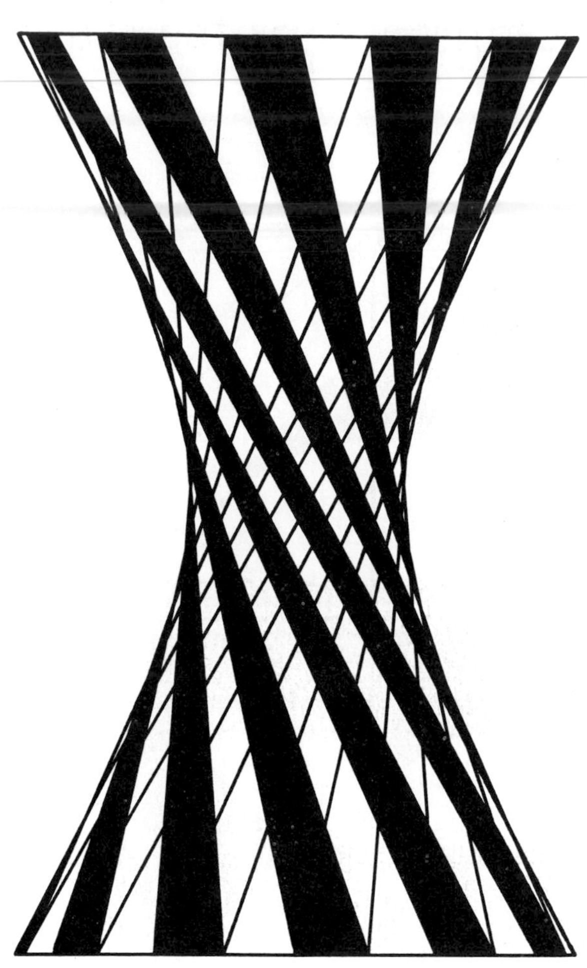

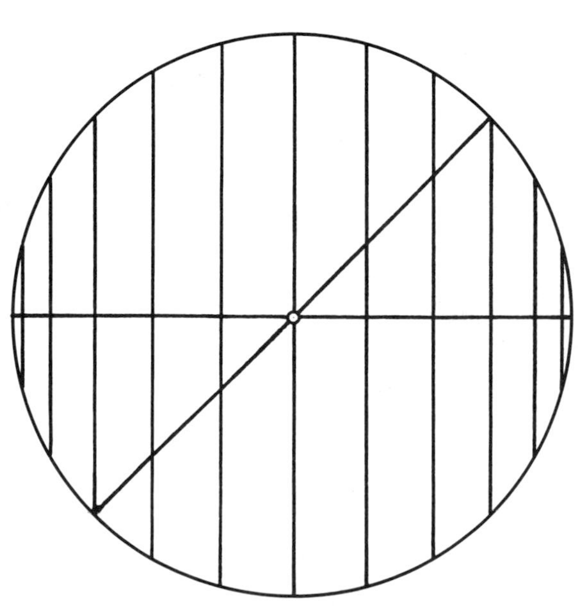

Helix.

Axial slope – 5 to 12.
Helix rises one diameter in 720°.

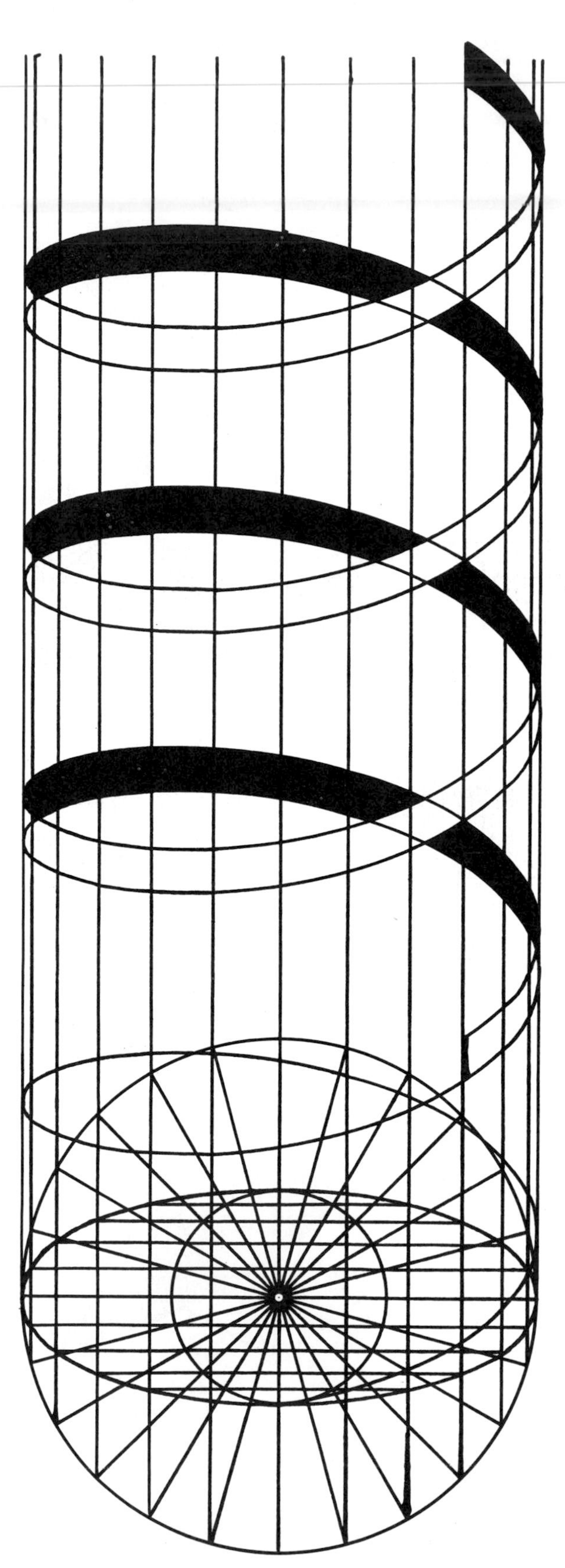

Intersections.
Planes and Cones.

Intersections.
Cylinders and Spheres.

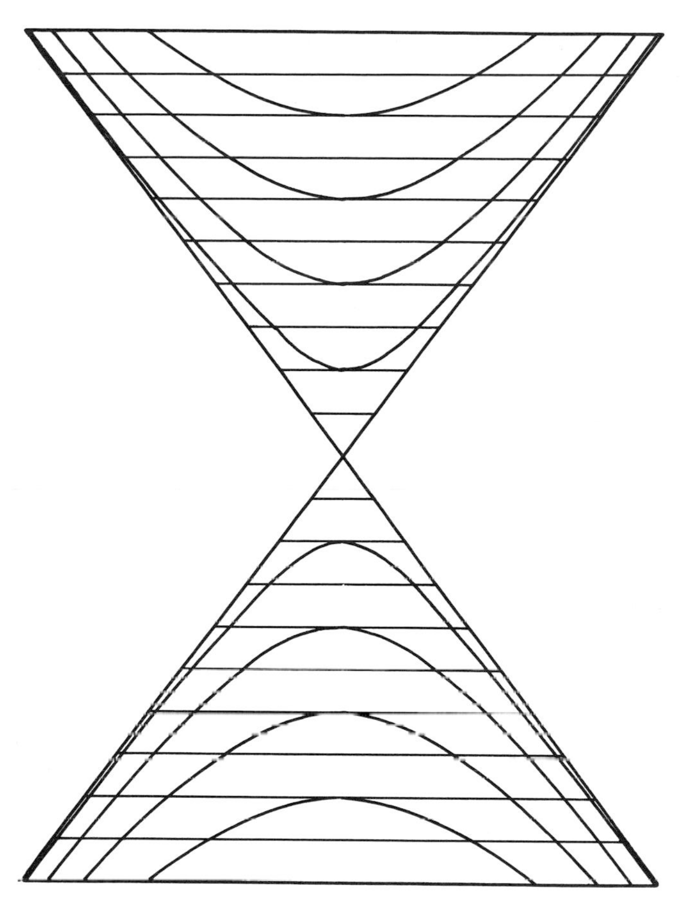

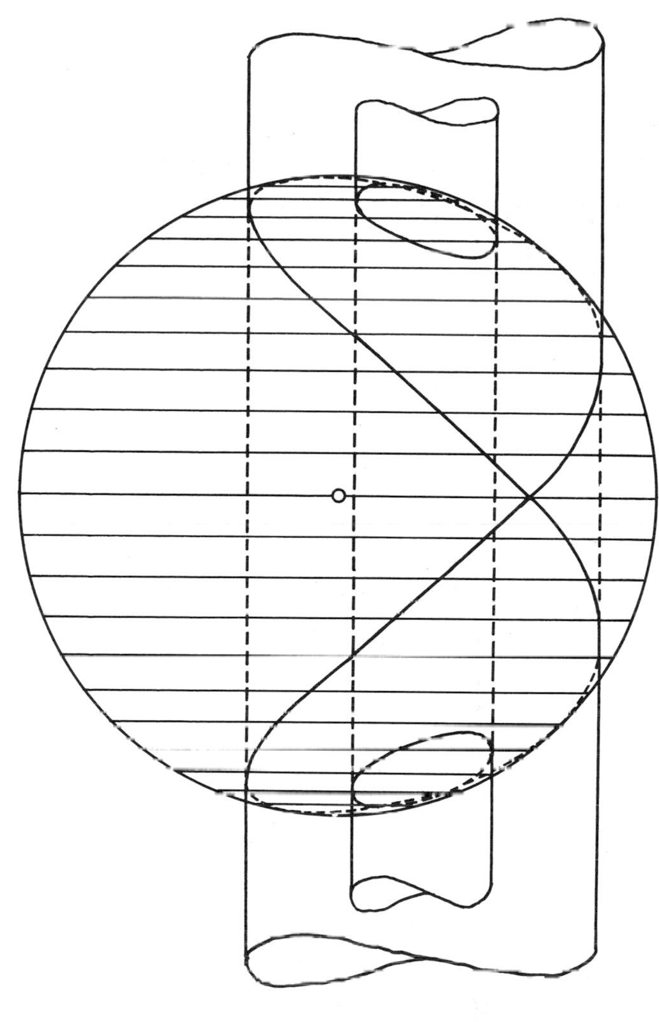

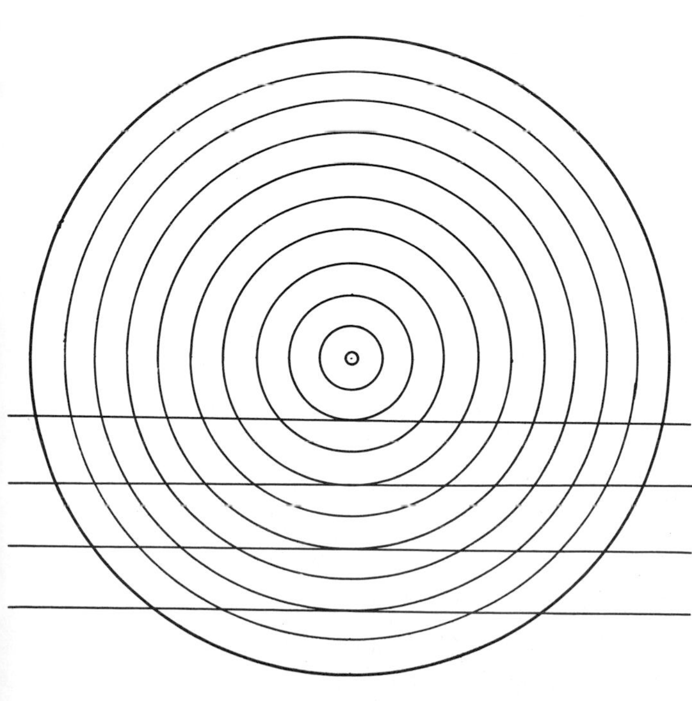

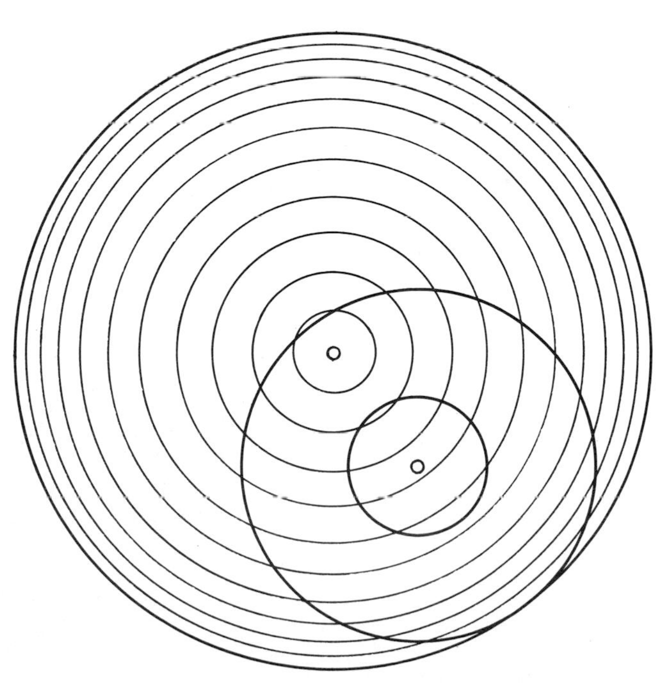

Plane Sections of Torus.

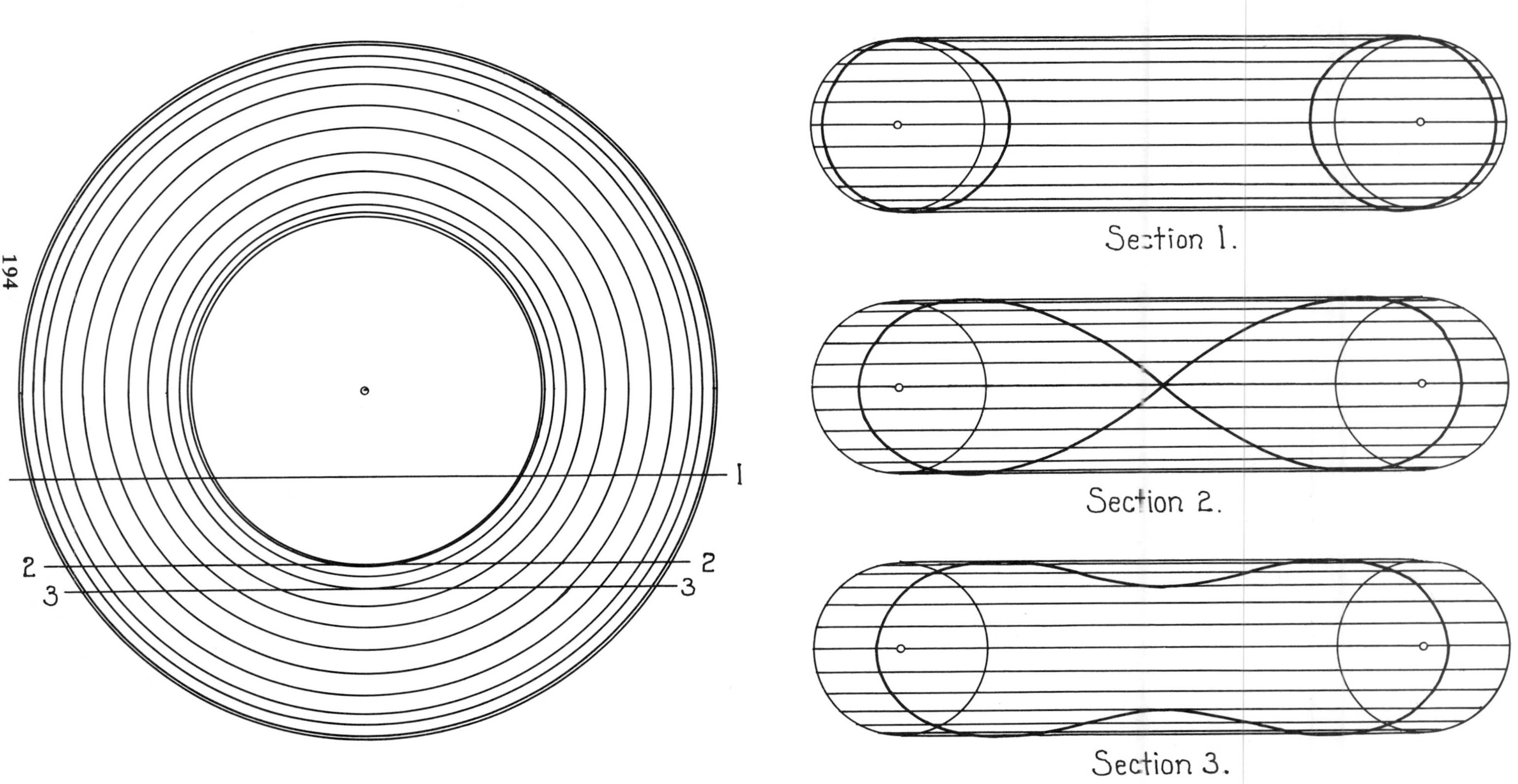

The Earth with 15° Parallels.

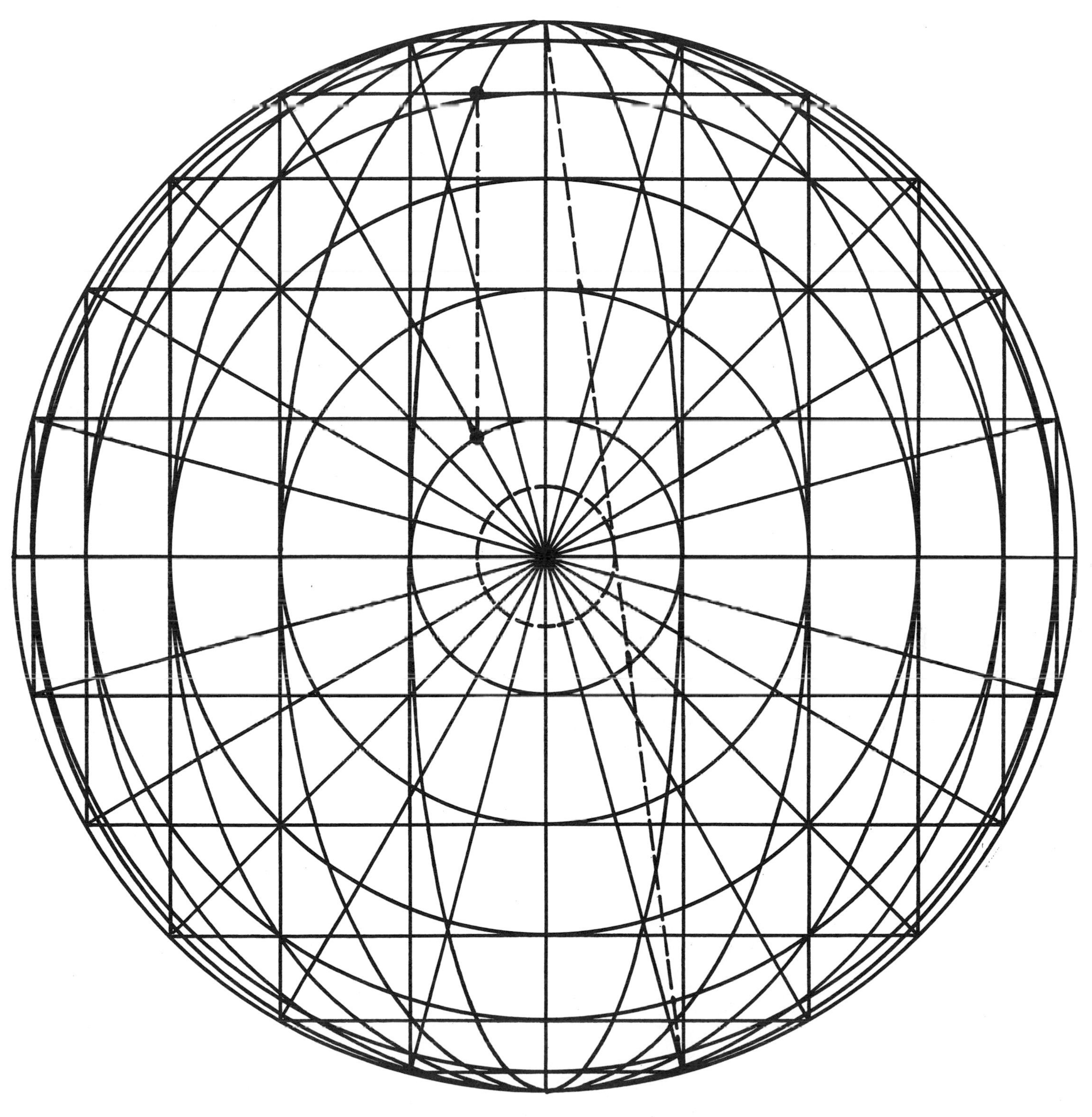

section VI

SPIRALS

Archimedean Spiral.

The radius of this Archimedean spiral lengthens at the rate of $\frac{1''}{16}$ per turn of 30°.

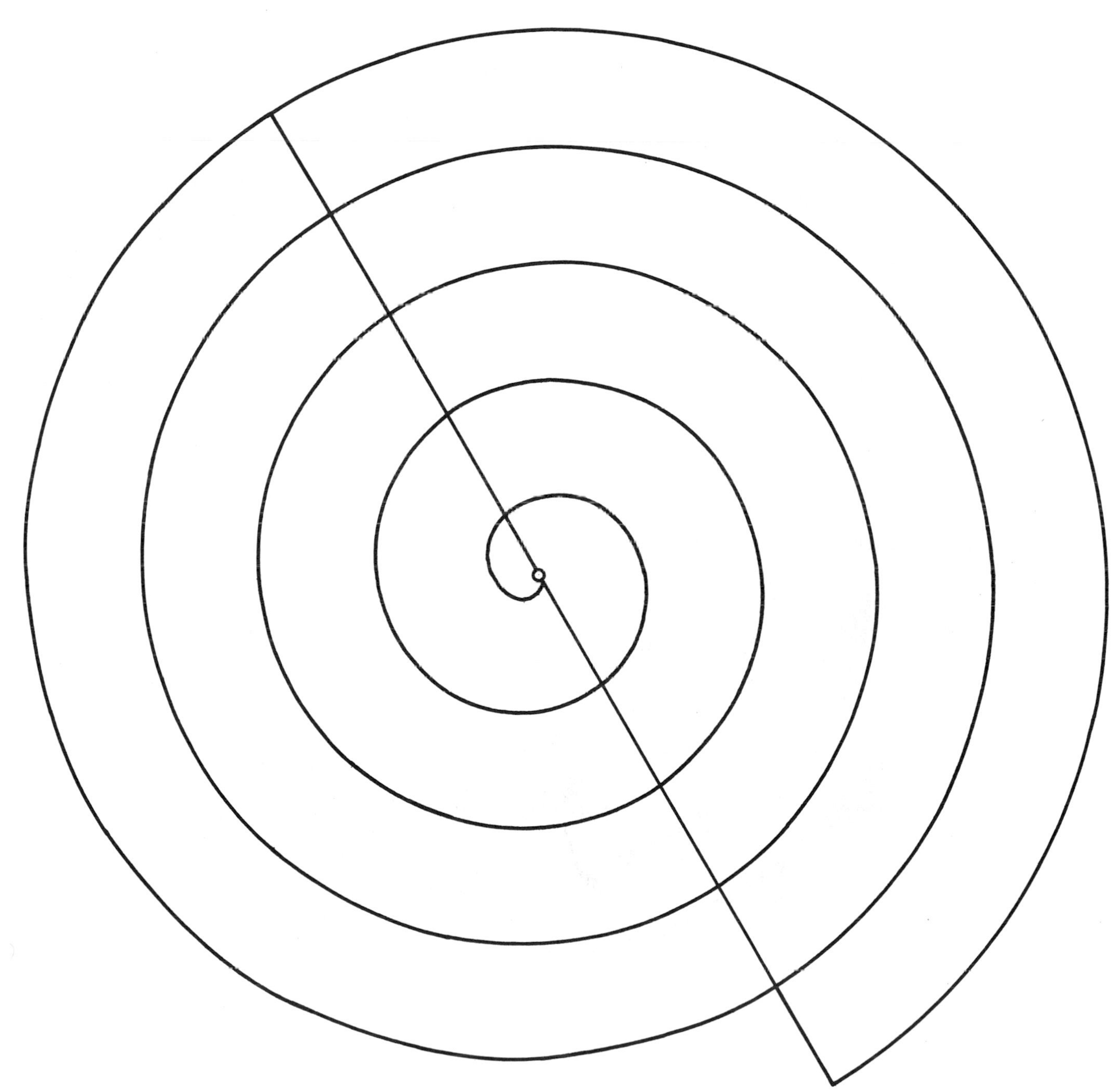

Archimedean Spirals.

Logarithmic Spiral.

The radius of this logarithmic spiral lengthens at the rate of 7% per turn of 36°.

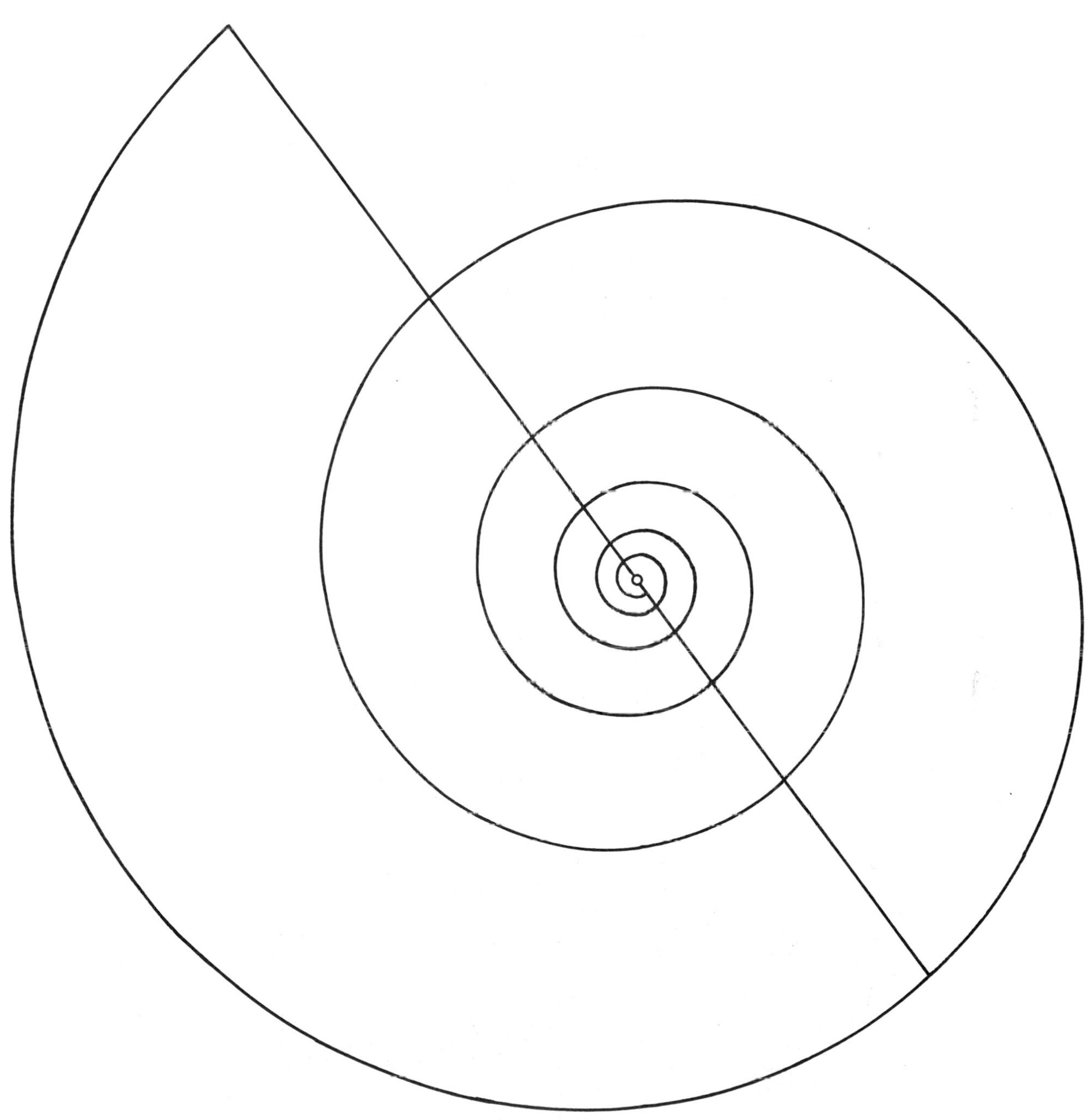

Logarithmic Spirals.

Baravalle Spirals in Squares.

Sides of successive squares have ratio of $\frac{1}{\sqrt{2}}$ or 0.707.

Baravalle Spirals in Hexagons.

Sides of successive hexagons have ratio of $\frac{1}{2}\sqrt{3}$ or 0.866.

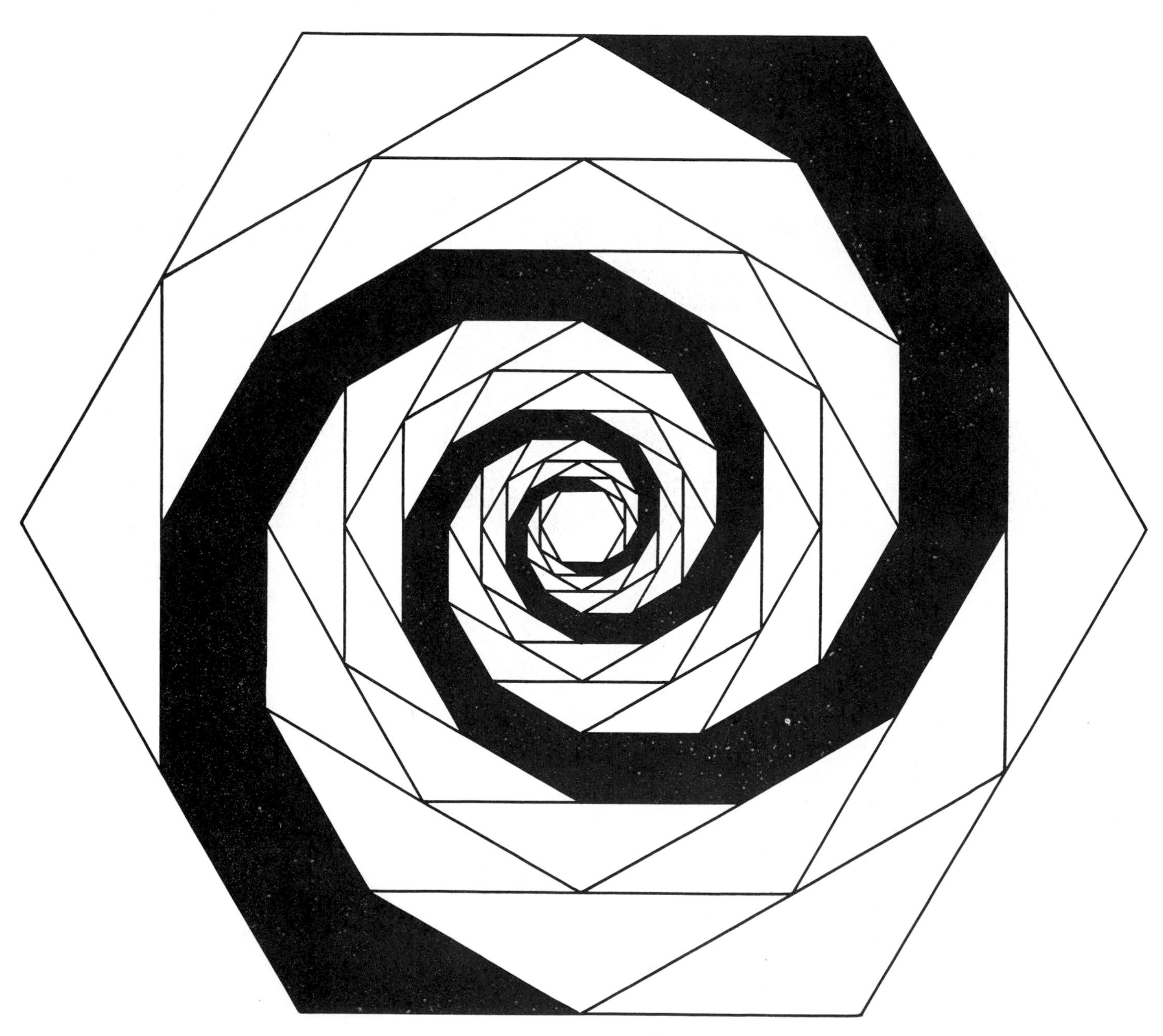

Baravalle Spirals in Octagons.

Sides of successive octagons have ratio of $\frac{1}{2}\sqrt{2+\sqrt{2}}$ or 0.924.

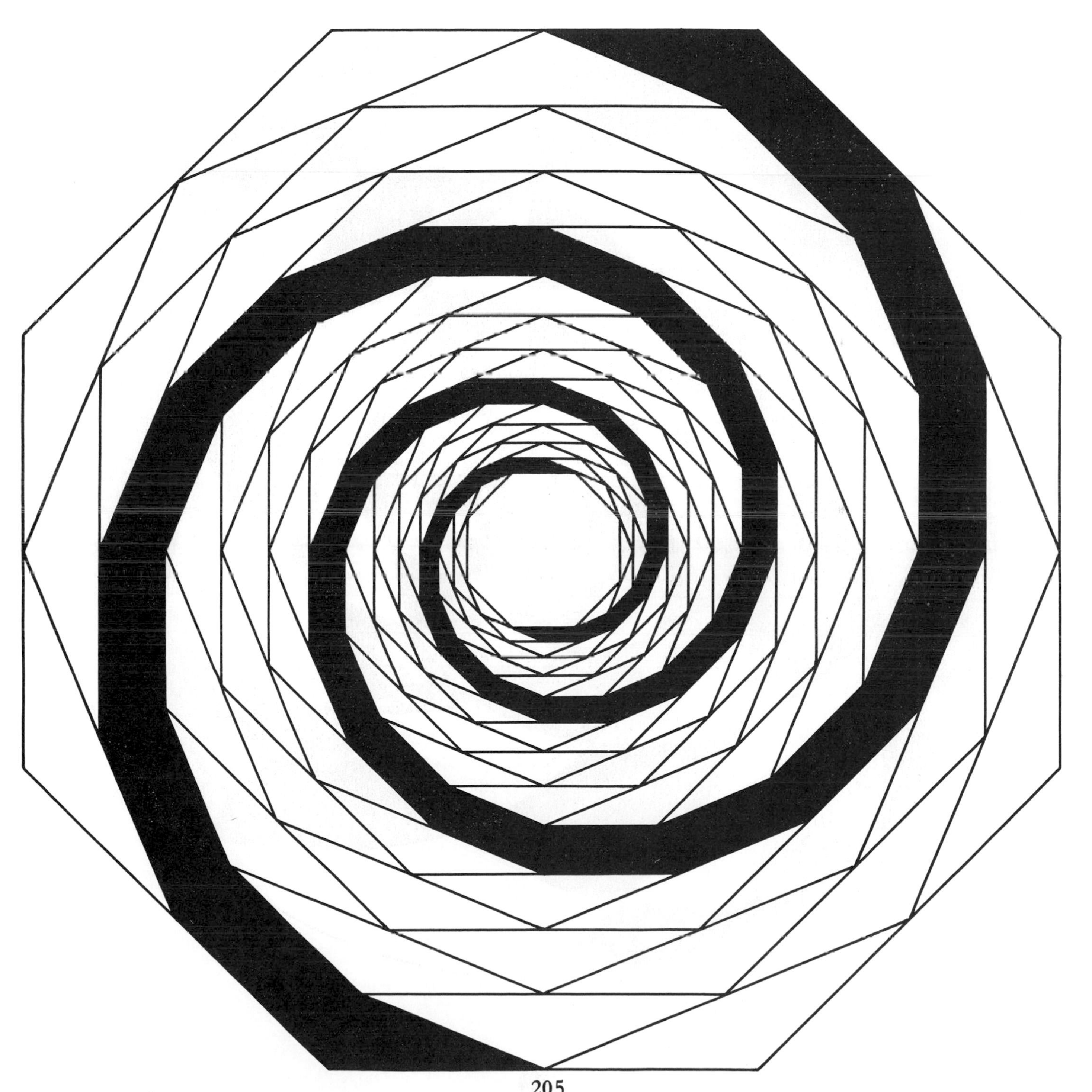

Fibonacci Spiraling.

5 clockwise spirals. Radii lengthen 61.8 % per 1/5th circle turn.
8 counter-clockwise spirals. Radii lengthen 61.8% per 1/8th circle turn.
13 axial radii.

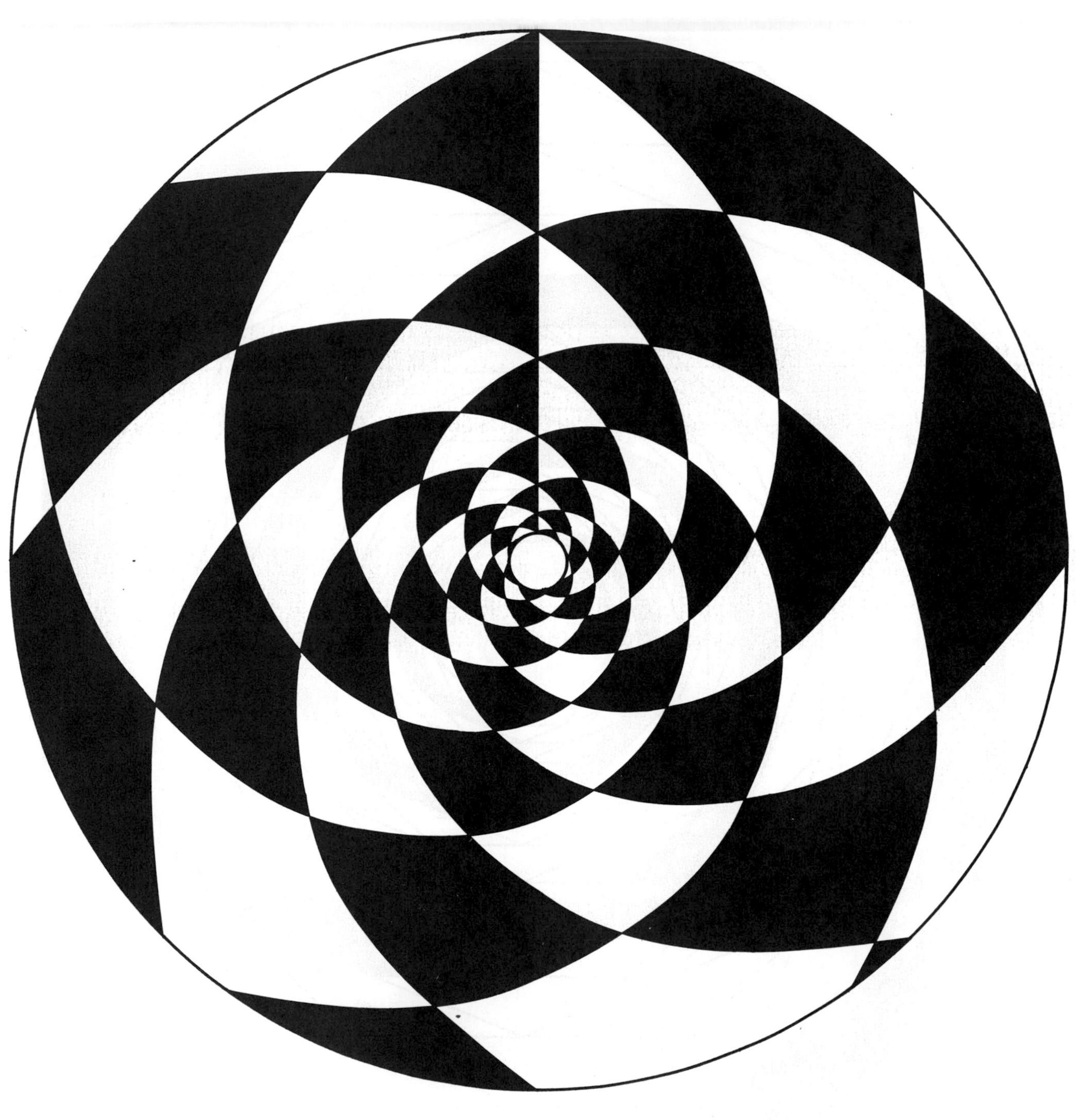

Fibonacci Spiraling.

5 clockwise spirals. Radii lengthen 28.1% per 1/5th circle turn.
8 counter-clockwise spirals. Radii lengthen 28.1% per 1/8th circle turn.
13 axial radii.

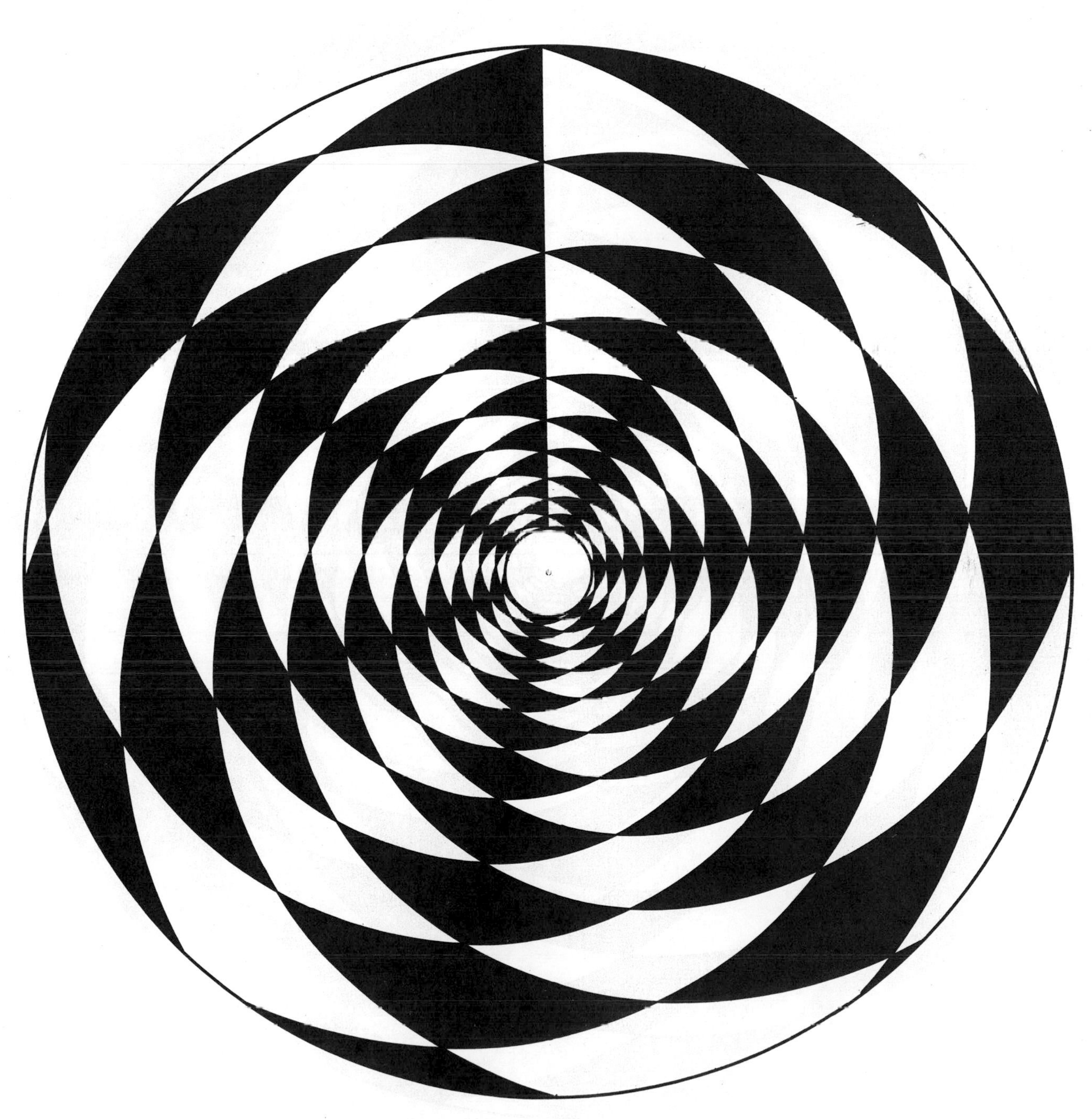

Fibonacci Spiraling.

8 clockwise spirals. Radii lengthen 20% per 1/8th circle turn.
13 counter-clockwise spirals. Radii lengthen 20% per 1/13th circle turn.
21 axial radii.

Commensurate Squares.

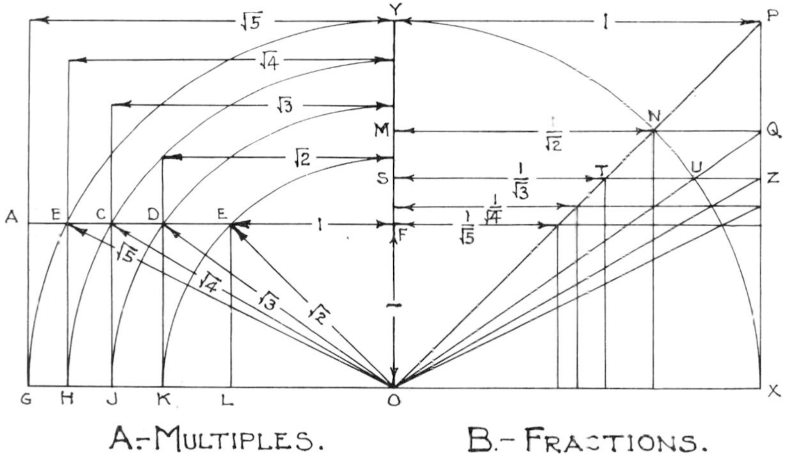

A.- Multiples. B.- Fractions.

A.- To draw squares with areas of 2,3,4,5 etc., times area of a given square.

Sides and area of given square, OFEL, are considered as unity. Draw diagonal, OE. It is √2 long. Extend side, EF, to A and OL to G. Draw arc, EK. The √2 square erected on base, OK, has twice area of given square. Draw diagonal, OD. Since right triangle, ODK, has an altitude of 1 and base of √2, hypotenuse, OD, is √3 long. Draw arc, DJ. The √3 square erected on base, OJ, has three times area of given square. Diagonal, OC, is √4 long. Repeat process to get number of commensurate squares desired.

B.- To draw squares with areas of $\frac{1}{2}, \frac{1}{3}, \frac{1}{4}, \frac{1}{5}$, etc., area of a given square.

Sides and area of given square, OYPX, are considered as unity. Draw diagonal, OP. It is √2 long. Inscribe arc, YNX, with radius of unity. Through intersection, N, of arc and diagonal, draw MQ parallel to YP. MN is $\frac{1}{\sqrt{2}}$ long. It is side of square having half of area of given square. Draw OQ and then SZ through U parallel to YP. ST is $\frac{1}{\sqrt{3}}$ long. It is side of square having one third area of given square. The process can be repeated indefinitely.

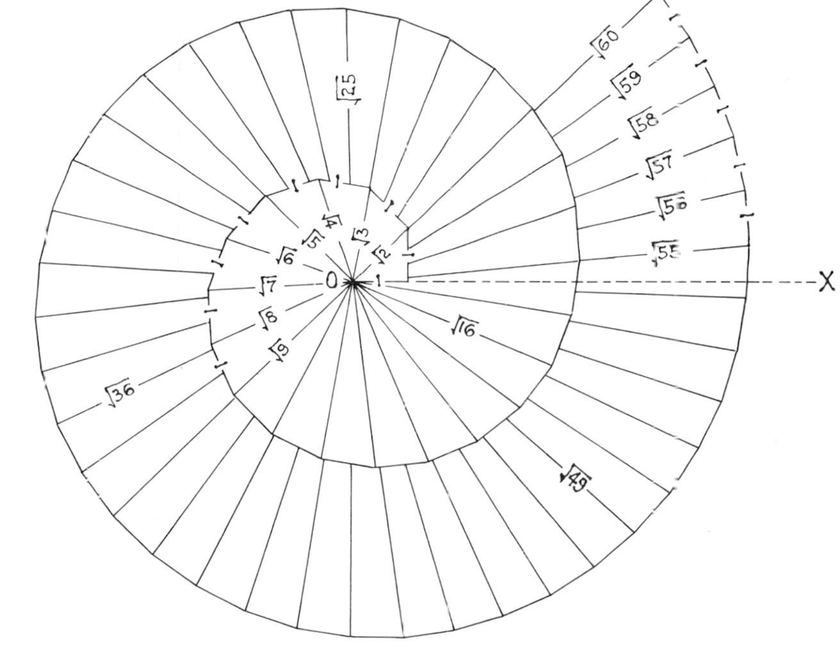

Square Root Spiral.

No.	√No.	Azimuth.	No.	√No.	Azimuth.	No.	√No.	Azimuth.	No.	√No.	Azimuth.
1	1.00000	00° 00' 00"	16	4.00000	337°06'48"	31	5.56776	516°06'39"	46	6.78233	655°09'06"
2	1.41421	45° 00' 00"	17	4.12311	351°09'43"	32	5.65685	526°17'35"	47	6.85565	663°32'20"
3	1.73205	80° 15' 58"	18	4.24264	364°47'42"	33	5.74456	536°19'05"	48	6.92820	671°50'16"
4	2.00000	110°15'58"	19	4.35890	378°03'28"	34	5.83095	546°11'35"	49	7.00000	680°03'04"
5	2.23607	136°49'52"	20	4.47214	390°58'43"	35	5.91608	555°55'28"	50	7.07107	688°10'52"
6	2.44949	160°55'33"	21	4.58258	403°34'59"	36	6.00000	565°31'06"	51	7.14143	696°13'51"
7	2.64575	183°08'01"	22	4.69042	415°53'35"	37	6.08276	574°58'41"	52	7.21110	704°12'07"
8	2.82843	203°50'18"	23	4.79583	427°55'42"	38	6.16441	584°19'00"	53	7.28011	712°05'50"
9	3.00000	223°18'25"	24	4.89898	439°42'24"	39	6.24500	593°31'52"	54	7.34847	719°55'06"
10	3.16228	241°44'32"	25	5.00000	451°14'37"	40	6.32456	602°47'43"	55	7.41620	727°40'03"
11	3.31662	259°17'26"	26	5.09902	462°33'13"	41	6.40312	611°46'43"	56	7.48331	735°20'49"
12	3.46410	276°04'09"	27	5.19615	473°38'58"	42	6.48075	620°39'24"	57	7.54983	742°57'30"
13	3.60555	292°10'17"	28	5.29150	484°32'34"	43	6.55744	629°25'43"	58	7.61577	750°30'12"
14	3.74166	307°40'22"	29	5.38516	495°14'40"	44	6.63325	638°05'57"	59	7.68115	758°09'02"
15	3.87298	322°38'09"	30	5.47723	505°45'51"	45	6.70820	646°40'22"	60	7.74597	765°34'07"

RECTANGULAR SPIRALS.

CD is perpendicular to AB. All segments of spiral are parallel to sides of rectangle. The width to length ratio of the rectangle is the ratio of successive segments of the spiral. The spirals increase in intricacy as the width to length ratio approaches unity.

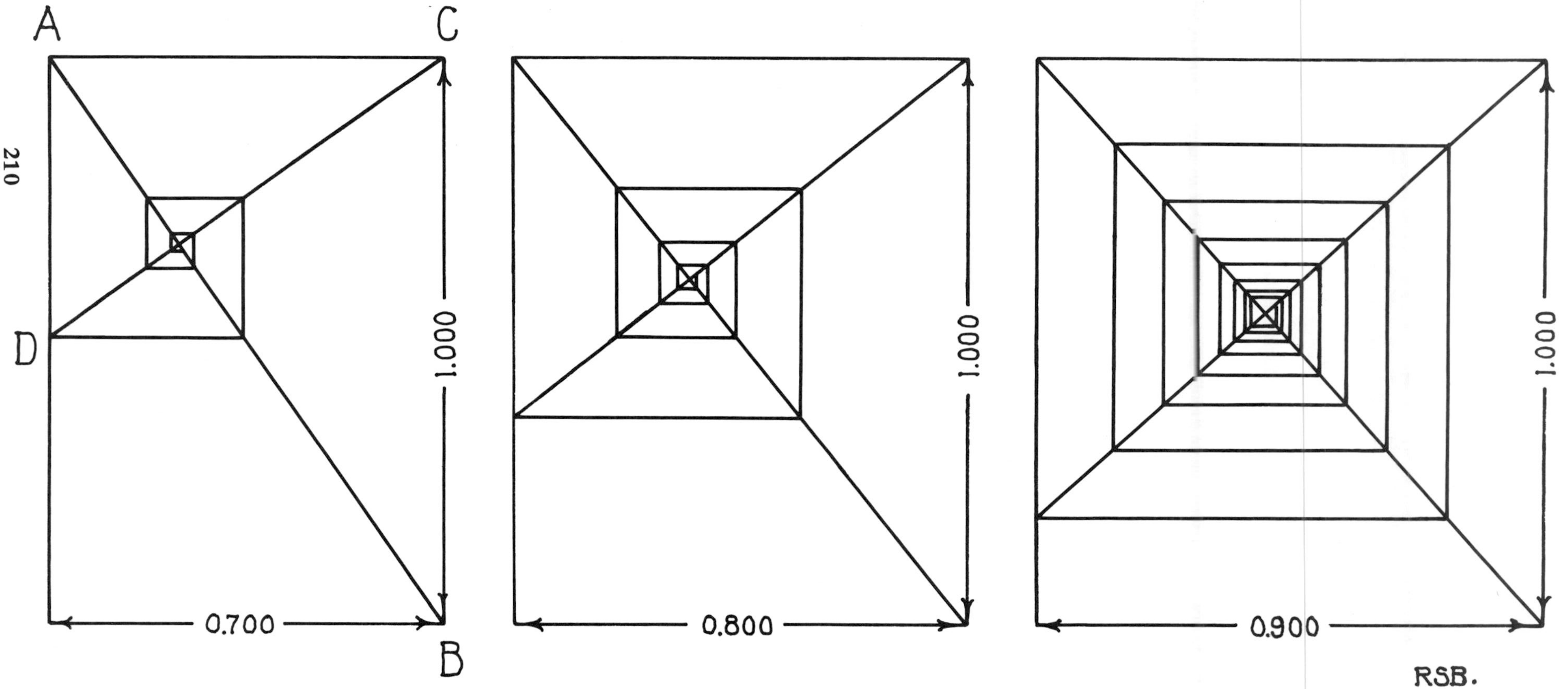

A
C
D
B
1.000
0.700
1.000
0.800
1.000
0.900

RSB.

Chords of spiral are in $\sqrt{k}$ ratio. $\sqrt{k} = 0.7862$.

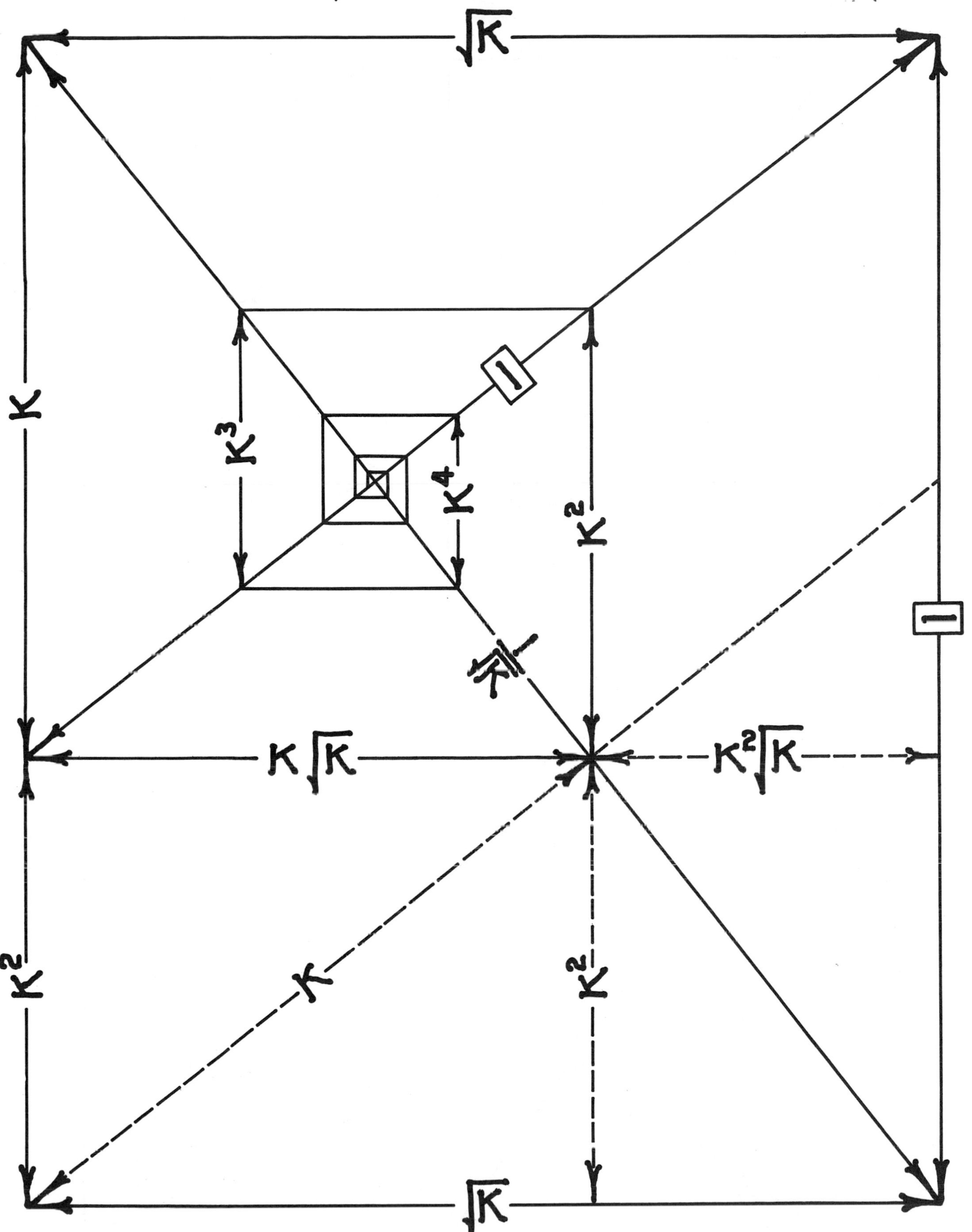

No other rectangle can be divided into three similar rectangles.

Rectangular and Rhomboidal Spirals.

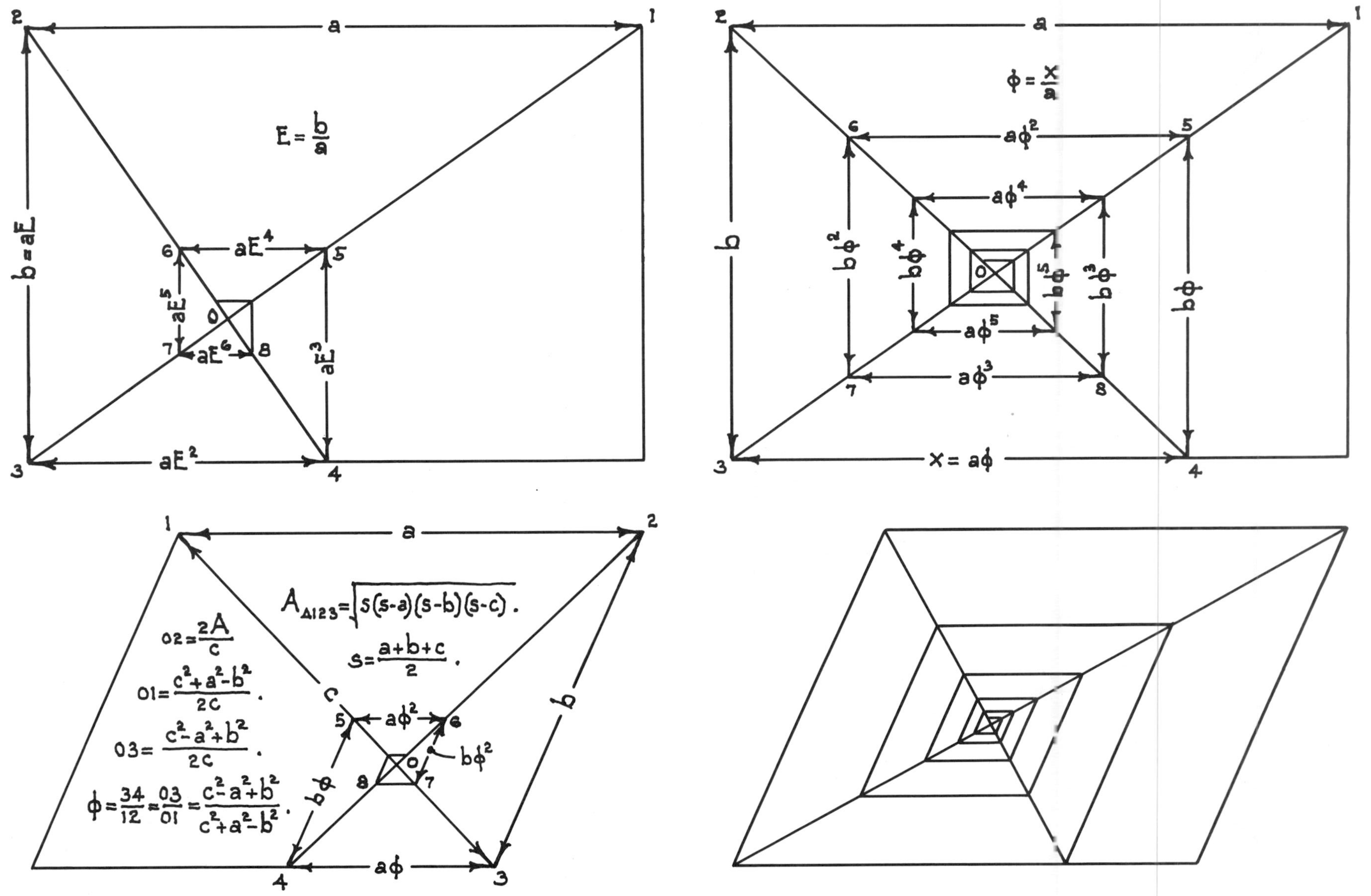

$E = \frac{b}{a}$

$b = aE$, aE^2, aE^3, aE^4, aE^5, aE^6

$\phi = \frac{x}{a}$

$x = a\phi$, $a\phi^2$, $a\phi^3$, $a\phi^4$, $a\phi^5$, $b\phi$, $b\phi^2$, $b\phi^3$, $b\phi^4$, $b\phi^5$

$$A_{\Delta 123} = \sqrt{s(s-a)(s-b)(s-c)}.$$

$$s = \frac{a+b+c}{2}.$$

$$02 = \frac{2A}{c}$$

$$01 = \frac{c^2+a^2-b^2}{2c}.$$

$$03 = \frac{c^2-a^2+b^2}{2c}.$$

$$\phi = \frac{34}{12} = \frac{03}{01} = \frac{c^2-a^2+b^2}{c^2+a^2-b^2}.$$

section VII

TRIANGLE RELATIONSHIPS

THE NINE POINT CIRCLE IN TRIANGLES.

Perpendiculars at midpoints A', B' and C' intersect at O, the center of the bounding circle. Altitudes AA'', BB'' and CC'' intersect at orthocenter, X. E_a, E_b and E_c are midpoints of AX, BX and CX. Q, midpoint of OX, is the center of the nine point circle which passes through points A', A'', B', B'', C', C'', E_a, E_b and E_c. This circle and the Euler triangle $E_aE_bE_c$ are half scale replicas of triangle ABC and its bounding circle.

Both triangles are units of a web centered on X.

The midposition of lines $C'E_b$ and $B'E_c$ in triangles AXB and AXC make them equal and perpendicular to E_bE_c. Diagonals $C'E_c$ and $B'E_b$ bisect each other at Q. Similarly the half diagonals of rectangle $A'E_cE_aC'$ show that points A' and E_a lie on circle Q. Right triangles $A'A''E_a$, $B'B''E_b$ and $C'C''E_c$ place points A'', B'' and C'' on circle Q.

The centroid P lies on the Euler line OX.

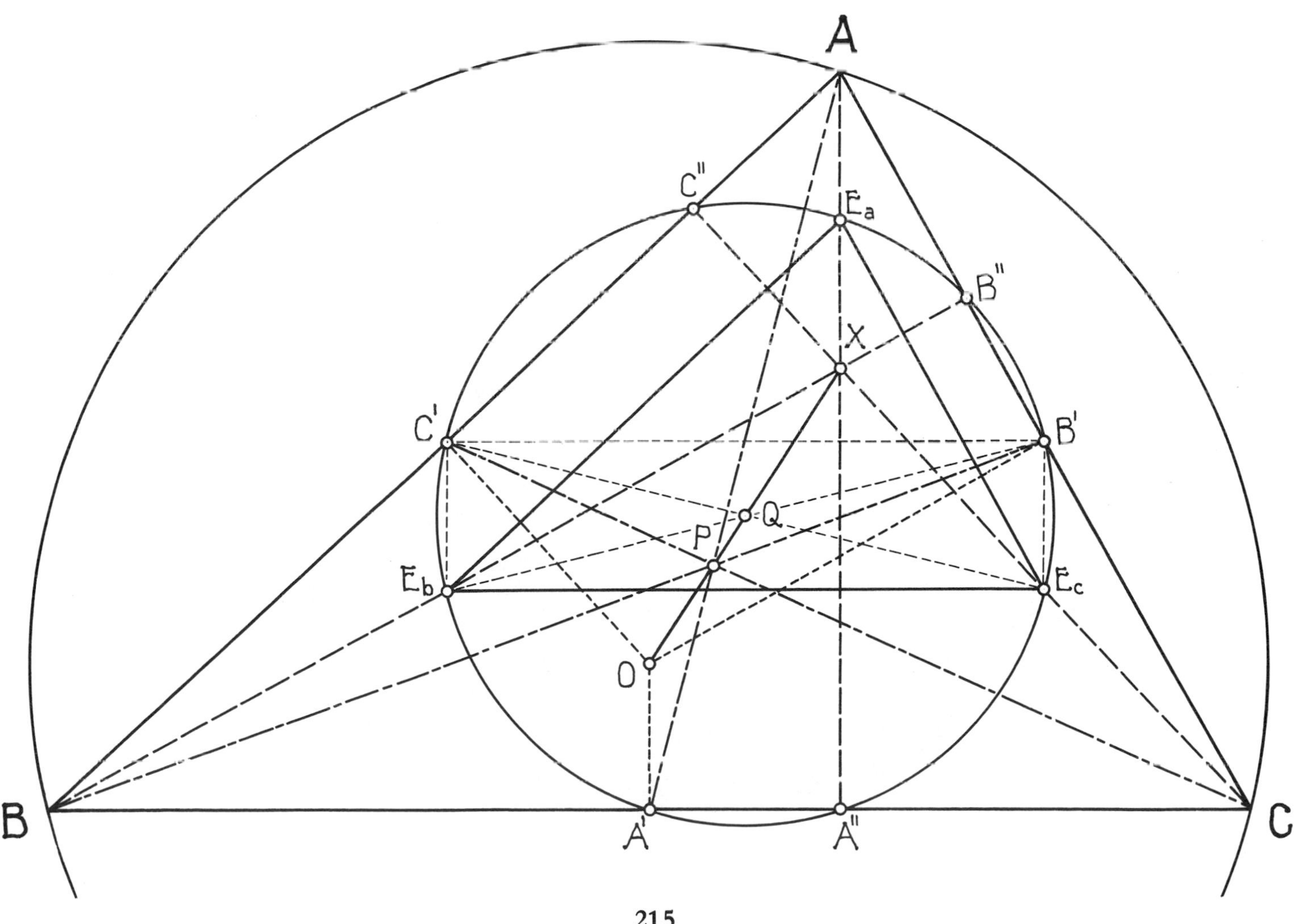

The Nine Circle Complex of Triangles.

A VARIATION OF THE APOLLONIUS PROBLEM

By Colonel Robert S. Beard

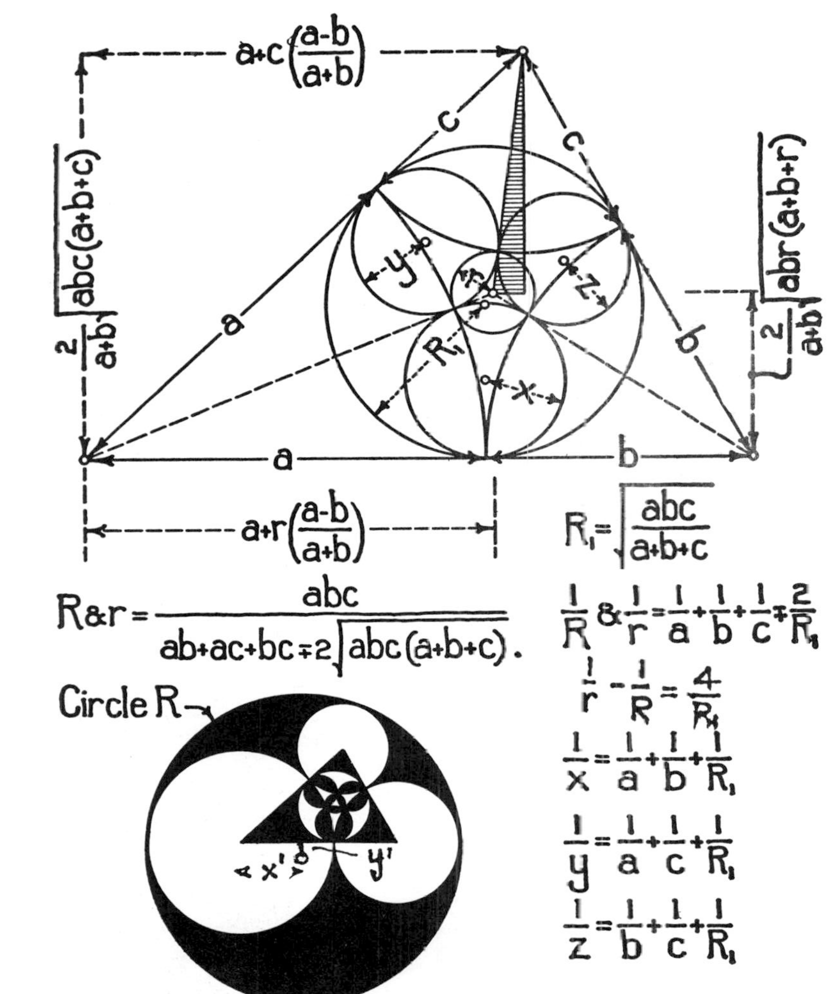

$$R \& r = \frac{abc}{ab+ac+bc \mp 2\sqrt{abc(a+b+c)}}.$$

$$R_1 = \sqrt{\frac{abc}{a+b+c}}$$

$$\frac{1}{R} \& \frac{1}{r} = \frac{1}{a} + \frac{1}{b} + \frac{1}{c} \mp \frac{2}{R_1}$$

$$\frac{1}{r} - \frac{1}{R} = \frac{4}{R_1}$$

$$\frac{1}{x} = \frac{1}{a} + \frac{1}{b} + \frac{1}{R_1}$$

$$\frac{1}{y} = \frac{1}{a} + \frac{1}{c} + \frac{1}{R_1}$$

$$\frac{1}{z} = \frac{1}{b} + \frac{1}{c} + \frac{1}{R_1}$$

Center of Circle R

$$x' = a - R\left\{\frac{a-b}{a+b}\right\}$$

$$y' = \frac{2}{a+b}\sqrt{abR(R-a-b)}.$$

ROBERT S. BEARD

In this figure a, b, and c are radii of three mutually tangent circular arcs. The lines joining their centers form a triangle with sides $a + b$, $a + c$ and $b + c$.

The tangent points of these circles are also the tangent points of the circle R_1 inscribed in the triangle, and of three mutually tangent circles x, y, and z. Circle r is constructed so as to be tangent to circles a, b, and c.

The triangle in the black and white circular figure is a scaled reduction of the large triangular figure. Circles a, b, and c are shown in full in this figure. They are internally tangent to the added black circle of radius R.

In the shaded right triangle in the top figure, the short leg, S, is the difference between the horizontal projections of the lines $a + c$ and $a + r$. The longer leg, L, is the difference between the vertical projections of these lines.

Hence we have

$$S = c\left(\frac{a-b}{a+b}\right) - r\left(\frac{a-b}{a+b}\right) = \frac{a-b}{a+b}(c-r).$$

$$L = \frac{2}{a+b}\sqrt{abc(a+b+c)} - \frac{2}{a+b}\sqrt{abr(a+b-r)}$$

or

$$L = \frac{2\sqrt{ab}}{a+b}\left(\sqrt{c(a+b+c)} - \sqrt{r(a+b+r)}\right).$$

The hypotenuse is $c + r$.

$$(c+r)^2 = L^2 + S^2 = \frac{4ab}{(a+b)^2}\left(\sqrt{c(a+b+c)} - \sqrt{r(a+b+r)}\right)^2 + \frac{(a-b)^2}{(a+b)^2}(c-r)^2$$

On simplification we get a second degree equation in r whose roots are

$$r = \frac{abc}{ab + ac + bc \pm 2\sqrt{abc(a+b+c)}}$$

The positive value of the square root term gives the value of the radius r shown in the figure. This is in agreement with the formula used by Dr. Kasner in *Scripta Mathematica*, Vol. IX, No. 1, page 19. The negative value surprisingly enough gives the value of the radius R to which circles a, b, and c are internally tangent.

When two of the circles a, b, and c are internally tangent to the third, the negative value of the radius of the outer circle is used in the formula. In this case circles R and r are also internally tangent to the outer circle.

The values of the radii of circles x, y, and z can be determined from the formula for the radius of a circle inscribed in a triangle.

Centers c and r and the tangent point of circles a and b are located on a hyperbola that has foci at the centers of the circles a and b. See *Scripta Mathematica*, Vol. XIX, No. 4, page 271. Similar reasoning proves center r* to be the point of intersection of three such hyperbolas having foci at the vertices of the triangle.

*and center R

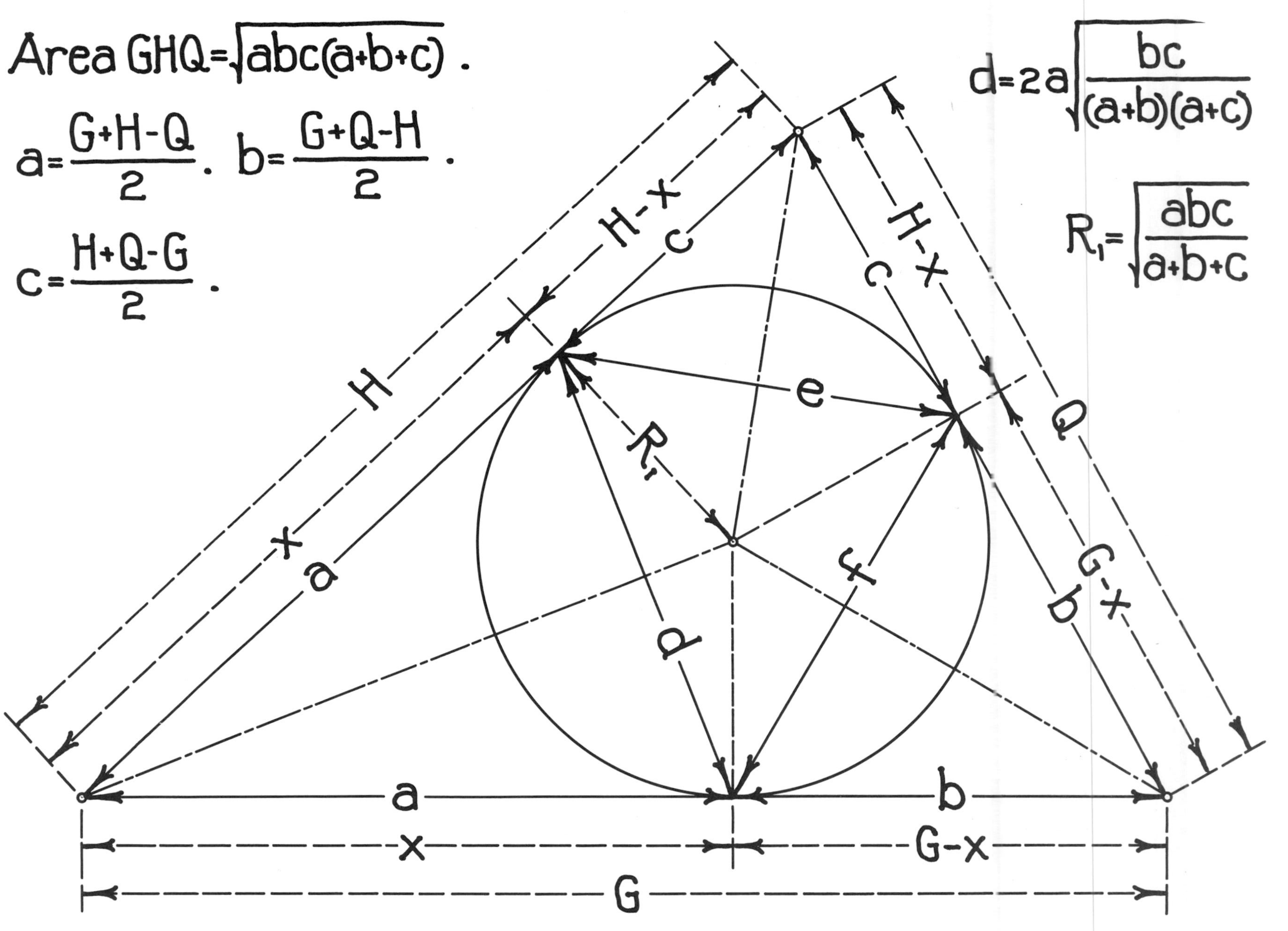

Area GHQ = $\sqrt{abc(a+b+c)}$.
$a = \frac{G+H-Q}{2}$. $b = \frac{G+Q-H}{2}$.
$c = \frac{H+Q-G}{2}$.
$d = 2a\sqrt{\frac{bc}{(a+b)(a+c)}}$
$R_1 = \sqrt{\frac{abc}{a+b+c}}$
H
H-x
c
x
a
H-x
c
Q
G-x
b
e
R_1
d
f
a
b
x
G-x
G

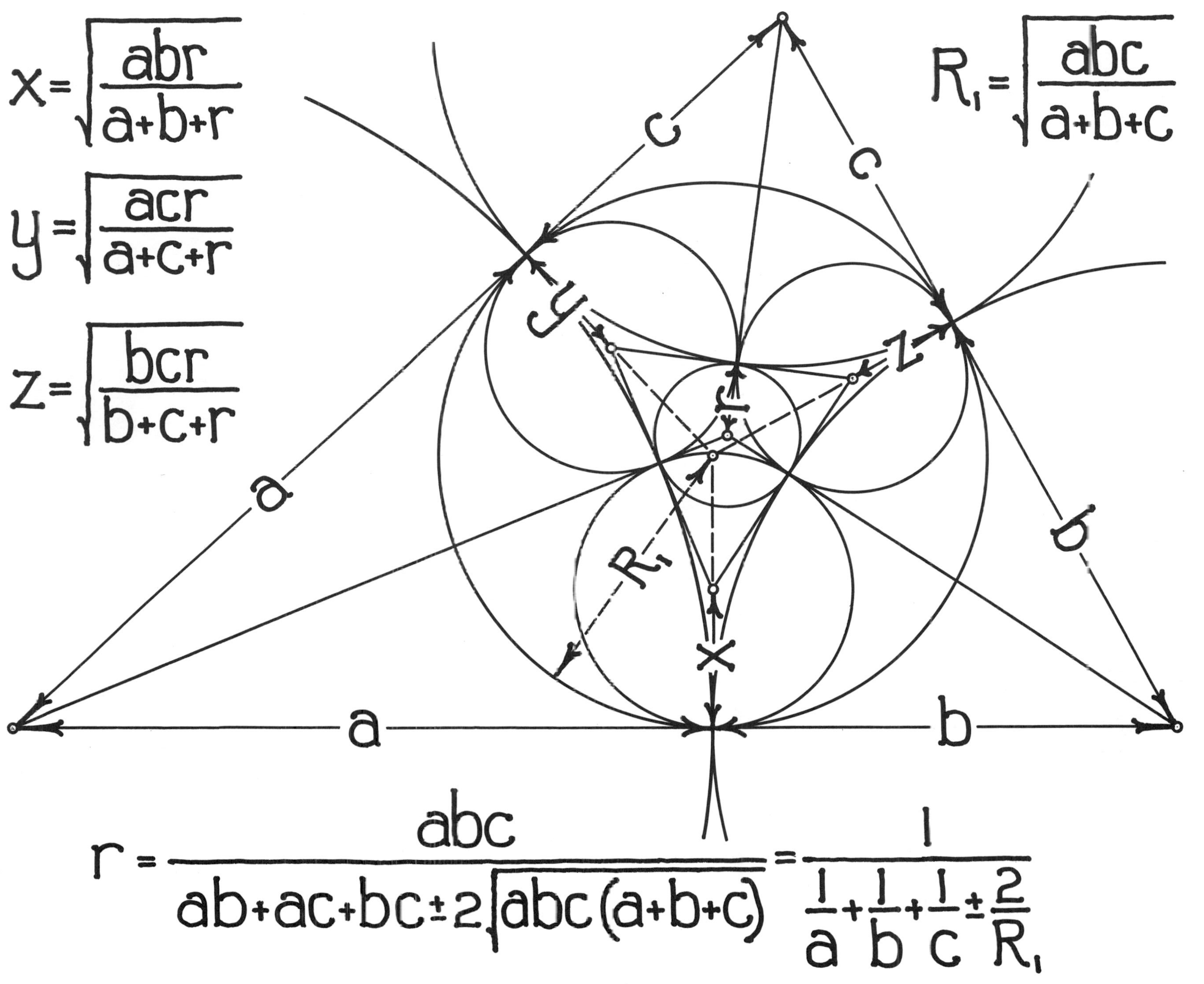

$R_1 = \sqrt{\frac{abc}{a+b+c}}$
$x = \sqrt{\frac{abr}{a+b+r}}$
$y = \sqrt{\frac{acr}{a+c+r}}$
$z = \sqrt{\frac{bcr}{b+c+r}}$
$r = \frac{abc}{ab+ac+bc \pm 2\sqrt{abc(a+b+c)}} = \frac{1}{\frac{1}{a}+\frac{1}{b}+\frac{1}{c} \pm \frac{2}{R_1}}$
a
a
b
b
c
c
x
y
z
r
R_1

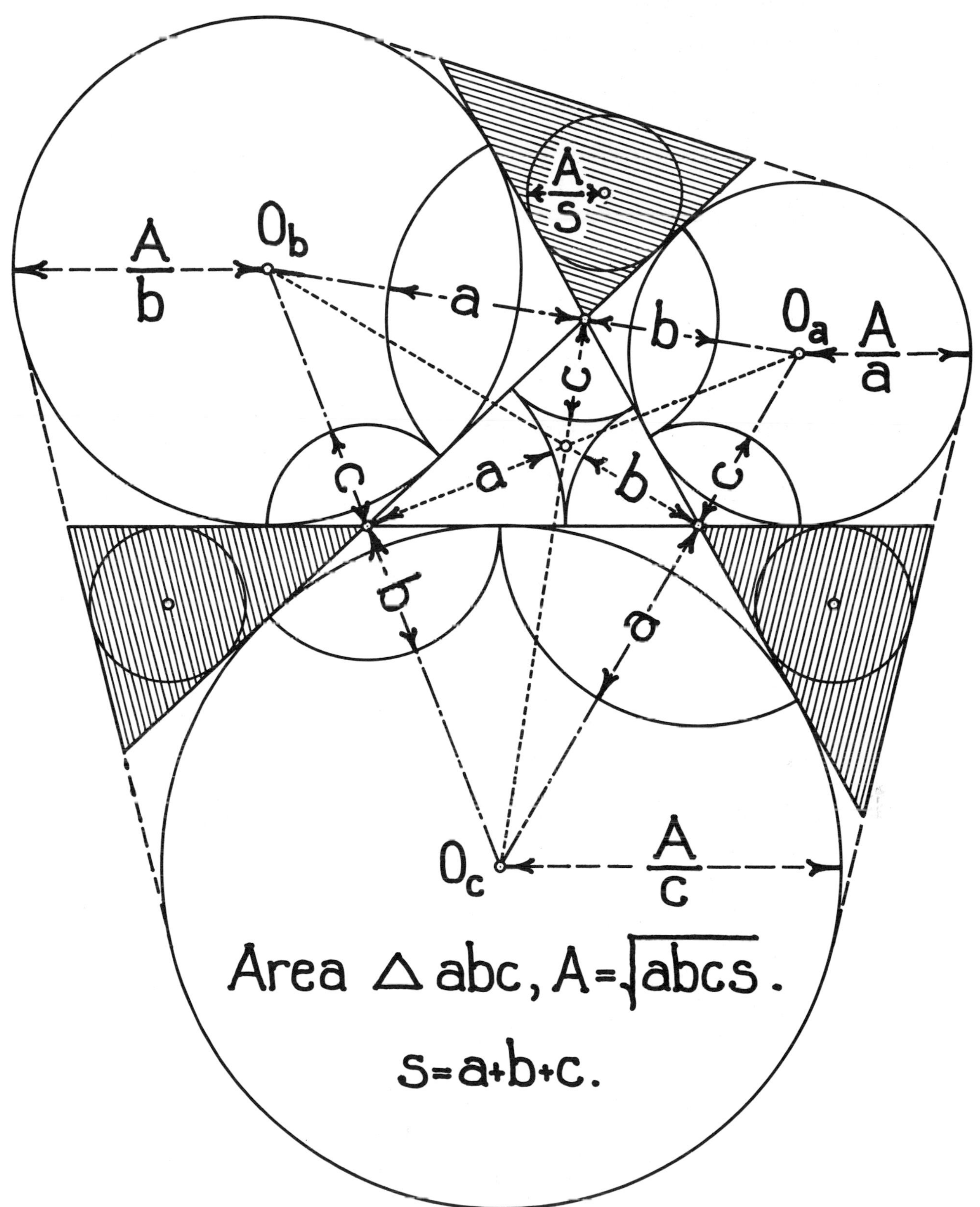
A/s
A/b
O_b
a
b
O_a
A/a
c
c
a
b
c
b
a
O_c
A/c
Area △ abc, A=√abcs.
s=a+b+c.

ENCIRCLING THE PARALLELOGRAM AND TRIANGLE.

When a circle centered on one vertex of a parallelogram has a radius equal to half of the sum of the sides and diagonal meeting at its center, circles centered on the other vertices that are tangent to that circle are tangent to each other.

When mutually tangent circles are centered on the vertices of a triangle, the circle at each vertex has a radius equal to half the perimeter of the triangle less the opposite side.

$$s=\frac{a+b+c}{2}=s_a+s_b+s_c$$

$$s_a=s-a=\frac{-a+b+c}{2}$$

$$s_b=s-b=\frac{a-b+c}{2}$$

$$s_c=s-c=\frac{a+b-c}{2}$$

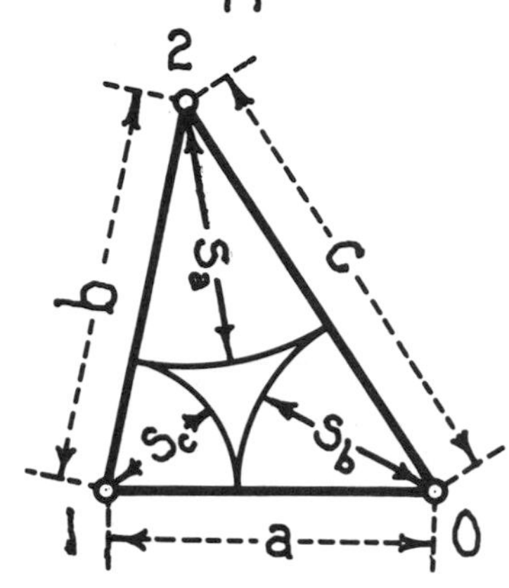

$$s^2+s_a^2+s_b^2+s_c^2=a^2+b^2+c^2.$$

$$\text{Area } \Delta 012=\sqrt{s\,s_a s_b s_c}$$

$$z=\sqrt{2a^2+2b^2-c^2}$$

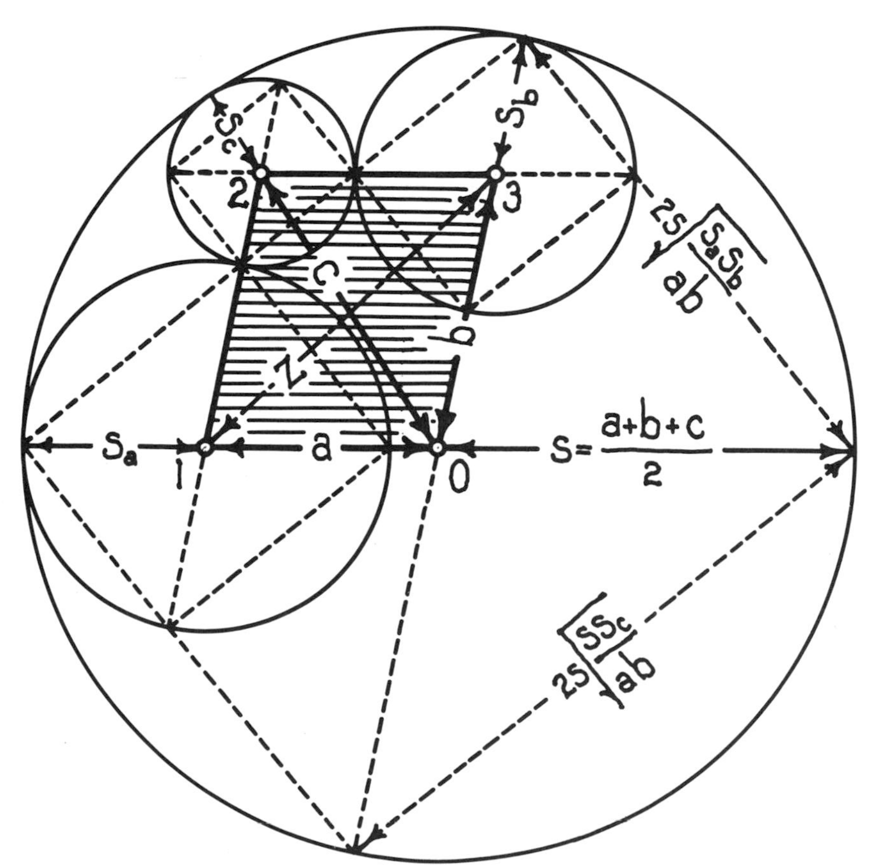

section VIII

PRIMITIVE TRIANGLES

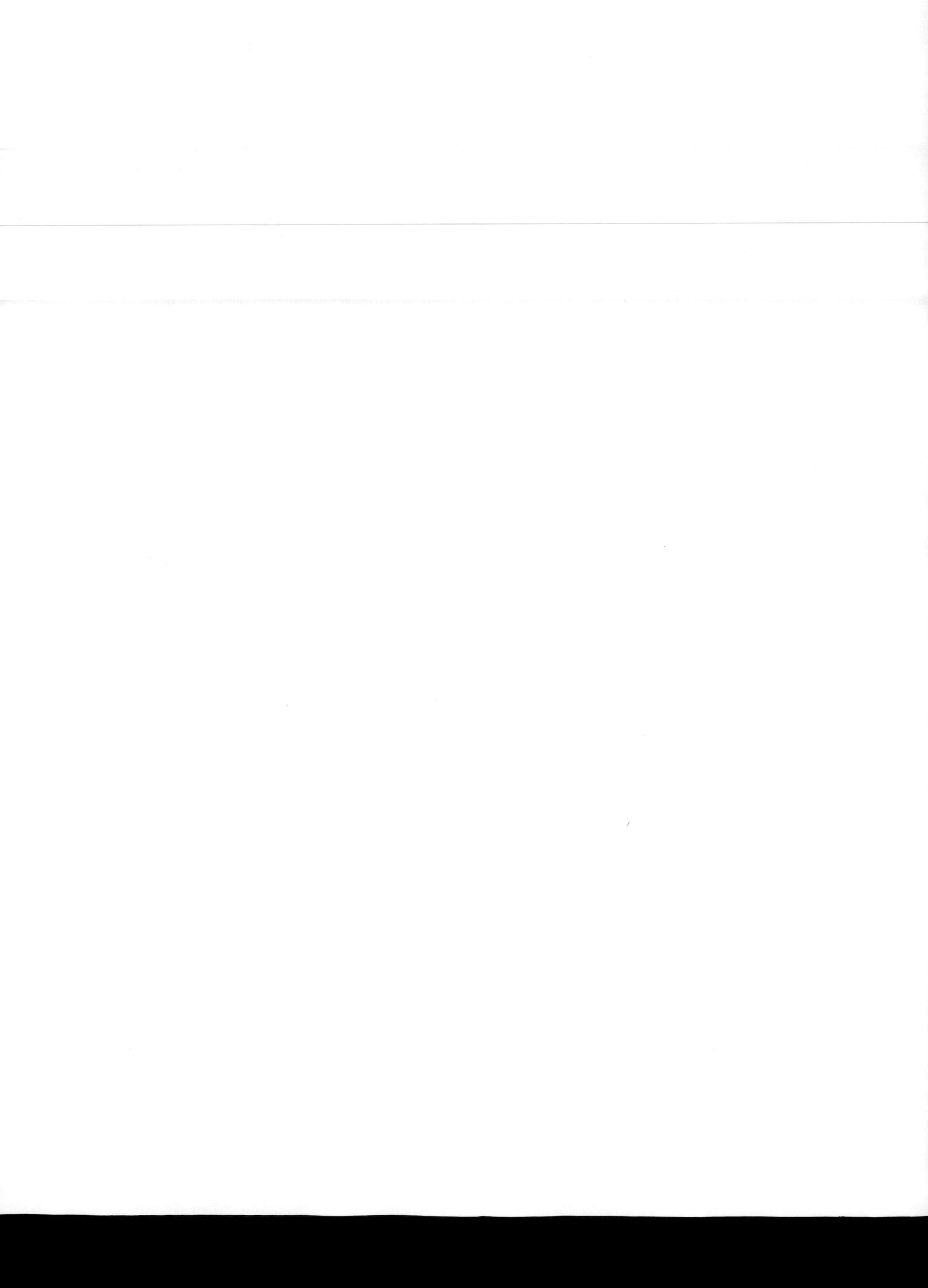

PRIMITIVE RIGHT TRIANGLES.

In any primitive right triangle, Figure 1, sides a, b and c are integers having no common factor. The hypotenuse, c, and one side, a, are odd. The other side, b, is even. The triangle is generated by the co-prime integers m and n. $m > n$. One integer is odd and the other is even. $p = m - n$. p is odd.

① $a = m^2 - n^2$. ② $b = 2mn$. ③ $c = m^2 + n^2$. See Figure 2.

④ $c - a = 2n^2$. ⑤ $c - b = (m-n)^2$ or p^2. ⑥ $m = p + n$.

⑦ $a = (p+n)^2 - n^2 = p^2 + 2pn$. See Fig 3.

⑧ $b = 2(p+n)n = 2pn + 2n^2$.

⑨ $c = (p+n)^2 + n^2 = p^2 + 2pn + 2n^2$.

⑩ $c = (a-r) + (b-r) = a + b - 2r$.

⑪ $r = \frac{a+b-c}{2}$

⑫ $r = \frac{1}{2}\left[(m^2-n^2) + 2mn - (m^2+n^2)\right]$

⑬ $r = mn - n^2$

⑭ $r = (m-n)n$

⑮ $r = pn$

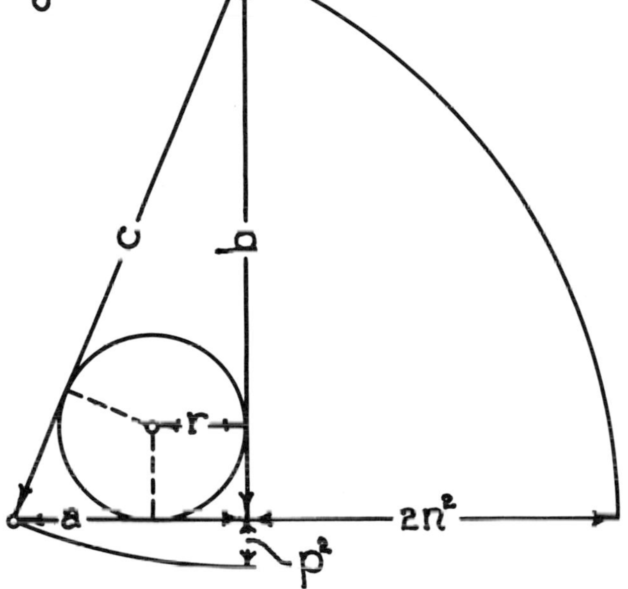

Figure 1.

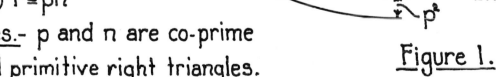

Notes.- p and n are co-prime in all primitive right triangles.

b is divisible by 4. Either a or b is divisible by 3. Either a, b or c is divisible by 5.

Odd Side Tabulation. n is the serial number of the triangle when listed with those having the same value of p.

Even Side Tabulation. p is the odd serial number of the triangle when listed with those having the same value of n.

PRIMITIVE RIGHT TRIANGLES.

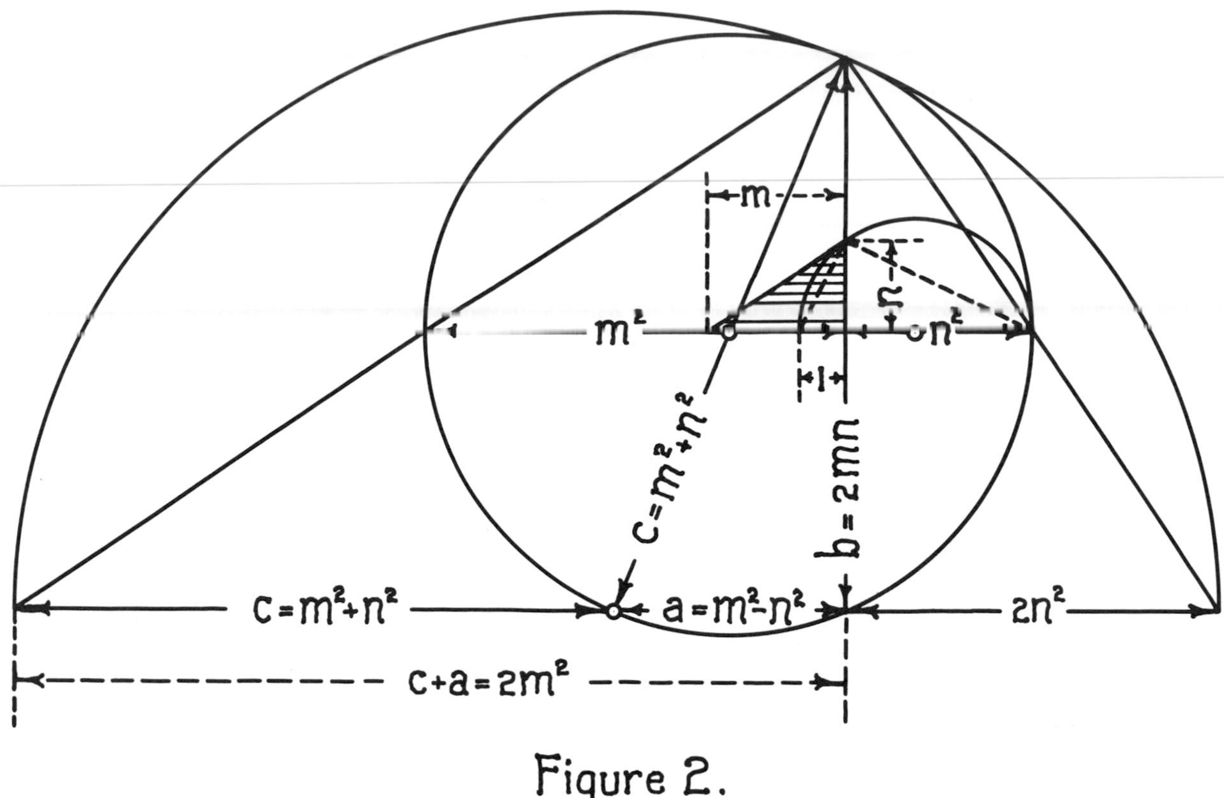

Figure 2.

<u>Note</u>:- To find the generators of any of these triangles reduce the fraction $\frac{c+a}{b}$ to the form $\frac{m}{n}$.

$$\frac{c+a}{b} = \frac{2m^2}{2mn} = \frac{m}{n}.$$

Examples.

$\frac{5+3}{4} = \frac{2}{1}$. $\frac{13+5}{12} = \frac{3}{2}$.

$\frac{17+15}{8} = \frac{4}{1}$. $\frac{25+7}{24} = \frac{4}{3}$.

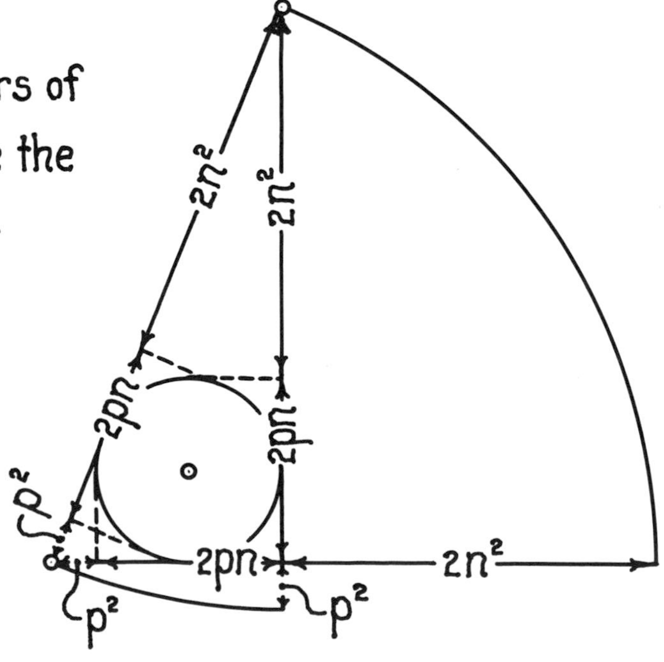

Figure 3.

Primitive Right Triangles.

(Odd Side Tabulation.)

$a^2+b^2=c^2$. $c-a=2n^2$. $c-b=p^2$. Odd-(•). Even-(••).

$a=(2n+p)p$. $b=2n(n+p)$. $c=b+p^2$.

n.	p=1.			p=3.			n.	p=5.			p=7.			n.
	a.	b.	c.	a.	b.	c.		a.	b.	c.	a.	b.	c.	
1	3	4	5	15	8	17	1	35	12	37	63	16	65	1
2	5	12	13	21	20	29	2	45	28	53	77	36	85	2
3	7	24	25	—	—	—	3	55	48	73	91	60	109	3
4	9	40	41	33	56	65	4	65	72	97	105	88	137	4
5	11	60	61	39	80	89	5	—	—	—	119	120	169	5
6	13	84	85	—	—	—	6	85	132	157	133	156	205	6
7	15	112	113	51	140	149	7	95	168	193	—	—	—	7
8	17	144	145	57	176	185	8	105	208	233	161	240	289	8
9	19	180	181	—	—	—	9	115	252	277	175	288	337	9
10	21	220	221	69	260	269	10	—	—	—	189	340	389	10
11	23	264	265	75	308	317	11	135	352	377	203	396	445	11
12	25	312	313	—	—	—	12	145	408	433	217	456	505	12

n.	p=9.			p=11.			n.	p=13.			p=15.			n.
	a.	b.	c.	a.	b.	c.		a.	b.	c.	a.	b.	c.	
1	99	20	101	143	24	145	1	195	28	197	255	32	257	1
2	117	44	125	165	52	173	2	221	60	229	285	68	293	2
3	—	—	—	187	84	205	3	247	96	265	—	—	—	3
4	153	104	185	209	120	241	4	273	136	305	345	152	377	4
5	171	140	221	231	160	281	5	299	180	349	—	—	—	5
6	—	—	—	253	204	325	6	325	228	397	—	—	—	6
7	207	224	305	275	252	373	7	351	280	449	435	308	533	7
8	225	272	353	297	304	425	8	377	336	505	465	368	593	8
9	—	—	—	319	360	481	9	403	396	565	—	—	—	9
10	261	380	461	341	420	541	10	429	460	629	—	—	—	10
11	279	440	521	—	—	—	11	455	528	697	555	572	797	11
12	—	—	—	385	552	673	12	481	600	769	—	—	—	12

Primitive Right Triangles.

(Even Side Tabulation.)

$a^2 + b^2 = c^2$. $c - a = 2n^2$. $c - b = p^2$. Odd-(•). Even-(••).

$b = 2n(n+p)$. $a = (2n+p)p$. $c = a + 2n^2$.

p.	n=1.			n=2.			p.	n=3.			n=4.			p.
	b.	a.	c.	b.	a.	c.		b.	a.	c.	b.	a.	c.	
1	4	3	5	12	5	13	1	24	7	25	40	9	41	1
3	8	15	17	20	21	29	3	—	—	—	56	33	65	3
5	12	35	37	28	45	53	5	48	55	73	72	65	97	5
7	16	63	65	36	77	85	7	60	91	109	88	105	137	7
9	20	99	101	44	117	125	9	—	—	—	104	153	185	9
11	24	143	145	52	165	173	11	84	187	205	120	209	241	11
13	28	195	197	60	221	229	13	96	247	265	136	273	305	13
15	32	255	257	68	285	293	15	—	—	—	152	345	377	15
17	36	323	325	76	357	365	17	120	391	409	168	425	457	17
19	40	399	401	84	437	445	19	132	475	493	184	513	545	19
21	44	483	485	92	525	533	21	—	—	—	200	609	641	21
23	48	575	577	100	621	629	23	156	667	685	216	713	745	23

p.	n=5.			n=6.			p.	n=7.			n=8.			p.
	b.	a.	c.	b.	a.	c.		b.	a.	c.	b.	a.	c.	
1	60	11	61	84	13	85	1	112	15	113	144	17	145	1
3	80	39	89	—	—	—	3	140	51	149	176	57	185	3
5	—	—	—	132	85	157	5	168	95	193	208	105	233	5
7	120	119	169	156	133	205	7	—	—	—	240	161	289	7
9	140	171	221	—	—	—	9	224	207	305	272	225	353	9
11	160	231	281	204	253	325	11	252	275	373	304	297	425	11
13	180	299	349	228	325	397	13	280	351	449	336	377	505	13
15	—	—	—	—	—	—	15	308	435	533	368	465	593	15
17	220	459	509	276	493	565	17	336	527	625	400	561	689	17
19	240	551	601	300	589	661	19	364	627	725	432	665	793	19
21	260	651	701	—	—	—	21	—	—	—	464	777	905	21
23	280	759	809	348	805	877	23	420	851	949	496	897	1025	23

Trains of Circles from Primitive Right Triangles.

Series A. The dotted rectangle in figure A2, sheet 2/3 is formed by primitive right triangles having their even sides, b, one unit shorter than their common hypotenuse, c.

Compute the radii of the mutually tangent circles centered on the vertices of the rectangle from the equations for such circles centered on the vertices of any parallelogram.

The two upper circles are units of a train of circles that have centers on an ellipse with foci at vertices f_1 and f_2.

Number the train circles as indicated in figure A6.

The A6 equations give the radius of any train circle, q, and the coordinates of its center.

The train circle over f_1 has the same number as the serial number of the base triangle.

Series B. The odd sides, a, of the base triangles are two units shorter than the hypotenuse, c.

Number the train circles as indicated in figure B5.

The B5 equations give r, x and y values for any circle, u.

Triangles A. c-b=1.

sr.no.	a.	b.	c.
1.	3	4	5
2.	5	12	13
3.	7	24	25
4.	9	40	41
5.	11	60	61
6.	13	84	85
7.	15	112	113
8.	17	144	145
9.	19	180	181
10.	21	220	221

Triangles B. c-a=2.

sr.no.	b.	a.	c.
1.	4	3	5
2.	8	15	17
3.	12	35	37
4.	16	63	65
5.	20	99	101
6.	24	143	145
7.	28	195	197
8.	32	255	257
9.	36	323	325
10.	40	399	401

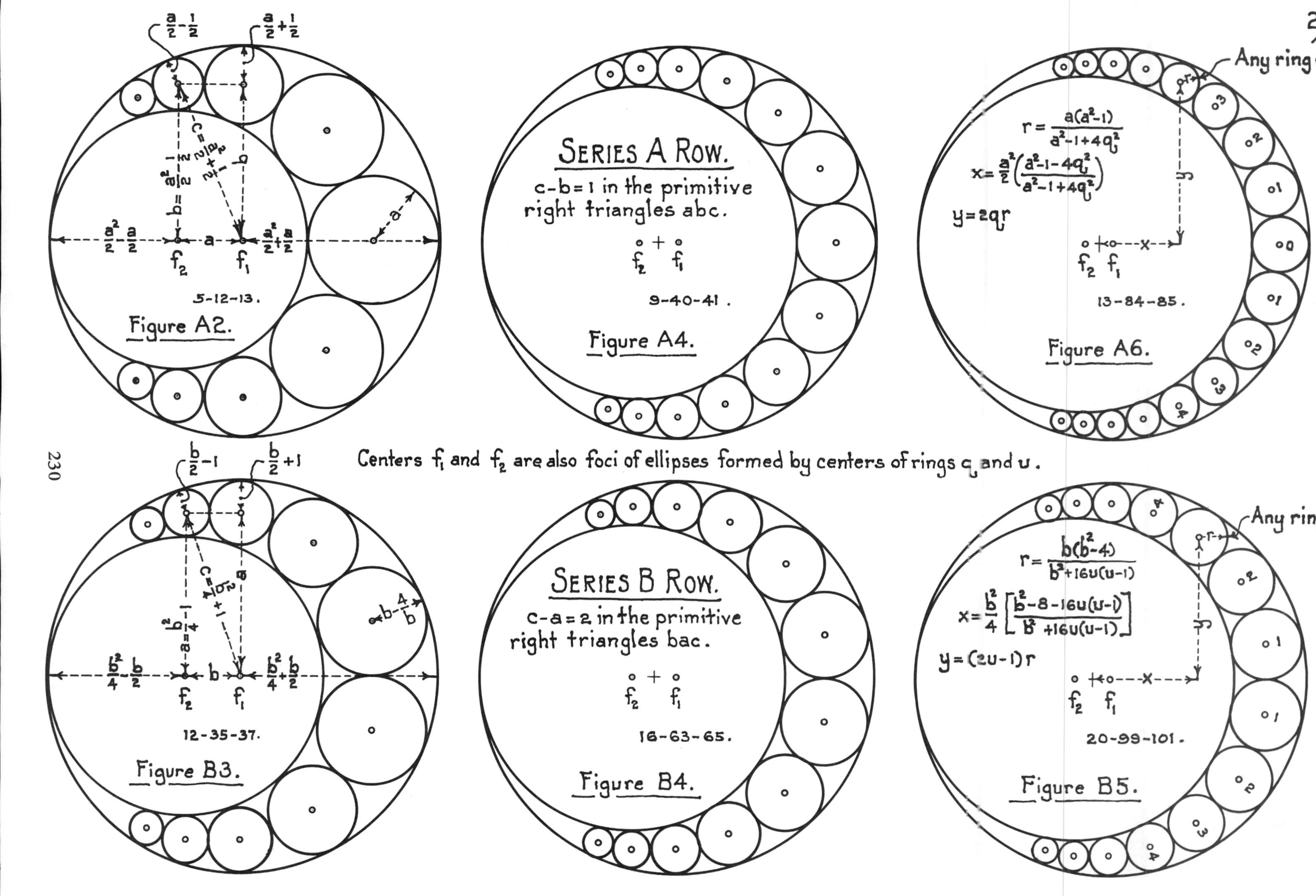

2/3
$\frac{a}{2}-\frac{1}{2}$
$\frac{a}{2}+\frac{1}{2}$
$c=\frac{a^2}{2}+\frac{1}{2}$
$b=\frac{a^2}{2}-\frac{1}{2}$
$\frac{a^2}{2}-\frac{a}{2}$
a
$\frac{a^2}{2}+\frac{a}{2}$
f_2
f_1
5-12-13.
Figure A2.
SERIES A ROW.
c-b=1 in the primitive
right triangles abc.
f_2 + f_1
9-40-41.
Figure A4.
Any ring q.
$r=\frac{a(a^2-1)}{a^2-1+4q^2}$
$x=\frac{a^2}{2}\left(\frac{a^2-1-4q^2}{a^2-1+4q^2}\right)$
$y=2qr$
f_2 f_1
13-84-85.
Figure A6.
Centers f_1 and f_2 are also foci of ellipses formed by centers of rings q and u.
$\frac{b}{2}-1$
$\frac{b}{2}+1$
$c=\frac{b^2}{4}+1$
$a=\frac{b^2}{4}-1$
$\frac{b^2}{4}-\frac{b}{2}$
b
$\frac{b^2}{4}+\frac{b}{2}$
$b-\frac{4}{b}$
f_2
f_1
12-35-37.
Figure B3.
SERIES B ROW.
c-a=2 in the primitive
right triangles bac.
f_2 + f_1
16-63-65.
Figure B4.
Any ring u.
$r=\frac{b(b^2-4)}{b^2+16u(u-1)}$
$x=\frac{b^2}{4}\left[\frac{b^2-8-16u(u-1)}{b^2+16u(u-1)}\right]$
$y=(2u-1)r$
f_2 f_1
20-99-101.
Figure B5.

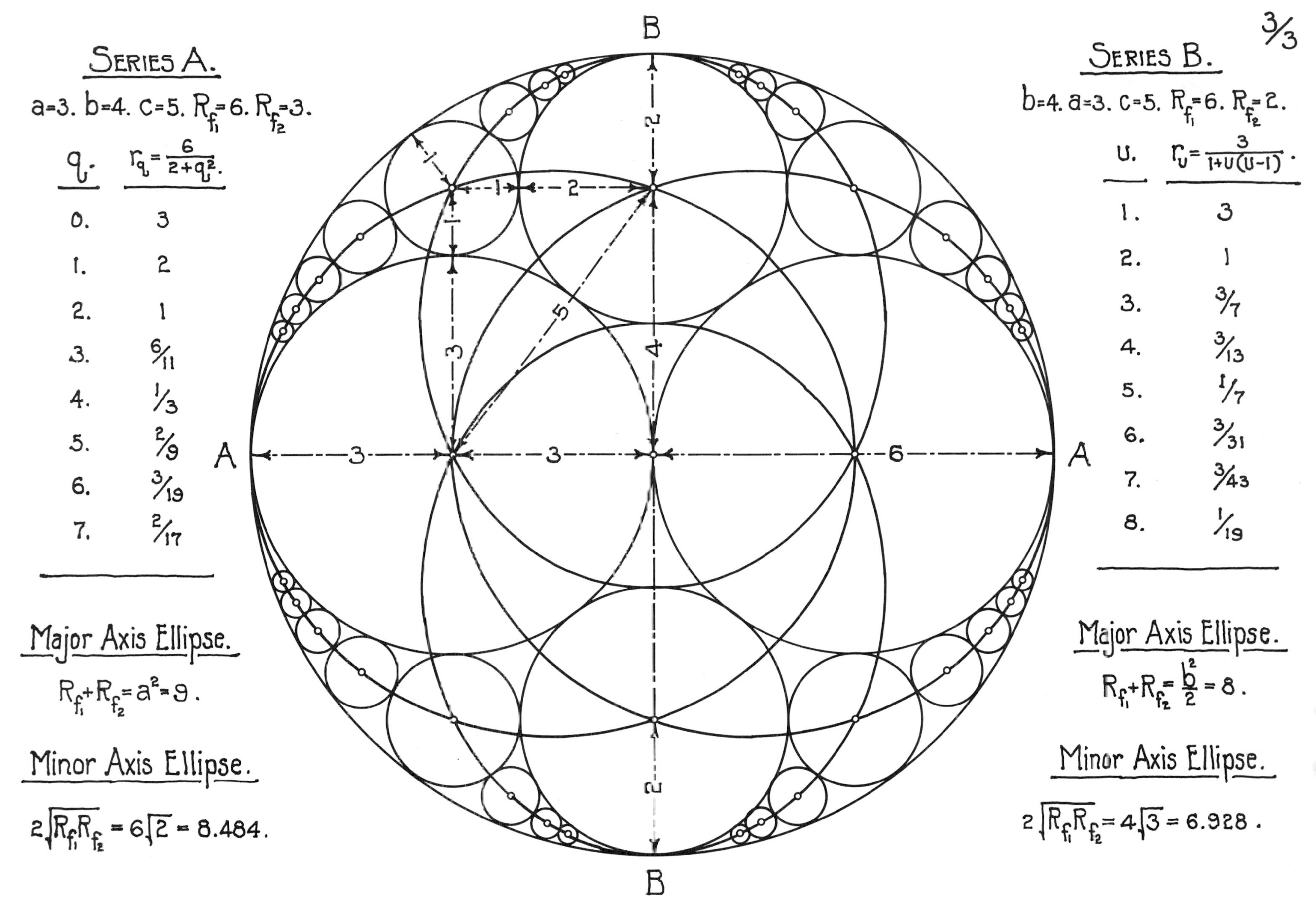
3/3
SERIES A.
a=3. b=4. c=5. R_{f_1}=6. R_{f_2}=3.
q. $r_q = \frac{6}{2+q^2}$.
0. 3
1. 2
2. 1
3. 6/11
4. 1/3
5. 2/9
6. 3/19
7. 2/17
Major Axis Ellipse.
$R_{f_1}+R_{f_2}=a^2=9$.
Minor Axis Ellipse.
$2\sqrt{R_{f_1}R_{f_2}}=6\sqrt{2}=8.484$.
SERIES B.
b=4. a=3. c=5. R_{f_1}=6. R_{f_2}=2.
u. $r_u = \frac{3}{1+u(u-1)}$.
1. 3
2. 1
3. 3/7
4. 3/13
5. 1/7
6. 3/31
7. 3/43
8. 1/19
Major Axis Ellipse.
$R_{f_1}+R_{f_2}=\frac{b^2}{2}=8$.
Minor Axis Ellipse.
$2\sqrt{R_{f_1}R_{f_2}}=4\sqrt{3}=6.928$.
A
A
B
B
3
3
6
2
1
1
1
3
5
4
2
2

section IX

MISCELLANEOUS

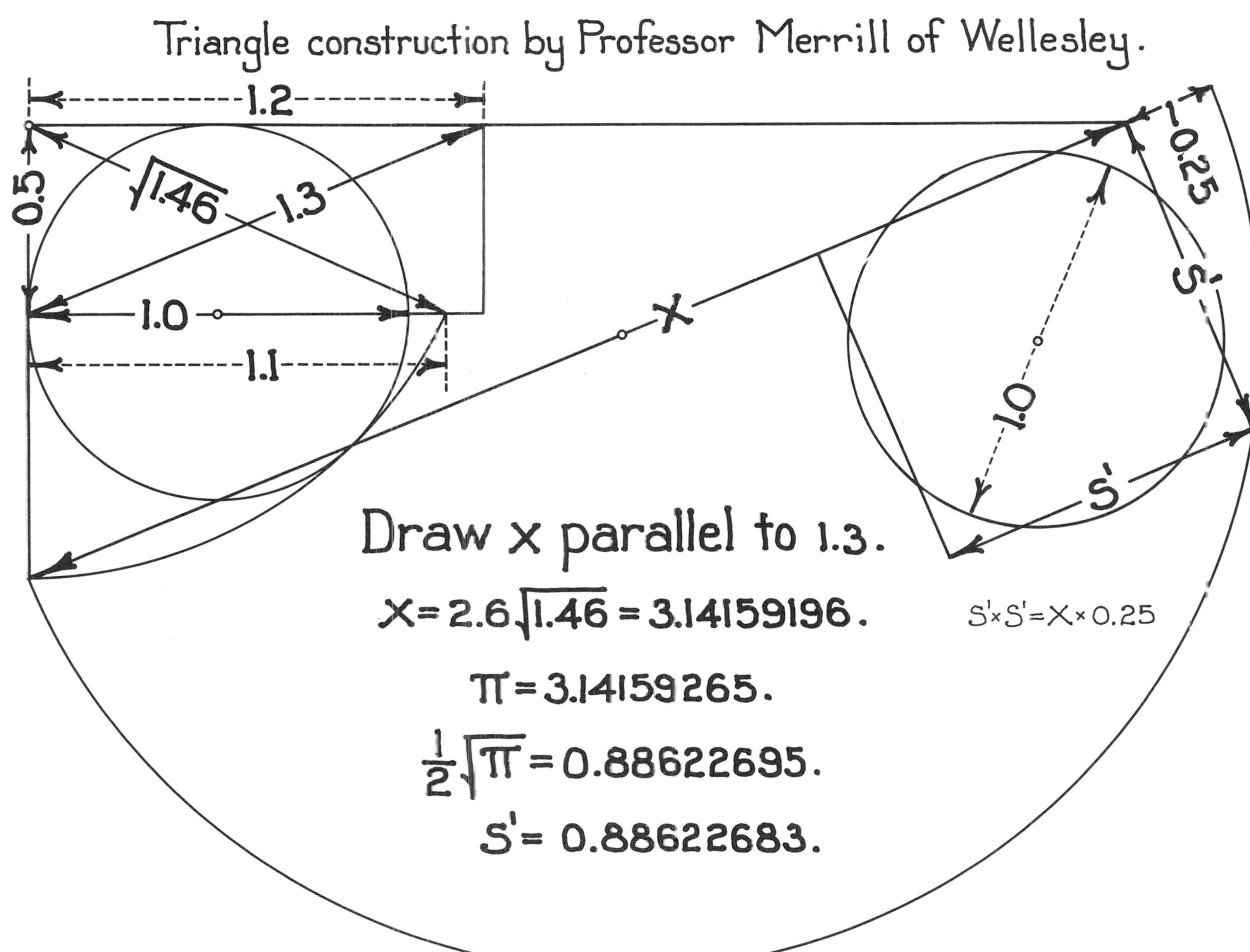
SQUARING THE CIRCLE.
Triangle construction by Professor Merrill of Wellesley.
1.2
0.5
√1.46
1.3
1.0
1.1
X
0.25
S'
1.0
S'
Draw x parallel to 1.3.
X=2.6√1.46 = 3.14159196.
π=3.14159265.
½√π = 0.88622695.
S'= 0.88622683.
S'×S'=X×0.25

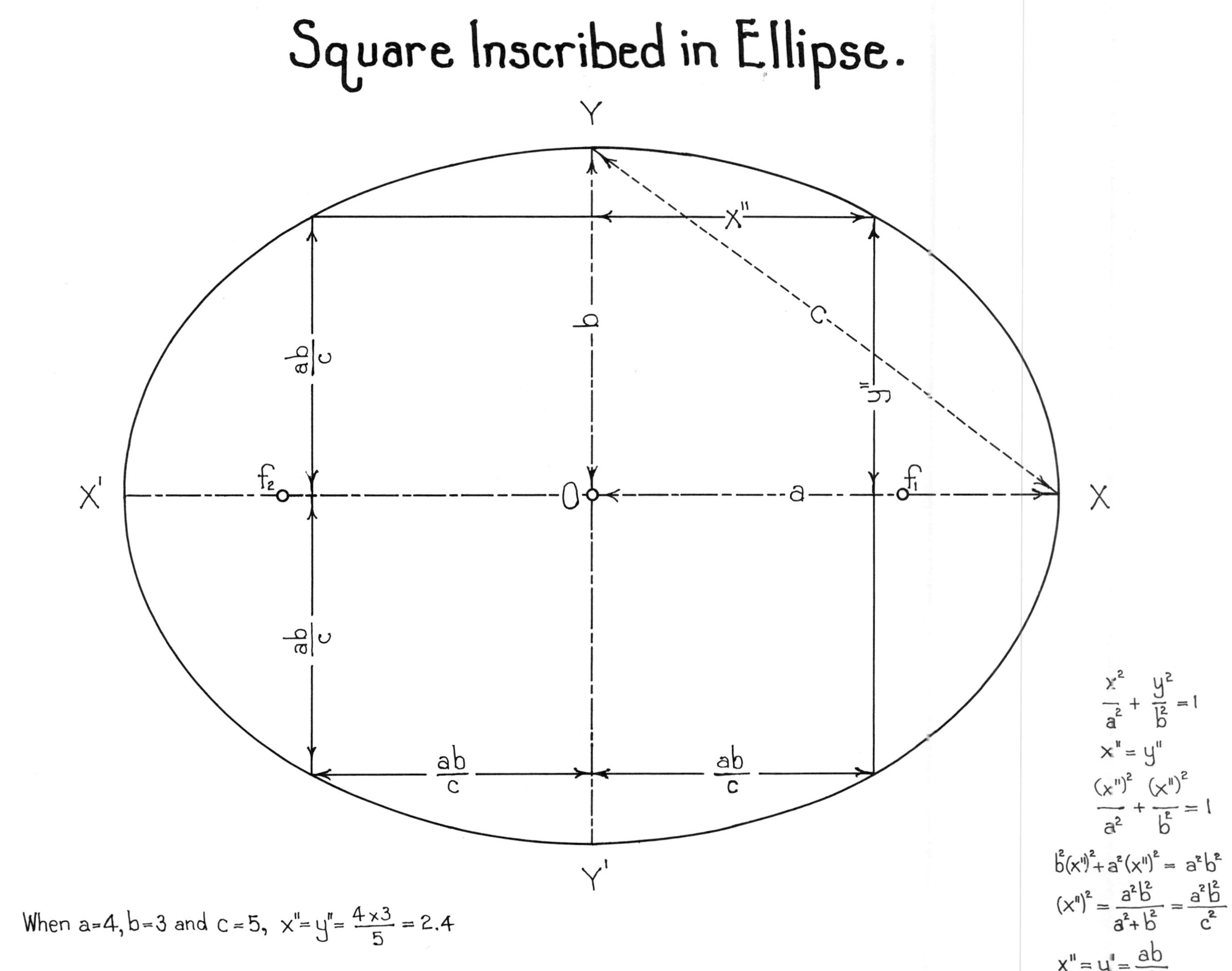

Square Inscribed in Ellipse.
Y
Y'
X
X'
O
f_1
f_2
a
b
c
x''
y''
$\frac{ab}{c}$
$\frac{ab}{c}$
$\frac{ab}{c}$
$\frac{ab}{c}$
When a=4, b=3 and c=5, $x''=y''=\frac{4\times 3}{5}=2.4$
$\frac{x^2}{a^2}+\frac{y^2}{b^2}=1$
$x''=y''$
$\frac{(x'')^2}{a^2}+\frac{(x'')^2}{b^2}=1$
$b^2(x'')^2+a^2(x'')^2=a^2b^2$
$(x'')^2=\frac{a^2b^2}{a^2+b^2}=\frac{a^2b^2}{c^2}$
$x''=y'=\frac{ab}{c}$

YANG AND YIN.

Ancient Chinese symbol for the secret of life, the cosmic power, Tao.

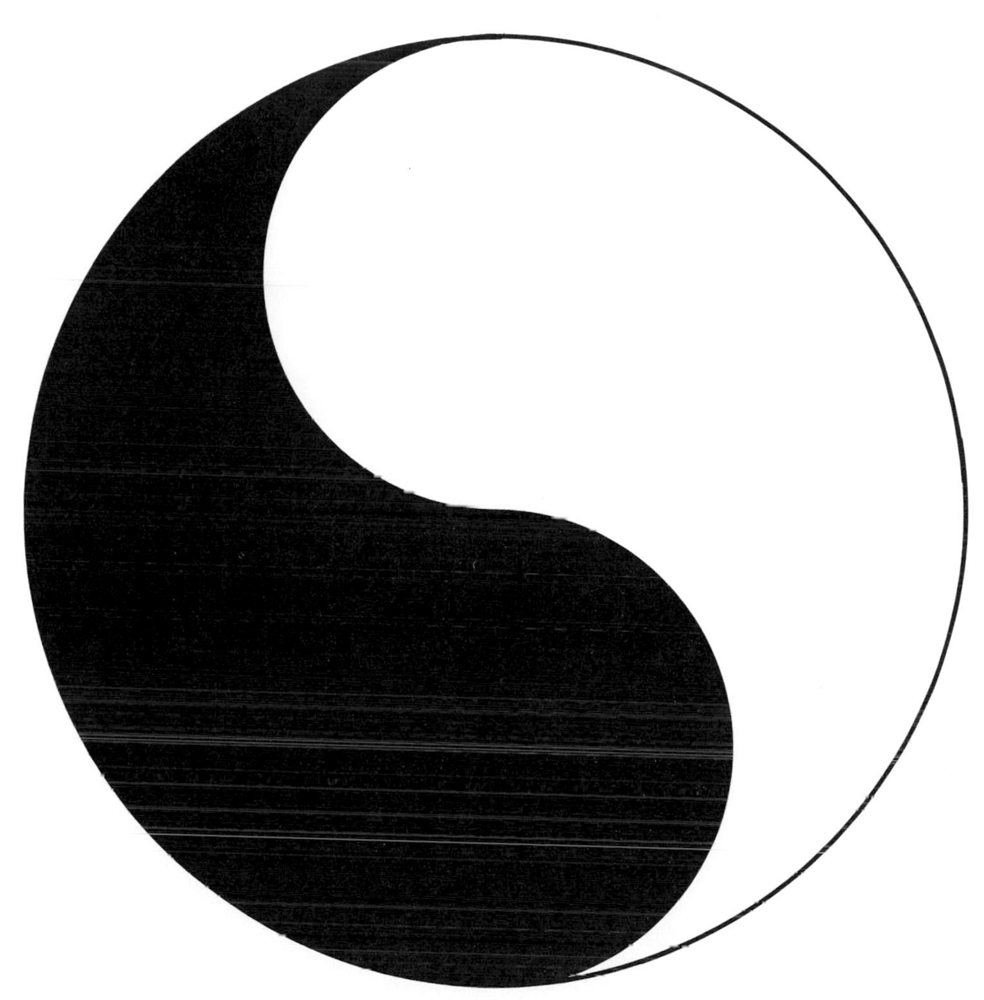

Positive and negative phases.-Sun and moon. Male and female. Good and evil. Life and death. Appears on Korean national flag.